# God-Breathed

*The Divine Inspiration of the Bible*

# GOD-BREATHED
*The Divine Inspiration of the Bible*

Louis Gaussen

*Translated by David Scott*

*Edited by John Robbins*

The Trinity Foundation

Cover: The Grand Teton Range, Wyoming
Photograph courtesy of Kevin Reed

*God-Breathed:*
*The Divine Inspiration of the Bible*
Copyright 2001 John W. Robbins
Published in the United States of America
ISBN: 0-940931-57-5

# Contents

Foreword  7
Analysis  12
Translator's Preface  21
Prefatory Observations  25

CHAPTER 1
DEFINITION OF THEOPNEUSTIA  38

*Theopneustia Defined  38*
*Theopneustia Asserted  39*
*Theopneustia Rejected  40*
*Theopneustia Further Defined and Stated  45*
*On the Individuality of the Sacred Writers  49*

CHAPTER 2
SCRIPTURAL PROOF OF THE DIVINE INSPIRATION  66

*All Scripture Is Divinely Inspired  66*
*All the Prophetic Utterances Are Given by God  67*
*All the Scriptures of the Old Testament Are Prophetic  74*
*All the Scriptures of the New Testament Are Prophetic  78*
*The Examples of the Apostles and of Their Master
Attest that, in Their View, All the Words
of the Holy Books Are Given by God  91*

CHAPTER 3
BRIEF DIDACTIC ABSTRACT OF THE
DOCTRINE OF THE DIVINE INSPIRATION  106

*Catechetical Sketch of the Main Points of the Doctrine  106*
*On the Adversaries and Defenders of This Doctrine  134*

5

## Chapter 4
### Examination of Objections 145

*The Translations 145*
*Use of the Septuagint Translation 151*
*The Various Readings 154*
*Errors of Reasoning or of Doctrine 183*
*Errors in Narratives; Contradictions in the Facts 190*
*Errors Contrary to Natural Philosophy 219*
*The Declarations of Paul Himself 241*

## Chapter 5
### Examination of Evasions 245

*Might Not Inspiration Pertain to the Thoughts Only, Without Extending to the Words? 245*
*Should We Except from Inspiration the Historical Books? 254*
*Will the Apparent Insignificance of Certain Details in the Bible Authorize Their Being Excepted from Inspiration? 270*

## Chapter 6
### Sacred Criticism, in the Relations It Bears to Divine Inspiration 284

*Sacred Criticism Is a Scientific Inquirer, and Not a Judge 285*
*Let Sacred Criticism Be an Historian, Not a Soothsayer 289*
*Sacred Criticism Is the Doorkeeper of the Temple, Not Its God 294*

## Chapter 7
### Conclusion 305

*Retrospect 305*
*The Bible Above Everything 310*

Index 319
Scripture Index 341
The Crisis of Our Time 349
Intellectual Ammunition 356

# Foreword

FRANÇOIS Samuel Robert Louis Gaussen is little known in the United States, even among those who profess to be Reformed. Born in Geneva, Switzerland, on August 25, 1790, Gaussen's principal ministry was in Geneva, where he died on June 18, 1863.

Two years after completing his studies at the University of Geneva, he was appointed minister at Satigny, near Geneva, in 1816, where he succeeded Cellerier, one of the few members of the Swiss clergy who believed and taught Biblical Christianity, and who exercised a profound influence on the formation of Gaussen's own theological convictions. Under Cellerier's influence and that of the Scotch layman Robert Haldane, Gaussen became an ardent champion of Reformed theology in Switzerland.

About this time there was a renewal of interest in Biblical Christianity in French Switzerland, the *Reveil*. This awakening coincided with Haldane's visit to Geneva in 1817, where he began a weekly Bible study on the *Epistle to the Romans* for the theological students at the University. Because of interest in his lectures from both students and professors, Haldane had to move the study from his apartment to larger quarters. On May 7, 1817, the *Vénérable Compagnie des Pasteurs de Genève*, concerned about the growth of Christianity in their city, issued an order virtually prohibiting the preaching of certain important Christian doctrines. Gaussen and his predecessor at Satigny, Cellerier, protested against this ruling, chiefly by republishing a new French edition of the *Second Helvetic Confession*, to which they added a preface asserting that a church must have a declaration of faith, and that the *Second Helvetic Confession* correctly voiced their personal convictions.

Gaussen continued to pursue his ministerial duties in Satigny, and held religious meetings in his own home, as well as in his mother's home in Geneva, striving to reform the National Church, but not advocating separation from it. At Geneva, which gradually became the center of his activity, Gaussen founded a missionary society that held meetings, first in private houses and later in the church building. In 1828, through the intervention of the *Vénérable Compagnie des Pasteurs,* new members were elected to the missionary society's governing board whom Gaussen considered errant in their views, and he withdrew from the society. This conflict with the clergy of Geneva was typical of frequent storms that affected his career. (Christ's conflict with the clergy of Jerusalem was, of course, another and more important instance of the ancient opposition between ecclesiastical authority and truth.) Calvin's catechism had long been used as a basis for the instruction of the young, but in 1827 the *Vénérable Compagnie des Pasteurs* substituted another catechism and ordered Gaussen to use it. He tried to do so, but found it unsatisfactory because of its Rationalism. The clergy of Geneva then lodged a complaint against him for refusing to obey their order, and after a lengthy dispute he was finally censured by the *Vénérable Compagnie des Pasteurs* and deprived of his right to take part in its meetings for a period of one year.

With his friends and fellow Christians, Merle d'Aubigne and Galland, Gaussen now founded the Evangelical Society to distribute Bibles and tracts, and to interest the public in missionary work among the heathen. Shortly afterward, the Evangelical Society decided to found a school for the dissemination of Christian doctrine, and this resolve was disclosed to the State Councilor of Geneva, as well as to the churches, in circular letters signed by Galland, Merle d'Aubigne, and Gaussen. Because of this, Gaussen was deposed from the ministry by the Consistory on September 30, 1831, and his two colleagues were suspended from the ministry. For two years Gaussen traveled through Italy and England, awakening strong sympathy for his cause in the latter country, and warning all that the Roman Catholic Church was a threat to Christianity. In 1834 he returned to Geneva and accepted the position of Professor of Systematic Theology at the *Oratoire,* the newly established Evangelical theological school.

Gaussen was a strict Reformed theologian, and he deviated from Reformed doctrines only with regard to his theory of predestination, for he denied supralapsarianism. During his career, Gaussen published books in three major divisions of theology: the deity of Christ, which was denied by the Rationalistic clergy of Switzerland; prophecies; and the divine authority of Holy Scripture. In addition to *Théopneustie* (Geneva, 1840; first English translation, *Theopneustia: The Plenary Inspi-*

*ration of the Holy Scriptures,* London, 1841), in which he argued that the entire Old and New Testaments were verbally inspired by God, an argument that was attacked by members of his own theological school, Gaussen wrote, in vindication of his position, *Le Canon des Saintes Écritures* (Lausanne, 1860; English translation, *Canon of the Holy Scriptures as Viewed Through Science and Faith,* London, 1862). He was the author of numerous other works, including *Geneva and Jerusalem,* 1844; *Geneva and Rome,* 1844; *Lessons for the Young,* 1860; *Leçons sur Daniel* (3 volumes, uncompleted, 1861; English translation, *The Prophet Daniel Explained,* 1873-74), consisting of several of his lectures on *Daniel; Les premiers chapîtres de l'Exode,* and *Le prophète Jonas* (the latter two published posthumously). His works enjoyed a wide circulation both in England and in France during the nineteenth century.

Gaussen's defense of the full and detailed inspiration of Scripture by God is one of the principal works on this subject by any Christian theologian. He advocates what has come to be called the "organic" view of inspiration, a word that unfortunately conveys little information to the reader's mind. His view, based firmly and completely on Scripture itself, is that God not only controlled which words, phrases, sentences, and paragraphs were to be set down as Scripture, but also controlled all human history so that at the exact time chosen, the author of those words would be properly prepared and available to write the words that God dictated to him. The result is an exact statement of God's thoughts in human language, language perfectly adequate to express divine thoughts.

Like Calvin before him, Gaussen frequently used the words "dictate" and "dictation" to explain the Bible's view of its own inspiration. For the past two centuries, and especially during the twentieth century, the "dictation view of inspiration" has been ridiculed by those who do not believe the Bible. But the problem with the liberals' view of dictation is not that it is too strict, but that it is not nearly strict enough. Gordon Clark explained in his book *God's Hammer: The Bible and Its Critics*:

> When God wished to make a revelation (at the time of the exodus or of the captivity) he did not suddenly look around as if caught unprepared, and wonder what man he could use. We cannot suppose that he advertised for a stenographer, and, when Moses and Jeremiah applied for the position, that God dictated his message. The relation between God and a prophet was not like that at all. A boss must take what he can get;

he depends on the high school or business college to have taught the applicant shorthand and typing. But if we consider the omnipotence and wisdom of God, a very different picture emerges. God is the Creator. He made Moses. And when God wanted Moses to speak for him, he said, "Who has made man's mouth?... Have not I, the Lord?".... To this end he so controlled events that Moses was born at a given date, placed in the water to save him from an early death, found by Pharaoh's daughter, given the best Egyptian education possible, driven into the wilderness to learn patience, and in every detail so prepared by heredity and environment that when the time came Moses' mentality and literary style were instruments precisely fitted to speak God's words.... Verbal inspiration therefore must be understood in connection with the complete system of Christian doctrine. It may not be detached therefrom, and *a fortiori* it may not be framed in an alien view of God. Verbal inspiration is integral with the doctrines of providence and predestination. When the liberals surreptitiously deny predestination in picturing God as dictating to stenographers, they so misrepresent verbal inspiration that their objections do not apply to the God of the Bible. The trouble is not, as the liberals think, that the boss controls the stenographer too completely; on the contrary, the analogy misses the mark because the boss hardly controls the stenographer at all.

One reason the republication of Gaussen's book is necessary in the twenty-first century is the widespread ignorance of the doctrine of divine inspiration of Scripture even among those who profess to be Christians. As Gordon Clark wrote: "No discussion of inspiration can contribute much of value without taking into account the elementary Scriptural data. These data must be kept in mind. Yet, unfortunately, a number of these details may have faded from our aging memories. More unfortunately, the younger generation – owing to the low standards of many seminaries – may never have learned the Scriptural data." Of course, it is not only the seminaries that are to blame; the churches are also culpable. Indeed, if there has been any decrease in ignorance of Christian doctrine in the last 50 years, it is largely through the instrumentality of ordinary Christians, not seminaries and denominations.

In his recommendation of Gaussen's book, Charles Spurgeon wrote: "The turning-point of the battle between those who hold 'the faith once delivered to the saints' and their opponents lies in the true and real inspiration of the Holy Scriptures. This is the Thermopylae of Christendom.... In this work the author proves himself a master of holy argument. Gaussen charms us as he proclaims the Divine veracity of Scripture. His testimony is clear as a bell." And it is such clarity, boldness, and fidelity to the Word of God that God desires in all his people.

JOHN ROBBINS

# Analysis

## Chapter I
### Definition of Theopneustia

I. *Theopneustia* defined
II. *Theopneustia* asserted, not explained
III. *Theopneustia* rejected as to its existence, universality, plenitude
   A. By some four degrees distinguished, *viz.*, superintendence, elevation, direction, suggestion
   B. This book designs, therefore to prove existence, universality, plenitude.
   C. Man's part in God's book; illustration from Pascal and Newton
IV. *Theopneustia* (further) defined and stated
   A. Neither *a priori* ("necessary"), nor from beauty, wisdom, etc., of Scriptures, but solely on divine declaration
   B. This addressed, of course, to those who admit Scriptures
   C. Scriptures declare their own inspiration.
V. Individuality of sacred writers, false inferences; different statement thereon
   A. Reply: human individuality acknowledged
   B. God's acting
   C. What is God's style?
   D. Human personality, how employed
   E. Inconsistency of objection to (alleged) difficulty
   F. Intermittent inspiration is complicated, rash, childish.
   G. "All Scripture is given by inspiration of God."
   H. Inspiration in book, not in man; three illusions: excitation, degree, already known
   I. Different styles – one God: illustration from music, Freiburg
   J. This individuality gives beauty, variety, unity, harmony.

## Chapter 2
## Scriptural Proof of Theopneustia

I. All Scripture is divinely inspired (*2 Timothy* 3:16)
II. All prophetic utterances given by God
   A. *2 Peter* 1:20, 21
   B. What is a prophet?
   C. The prophets, in the Bible, speak the words of Jehovah
   D. False prophets
   E. Scripture prophecies "the words of God in the mouth of man"
   F. Scripture prophecies sometimes without foresight, knowledge, or even desire, of prophets
   G. Occasional gift of prophecy
   H. Church of Corinth had (*1 Corinthians* 12:4-11):
      1. Diversities of gifts
      2. Divided severally
      3. The subject of desire
      4. Different forms
      5. Words of the Holy Spirit spoken by man
      6. Of long continuance
      7. Prophets not absolutely passive
   I. Hence, *2 Peter* 1:20, 21 establish plenary and entire inspiration of Scriptures: These are written prophecies.
III. All Old Testament Scriptures are prophetic.
   A. *2 Peter* 3:15, 16
   B. *2 Peter* 3:2 – hence, writings of apostles are written prophecies
   C. Writers of New Testament superior to writers of Old Testament, in
      1. Mission
      2. Promises
      3. Gifts
      4. Rank
   D. Apostles are prophets (*Romans* 16:25); more than prophets (*Matthew* 11:9, 11); above the prophets.
   E. Were Mark and Luke prophets?
   F. *Luke* 1:1-4
   G. Inspiration does not imply ecstasy.

IV. Testimony of Apostles and the Lord Jesus Christ
   A. Paul (*Epistle to the Hebrews*)
   B. The Lord Jesus Christ
      1. (Unconscious blasphemy of Rationalists)
      2. In the temple (*Luke* 2:41)
      3. The temptation (*Matthew* 4)
      4. At Nazareth (*Luke* 4:16)
      5. Before Sadducees (*Matthew* 22:32)
      6. Before Pharisees (*Matthew* 22:43)
      7. On the cross (*Matthew* 27:46)
      8. After resurrection (*Luke* 24:26)
      9. *Luke* 16:17, and *Matthew* 5:18
      10. *John* 10:22-40
      11. The Scripture cannot be broken (*John* 10:35): hence plenary verbal inspiration

## Chapter 3
### Didactic Abstract of the Doctrine

I. Catechetical sketch
   A. Inspiration: its effects
   B. Degrees of inspiration: mediate revelation
   C. Inspiration and illumination: These differ in kind, characteristics, degree.
   D. Miraculous gifts intermittent: inspiration by intervals
   E. Language fallible when uninspired
   F. Inspiration differs from illumination in essence; infallibility of sacred writers depends solely on inspiration: inspired words, miraculous words of God; our faith not in illumination of writers, but in inspiration of writings: one has degrees; other has no degrees: It goes to heart of God.
   G. Much harm from confusion; either the Word of God degraded, or uninspired writings exalted
   H. Rationalists the former, Jews and Roman Catholics the latter
   I. The Jewish Talmud
   J. Papal traditions
   K. Inspiration shows impulsion (will) and suggestion: internal and external (understanding): writers were living pens: they (and the occasion) prepared by God; their individuality sanctified

    L. All Scripture (Old Testament and New Testament) equally inspired
    M. The authenticity of each book an historical question
    N. Test of Reformed churches; of Luther
    O. Jews bear testimony to the authenticity of each book of Old Testament
    P. Catholic church bears testimony to each book of New Testament
    Q. Apocrypha; no addition to New Testament
    R. Church a depository of Scripture: that (an historical document) declares its own plenary inspiration
II. Adversaries and defenders
    A. Adversaries – to eighth century among heretics (except Theodore of Mopsuestia)
        1. second century, Gnostics
        2. third century, Manicheans
        3. fourth century, Anomeans
        4. fifth century, Theodore of Mopsuestia
        5. seventh century, Mohammed
        6. twelfth and thirteenth centuries, Talmudistic Jews – Moses Maimonides
        7. sixteenth century, Socinus and Castellio
        8. seventeenth century, Fanatics, Roman Catholics, Rationalists
        9. eighteenth century, Rationalists
    B. Defenders – whole church to days of Reformation. Rudelbach gives review of first eight centuries; proves that:
        1. Ancient church teaches Old and New Testament canonical writings inspired
        2. Teaches infallibility of Scripture
        3. Teaches nothing erroneous, useless, superfluous therein
        4. Teaches doctrine same throughout
        5. Teaches passive intelligent inspiration
        6. Teaches inecstatic inspiration
        7. Teaches verbal inspiration
        8. She respectfully quotes, etc.; reconciles, etc.
        9. She admits liberty in phenomena
       10. She fixes relations; proves; replies

## Chapter 4
## Objections Examined

I. Translations
   A. Are they inspired?
      1. Insignificant objection; really no objection; not bearing against fact of verbal inspiration; only contests advantage
      2. Difference of original and translated text
         (a) Sacred writers rendered Divine thoughts by sensible symbols
         (b) Original text written at given moment by single man
         (c) Translators learned; sacred writers illiterate
         (d) Thought of God only found in expression of sacred writer; but translators have Divine text
         (e) Possible faults as to original text boundless, as to translation limited
            (1) Hence, limitation of doubt
            (2) God required for one, man sufficed for other

II. Use of Septuagint in New Testament
   A. How did apostles use Septuagint? Illustration
   B. When Septuagint correct, quoted verbatim
   C. When Septuagint incorrect, amended
   D. When Septuagint in particular sense, paraphrased

III. Various readings
   A. Inspiration and integrity of present copies not to be confounded
   B. Objection is against present integrity; a question of history, criticism
   C. Modern researches, unimportant results: Buchanan, Massoretics
   D. Divine care of Old and New Testament text
   E. Osterwald and Martin – illustration, comparison
   F. Received text and all Greek manuscripts
   G. Received text and Griesbach (*Epistle to Romans*)
   H. Received text and Griesbach results examined
   I. Received text and Griesbach (*Epistle to Galatians*)
   J. Received text and Griesbach (and Scholz) new readings

K. Limitation of doubt – Benelius
L. All churches have same Hebrew Old Testament, Greek New Testament
IV. Errors of reasoning or doctrine
    A. (Supposed) reasonings, quotations, superstitions, prejudices, etc.; Jerome
    B. Reply:
        1. Protest
        2. Inconsistency – involve abandonment of principles
        3. Where stop?
        4. Human vanity, ignorance
V. Errors in narratives – contradictions in facts (supposed) dates, allusions, etc.
    A. Scriptures always adversaries and defenders
    B. Ease of general assertion
    C. Precipitate judgment: various causes:
        1. Brevity
        2. Two date-commencements
        3. Different designs in Gospels
        4. Mistranslations, contrary meanings
        5. Repeated acts, discourses
        6. Disregard of various readings
        7. Point of narration not discerned
        8. Want of care in chronology
VI. Errors in natural philosophy
    A. *Joshua* 10:12 – illustration
    B. Popular language of Scripture – illustrations, Herschel, Airey, etc.
    C. Two grand facts – God says true; knows more directly than us
    D. First fact: No physical error in the Word of God
        1. Ancient and modern false theologies
        2. Scriptures: no blunders, absurdities; various, and true; poetical, and true
    E. Second fact: Intimations escape of knowledge of the Almighty. Profound science as to:
        1. Earth
        2. Heavens

      3. Light
      4. Planets
      5. Air
      6. Mountains, primary – secondary
      7. Races of men
      8. Seas
      9. Submarine fires
      10. Subterranean waters
      11. Languages of men
      12. Stars
      13. Heaven
   F. God turns objections into testimonies – difficulties into proof
VII. Declarations of Paul (*1 Corinthians* 7:10, 12, 25, *etc.*)

## Chapter 5
### Evasions Examined

I. Does inspiration pertain to thoughts only, or to words also?
  A. Some confine to thoughts only
  B. Reply:
    1. Contrary to testimony – a Scripture of letters and words
    2. Irrational also – language, the mirror of the soul
    3. Leads further – "errors (more) in ideas (than) in words"
    4. Gratuitous hypothesis: useless
    5. Extreme inconsistency
    6. Question relates to book, not to writers: latter sometimes, former always, inspired – unwilling prophets
II. The historical books, should they be excepted from inspiration?
  A. Some think their inspiration unnecessary
  B. Reply:
    1. To them Old Testament prophets and New Testament apostles give striking, most respectful testimony.
    2. Our Lord's manner of quotation
    3. They reveal the character of God.
    4. They reveal the deep things of man.
    5. They reveal the angelic nature and office.
    6. They are full of the future.
    7. Their dramatic power and indefinable charm

8. Divine brevity – reserve
9. Divine prudence, foresight, wisdom
III. Details (insignificant), do they deserve exception?
   A. Paul
   B. Important insight, lessons, inferences

## Chapter 6
### Sacred Criticism, Its Relation to Divine Inspiration

I. Criticism a scientific inquirer, not a judge – else faith undermined and overthrown
II. Criticism an historian, not a soothsayer – else encourages impertinent and idle questions
III. Criticism the doorkeeper, not the God, of the temple
   A. Advice – illustration, a Roman traveler
   B. Counsel (the argument), study the Bible by and for itself
   C. The Bible its own witness
   D. The Bible: its majesty, beauty – above all Divine sanction in smallest parts
      1. Testimony of ministers
      2. Interpreters
      3. Believers – Luther – Augustine
   E. Take and read.

## Chapter 7
### Conclusion

I. Retrospect
   A. Inspiration not a system, but a fact; the book is inspired; we have to do with its words, not writers.
   B. Scripture entirely the word of man and God; human individuality; not gradual intermittent inspiration, but "everywhere and entirely" from God; this established by Scripture
   C. Scripture declares all prophetic words given by God; all Old, all New Testament prophetic, warranted by God; examples of the apostles and of the Lord Jesus Christ
   D. Objections considered; translations, readings, Septuagint in New Testament, philosophical errors, words of Paul
   E. Other objections: verbal inspiration contested, historical writings excluded, insignificant details, etc.

II. Religious: Bible above everything (Christian)
    A. Something above Bible, namely:
        1. Judaism
        2. Romanism
        3. Impure Protestantism
        4. Mysticism
    B. Light and growing radiance of Scriptures
    C. Grace and glory
    D. "The whole written Word is inspired by God."

# Translator's Preface

SOON AFTER the first publication of the *Theopneustia,* the late Rev. Dr. Welsh wrote to me, urging me to translate it for the press. A series of other engagements prevented me from doing so for several years. At last, in answer to a call for a cheaper and less bulky translation than one that had meanwhile appeared in London, I applied myself to the task, and had completed it before seeing what my predecessor had published in the south. The present translation being from the latest French edition, has the advantage of all the author's improved arrangement.

The importance of the subject, the high character of the author, and the admirable manner in which he has acquitted himself, required that no ordinary pains should be bestowed in doing him justice. These pains I have not spared.

I have endeavored, as far as I could, to give the texts quoted from Scripture in the precise words of our authorized version, and to secure the utmost possible correctness in the references. The headings at the top of the pages will, it is hoped, be of considerable use to the student.

After consulting an eminent authority as to the propriety of the change, "plenary inspiration," "divine inspiration," or "verbal inspiration," have been substituted throughout for the term *Theopneustia,* borrowed by the author from the Greek, and retained on the title-page. It was thought that the frequent recurrence of so unusual a word might repel ordinary readers, and make it appeal that the book was exclusively for the learned.

At a time when almost all religious controversies seem to turn, more or less, on the question, How far the Holy Scriptures are inspired? and when persons of all ranks and classes are called upon to arm themselves against various errors having their root in false or inadequate views on this subject, it seems hardly possible to overrate the value of the work now before the reader. Nor is it only as a work of controversy that it is invaluable. It is imbued throughout with a spirit of affectionate earnestness and glowing piety, which, even when it makes the greatest demand on the intellect, never suffers the heart to remain cold. Add to this, the wonderful copiousness of the illustrations, which the author seems to borrow with equal ease from the simplest objects in nature, the deepest wells of learning, the remotest deductions of science, and the history at once of the most ancient and most modern times. In short, as we accompany him from page to page and chapter to chapter, we seem not so much to be reading a book, as to be listening to a devout and accomplished friend, expatiating on a favorite subject – a subject of the very greatest importance, and one amid all the details of which he is quite at home.

David D. Scott<br>Glasgow

# God-Breathed

*The Divine Inspiration of the Bible*

# Prefatory Observations

A GLANCE at this book and its title may have prepossessed certain minds against it, by creating two equally erroneous impressions. These I am compelled to dissipate.

The Greek title "Theopneustia," although borrowed from Paul, and although it has long been used in Germany, from not having found its way into our language, may, no doubt, have led more than one reader to say to himself of the subject here treated, that it is too learned and abstruse (*scientifique*) to be popular, and too little popular to be important.

Yet I am bold to declare that if anything has given me at once the desire and the courage to undertake it, it is just the double conviction I entertain of its importance and its simplicity.

First of all, I do not think that after we have come to know that Christianity is divine, there can be presented to our mind any question bearing more essentially on the vitality of our faith than this: "Does the Bible come from God? Is it altogether from God? Or may it not be true, as some have maintained, that there occur in it maxims purely human, statements not exactly true, exhibitions of vulgar ignorance and ill-sustained reasoning? – in a word, books, or portions of books, foreign to the interests of the faith, subject to the natural weakness of the writer's judgment, and alloyed with error?" Here we have a question that admits of no compromise, a fundamental question – a question of life. It is the first that confronts you on opening the Scriptures, and with it your religion ought to commence.

Were it the case, as you whom I now address will have it, that all in the Bible is not important, does not bear upon the faith, and does not relate to Jesus Christ; and were it the case, taking another view, that in that book there is nothing inspired except what, in your opinion, is important, does bear upon the faith, and does relate to Jesus Christ; then your Bible is quite a different book from that of the fathers, of the

Reformers, and of the saints of all ages. It is fallible; theirs was perfect. It has chapters or parts of chapters, it has sentences and expressions, to be excluded from the number of the sentences and expressions that are God's; theirs was "all given by inspiration of God," "all profitable for doctrine, for reproof, for correction, for instruction in righteousness, and for rendering the man of God perfect by faith in Christ Jesus" (2 Timothy 3:16-17). In that case, one and the same passage is, in your judgment, as remote from what it was in theirs as Earth is from Heaven.

You may have opened the Bible, for example, at the 45<sup>th</sup> *Psalm*, or at the *Song of Songs;* and while you will see nothing there but what is most human in the things of the Earth – a long epithalamium, or the love communings of a daughter of Sharon and her young bridegroom – they read there of the glories of the church, the endearments of God's love, the deep things of Jesus Christ – in a word, all that is most divine in the things of Heaven; and if they found themselves unable to read of those things there, they knew at least that they were there, and there they tried to find them.

Suppose now that we both take up one of Paul's epistles. While one of us will attribute such or such a sentence, the meaning of which he fails to seize, or which shocks his carnal sense, to the writer's Jewish prejudices, to the most common intentions, to circumstances altogether human; the other will set himself, with profound respect, to scan the thoughts of the Holy Spirit: He will believe these perfect even before he has caught their meaning, and will put any apparent insignificance or obscurity to the account of his own dullness or ignorance alone.

Thus, while in the Bible of the one all has its object, its place, its beauty, and its use, as in a tree, branches and leaves, vessels and fibers, epidermis and bark even, have all theirs; the Bible of the other is a tree of which some of the leaves and branches, some of the fibers and the bark, have not been made by God.

But there is much more than this in the difference between us; for not only, according to your reply, we shall have two Bibles, but no one can know what your Bible really is.

It is human and fallible, say you, only in a certain measure; but who shall define that measure? If it be true that man, in putting his baneful impress upon it, have left the stains of humanity there, who shall determine the depth of that impression, and the number of those stains? You have told me that it has its human part; but what are the limits of that part, and who is to fix them for me? Why, no one. These everyone must determine for himself, at the bidding of his own judgment; in other words, this fallible portion of the Scriptures will be enlarged in the inverse ratio of our being illuminated by God's light, and a man will deprive himself of communications from above in the very proportion that he has need of them; in like manner as we see idolaters make to themselves divinities that are more or less impure, in proportion as they themselves are more or less alienated from the living and holy God! Thus, then, everyone will curtail the inspired Scriptures in different proportions, and making for himself an infallible rule of that Bible, so corrected by himself, will say to it: "Guide me henceforth, for you are my rule!" like those makers of graven images of whom Isaiah speaks, who make to themselves a god, and say to it, "Deliver me, for you are my god" (*Isaiah* 44:17).

But this is not all; what follows is of graver import still. According to your reply, it is not the Bible only that is changed – it is you.

Yes, even in presence of the passages which you have most admired you will have neither the attitude nor the heart of a believer! How can that be, after you have summoned these along with the rest of the Scriptures before the tribunal of your judgment, there to be pronounced by you divine, or not divine, or semi-divine? What authority for your soul can there be in an utterance which for you is infallible only in virtue of yourself? Had it not to present itself at your bar, along with other sayings of the same book, which you have pronounced to be wholly or partly human? Will your mind, in that case, put itself into the humble and submissive posture of a disciple, after having held the place of a judge? This is impossible. The deference you will show to it will be that perhaps of acquiescence, never that of faith; of approval, never of adoration. Do you tell me that you will believe in the divinity of the passage? But then it is not in God that you will believe, but in yourself! This utterance pleases, but does not govern you; it stands before you like a lamp; it is not within you as an unction from above – a principle of light, a fountain of life! I do not believe there ever was a pope, however possessed with notions of the importance of his own priestly office, who could confidently address his prayers to a dead person, whom he had himself, by canonizing him of his own plenary authority, raised to the rank of the demigods. How, then, shall a reader of the Bible, who has himself canonized a passage of the Scriptures, however possessed with a high idea of his own wisdom, possibly have the disposition of a true believer with regard to such a passage? Will his mind come down from his pontifical chair and humble itself before this utterance of thought, which, but for himself, would remain human, or at least doubtful? No one tries to fathom the meaning of a passage which he has himself legitimated, only in virtue of a meaning which he thinks he has already found. One submits only by halves to an authority which he has had it in his power to decline, and which he has once held to be doubtful. One worships but imperfectly what he has first degraded.

Besides, and let this be carefully noted, inasmuch as the entire divinity of such or such a passage of the Scriptures depends, in your view, not on its being found in the book of God's oracles, but on its presenting certain traits of spirituality and wisdom to your wisdom and your spirituality, the sentence that you pass cannot always be so exempt from hesitation as that you shall not retain, with regard to it, some of the doubts with which you set out. Hence your faith will necessarily participate in your uncertainties, and will be itself imperfect, undecided, conditional. As is the sentence, so will be the faith; and as is the faith, so will be the life. But such is not the faith, neither is such the life of God's elect.

But what will better show the importance of the question which is about to occupy us is, that if one of the two systems to which it may lead have, as we have said, all its root imbued with scepticism, its fruit inevitably will be a new unbelief.

How do we come to see that so many thousands can every morning and evening open their Bibles without once perceiving there doctrines which it teaches with the utmost clearness? How can they thus, during many a long year, walk on in darkness with the Sun in their hands? Do they not hold these books to be a revelation from God? Yes, but prepossessed with false notions of the divine inspiration, and believing that there still exists in Scripture an alloy of human error – they are compelled to find in it, nevertheless, reasonable utterances of thought, in order to their being authorized to believe these divine – they make it their study, as if unconsciously, to give these a meaning that their own wisdom approves; and thus not only do they render themselves incapable of recognizing therein the wisdom of God, but they lower the Scriptures in their own respect. In reading Paul's epistles, for example, they will do their utmost to find in them man's justification by the law, his native innocence and bent towards that which is good, the moral omnipotence of his will – the merit of his works. But, then, what happens? Alas! Just that after having given the sacred writer such forced meanings, they find his language so ill-conceived for his assumed object, such ill-chosen terms for what he is made to say, and such ill-sustained reasonings, that, as if in spite of themselves, they lose any respect felt for the letter of the Scriptures, and plunge into rationalism. It is thus that, after having commenced with unbelief, they reap a new unbelief as the fruit of their study; darkness becomes the recompense of darkness, and that terrible saying of Christ is fulfilled, "From him that has not shall be taken away even that which he has."

Such, then, it is evident, is the fundamental importance of the great question with which we are about to be occupied.

According to the answer which you, to whom we now address ourselves, make to it, the arm of God's Word is palsied for you; the sword of the Spirit has become blunted – it has lost its temper and its power to pierce. How could it henceforth penetrate your joints and marrow? How could it become stronger than your lusts, than your doubts, than the world, than Satan? How could it give you energy, victory, light, peace? No! It possibly may happen, at wide intervals of time, by a pure effect of God's unmerited favor, that, in spite of this dismal state of a soul, a divine utterance may come and seize it unawares; but it does not remain the less true, that this disposition that judges the Scriptures and doubts beforehand of their universal inspiration is one of the greatest obstacles that we can oppose to their acting with effect. "The word spoken," says Paul, "did not profit, not being mixed with faith in them who heard it" (*Hebrews* 4:2); while the most abundant benedictions of that same Scripture were at all times the lot of the souls which received it, "not as the word of man, but which it is truly, as the Word of God, working effectually in them who believe" (*1 Thessalonians* 2:13).

It will thus be seen that this question is of immense importance in its bearing upon the vitality of our faith; and we are entitled to say that between the two answers that may be made to it, there lies the same great gulf that must have separated two Israelites who might both have seen Jesus Christ in the flesh, and both equally owned him as a prophet; but one of whom, looking to his carpenter's dress, his poor fare, his hands inured to labor, and his rustic retinue, believed further, that he was not exempt from error and sin, as an ordinary prophet; while the other recognized in him Immanuel, the Lamb of God, the everlasting God, our Righteousness, the King of kings, the Lord of lords.

The reader may not yet have admitted each of these considerations; but he will at least admit that I have said enough to be entitled to conclude that it is worth while to study such a question, and that, in weighing it, you hold in your hands the most precious interests of the people of God. This is all I desired in a preface. It was the first point to which I wished to direct the reader's attention beforehand, and now comes the second.

If the study of this doctrine be the duty of all, that study is also within the reach of all; and the author scruples not to say that in writing his book the dearest object of his ambition has been to make it level to the comprehension of all classes of readers.

Meanwhile, he thinks he hears many make this objection. You address yourself to men of learning, they will say; your book is no concern of ours: We confine ourselves to religion, but here you give us theology.

Theology no doubt! But, what theology? Why, that which ought to be the study of all the heirs of eternal life, and with respect to which a very child may be a theologian.

Religion and theology! Let us explain what we mean; for often are both these terms abused to the injury of both, by people presuming to set the one against the other. Is not theology defined in all our dictionaries as "the science which has for its object, God and his revelation"? Now, when I was a boy at school, the catechism of my childhood made this the designation of my religion. "It is the science," it told me, "that teaches us to know God and his Word, God and his counsels, God in Christ." So, then, there is no difference between them, in object, means, or aim. Their object is truth; their means, the Word of God; their aim, holiness. "Sanctify them, O Father, by your truth: Your Word is truth!" Such is the aim contemplated by both, as it was that of their dying Master. How, then, shall we distinguish the one from the other? By this alone – that theology is religion studied more methodically, and with the aid of more perfect instruments.

Men have contrived, no doubt, to make, under the name of theology, a confused compound of philosophy, or the traditions of men with God's Word; but that was not theology – it was only scholastic philosophy.

It is true that the term *religion* is not always employed in its objective sense, to signify the science that embraces the truths of our faith; but it is used also, with a subjective meaning, to designate rather the sentiments which those truths foster in the hearts of believers. Let these two meanings be kept distinct. This is what we may do, and ought to do; but to oppose the one to the other, by calling the one *religion*, the other *theology*, were a deplorable absurdity. This would be to maintain, in other terms, that one might have the religious sentiments without the religious doctrines from which alone they spring; this would imply that you would have a man to be moral without having any religious tenets, pious without belief, a Christian without Christ, an effect without a cause – living, without a soul! Deplorable illusion! "Holy Father, this is life eternal, that they might know you, the only true God, and Jesus Christ whom you have sent" (*John* 17:3).

But even were it rather in its objective sense that people set themselves to oppose religion to theology – that is to say, the religion a Christian learns in his native tongue in his Bible, to the religion which a more accomplished person would study in the same Bible with the aid of history and of the learned languages – still I would say, even in this case, Distinguish between the two; don't oppose them to each other! Ought not every true Christian to be a theologian as far as he can? Is he not enjoined to be learned in the Word of God, nurtured in sound doctrine, rooted and established in the knowledge of Jesus Christ? And was it not to the multitude that our Lord said, in the midst of the street, "Search the Scriptures" (*John* 5:39).

Religion, then, in its objective meaning, bears the same relation to theology that the globe does to astronomy. They are distinct, and yet united; and theology renders the same services to religion that the astronomy of the geometrician offers to that of seamen. A ship captain might, no doubt, do without the *Mécanique Céleste* in finding his way to the seas of China, or in returning from the Antipodes; but even then it is to that science that, while traversing the ocean with his elementary notions he will owe the advantage he derives from his formulas, the accuracy of his tables, and the precision of the methods which give him his longitudes, and set his mind at ease as to the course he is pursuing. Thus too, the Christian, in order to his traversing the ocean of this world, and to his reaching the haven to which God calls him, may dispense with the ancient languages and the lofty speculations of theology; but, after all, the notions of religion with which he cannot dispense, will receive, in a great measure, their precision and their certainty from theological science. And while he steers toward eternal life with his eyes fixed on the compass which God has given him, still it is to theology that he will owe the certainty that that heavenly magnet is the same that it was in the days of the apostles – that the instrument of salvation has been placed intact in his hands, that its indications are faithful, and that the needle never varies.

There was a time when all the sciences were mysterious, professing secrecy, having their initiated persons, their sacred language, and their freemasonry. Physical science, geometry, medicine, grammar, history – everything was treated of in Latin. Men soared aloft in the clouds, far above the vulgar crowd; and would drop now and then from their bark sublime a few detached leaves, which we were bound to take up respectfully, and were not allowed to criticize. Nowadays, all is changed. Genius glories in making itself intelligible to the mass of mankind; and after having mounted up to the ethereal regions of science, there to pounce upon truth in her highest retreats, it endeavors to find a method of coming down again, and approaching near enough to let us know the paths it has pursued, and the secrets it has discovered. But if such be at present the almost universal tendency of the secular sciences, it has been at all times the distinctive character of true theology. That science is at the service of all. The others may do without the people, as the people may do without them; true theology, on the contrary, has need of flocks, as they again have need of it. It preserves their religion; and their religion preserves it in turn. Woe to them when their theology languishes, and does not speak to them! Woe to them when the religion of the flocks leave it to go alone, and no longer esteems it! We ought then, both for its sake and for theirs, to hold that it should speak to them, listen to them, study in their sight, and keep its schools open to them as our churches are.

When theology occupies the professor's chair in the midst of Christian flocks, its relations with them, constantly keeping before its eyes the realities of the Christian life, constantly recall to it also the realities of science: man's misery, the counsels of the Father, the Redeemer's cross, the consolations of the Holy Spirit, holiness, eternity. Then, too, the church's conscience, repressing its wanderings, overawes its hardihood, compels it to be serious, and corrects the effects of that familiarity, so readily running into profaneness, with which the science of the schools puts forth its hand and touches holy things. In speaking to it, day after day, of that life which the preaching of the doctrines of the cross nourishes in the church (a life, without the knowledge of which all its learning would be as incomplete as the natural history of man were it derived from the study of dead bodies), the religion of the flocks disengages theology from its excessive readiness to admire those branches of knowledge which do not sanctify. It often repeats to it the question addressed by Paul to the perverted science of the Galatians: "Did you receive the Spirit by the works of the law, or by the hearing of faith?" It disabuses it of the wisdom of man; it imbues it with reverence for the Word of God, and (in that holy Word) for those doctrines of the righteousness of faith which are "the power of God our Saviour," and which ought to penetrate the whole soul of its science. Thus does religion teach theology practically how to associate, in its researches, the work of the conscience with that of the understanding, and never to seek after God's truth but under the combined lights of study and prayer.

And, on the other hand, theology renders in its turn, to Christian flocks, services with which they cannot long dispense without damage. Theology watches over the religion of a people, to see that the lips of the priest keep knowledge, and that the law may be had from his mouth. Theology preserves purity of doctrine in the holy ministry of the Gospel, and the just balancing of all truths in preaching. Theology assures the simple against the confident assertions of a science inaccessible to them. Theology goes for its answers to the same quarters whence those assertions have come; which puts its finger on the sophisms of the adversaries of truth, overawes them by its presence, and compels them, before the flocks, to avoid exaggeration, and to put some reserve on the terms they employ. Theology gives the alarm at the first and so often decisive moment, when the language of religion among a people begins to decline from the truth, and when error, like a rising weed, sprouts and grows into a plant. It then gives timely warning, and people hasten to root it out.

It has ever happened that when flocks have been pious, theology has flourished. She has accomplished herself with learning; she has put due honor on studies that require vigorous effort; and, the better to capacitate herself for searching the Scriptures, not only has she desired to master all the sciences that can throw light upon them, but she has infused life into all other sciences, whether by the example of her own labors, or by gathering around her men of lofty minds, or by infusing into academical institutions a generous sentiment of high morality, which has promoted all their developments.

Thus it is that, in giving a higher character to all branches of study, theology has often ennobled that of a whole people.

But, on the contrary, when theology and the people have become indifferent to each other, and drowsy flocks have lived only for this world, then theology herself has given evident proofs of sloth, frivolity, ignorance, or perhaps of a love of novelties; seeking a profane popularity at any cost; affecting to have made discoveries that are only whispered to the ear, that are taught in academies, and never mentioned in the churches; keeping her gates shut amid the people, and at the same time throwing out to them from the windows doubts and impieties with the view of ascertaining the present measure of their indifference; until at last she breaks out into open scandal, in attacking doctrines, or in denying the integrity or the inspiration of certain books, or in giving audacious denials to the facts which they relate.

Let a man beware of believing that the whole people do not before long feel the consequences of so enormous a mischief. They will suffer from it even in their temporal interests, and their national existence will be compromised. In degrading their religion, you proportionally lower their moral character; you leave them without a soul. All things take their measure, in a nation, according to the elevation that is given to Heaven among the people. If their Heaven be low, everything is affected by it, even on the Earth. All there becomes before long more confined and more creeping; the future becomes narrowed; patriotism becomes materialized; generous traditions drop out of notice; the moral sense loses its tone; material well-being engrosses all regard; and all conservative principles, one after another, disappear.

We conclude then, on the one hand, that there exists the most intimate union, not only between a people's welfare and their religion, but between their religion and true theology; and, on the other hand, that if there have always been most pertinent reasons for this science being taught as such, for all and before all, never was this character more necessary for it than when treating of the doctrine which is about to occupy us. It is the doctrine of doctrines; the doctrine that teaches us all others, and in virtue of which alone they are doctrines; the doctrine which is to the believer's soul what the air is to his lungs – necessary for birth in the Christian life – necessary for living in it – necessary for advancing in it to maturity, and persevering in it.

Such, then, has been the twofold view under which this work has been composed. Every part of it, I trust, will bear testimony to my serious desire to make it useful to Christians of all classes.

With this object I have thrown off the forms of the school. Without entirely relinquishing, I have abstained from multiplying quotations in the ancient tongues. In pressing the wonderful unanimity of Christian antiquity on this question, I have confined myself to general facts. In fine, when I have had to treat the various questions that bear upon this subject, and which must be introduced in order to complete the doctrine which it involves, I have thrown them all into a separate chapter. And even there, against the advice of some friends, I have employed a method considered by them out of harmony with the general tone of the book, but which to me has seemed fitted to enable the reader to take a clearer and more rapid view of the subject.

It is, then, under this simple and practical form that, in presenting this work to the church of God, I rejoice that I can recommend it to the blessing of him who preached in the streets, and who, to John the Baptist, pointed to this as the peculiar character of his mission: "To the poor the Gospel is preached" (*Matthew* 11:5; *Luke* 7:22).

Well will it be if these pages confirm in the simplicity and the blissfulness of their faith those Christians who, without learning, have already believed, through the Scriptures, in the full inspiration of the Scriptures! Well will it be if some weary and heavy-laden souls are brought to listen more closely to that God who speaks to them in every line of his holy book! Well will it be if, through anything said by us, some travelers Zionward (like Jacob on his pilgrimage at the stone of Bethel), after having reposed their wearied being with too much indifference on this book of God, should come to behold at last that mysterious ladder which rises from thence to Heaven, and by which alone the messages of grace can come down to their souls, and their prayers mount up to God! Would that I could induce them, in their turn, to pour the sacred unction of their gratitude and their joy, and that they also could exclaim, "Surely the Lord is in this place! This is the house of God, and the gate of Heaven!" (*Genesis* 28:17).

## GOD-BREATHED: THE DIVINE INSPIRATION OF THE BIBLE

For myself, I fear not to say, that in devoting myself to the labor this work has cost me, I have often had to thank God for having called me to it; for while engaged in it, I have more than once beheld the divine majesty fill with its brightness the whole temple of the Scriptures. Here have I seen all the tissues, coarse in appearance, that form the vesture of the Son of man, become white, as no fuller on Earth could whiten them; here have I often seen the Book illuminated with the glory of God, and all its words seem radiant; in a word, I have felt what one ever experiences when maintaining a holy and true cause, namely, that it gains in truth and in majesty the more we contemplate it.

O my God, give me to love this Word of yours, and to possess it, as much as you have taught me to admire it!

"All flesh is as grass, and all the glory of man is as the flower of the grass: The grass withers, the flower thereof fades, but the Word of God abides forever; and it is this Word which, by the Gospel, has been preached unto us" (*1 Peter* 1:24-25).

*Our object in this book is, with God's help, and on the sole authority of his Word, to set forth, establish, and defend the Christian doctrine of Divine Inspiration.*

Chapter 1

# Definition of Theopneustia

### Section I
### *Theopneustia Defined*

THIS TERM is used for the mysterious power which the Divine Spirit put forth on the authors of the Scriptures of the Old and New Testaments, in order to their composing these as they have been received by the church of God at their hands. "All Scripture," says an apostle, "is *theopneustic.*"[1]

This Greek expression, at the time when Paul employed it, was new perhaps even among the Greeks; yet though the term was not used among the idolatrous Greeks, such was not the case among the Hellenistic Jews. The historian Josephus,[2] a contemporary of Paul's, employs another closely resembling it in his first book against Apion, when, in speaking of all the prophets who composed, says he, the twenty-two sacred books of the Old Testament,[3] he adds, that they wrote *according to the pneustia* (or the inspiration) *that comes from God.*[4] And the Jewish philosopher Philo,[5] himself a contemporary of Josephus, in the account he has left us of his embassy to the emperor Caius, making use, in his turn, of an expression closely resembling that of Paul, calls the Scriptures "*theochrest* oracles;"[6] that is to say, oracles given under the agency and dictation of God.

Theopneustia is not a system, it is a fact; and this fact, like everything else that has taken place in the history of redemption, is one of the doctrines of our faith.

1. *2 Timothy* 3:16. *Theopneust*, less euphonious, would be more exact.
2. Page 1036, edit. Aurel, *Allob.* 1611.
3. See on this number our chapter 3, section 2, question 27.
4. Κατὰ τὴν ἐπίπνοιαν τὴν ἀπὸ τοῦ Θεοῦ.
5. Page 1022, edit. Francof.
6. Θεόχρηστα (ἐν χρησμῷ Θεοῦ).

## Section II
## Theopneustia Asserted

Meanwhile, it is of consequence for us to say, and it is of consequence that it be understood, that this miraculous operation of the Holy Spirit had not the sacred writers themselves for its object – for these were only his instruments, and were soon to pass away; but that its objects were the holy books themselves, which were destined to reveal from age to age, to the church, the counsels of God, and which were never to pass away.

The power then put forth on those men of God, and of which they themselves were sensible only in very different degrees, has not been precisely defined to us. Nothing authorizes us to explain it. Scripture has never presented either its manner or its measure as an object of study. What it offers to our faith is solely the inspiration of what they say – the divinity of the books they have written. In this respect it recognizes no difference among them. What they say, they tell us, is theopneustic: Their book is from God. Whether they recite the mysteries of a past more ancient than the creation, or those of a future more remote than the coming again of the Son of man, or the eternal counsels of the Most High, or the secrets of man's heart, or the deep things of God – whether they describe their own emotions, or relate what they remember, or repeat contemporary narratives, or copy over genealogies, or make extracts from uninspired documents – their writing is inspired, their narratives are directed from above; it is always God who speaks, who relates, who ordains or reveals by their mouth, and who, in order to this, employs their personality in different measures: for "the Spirit of God has been upon them," it is written, "and his word has been upon their tongue." And though it be always the word of man since they are always men who utter it, it is always, too, the Word of God, seeing that it is God who superintends, employs, and guides them. They give their narratives, their doctrines, or their commandments, "not with the words of man's wisdom, but with the words taught by the Holy Spirit;" and thus it is that God himself has not only put his seal to all these facts, and constituted himself the author of all these commands, and the revealer of all these truths, but that, further, he has caused them to be given to his church in the order, and in the measure, and in the terms which he has deemed most suitable to his heavenly purpose.

Were we asked, then, how this work of divine inspiration has been accomplished in the men of God, we should reply, that we do not know; that it is not necessary or advantageous for us to know; and that it is in the same ignorance, and with a faith quite of the same kind, that we receive the doctrine of the new birth and sanctification of a soul by the Holy Spirit. We believe that the Spirit enlightens that soul, cleanses it, raises it, comforts it, softens it. We perceive all these effects; we admire and we adore the cause; but we have found it our duty to be content never to know the means by which this is done. Be it the same, then, with regard to divine inspiration.

And were we, further, called to say at least what the men of God experienced in their bodily organs, in their will, or in their understandings, while engaged in tracing the pages of the sacred book, we should reply that the powers of inspiration were not felt by all to the same degree, and that their experiences were not at all uniform; but we might add that the knowledge of such a fact bears very little on the interests of our faith, seeing that, as respects that faith, we have to do with the book, and not with the man. It is the book that is inspired, and altogether inspired: to be assured of this ought to satisfy us.

## Section III
### *Theopneustia Rejected*

Three descriptions of men, in these late times, without disavowing the divinity of Christianity and without venturing to decline the authority of the Scriptures, have thought themselves authorized to reject this doctrine.

Some of these have disowned the very *existence* of this action of the Holy Spirit; others have denied its *universality*; others, again, its *plenitude*.

The first, like Dr. Schleiermacher,[7] Dr. De Wette, and many other German divines, reject all miraculous inspiration, and are unwilling to attribute to the sacred writers any more than Cicero accorded to the poets – *afflatum spiritus divini* – "a divine action of nature, an interior power resembling the other vital forces of nature."[8]

---

7. Schleiermacher, *Der Christliche Glaube,* Volume i, s. 115.
8. De Wette, *Lehrbuch Anmerk.* Twesten, *Vorlesungen über die Dogmatik,* Volume 1, page 424, etc.

## DEFINITION OF THEOPNEUSTIA

The second, like Dr. Michaëlis,[9] and like Theodore of Mopsuestia,[10] while admitting the existence of a divine inspiration, would confine it to a part only of the sacred books: to the first and fourth of the four *Evangelists*, for example; to a part of the *Epistles*, to a part of *Moses*, a part of *Isaiah*, a part of *Daniel*. These portions of the Scriptures, say they, are from God; the others are from man.

The third class, in fine, like M. Twesten in Germany, and like many divines in England,[11] extend, it is true, the notion of a divine inspiration to all parts of the Bible, but not to all equally (*nicht gleichmaessig*). Inspiration, as they understand it, might be universal indeed, but unequal; often imperfect, accompanied with innocent errors; and carried to very different degrees, according to the nature of different passages – of which degrees they constitute themselves, more or less, the judges.

Many of these, particularly in England, have gone so far as to distinguish four degrees of divine inspiration: The inspiration of *superintendence*, they have said, in virtue of which the sacred writers have been constantly preserved from serious error in all that relates to faith and life; the inspiration of *elevation*, by which the Holy Spirit, further, by carrying up the thoughts of the men of God into the purest regions of truth, must have indirectly stamped the same characters of holiness and grandeur on their words; the inspiration of *direction*, under the more powerful action of which the sacred writers were under God's guidance in regard to what they said and abstained from saying; finally, the inspiration of *suggestion*. Here, they say, all the thoughts, and even the words, have been given by God, by means of a still more energetic and direct operation of his Spirit.

"The Theopneustia," says M. Twesten, "extends unquestionably even to words, but only when the choice or the employment of them is connected with the religious life of the soul; for one ought, in this respect," he adds, "to distinguish between the Old and New Testament, between the Law and the Gospel, between history and prophecy, between narratives and doctrines, between the apostles and their apostolical assistants."

To our mind these are all fantastic distinctions; the Bible has not authorized them; the church of the first eight centuries of the Christian

---

9. Michaëlis, *Introduction to the New Testament*.
10. See our chapter 5, section 2, question 44.
11. Drs. Pye, Smith, Dick, Wilson.

era knew nothing of them, and we believe them to be erroneous in themselves, and deplorable in their results.

Our design then, in this book, in opposition to these three systems, is to prove the existence, the universality, and the plenitude of the divine inspiration of the Bible.

First of all, it concerns us to know if there has been a divine and miraculous inspiration for the Scriptures. We say that there has. Next, we have to know if the parts of Scripture that are divinely inspired are equally and entirely so; or, in other terms, if God has provided, in a certain though mysterious manner, that the very words of his holy book should always be what they ought to be, and that it should contain no error. This, too, we affirm to be the case. Finally, we have to know whether what is thus inspired by God in the Scriptures be a part of the Scriptures or the whole of the Scriptures. We say that it is the whole Scriptures – the historical books as well as the prophecies; the *Gospels* as well as the *Song of Solomon;* the *Gospels of Mark* and *Luke*, as well as those of *John* and *Matthew;* the history of the shipwreck of Paul in the waters of the Adriatic, as well as that of the shipwreck of the old world in the waters of the flood; the scenes of Mamre beneath the tents of Abraham, as well as those of the day of Christ in the eternal tabernacles; the prophetic prayers in which the Messiah, a thousand years before his first advent, cries in the *Psalms*, "My God, my God, why have you forsaken me?" "They have pierced my hands and my feet." "They have cast lots upon my vesture." "They look and stare at me" – as well as the narratives of them by John, Mark, Luke, or Matthew.

In other words, it has been our object to establish by the Word of God that the Scripture is from God, that the Scripture is throughout from God, and that the Scripture throughout is entirely from God.

Meanwhile, however, we must make ourselves clearly understood. In maintaining that all Scripture is from God, we are very far from thinking that man goes for nothing in it. We shall return in a subsequent section to this opinion; but we have felt it necessary to state it here. There, all the words are man's; as there, too, all the words are God's. In a certain sense, the *Epistle to the Romans* is altogether a letter of Paul's and in a still higher sense, the *Epistle to the Romans* is altogether a letter of God's.

Pascal might have dictated one of his *Provincial Letters* to some Clermont artisan, and another to the Abbess of Port-Royal. Could the former have been on that account less Pascalian than all the rest? Undoubtedly not. The great Newton, when he wished to hand over to the world his marvelous discoveries, might have employed some Cambridge youth to write out the fortieth, and some college servant the forty-first proposition of his immortal work, the *Principia*, while he might have dictated the remaining pages to Barrow and Halley. Should we any the less possess the discoveries of his genius, and the mathematical reasonings which lead us to refer to one and the same law all the movements in the universe? Would the whole work be any the less his? No, undoubtedly. Perhaps, however, someone at his leisure might have further taken some interest in knowing what were the emotions of those two great men, or the simple thoughts of that boy, or the honest musings of that domestic, at the time that their four pens, all alike docile, traced the Latin sentences that were dictated to them. You may have been told that the two latter, as they plied the quill, allowed their thoughts to revert indifferently to past scenes in the gardens of the city, or in the courts of Trinity College; while the two professors, following with the most intense interest every thought of their friend, and participating in his sublime career, like eaglets on their mother's back, sprang with him into the loftiest elevations of science, borne up by his mighty wings, soaring with delight into the new and boundless regions that he had opened to them. Nevertheless, you may have been told, among the lines thus dictated, there may have been some which neither the boy nor even the professors were capable of understanding. These details are of little consequence, you would have replied; I will not waste any time upon them; I will study the book. Its preface, its title, it first line, and its last line, all its theorems, easy or difficult, understood or not understood, are from the same author, and that is enough. Whoever the writers may have been, and however different the respective elevation of their thoughts, their hand, faithful to its task, and superintended while engaged in it, has equally traced their master's thoughts on the same roll of paper; and there I can always study, with equal confidence, in the very words of his genius, the mathematical principles of Newton's philosophy.

Such is the fact of the divine inspiration of the Scriptures; nearly to this extent, that in causing his books to be written by inspired men, the Holy Spirit has almost always, more or less, employed the instrumentality of their understanding, their will, their memory, and all the powers of their personality, as we shall before long have occasion to repeat. And it is thus that God, who desired to make known to his elect in a book that was to last forever the spiritual principles of divine philosophy, has caused its pages to be written in the course of a period of sixteen hundred years, by priests, by kings, by warriors, by shepherds, by publicans, by fishermen, by scribes, by tentmakers, associating their affections and their faculties therewith, more or less, according as he deemed fit. Such, then, is God's book. Its first line, its last line, all its teachings, understood or not understood, are by the same author; and that ought to suffice for us. Whoever may have been the writers – whatever their circumstances, their impressions, their comprehension of the book, and the measure of their individuality in this powerful and mysterious operation – they have all written faithfully and under superintendence in the same roll, under the guidance of one and the same Master, for whom a thousand years are as one day; and the result has been the Bible. Therefore, I will not lose time in idle questions; I will study the book. It is the word of Moses, the word of Amos, the word of John, the word of Paul; but still the thoughts expressed are God's thoughts, and the words are God's words. "You, Lord, have spoken by the mouth of your servant David." "The Spirit of the Lord spoke by me," said he, "and his word was in my tongue."[12]

It would then, in our view, be holding very erroneous language to say that certain passages in the Bible are man's, and certain passages in the Bible are God's. No; every verse without exception is man's; and every verse without exception is God's, whether we find him speaking there directly in his own name, or whether he employs the entire personality of the sacred writer. And as Bernard has said of the living works of the regenerated man, "that our will does nothing there without grace, but that grace does nothing there without our will;" so ought we to say that in the Scriptures God has done nothing but by man, and man has done nothing but by God.

In fact, it is with divine inspiration as with efficacious grace. In the operations of the Holy Spirit while causing the sacred books to be written, and in those of the same divine agent while converting a soul, and causing it to advance in the ways of sanctification, man is in different respects entirely active and entirely passive. God does all there; man

---

12. *Acts* 4:25; *2 Samuel* 23:1-2. See chapter 2, section 2.

does all there; and it may be said for both of these works what Paul said of one of them to the Philippians, "It is God that works in you *to will and to do.*"[13] Thus you will see that in the Scriptures the same operations are attributed alternately to God and to man. God converts, and it is man that converts himself. God circumcises the heart, God gives a new heart; and it is man that should circumcise his heart, and make himself a new heart. "Not only because, in order to obtain such or such an effect, we ought to employ the means to obtain such or such an effect," says the famous President Edwards in his admirable remarks against the errors of the Arminians, "but because this effect itself is our act, as it is our duty; *God producing all, and we acting all.*"[14]

Such, then, is the Word of God. It is God speaking in man, God speaking by man, God speaking as man, God speaking for man! This is what we have asserted, and must now proceed to prove. Possibly, however, it will be as well that we should first give a more precise definition of this doctrine.

## Section IV
## *Theopneustia Further Defined and Stated*

In point of theory, it were allowable to say that a religion might be divine without the books that teach it being miraculously inspired. It were possible, for example, to figure to ourselves a Christianity without divine inspiration; and one might conceive, perhaps, that all the miracles of our faith have been performed with the single exception of this one. On this supposition (which nothing authorizes), the everlasting Father would have given his Son to the world; the creating Word, made flesh, would have submitted for us to the death of the cross, and caused to descend from Heaven upon his apostles the spirit of understanding and the power of working miracles; but, all these mysteries of redemption once consummated, he might have relinquished to these men of God the care of writing, according to their own wisdom, our sacred books; and their writings would thus have presented no more than the natural language of their supernatural illuminations, of their convictions, and their charity. Such an order of things, no doubt, is but an idle supposition, directly opposed to the testimony which the Scriptures have ren-

---

13. *Philippians* 2:13.
14. Edwards' *Remarks,* page 251.

dered to what they are. But without saying here that it resolves nothing, and that, miracle for miracle, that of illumination is not less inexplicable than that of inspiration; without saying further, that the Word of God possesses a divine power which belongs to it alone – such an order of things, granting it were a reality, would have exposed us to innumerable errors, and plunged us into the most dismal uncertainty. Upon what testimony could, in that case, our faith have rested? On something said by men? But faith is founded only on the Word of God (*Romans* 10:17). In such a system, then, you would only have had a Christianity without Christians. Deprived of any security against the imprudence of the writers, you could not even have given their books the authority at present possessed in the church by those of Augustine, Bernard, Luther, and Calvin, or of so many other men whom the Holy Spirit enlightened with a knowledge of the truth. We are, in fact, sufficiently aware how many imprudent expressions and erroneous propositions have found their way into the midst even of the finest pages of those admirable doctors. And yet the apostles (on the supposition we have made) would have been far more subject to serious mistakes even than they were, since they would not have had, like the doctors of the church, a Word of God by which to direct their own; and since they themselves would have had to compose the whole language of religious science. (A science is more than half-formed when its language is formed.) What deplorable and inevitable errors must have necessarily accompanied, in their case, this revelation without divine inspiration! And in what deplorable doubts would their hearers have been left – errors in the selection of facts, errors in the appreciation of them, errors in the statement of them, errors in the mode of conceiving the relations they bear to doctrines, errors in the expression of those very doctrines, errors of omission, errors of language, errors of exaggeration, errors in adopting certain national prejudices, or prejudices arising from a man's rank or party, errors in the foresight of the future, and in judgments pronounced upon the past.

But, thanks be to God, it is not thus with our sacred books. They contain no error; they are written throughout by inspiration of God. "Holy men spoke as they were moved by the Holy Spirit;" they did so, "not with words that man's wisdom teaches, but with words which the Spirit of God taught;" in such sort, that not one of these words should be neglected, and that we are called to respect them and to study them, even to their smallest iota and their slightest jot: for "this Scripture is pure; like silver refined seven times, it is perfect."

These assertions, which are themselves testimonies of the Word of God, have already comprised our last definition of *Theopneustia*, and lead us to characterize it, finally, as that inexplicable power which the Divine Spirit put forth of old on the authors of Holy Scripture, in order to their guidance even in the employment of the words they used, and to preserve them alike from all error and from all omission.

This new definition, which might appear complex, is not so really; for the two traits of which it is composed are equivalent, and to admit the one is to accept the other.

We propose them disjunctively to the assent of our readers, and we offer them the alternative of accepting either. One has more precision, the other more simplicity, in so far as it presents the doctrine under a form more disengaged from all questions relative to the mode of inspiration, and to the secret experiences of the sacred writers. Let either be fully accepted, and then there will have been rendered to the Scriptures the honor and the credit to which they are entitled.

What we propose, therefore, is to establish the doctrine of divine inspiration under one or other of these two forms:

The Scriptures are given and warranted by God, even in their language; and, the Scriptures contain no error (whereby we understand that they say all that they ought to say, and that they do not say what they ought not to say).

Now, how shall a man establish this doctrine? By the Scriptures, and only by the Scriptures. Once that we have recognized these as true, we must go to them to be taught what they are; and once that they have told us that they are inspired of God, it belongs to them further to tell us how they are so, and how far they are so.

To attempt the proof of their inspiration *a priori* – by arguing from that miracle being necessary for the security of our faith – would be to adopt a feeble mode of reasoning, and almost to imitate, in one sense, the presumption which, in another sense, imagines *a priori* four degrees of divine inspiration. Further, to think of establishing the entire inspiration of the Scriptures on the consideration of their beauty, their constant wisdom, their prophetic foresight, and all the characters of divinity which occur in them, would be to build on arguments no doubt just, but contestable, or at least contested. It is solely on the declarations of

Holy Scripture, therefore, that we have to take our stand. We have no authority but that for the doctrines of our faith; and divine inspiration is just one of those doctrines.

Here, however, let us anticipate a misapprehension. It may happen that some reader, still but feebly established in his Christianity, mistaking our object, and thinking to glance through our book in search of arguments which may convince him, might find himself disappointed, and might conceive himself authorized to charge our line of argument with some vicious reasoning, as if we wanted to prove in it the inspiration of the Scriptures by the inspiration of the Scriptures. It is of consequence that we should put him right. We have not written these pages for the disciples of Porphyry, or of Voltaire, or of Rousseau; and it has not been our object to prove that the Scriptures are worthy of belief. Others have done this, and it is not our task. We address ourselves to men who respect the Scriptures, and who admit their veracity. To these we attest, that, being true, they say that they are inspired; and that, being inspired, they declare that they are so throughout: Whence we conclude that they necessarily must be so.

Certainly, of all truths, this doctrine is one of the simplest and the clearest to minds meekly and rationally submissive to the testimony of the Scriptures. No doubt modern theologians may be heard to represent it as full of uncertainties and difficulties; but they who have desired to study it only by the light of God's Word have been unable to perceive those difficulties, or to find those uncertainties. Nothing, on the contrary, is more clearly or oftener taught in the Scriptures than the inspiration of the Scriptures. Accordingly, the ancients knew nothing on this subject of the embarrassments and the doubts of the doctors of the present day: For them the Bible was from God, or it was not from God. On this point antiquity presents an admirable unanimity.[15] But since the moderns, in imitation of the Talmudistic Jews and Rabbins of the Middle Ages, have imagined learned distinctions between four or five different degrees of inspiration, who can wonder that for them difficulties and uncertainties have been multiplied? Contesting what the Scriptures teach, and explaining what the Scriptures do not teach, it is easy

---

15. See on this subject the learned dissertation in which Dr. Rudelbach establishes the sound doctrines of inspiration historically, as we have sought to establish them by Scripture (*Zeitschrift für die gesammte Lutherische Theologie und Kirche*, von Rudelbach und Guericke, 1840).

to see how they come to be embarrassed; but for this they have only their own rashness to blame.

So very clear, indeed, is this testimony that the Scriptures render to their own inspiration, that one may well feel amazed that, among Christians, there should be any diversities of opinion on so well-defined a subject. But the evil is too easily explained by the power of preconceived opinions. The mind once wholly preoccupied by objections of its own raising, sacred passages are perverted from their natural meaning in proportion as those objections present themselves; and, by a secret effort of thought, people try to reconcile these with the difficulties that embarrass them. The plenary inspiration of the Scriptures is, in spite of the Scriptures, denied (as the Sadducees denied the resurrection), because the miracle is thought inexplicable; but we must recollect the answer made by Jesus Christ, "Do you not therefore err, because you know not the Scriptures, nor the power of God?" (*Mark* 12:24, 27). It is, therefore, because of this too common disposition of the human mind that we have thought it best not to present the reader with our Scriptural proofs until after having completed our definition of divine inspiration, by an attentive examination of the part to be assigned in it to the individuality of the sacred writers. This will be the subject of the following section. No less do we desire being able to present the reader with a more didactic expression of the doctrine that occupies us, and of some of the questions connected with it; but we have thought that a more fitting place might be found for this development elsewhere, partly because it will be more favorably received after our Scriptural proofs shall have been considered; partly because we have no desire, by employing the forms of the school, to repel, at the very threshold, unlearned readers who may have taken up these pages with the idea of finding something in them for the edification of their faith.

## Section V
### *On the Individuality of the Sacred Writers*

The individuality of the sacred writers, so profoundly stamped on the books they have respectively written, seems to many impossible to be reconciled with a plenary inspiration. No one, say they, can read the Scriptures without being struck with the differences of language, conception, and style discernible in their authors; so that even were the titles of the several books to give us no intimation that we were passing from one author to another, still we should almost instantly discover, from the change of their character, that we had no longer to do with the same writer, but that a new personage had taken the pen. This diversity reveals itself even on comparing one prophet with another prophet, and one apostle with another apostle. Who could read the writings of Isaiah and Ezekiel, of Amos and Hosea, of Zephaniah and Habakkuk, of Jeremiah and Daniel, and proceed to study those of Paul and Peter or of John without observing, with respect to each of them, how much his views of the truth, his reasonings, and his language, have been influenced by his habits, his condition in life, his genius, his education, his recollections – all the circumstances, in short, that have acted upon his outer and inner man? They tell us what they saw, and just as they saw it. Their memory is put into requisition, their imagination is called into exercise, their affections are drawn out – their whole being is at work, and their moral physiognomy is clearly delineated. We are sensible that the composition of each has greatly depended, both as to its essence and its form, on its author's circumstances and peculiar turn of mind. Could the son of Zebedee have composed the *Epistle to the Romans*, as we have received it from the Apostle Paul? Who would think of attributing to him the *Epistle to the Hebrews?* And although the epistles general of Peter were without their title, who would ever think of ascribing them to John? It is thus, likewise, with the evangelists. All four are very distinctly recognizable, although they all speak of the same Master, profess the same doctrines, and relate the same acts. Such, we are told, is the fact, and the following consequences are boldly deduced from it:

Were it God who speaks alone and constantly in the Scriptures, we should see in their various parts an uniformity which is not to be found there.

It must be admitted that two different impulses have acted at the same time on the same authors, while they were composing the Scriptures; the natural impulses of their individuality, and the miraculous impulses of inspiration.

There must have resulted from the conflict, the concurrence, or the balanced action, of these two forces – an inspiration variable, gradual, sometimes entire, sometimes imperfect, and often even reduced to the feeble measure of a mere superintendence.

The variable power of the Divine Spirit, in this combined action, must have been in the ratio of the importance and the difficulty of the matters treated of by the sacred author. He might even have abstained from any intervention when the judgment and the recollections of the writer could suffice, inasmuch as God never performs useless miracles.

"It belongs not to man to say where nature ends and where inspiration begins," says Bishop Wilson.[16]

"The exaggeration we find in the notions which some have entertained of inspiration," says Dr. Twesten, "does not consist in their having extended them to all, but in their having extended them to all equally. If inspiration does not exclude the personal action of the sacred authors, no more does it destroy all influence proceeding from human imperfection. But we may suppose this influence to be more and more feeble in the writers, in proportion as the matter treated of is more intimately related to Christ."[17]

Dr. Dick recognizes three degrees of inspiration in the Holy Scriptures: "1. There are many things in the Scriptures which the writers might have known, and probably did know, by ordinary means.... In these cases, no supernatural influence was necessary to enlighten and invigorate their minds; it was only necessary that they should be infallibly preserved from error. 2. There are other passages of Scripture, in composing which the minds of the writers must have been supernaturally endowed with more than ordinary vigor.... It is manifest, with respect to many passages of Scripture, that the subjects of which they treat must have been directly revealed to the writers."[18]

Hence it follows, that if this plenary inspiration were sometimes necessary, still, with respect to matters at once easy and of no religious importance, there might be found in the Scriptures some harmless errors, and some of those stains ever left by the hand of man on all he touches. While the energies of the Divine Mind, by an action always powerful, and often victorious, enlarged the comprehension of the men of God, purified their affections, and led them to seek out, from among all their recollections of the past, those which might be most usefully transmitted to the church of God, the natural energies of their own minds, left to themselves in so far as regarded all details of no consequence either to faith or virtue, may have led to the occurrence in the

16. *Lectures on the Evidences of Christianity*, page 506.
17. Vories, *Über die Dogmatik*, Volume 1.
18. See *An Essay on the Inspiration of the Holy Scriptures* by the late John Dick, D.D. Fourth edition, Glasgow, 1840, chapter 1.

Scriptures of some mixture of inaccuracy and imperfection. "We must not therefore," says M. Twesten, "attribute an unlimited infallibility to the Scripture, as if there were no error there. No doubt God is truth, and in matters of importance all that is from him is truth; but if all be not of equal importance, all does not then proceed equally from him; and if inspiration does not exclude the personal action of the sacred authors, no more does it destroy all influence of human imperfection."[19]

All these authors include in their assumptions and conclusions the notion that there are some passages in the Scriptures quite devoid of importance, and that there are others alloyed with error. We shall before long repel with all our might both these imputations; but this is not yet the place for it. The only question we have to do with here is that respecting the living and personal form under which the Scriptures of God have been given to us, and its alleged incompatibility with the fact of a plenary inspiration. To this we proceed to reply.

We begin by declaring how far we are from contesting the fact alleged, while, however, we reject the false consequences that are allegedly deduced from it. So far are we from not acknowledging this human individuality stamped throughout on our sacred books, that, on the contrary, it is with profound gratitude – with an ever-growing admiration – that we contemplate this living, actual, dramatic, human character diffused with so powerful and charming an effect through all parts of the book of God. Yes (we cordially unite with the objectors in saying it), here is the phraseology, the tone, the accent of a Moses; there, of a John; here, of an Isaiah; there, of an Amos; here, of a Daniel or of a Peter; there, of a Nehemiah; there again of a Paul. We recognize them, listen to them, see them. Here, one may say, there is no room for mistake. We admit the fact; we delight in studying it; we profoundly admire it – and we see in it, as we shall have occasion more than once to repeat, one additional proof of the divine wisdom which has dictated the Scriptures.

Of what consequence to the fact of the divine inspiration is the absence or the concurrence of the sacred writers' affections? Cannot God equally employ them or dispense with them? He who can make a statue speak, can he not, as he pleases, make a child of man speak? He who rebuked by means of a dumb animal the madness of one prophet,

---

19. *Ut supra.*

can he not put into another prophet the sentiments or the words which suit best the plan of his revelations? He that caused to come forth from the wall a hand, without any mind of its own to direct it, that it might write for him those terrible words, "*Mene, mene, tekel, upharsin*" (*Daniel* 5:25), could he not equally guide the intelligent and pious pen of his apostle, in order to its tracing for him such words as these: "*I say the truth in Christ, and my conscience bears me witness in the Holy Spirit, that I have great heaviness and continual sorrow in my heart for my brethren, my kinsmen according to the flesh, and who are Israelites*" (*Romans* 9:1-4)? Know you how God acts, and how he abstains from acting? Will you teach us the mechanism of inspiration? Will you say what is the difference between its working where individuality is discoverable, and its working where individuality is not discoverable? Will you explain to us why the concurrence of the thoughts, the recollections, and the emotions of the sacred writers, should diminish aught of their *theopneustia*? And will you tell us whether this very concurrence may not form part of it? There is a gulf interposed between the fact of this individuality and the consequence you deduce from it; and your understanding is no more competent to descend into that gulf to contest the reality of *theopneustia* than ours is to explain it. Was there not a great amount of individuality in the language of Caiaphas when that wicked man, full of the bitterest spite, abandoning himself to the counsels of his own evil heart, and little dreaming that he was giving utterance to the words of God, cried out in the Jewish council, "You know nothing at all nor consider that it is expedient for us that one man should die for the people"? Certainly there was in these words, we should say, abundance of individuality; and yet we find it written that Caiaphas *spoke this not of himself* (ἀφ' ἑαυτοῦ), but that, being high priest for that year, "he prophesied," unconsciously, that Jesus should die, "in order that he might gather into one the children of God that were scattered abroad" (*John* 11:49-52).

Why, then, should not the same Spirit in order to the utterance of the words of God, employ the pious affections of the saints, as well as the wicked and hypocritical thoughts of his most detestable adversaries?

When a man tells us that if, in such or such a passage, the style be that of Moses or of Luke, of Ezekiel or of John, then it cannot be that of God – it were well that he would let us know what is God's style. One would call our attention, forsooth, to the accent of the Holy Spirit –

would show us how to recognize him by the peculiar cast of his phraseology, by the tone of his voice; and would tell us wherein, in the language of the Hebrews or in that of the Greeks, his supreme individuality reveals itself!

It should not be forgotten that the sovereign action of God, in the different fields in which it is displayed, never excludes the employment of second causes. On the contrary, it is in the concatenation of their mutual bearings that he loves to make his mighty wisdom shine forth. In the field of creation he gives us plants by the combined employment of all the elements – heat, moisture, electricity, the atmosphere, light, the mechanical attraction of the capillary vessels, and the manifold operations of the organs of vegetation. In the field of providence, he accomplishes the development of his vastest plans by means of the unexpected concurrence of a thousand million human wills, alternately intelligent and yielding, or ignorant and rebellious. "Herod and Pilate, with the Gentiles and the people of Israel" (influenced by so many diverse passions), "were gathered together," he tells us, only "to do whatsoever his hand and counsel had determined before to be done" (*Acts* 4:27-28). Thus, too, in the field of prophecy does he bring his predictions to their accomplishment. He prepares, for example, long beforehand, a warlike prince in the mountains of Persia, and another in those of Media; the former of these he had indicated by name two hundred years before; he unites them at the point named with ten other nations against the empire of the Chaldeans; he enables them to surmount a thousand obstacles; and makes them at last enter the great Babylon at the moment when the seventy years, so long marked out for the captivity of the Jewish people, had come to a close. In the field of his miracles, even, he is pleased still to make use of second causes. There he had only to say, "Let the thing be," and it would have its being; but he desired, by employing inferior agents, even in that case to let us know that it is he that gives power to the feeblest of them. To divide the Red Sea, he not only causes the rod of Moses to be stretched out over the deep – he sends from the east a mighty wind, which blows all night, and makes the waters go back. To cure the man that was born blind, he makes clay and anoints his eyelids. In the field of redemption, instead of converting a soul by an immediate act of his will, he presents motives to it, he makes it read the Gospel, he sends preachers to it, and thus it is that, while it is he who "gives us to will and to do according to his good pleasure" (*Philippians* 2:13), he "begets us by his own will, by the Word of truth" (*James* 1:18). Well, then, why should it not be thus in the field of inspiration (*theopneustia*)? Wherefore, when he sends forth his Word, should he not cause it to enter the understanding, the heart, and the life of his servants, as he puts it upon their lips? Wherefore should he not associate their personality with what they reveal to us? Wherefore should not their sentiments, their history, their experiences, form part of their inspiration (*theopneustia*)?

What may, moreover, clearly expose the error involved in this alleged difficulty is the extreme inconsistency shown in the use that is made of it. In fact, in order to impugn the plenary inspiration of certain portions of the Scriptures, the individuality with which they are marked is insisted on; and yet it is admitted that other parts of the sacred books, in which this character is equally manifest, must have been given directly by God, even to the most minute details. Isaiah, Daniel, Jeremiah, Ezekiel, and the author of the *Apocalypse* have each stamped upon their prophecies their peculiar style, features, manner – in a word, their mark; just as Luke, Mark, John, Paul, and Peter have been able to do in their narratives, or in their letters. There is no validity, then, in the objection. If it proved anything, it would prove too much.

What still further strikes us in this objection, and in the intermittent system of inspiration with which it is associated, is its triple character of complication, rashness, and childishness. Complication, for it is assumed that the divine action in dictating the Scriptures intermitted or fell off as often as the passage falls in the scale of difficulty, or in the scale of importance; and thus God is made to retire or advance successively in the mind of the sacred writer during the course of one and the same chapter, or one and the same passage! Rashness, for the majesty of the Scriptures not being recognized, it is boldly assumed that they are of no importance and require no wisdom beyond that of man except in some of their parts. We add childishness; one is afraid, it is alleged, to attribute to God useless miracles – as if the Holy Spirit, after having, as is admitted, dictated, word for word, one part of the Scriptures, must find less trouble in doing nothing more elsewhere than aiding the sacred author by enlightening him, or leaving him to write by himself under mere superintendence!

But this is by no means all. What most of all makes us protest against a theory according to which the Scriptures are classed into the *inspired*, the *half-inspired*, and the *uninspired* (as if this sorry doctrine necessarily flowed from the individuality stamped upon them), is its direct opposition to the Scriptures. One part of the Bible is from man (people venture to say), and the other part is from God. And yet, mark what its own language on the subject is. It protests that "*all Scripture is given by inspiration of God*" (2 *Timothy* 3:16). It points to no exception. What right, then, can we have to make any, when Scripture itself admits none? Just because people tell us, if there be in the Scriptures a certain number of passages which could not have been written except under plenary inspiration, there are others for which it would have been enough for the author to have received some eminent gifts, and others still which might have been composed even by a very ordinary person! Be it so; but how does this bear upon the question? When you have been told who the author of a book is, you know that all that is in that book is from him – the easy and the difficult, the important and the unimportant. If, then, the whole Bible "is given by inspiration of God," of what consequence is it to the question that there are passages in your eyes more important or more difficult than others? The least among the companions of Jesus might no doubt have given us that fifth verse of the eleventh chapter of *John*, "Now Jesus loved Martha, and her sister, and Lazarus;" as the most petty schoolmaster also might have composed that first line of *Athalie*, "Into his temple, lo! I come, Jehovah to adore." But were we told that the great Racine employed some village schoolmaster to write out his drama, at his dictation, should we not continue, nevertheless, still to attribute to him all its parts – its first line, the notation of the scenes, the names of the *dramatis personæ*, the indications of their exits and their entrances, as well as the most sublime strophes of his choruses? If, then, God himself declares to us his having dictated the whole Scripture, who shall dare to say that that fifth verse of the eleventh chapter of *John* is less from God than the sublime words with which the *Gospel* begins, and which describe to us the eternal Word? Inspiration, no doubt, may be perceptible in certain passages more clearly than in others; but it is not, on that account, less real in the one case than in the other.

In a word, were there some parts of the Bible without inspiration, no longer could it be truly said that the whole Bible is divinely inspired. No longer would it be throughout the Word of God. It would have deceived us.

Here it is of special importance to remark that this fatal system of a gradual, imperfect, and intermittent inspiration, has its origin in that misapprehension to which we have more than once had occasion to advert. It is because people have almost always wished to view inspiration in the man, while it ought to have been seen only in the book. It is "*All Scripture*," it is *all that is written*, that is inspired of God (2 *Timothy* 3:16). We are not told, and we are not asked, how God did it. All that is attested to us is that he has done it. And what we have to believe is simply that, whatever may have been the method he took for accomplishing it.

To this deceptive point of view, which some have thought good to take in contemplating the fact of inspiration, the three following illusions may be traced:

First, in directing their regard to inspiration in the sacred author, people have naturally been led to figure it to themselves as an *extraordinary excitation* in him, of which he was conscious, which took him out of himself, which animated him, after the manner of the ancient Pythonesses, with an *afflatu divino*, a divine fire, easily discernible, in such sort, that wherever his words are simple, calm, familiar, they have been unable to see how divine inspiration could be attributed to him.

Next, in contemplating inspiration in persons, people have further been led to attribute to it *different degrees* of perfection, seeing they knew that the sacred authors had themselves received very different measures of illumination and personal holiness. But if you contemplate inspiration in the book, then you will immediately perceive that it cannot exist there in degrees. A word is from God, or it is not from God. If it be from God, it is not so after two different fashions. Whatever may have been the spiritual state of the writer, if all he writes be divinely inspired, all his words are from God. And (mark well) it is according to this principle that no Christian will hesitate, any more than Jesus Christ has done, to rank the Scriptures of Solomon with those of Moses, any more than those of Mark or of Matthew with those of the disciple whom Jesus loved – nay, with the words of the Son of God himself. They are all from God.

Finally, by a third illusion, from contemplating inspiration in the men who wrote the Scriptures, not in the Scriptures which they wrote, people have been naturally led to deem it absurd that God should *reveal* miraculously to anyone *what that person knew already*. They would, on this ground, deny the inspiration of those passages in which the sacred writers simply tell what they had seen, or simply state opinions, such as any man of plain good sense might express without being inspired. But it will be quite otherwise the moment inspiration is viewed, not as *in the writer*, but as *in that which is written*. Then it will be seen that all has been traced under God's guidance – both the things which the writer knew already and those of which he knew nothing. Who is not sensible, to give an example, that the case in which I should dictate to a student a book on geometry altogether differs from that in which, after having instructed him more or less perfectly in that science, I should employ him to compose a book on it himself under my auspices? In the latter work, it is true, he would require my intervention only in the difficult propositions; but then, who would think of saying the book was mine? In the former case, on the contrary, all parts of the book, easy and difficult alike, from the quadrature of the transcendental curves to the theory of the straight line or of the triangle, would be mine. Well, then, so is it with the Bible. It is not, as some will have it, a book which God employed men, whom he had previously enlightened, to write under his auspices. No – it is a book which he dictated to them; it is the Word of God; the Spirit of the Lord spoke by its authors, and his words were upon their tongues.

That the style of Moses, Ezekiel, David, Luke, and John may be at the same time God's style, is what a child might tell us.

Let us suppose that some modern French author had thought good, at the commencement of the present century, to aim at popularity by borrowing for a time the style, we shall say, of Chateaubriand; might it not then be said with equal truth, but in two different senses, that the style was the author's and yet the style too of Chateaubriand? And if, to save the French from some terrible catastrophe by bringing them back to the Gospel, God should condescend to employ certain prophets among them, by the mouths of whom he should proclaim his message, would not these men have to preach in French? What, then, would be their style, and what would you require in it, in order to its being recognized as that of God? If such were his pleasure, one of these prophets might speak like Fénelon, another like Bonaparte; in which case there is no doubt that it would be, in one sense, the curt, barking, jerking style of the great captain; also, and in the same sense, the sustained and varied flow of the priest of Cambray's rounded eloquence; while in another, and a higher and truer sense, it would, in both these mouths, be the style of God, the manner of God, the Word of God. No doubt, on every occasion on which he has revealed himself, God might have caused an awful voice to resound from Heaven, as of old from the top of Sinai, or on the banks of the Jordan.[20] His messengers, at least, might have been only angels of light. But even then what languages would these angels have spoken? Evidently those of the Earth! And if he found it advantageous on this Earth to substitute for the syntax of Heaven and the vocabulary of the archangels, the words and the constructions of the Hebrews or the Greeks, why not equally have borrowed their manners, style, and personality?

There is no doubt that he did this, but not so as that anything was left to chance. "Known unto him are all his works from the beginning of the world;"[21] and just as, year after year, he causes the tree to put forth its leaves as well for the season when they respire the atmospheric elements, and, cooperating with the process at the roots, can safely draw nourishment from their juices, as for that in which the caterpillars that are to spin their silk on its branches are hatched and feed upon them; just as he prepared a gourd for the very place and the very night on which Jonah was to come and seat himself to the east of Nineveh, and when the next morning dawned, a gnawing worm when the gourd was to be withered; so, too, when he would proceed to the most important of his doings, and cause that Word to be written which is to outlast the heavens and the Earth, the Lord God could prepare long beforehand each of those prophets for the moment and for the testimony to which he had foreordained them from eternity. He chose them, in succession, for their several duties, from among all men born of women; and, with respect to them, fulfilled in its perfection that saying, "Send, O Lord, by the hand you should send."[22]

As a skillful musician, when he would execute a long score by himself, takes up by turns the funereal flute, the shepherd's pipe, the merry fife, or the trumpet that summons to battle; so did Almighty God, when he would make us hear his eternal word, choose out from of old the instruments which it seemed fit to him to inspire with the breath of his

20. *Exodus* 19; *John* 12:29.
21. *Acts* 15:18.
22. *Exodus* 4:13.

Spirit. "He chose them before the foundation of the world, and separated them from their mother's womb."²³

Has the reader ever paid a visit to the astonishing organist, who so charmingly elicits the tourists' tears in the cathedral at Freiburg, as he touches one after another his wondrous keys, and greets your ear by turns with the march of warriors on the riverside, the voice of prayer sent up from the lake during the fury of the storm, or of thanksgiving when it is hushed to rest? All your senses are electrified, for you seem to have seen all, and to have heard all. Well, then, it was thus that the Lord God, mighty in harmony, applied as it were, the finger of his Spirit to the stops which he had chosen for the hour of his purpose, and for the unity of his celestial hymn. He had from eternity before him all the human stops which he required; his Creator's eye embraces at a glance this range of keys stretching over threescore centuries; and when he would make known to our fallen world the everlasting counsel of his redemption, and the coming of the Son of God, he put his left hand on Enoch, the seventh man from Adam,²⁴ and his right on John, the humble and sublime prisoner of Patmos. The celestial anthem, seven hundred years before the flood, began with these words, "Behold, the Lord comes with ten thousand of his saints, to execute judgment upon all" (*Jude* 14-15); but already, in the mind of God, and in the eternal harmony of his work, the voice of John had answered to that of Enoch, and closed the hymn, three thousand years after him, with these words, "Behold, he comes with clouds, and every eye shall see him, and they also which pierced him! Even so, Lord Jesus, come quickly. Amen!" (*Revelation* 1:7; 22:20). And during this hymn of thirty centuries, the Spirit of God never ceased to breathe in all his messengers; the angels, an apostle tells us, desired to look into its wondrous depths.²⁵ God's elect were moved, and life eternal came down into the souls of men.

Between Enoch and John, listen to Jeremiah, twenty-four centuries after the one, and seven hundred years before the other, "Before I formed you in the belly," says the Lord, "I knew you; and before you came forth out of the womb I sanctified you, and I ordained you a prophet unto the nations."²⁶ In vain did this alarmed man

---

23. *Galatians* 1:15; *Ephesians* 1:4.
24. *Jude* 14.
25. *1 Peter* 1:12.
26. *Jeremiah* 1:5-7.

## DEFINITION OF THEOPNEUSTIA

exclaim, "Ah, Lord God! behold, I cannot speak, for I am a child." The Lord answered him, "Say not, I am a child, for you shall speak whatsoever I command you;" and the Lord put forth his hand and touched his mouth, "Behold" said he, "I have put my words in your mouth."

Between Enoch and Jeremiah, listen to Moses. He, too, struggles on Mount Horeb against the call of the Lord: "Alas, O my Lord, I am not eloquent; send, I pray you, by the hand of him whom you will send." But the anger of the Lord is kindled against Moses. "Who has made man's mouth?" he says to him. "Now, therefore, go, and I will be with your mouth, and will teach you what you shall say."[27]

Between Jeremiah and John, listen to Paul of Tarsus: "When it pleased God, who separated me from my mother's womb, to reveal his Son in me, he called me by his grace, that I might preach him among the heathen."[28]

You see, then, it was sometimes the artless and sublime simplicity of John; sometimes the impassioned, elliptical, rousing, and logical energy of Paul; sometimes the fervor and solemnity of Peter; it was Isaiah's magnificent, and David's lyrical, poetry; it was the simple and majestic narratives of Moses, or the sententious and royal wisdom of Solomon – yes, it was all this; it was Peter, it was Isaiah, it was Matthew, it was John, it was Moses; yet it was God.

"Are not all these which speak Galileans?" (*Acts* 2:7) the people exclaimed on the day of Pentecost; yes, they are so; but the message that is on their lips comes from another country – it is from Heaven. Listen to it; for tongues of fire have descended on their heads, and it is God that speaks to you by their mouths.

Finally, we would desire that people should understand that this human individuality to which our attention is directed in the Scriptures, far from leaving any stain there, or from being an infirmity there, stamps upon them, on the contrary, a divine beauty, and powerfully reveals to us their inspiration.

Yes, we have said that it is God who speaks to us there, but it is also man; it is man, but it is also God. Admirable Word of God! It has been made man in its own way, as the eternal Word was! Yes, God has made

---

27. *Exodus* 4:10, etc.
28. *Galatians* 1:15-16.

it also come down to us full of grace and truth, like unto our words in all things, yet without error and sin! Admirable Word, divine Word, yet withal full of humanity, much-to-be-loved Word of my God! Yes, in order to our understanding it, it had of necessity to be put upon mortal lips, that it might relate human things; and, in order to attract our regard, it was required to invest itself with our modes of thinking, and with all the emotions of our voice; for God well knew whereof we are made. But we have recognized it as the Word of the Lord, mighty, efficacious, sharper than a two-edged sword; and the simplest among us, on hearing it, may say like Cleopas and his friend, "Did not our heart burn within us while he spoke to us?" (*Luke* 24:32).

With what a mighty charm do the Scriptures, by this abundance of humanity, and by all this personality with which their divinity is invested, remind us that the Lord of our souls, whose touching voice they are, does himself bear a human heart on the throne of God, although seated on the highest place, where the angels serve him and adore him forever! It is thus, also, that they present to us not only that double character of variety and unity which already embellishes all the other worlds of God, as Creator of the heavens and the Earth; but, further, that mingling of familiarity and authority, of sympathy and grandeur, of practical details and mysterious majesty, of humanity and divinity, which is recognizable in all the dispensations of the same God, as Redeemer and Shepherd of his church.

It is thus, then, that the Father of mercies, while speaking in his prophets, found it advantageous not only to employ their manner as well as their voice, and their style as well as their pen; but, further, often to put in operation their whole faculties of thought and feeling. Sometimes, in order to show us his divine sympathy there, he has deemed it fitting to associate their own recollections, their human convictions, their personal experiences, and their pious emotions, with the words he dictated to them; sometimes, in order to remind us of his sovereign intervention, he has preferred dispensing with this unessential concurrence of their recollections, affections, and understanding.

Like Immanuel, full of grace and truth; at once in the bosom of God and in the heart of man; mighty and sympathizing; heavenly and of the Earth; sublime and lowly; awful and familiar; God and man! Accordingly it bears no resemblance to the god of the Rationalists. They, after having, like the disciples of Epicurus, banished the Divinity far from man into a third Heaven, would have had the Bible also to have kept itself there. "Philosophy employs the language of the gods," says the too famous Strauss of Ludwigsburg, "while religion makes use of the language of men." No doubt she does so; she has recourse to no other; she leaves to the philosophers and to the gods of this world their empyrean and their language.

Studied under this aspect, considered in this character, the Word of God stands forth without its like; it presents attractions quite unequalled; it offers to men of all times, all places, and all conditions beauties ever fresh; a charm that never grows old, that always satisfies, never palls. With it, what we find with respect to human books is reversed; for it pleases and fascinates, extends and rises in your regard the more assiduously you read it. It seems as if the book, the more it is studied and studied over again, grows and enlarges itself, and that some kind unseen being comes daily to stitch in some fresh leaves. And thus it is that the souls, alike of the learned and the simple, who have long nourished themselves on it, keep hanging upon it as the people hung of old on the lips of Jesus Christ.[29] They all think it incomparable; now powerful as the sound of mighty waters; now soft and gentle like the voice of the spouse to her bridegroom, but always perfect, "always restoring the soul, and making wise the simple."[30]

To what book, in this respect, would you liken it? Go and put beside it the discourses of Plato, or Seneca, or Aristotle, or Saint-Simon, or Jean-Jacques Rousseau. Have you read Mohammed's books? Listen to him but for one hour, and your ears will tingle while beaten on by his piercing and monotonous voice. From the first page to the last, it is still the same sound of the same trumpet, still the same Medina horn, blown from the top of some mosque, minaret, or war-camel; still sybilline oracles, shrill and harsh, uttered in an unvarying tone of command and threat, whether it ordain virtue or enjoin murder; ever one and the same voice, surly and blustering, having no bowels, no familiarity, no tears, no soul, no sympathy.

After trying other books, if you experience religious longings, open the Bible; listen to it. Sometimes you find here the songs of angels, but of angels that have come down among the children of Adam. Here is the

---

29. *Luke* 19:48: ὁ λαὸς γὰρ, κ. τ. λ.
30. *Psalm* 19:7.

deep sounding organ of the Most High, but an organ that serves to soothe man's heart and to rouse his conscience, alike in shepherds' cots and in palaces; alike in the poor man's garrets and in the tents of the desert. The Bible, in fact, has lessons for all conditions; it brings upon the scene both the lowly and the great; it reveals equally to both the love of God, and unveils in both the same miseries. It addresses itself to children; and it is often children that show us there the way to Heaven and the great things of Jehovah. It addresses itself to shepherds and herdsmen; and it is often shepherds and herdsmen who lift up their voices there, and reveal to us the character of God. It speaks to kings and to scribes, and it is often kings and scribes that teach us there man's wretchedness, humiliation, confession, and prayer. Domestic scenes, confessions of conscience, pourings forth of prayer in secret, travels, proverbs, revelations of the depths of the heart, the holy courses pursued by a child of God, weaknesses unveiled, falls, recoveries, inward experiences, parables, familiar letters, theological treatises, sacred commentaries on some ancient Scripture, national chronicles, military annals, political statistics, descriptions of God, portraits of angels, celestial visions, practical counsels, rules of life, solutions of cases of conscience, judgments of the Lord, sacred hymns, predictions of future events, narratives of what passed during the days preceding our creation, sublime odes, inimitable pieces of poetry; all this is found there by turns; and all this meets our view in most delightful variety, and presenting a whole whose majesty, like that of a temple, is overpowering. Thus it is, that, from its first to its last page, the Bible necessarily combined with its majestic unity the indefinable charm of human-like instruction – familiar, sympathetic, personal – and the charm of a drama extending over forty centuries. In the Bible of Desmarets, it is said, "There are fords here for lambs, and there are deep waters where elephants swim."

But behold, at the same time, what unity, and, lo! what innumerable and profound harmonies in this immense variety! Under all forms it is still the same truth; ever man lost, and God the Saviour; ever man with his posterity coming forth out of Eden and losing the tree of life, and the second Adam with his people re-entering paradise, and regaining possession of the tree of life; ever the same cry uttered in tones innumerable, "O heart of man, return to your God, for he pardons! We are in the gulf of perdition; let us come out of it; a Saviour has gone down into it.... He bestows holiness as he bestows life."

"Is it possible that a book at once so sublime and so simple can be the work of man?" was asked of the philosophers of the last century by one who was himself too celebrated a philosopher. And all its pages have replied, No – it is impossible; for everywhere, traversing so many ages, and whichever it be of the God-employed writers that holds the pen, king or shepherd, scribe or fisherman, priest or publican, you everywhere perceive that one same Author, at a thousand years' interval, and that one same eternal Spirit, has conceived and dictated all; everywhere, at Babylon as at Horeb, at Jerusalem as at Athens, at Rome as at Patmos, you will find described the same God, the same world, the same men, the same angels, the same future, the same Heaven: Everywhere whether it be a poet or a historian that addresses you, whether it be in the plains of the desert in the age of Pharaoh, or in the prisons of the Capitol in the days of the Caesars – everywhere in the world the same ruin, in man the same impotency; in the angels the same elevation, the same innocence, the same charity; in Heaven the same purity, the same happiness, the same meeting together of truth and mercy, the same mutual embracing of righteousness and peace; the same counsels of a God who blots out iniquity, and who, nevertheless, does not clear the guilty.

We conclude, therefore, that the abundance of humanity to be found in the Scriptures, far from compromising their divine inspiration, is only one further mark of their divinity.

## Chapter 2
# Scriptural Proof of the Divine Inspiration

Let us open the Scriptures. What do they say of their inspiration?

*Section I*
*All Scripture Is Divinely Inspired*

WE SHALL commence by reproducing here that oft-repeated passage, *2 Timothy* 3:16, "All Scripture is given by inspiration of God;"[1] that is to say, all parts of it are given by the Spirit or by the breath of God.

This statement admits of no exception and of no restriction. Here there is no exception; it is all Scripture; it is *all that is written* (πᾶσα γραφή); meaning thereby the thoughts after they have received the stamp of language. No restriction; all Scripture is in such wise a work of God, that it is represented to us as uttered by the divine breathing, just as human speech is uttered by the breathing of a man's mouth. The prophet is the mouth of the Lord.

The purport of this declaration of Paul remains the same in both the constructions that may be put upon his words, whether we place, as our versions do, the affirmation of the phrase on the word θεόπνευστος (divinely inspired), and suppose the verb to be understood ("all Scripture is divinely inspired, profitable...") or, making the verb apply to the words that follow, we understand θεόπνευστος (divinely inspired) only as a determinative adjective ("all Scripture divinely inspired of God, is profitable..."). This last construction would even give more force than the first to the apostle's declaration. For then, as his statement would necessarily relate to the whole Scripture of the *Holy Letters* (τὰ ἱερὰ

---

1. See further upon this passage, our chapter 3, question XXVII (page 123).

## SCRIPTURAL PROOF OF THE DIVINE INSPIRATION

γράμματα), of which he had been speaking, his statement would assume, as an admitted and incontestable principle, that the simple mention of the *Holy Letters* implies of itself that *Scriptures inspired by God* are meant.

Nevertheless, it will be proper to give a further expression of this same truth by some other declaration of our holy books.

### Section II
### All the Prophetic Utterances Are Given by God

Peter in his second epistle, at the close of the first chapter, thus expresses himself: "Knowing this first, that no Scripture is of any private interpretation, for the prophecy came not in old time by the will of man, but holy men of God spoke as they were moved by the Holy Spirit." Note on this passage:

1. That it relates to *written* revelations (προφητεία γραφῆς);

2. That *never* (οὐ ποτέ) did any of these come through the impulsion or the government of a *will of man;*

3. That it was as *urged* or moved by the Holy Spirit that those holy men wrote and spoke.

4. Finally, that their writings are called by the name of *prophecy.*

It will be proper then, before we proceed farther, to have the Scriptural meaning of these words, *prophecy, prophesy, prophet* (נָבִיא), precisely determined; because it is indispensable for the investigation with which we are occupied, that this be known, and because the knowledge of it will throw much light on the whole question.

Various and often very inaccurate meanings have been given to the Biblical term *prophet*; but an attentive examination of the passages in which it is employed will soon convince us that it constantly designates, in the Scriptures, "a man whose mouth utters the words of God."

Among the Greeks, this name was at first given only to the interpreter and the organ of the *vaticinations* pronounced in the temples (ἐξηγητὴς ἔνθεως μαντείων). This sense of the word is fully explained by a passage in the *Timæus* of Plato.[2] The most celebrated prophets of pagan antiquity were those of Delphos. They conducted the Pythoness to the tripod and were charged with the interpretation of the oracles of the god, or the putting of them into writing. And it was only afterward, by an extension of this its first meaning, that the name

---

2. Volume IX, ed. Bipont., page 392.

## GOD-BREATHED: THE DIVINE INSPIRATION OF THE BIBLE

of prophet was given among the Greeks to poets, who, commencing their songs with an invocation of Apollo and the Muses, were deemed to give utterance to the language of the gods, and to speak under their inspiration.

A prophet, in the Bible, is a man, then, in whose mouth God puts the words which he wishes to be heard upon Earth; and it was further by allusion to the fulness of this meaning that God said to Moses[3] that Aaron should be his prophet unto Pharaoh, according as he had told him (*Exodus* 4:16): "He shall be to you instead of a mouth, and you shall be to him instead of God."

Mark, in Scripture, how the prophets testify of the Spirit who makes them speak, and of the wholly divine authority of their words: You will ever find in their language one uniform definition of their office, and of their inspiration. They speak; it is no doubt their voice that makes itself heard; it is their person that is agitated; it is, no doubt, their soul also that often is moved; but their words are not only theirs; they are, at the same time, the words of Jehovah.

"The mouth of the Lord has spoken;" "the Lord has spoken," they say unceasingly.[4] "I will open my mouth in the midst of them," says the Lord to his servant Ezekiel. "The Spirit of the Lord spoke by me, and his Word was in my tongue," said the royal psalmist.[5] "Hear the Word of the Lord!" It is thus that the prophets announce what they are about to say.[6] "Then was the Word of the Lord upon me," is what they often say. "The Word of God came unto Jeremiah;" "the Word of God came to Nathan," "the Word of God came unto John in the wilderness;"[7] "the word that came to Jeremiah from the Lord;"[8] "the burden of the Word of the Lord by Malachi;"[9] "the Word of the Lord that came unto Hosea;"[10] "In the second year of Darius, came the Word of the Lord by Haggai, the prophet."[11]

---

3. *Exodus* 7:1.
4. *Micah* 4:4; *Jeremiah* 9:12; 13:15; 30:4; 50:1; 51:12; *Isaiah* 8:11; *Amos* 3:1; *Exodus* 4:30; *Deuteronomy* 18:21-22; *Joshua* 24:2.
5. *2 Samuel* 23:1-2.
6. *Isaiah* 28:14; *Jeremiah* 19:3; 10:1; 17:20.
7. *1 Kings* 12:22; *1 Chronicles* 17:3; *Luke* 3:2.
8. *Jeremiah* 11:1; 7:1; 18:1; 21:1; 26:1; 27:1; 30:1; and in many other places. See *Ezekiel* 1:3; *Jeremiah* 1:1-2, 9, 14; *Ezekiel* 3:4, 10-11; *Hosea* 1:1-2, etc.
9. *Malachi* 1:1.
10. *Hosea* 1:1.
11. *Haggai* 1:1.

## SCRIPTURAL PROOF OF THE DIVINE INSPIRATION

This Word came down upon the men of God when he pleased, and often in the most unlooked-for manner.

It is thus that God, when he sent Moses, said to him, "I will be with your mouth;"[12] and that, when he made Balaam speak, "he put a word in Balaam's mouth."[13] The apostles, too, quoting a passage from David in their prayer, express themselves in these words: "You, Lord, have said by the mouth of your servant David."[14] And Peter, addressing the multitude of the disciples: "Men and brethren, this Scripture must needs have been fulfilled, which the Holy Spirit by the mouth of David spoke before concerning Judas."[15] The same apostle also, in the holy place, under Solomon's Porch, cried to the people of Jerusalem, "But those things which God before had showed by the mouth of all his prophets, that Christ should suffer, he has so fulfilled."[16]

In the view of the apostles, then, David in his *Psalms*, and all the prophets in their writings, whatever might be the pious emotions of their souls, were only the mouth of the Holy Spirit. It was David who spoke; it was the prophets who showed; but it was also God that spoke by the mouth of David, his servant; it was God who showed by the mouth of all his prophets (*Acts* 1:16; 3:18, 21; 4:25).

And, yet again, let the reader be so good as carefully to examine, as it stands in the Greek, that expression which recurs so often in the Gospel, and which is so conclusive, "That it might be fulfilled which was spoken by the prophet, (and even) which was spoken of the Lord by the Prophet, ($\Delta IA$ τοῦ προφήτου, and even, $\Upsilon\Pi O$ τοῦ Κυρίου $\Delta IA$ τοῦ προφήτου), saying...."[17]

It is in a quite analogous sense that Holy Scripture gives the name of *prophets* and of *false prophets* to impostors who lied among the Gentiles in the temples of the false gods, whether they were only common cheats, falsely pretending to visions from God, or whether they were really the mouth or an occult power, of a malevolent angel, of a spirit of Python.[18]

---

12. *Exodus* 4:12, 15.
13. ἐνέβαλεν (οἱ, ὁ); *Numbers* 23:5.
14. *Acts* 4:25.
15. *Acts* 1:16.
16. *Acts* 3:18.
17. *Matthew* 1:22; 2:5, 15, 23; 13:35; 21:4; 27:9; 4:14; 8:17; 12:17.
18. *Acts* 13:6; *Jeremiah* 29:1-8; *2 Kings* 18:19. The LXX often renders נָבִיא by ψευδοπροφήτης (*Jeremiah* 6:13; 26:7-8, 11, 16; 29:1, 8; *Zechariah* 13:2).

And it is, further, in the same sense that Paul, in quoting a verse of Epimenides, a poet, priest, and soothsayer among the Cretans, called him "one of their prophets," because all the Greeks consulted him as an oracle; because Nicias was sent into Crete by the Athenians to fetch him to purify their city; and because Aristotle, Strabo,[19] Suidas,[20] and Diogenes Laërtius[21] tell us that he undertook to foretell the future, and to discover things unknown.

From all these quotations, accordingly, it remains established, that in the language of the Scriptures the prophecies are "the words of God put into the mouth of man."

Accordingly, it is by a manifest abuse also, that in common language people seem to understand no more by that word than a miraculous *prediction*. The prophecies could reveal the past as well as the future; they pronounced God's judgments; they interpreted his Word; they sang his praises; they consoled his people; they exhorted souls to holiness; they testified of Jesus Christ.

And as "no prophecy came by the will of man,"[22] a prophet, as we have already intimated, was such only at intervals, "and as the Spirit gave him utterance" (*Acts* 2:4).

A man prophesied sometimes without foreseeing it, sometimes too without knowing it, and sometimes even without desiring it.

I have said, without foreseeing it; and often at the very moment when he could least expect it. Such was the old prophet of Bethel (*1 Kings* 13:20). I have said, without knowing it; such was Caiaphas (*John* 11:51). Finally, I have said, without desiring it; such was Balaam, when, wishing three times to curse Israel, he could not, three successive times, make his mouth utter any words but those of benediction (*Numbers* 23, 24).

We shall give other examples to complete the demonstration of what a prophecy generally is, and thus to arrive at a fuller comprehension of the extent of the action of God in what Peter calls *written prophecy* (προφητείαν γραφῆς).

We read in the eleventh chapter of *Numbers* (verses 25-29), that, as soon as the Lord made the Spirit to rest upon the seventy elders, "they

---

19. *Georg.*, Book x.
20. In voce Επίμεν.
21. *Vita Epimen.*
22. *2 Peter* 1:21.

prophesied;" but (it is added) "they did not cease." The Spirit, then, came upon them at an unexpected moment, and after he had thus "spoken by them," and his word "had been upon their tongue" (*2 Samuel* 23:2), they preserved nothing more of this miraculous gift, and were prophets only for a day.

We read in the *First Book of Samuel* (10:11), with what unforeseen power the Spirit of the Lord seized young king Saul at the moment when, as he sought for his father's she asses, he met a company of prophets who came down from the holy place. "What is this that is come to the son of Kish?" said they one to another. "Is Saul also among the prophets?"

We read at the nineteenth chapter something still more striking. Saul sends to Ramah men who were to take David; but no sooner did they meet Samuel and the company of prophets over whom he was set than the Spirit of the Lord came upon these men of war, and "they also prophesied." Saul sends others, and "they also prophesy." Saul at last goes thither himself, and he also prophesied all that day and all that night before Samuel." "The Spirit of God," we are told, "was upon him."

But it is particularly by an attentive study of the twelfth and fourteenth chapters of the *First Epistle to the Corinthians* that one obtains an exact knowledge of what the action of God, and the part assigned to man severally, were in prophecy.

The apostle there gives the Church of Corinth the rules that were to be followed in the use of this miraculous gift. His counsels will be found to throw much light on this important subject. One will then recognize at once the following facts and principles:

1. The Holy Spirit at that time conferred upon the faithful, for the common advantage, a great variety of gifts (12:8-10); to one that of miracles; to another that of healing; to another, discerning of spirits; to another, divers kinds of tongues, which the man himself did not understand when he spoke them;[23] to another, the interpretation of tongues; to another, in fine, prophecy – that is uttering with his own tongue words dictated by God.

---

23. That the man who spoke in tongues had not studied the language in which he spoke does not imply that he did not understand that language. In fact, he did understand, for he was edified by his own speaking, as Paul says, in *1 Corinthians* 14:4. One cannot be edified by words one cannot understand. – Editor.

2. One and the selfsame Spirit divided severally as he would these different miraculous powers.[24]

3. These gifts were a just subject of Christian desire and ambition (ζηλοῦτε, 14:1, 39). But the one that was to be regarded as the most desirable of all was that of prophesying; for one could speak an unknown tongue without edifying anybody [except those who understood the language – *Editor*], and that miracle was "useful rather to the unbelievers than to believers;" whereas "he that prophesied spoke unto men to edification, and exhortation, and comfort" (*1 Corinthians* 14:1-3).

4. That prophecy – that is to say, those words that fell miraculously on the lips that the Holy Spirit had chosen for such an office – that prophecy assumed very different forms. Sometimes the Spirit gave a *Psalm*, sometimes a doctrine, sometimes a revelation; sometimes, too, it was a miraculous interpretation of that which others had miraculously expressed in foreign tongues.[25]

5. In those prophecies there was evidently a work of God and a work of man. They were the words of the Holy Spirit; but they were also the words of the prophet. It was God that spoke, but in men, by men, for men; and there you would have found, as on other occasions, the sound of their voice – perhaps also the habitual peculiarities of their style – perhaps, moreover, allusions to their own experience, to their position at the time, to their individuality.

6. These miraculous facts continued in the primitive church throughout the long career of the apostles. Paul, who wrote his letter to the Corinthians twenty years after the death of Jesus Christ, speaks of them as a common and habitual order of things, for some time existing among them, and which ought still to continue.

7. The prophets, although they were the mouth of God to make his words heard, were not, however, absolutely passive while engaged in prophesying.

"The spirits of the prophets," says Paul, "are subject to the prophets" (*1 Corinthians* 14:32), that is to say, that the men of God, while his prophetic word was on their lips, could nevertheless check its escape by the repressive action of their own wills; nearly as a man suspends, when he wishes to do so, the almost involuntary course of his respiration.

---

24. Verse 11. See also *Ephesians* 4:7 and *Acts* 19:1-6.
25. Verses 26–31; and *1 Samuel* 10:6; 18:10.

## SCRIPTURAL PROOF OF THE DIVINE INSPIRATION

Thus, for example, if any revelation came upon one of those that were sitting, the first that spoke had then "to hold his peace, sit down, and let him speak."

Let us now apply these principles and these facts to the prophecy of Scripture (τῇ προφητείᾳ γραφῆς), and to the passage of Peter, for the explanation of which we have adduced them.

"No prophecy of the Scripture," says he, "is of any private interpretation, for the prophecy came not in old time by a will of man, but holy men of God spoke as they were moved by the Holy Spirit" (*2 Peter* 1:21).

Here, then, we have the plenary and entire inspiration of the Scriptures clearly established by the apostle; here we have the Scripture assimilated to those prophecies which we have just defined. It "came not by a will of man," it is entirely dictated by the Holy Spirit; it gives us the very words of God; it is entirely (ἔνθεος and θεόπνευστος) given by the breath of God.

Who would dare then, after such declarations, to maintain, that in the Scriptures the expressions are not inspired? They are written prophecies (πᾶσα προφητεία γραφῆς). One sole difficulty, accordingly, is all that can any longer be opposed to our conclusion. The testimony and the reasoning on which it rests are so clearly valid that one can elude them only by this objection. We agree, it will be said, that written prophecy (προφητεία γραφῆς) has, without contradiction, been composed by that power of the Holy Spirit which was put forth in the prophets; but the rest of the book, the *Epistles*, the *Gospels*, and the *Acts*, the *Proverbs*, the *Books of Kings*, and so many other purely historical writings, are not entitled to be put in the same rank.

Here, then, let us pause; and, before replying, see clearly the extent of our argument.

It ought already to be fully acknowledged that all that part of the Scriptures at least called *prophecy*, whatever it be, has been *completely dictated by God;* so that the words as well as the thoughts have been given by him.

But who now will permit us to establish a distinction between any one of the books of the Bible, and all the other books? Is not all given by prophecy? Certainly all has equally God's warrant; this is what we proceed to prove.

## Section III
### All the Scriptures of the Old Testament Are Prophetic

And, first of all, all the Scriptures are without distinction called *The Word of God*. This title is sufficient of itself to demonstrate to us that if Isaiah began his prophecies by inviting the heavens and the Earth to give ear because the Lord had spoken,[26] the same summons ought to come forth for us from all the books of the Bible, for they are all called "The Word of God." "Hear, O heavens, and give ear, O Earth; for the Lord has spoken!"

Nowhere shall we find a single passage that permits us to detach one single part of it as less divine than all the rest. When we say that this whole book is the Word of God, do we not attest that the very phrases of which it is composed have been given by him?

But the whole Bible is not only called *The Word of God*, (ὁ λόγος τοῦ Θεοῦ); it is called, without distinction, *The Oracles of God* (τὰ λόγια τοῦ Θεοῦ).[27] Who knows not what oracles were held to be in the ideas of men in ancient times? Was there a word that could more absolutely express a verbal and complete inspiration? And as if this term, which Paul employs, were not sufficient, we further hear Stephen, filled with the Holy Spirit, call them the *living oracles* (λόγια ζῶντα). "Moses," he says, "received the lively oracles, to give them unto us" (*Acts* 7:38).

All the Scriptures, then, without exception, are a continuous Word of God; they are his miraculous voice; they are his written prophecies and his lively oracles. Which of their various parts, then, would you dare to cut off? The apostles often distinguish two parts in them, when they call them *Moses* and *The Prophets*. Jesus Christ distinguished them into three parts[28] when he said to his apostles, "That all things must be fulfilled which were written in *Moses*, and in *The Prophets*, and in *The Psalms*, concerning me." According to this division, then, in which our Lord speaks according to the language of that time, the Old Testament would be made up of these three parts, *Moses, The Prophets*, and *The Psalms*; as the New Testament is composed of the *Gospels*, the *Acts*, the *Epistles*, and the *Book of the Revelation*. Which, then, of these three parts

26. Isaiah 1:2.
27. Romans 3:2.
28. Luke 24:44.

of the Old Testament, or which of these four parts of the New, would you dare to withdraw from the Scripture of the prophets (προφητείας γραφῆς), or from the inspired Word (ἐνθέου λόγου - γραφῆς θεοπνεύστου)?

Would it be *Moses*? But what is more holy and more divine in the whole Old Testament, than the writings of that man of God? He was in such sort a prophet that his holy books are placed above all the rest, and are called emphatically *The Law*. He was in such sort a prophet, that another prophet, speaking of his books alone, said, "The law of the Lord is perfect" (*Psalm 19:7*); "The words of the Lord are pure words, as silver tried in a furnace of earth, purified seven times" (*Psalm* 12:6). He was such a prophet of God that he is compared by himself to none but the Son of God. "This is that Moses," it is written, "who said to the children of Israel, A prophet shall the Lord your God raise up unto you of your brethren, *like unto me*; him shall you hear" (*Acts* 7:37). He was such a prophet that he was accustomed to preface his orders with these words: "Thus says the Lord." He was such a prophet that God said to him, "Who has made man's mouth? Have not I, the Lord? Now therefore go; and I will be with your mouth, and teach you what you shall say" (*Exodus* 4:11). Finally, he was such a prophet that it is written, "And there arose not a prophet since in Israel like unto Moses, whom the Lord knew face to face" (*Deuteronomy* 34:10).

What other part of the Old Testament, then, would you exclude from the prophetic Scriptures? Shall it be the second – that which Jesus Christ calls *The Prophets*, and which comprises all the Old Testament, exclusive of *Moses* and the *Psalms*, and sometimes exclusive of *Moses* alone? It is well worth noting that Jesus Christ, and the apostles, and the whole people habitually call by the name of prophets all the authors of the Old Testament. They were wont to say, in order to designate the whole Scriptures, "*Moses and The Prophets*" (*Luke* 24:25, 27, 44; *Matthew* 5:17; 7:12; 11:13; 22:40; *Luke* 16:16, 29, 31; 20:42; *Acts* 1:20; 3:21-22; 7:35, 37; 8:28; 26:22, 27; 28:23; *Romans* 1:2; 3:21; 10:5, etc.). Jesus Christ called all their books *The Prophets:* They were prophets. Joshua, then, was a prophet; the authors of the *Chronicles* were prophets, quite as Isaiah, Jeremiah, Ezekiel, Daniel, Hosea, and all the rest were, down to Malachi.

They wrote then, all of them, the prophetic Scriptures (προφητείαν γραφῆς); all, the words of which Peter has said, "that none of them came by a will of man;" all, those ἱερὰ γράμματα, those holy letters, which the apostle declares to be "divinely inspired."[29] The Lord said of all of them as of Jeremiah, "Lo, I have put my words in your mouth;"[30] and as of Ezekiel, "Son of man, go, speak unto them my words: Speak unto them, and tell them, Thus says the Lord God."[31]

That all the phrases, all the words, were suggested to them by God is demonstrated by a fact stated to us more than once, and in the study of their writings frequently brought under our eye, to wit – that they were charged to transmit to the church oracles, the meaning of which was to remain veiled to their own minds. Daniel, for example, declares more than once that he was unable to seize the prophetic meaning of the words that proceeded from his own lips, or were traced with his hand.[32] The types, impressed by God on all the events of primitive history, were not to be recognized till many centuries after the death of the men who were commissioned to relate to us their leading features; and the Holy Spirit informs us that the prophets, after having written out their sacred pages, set themselves to study them with the most respectful attention as they would have done with the other Scriptures, "searching what, or what manner of time the Spirit of Christ which was in them did signify when it testified beforehand the sufferings of Christ, and the glory that should follow."[33] Behold, then, these men of God bending over their own writings. There they ponder the words of God and the thoughts of God. Can this cause you any surprise, seeing that they have written for the elect of the Earth, and for the principalities and powers of Heaven, the doctrines and the glories of the Son of God, seeing these are things "into which the angels desire to look?"[34]

So much for *Moses* and for *The Prophets*; but what will you say of the *Psalms*? Shall we consider these less given by the spirit of prophecy than all the rest? Are not the authors of the *Psalms* always called *prophets*?[35] And if they are sometimes, like Moses, distinguished from the other prophets, is it not evidently in order that a place of greater

---

29. *2 Timothy* 3:16.
30. *Jeremiah* 1:9.
31. *Ezekiel* 3:10-11.
32. *Daniel* 12:4, 8-9; 8:27; 10:8, 21.
33. *1 Peter* 1:10-12.
34. *Ephesians* 3:10-11.
35. *Matthew* 13:35; for Asaph (*Psalm* 78).

eminence may be assigned them? "David was a prophet," says Peter (*Acts* 2:30). Mark what he himself says he is: "The Spirit of the Lord spoke by me," says he, "and *his word was upon my tongue*" (2 *Samuel* 23:1-2). What David wrote, and even his words in detail, "he wrote *speaking by the Holy Spirit*," said our Lord (*Mark* 12:36). The apostles also, quoting him (in their prayer) take care to say, "This Scripture must needs have been fulfilled which the Holy Spirit by the mouth of David spoke" (*Acts* 1:16). "Lord, you are God, who by the mouth of your servant David have said" (*Acts* 4:25). What do I say? These *Psalms* were to such a degree all dictated by the Holy Spirit that the Jews, and the Lord Jesus Christ himself call them by the name of *The Law*;[36] all their utterances had the force of *law;* their smallest words were from God. "Is it not written in your *law*?" said Jesus while quoting them, and in quoting them even for a single word (as we shall soon have occasion to show).

The whole Old Testament then is, in a Scriptural sense of the expression, a *written prophecy* (προφητεία γραφῆς). It is plenarily inspired therefore by God, seeing that, according to the testimony of Zachariah, "it is God who spoke by the mouth of his holy prophets, which have been since the world began;"[37] and because, according to that of Peter, "they spoke as they were moved by the Holy Spirit."[38]

It is true that thus far our reasonings, and the testimonies on which they are founded, directly relate to the books of the Old Testament only; and it might possibly be objected to us that as yet we have proved nothing for the New.

We shall begin, before we reply, with asking if it were likely that the Lord could have designed giving successive revelations to his people, and that, nevertheless, the latest and the most important of these should be inferior to the first? We would ask if it be rational to imagine that the first Testament, which contained only "the shadows of things that were to come," could have been dictated by God in all its contents; while the second Testament, which sets before us the grand object to

---

36. *John* 10:34. Paul (*Romans* 3:19) calls the whole Old Testament equally by the name of *law*, and more especially *Isaiah*, the *Proverbs*, and the *Psalms* (which he quotes). This remark has not escaped Chrysostom (*Homil.*, viii.) ἐνταῦθα τουσ ψαλμοὺς Νόμοι ἰκαλεσεν; and Theophylact adds, καὶ τὰ τοῦ Ἡσαίου.

37. *Luke* 1:70.

38. 2 *Peter* 1:21; see also *Matthew* 1:22; 22:43; *Mark* 12:36.

which all those shadows relate, and which describes to us the works, the character, the person, and the sayings even of the Son of God was to be less inspired than the first? We would ask if one can believe that the *Epistles* and the *Gospels*, which were destined to repeal many of the ordinances of *Moses and the Prophets*, could be less divine than *Moses and the Prophets*; and that the Old Testament could be throughout an utterance of thought on the part of God, while it was to be replaced, or at least modified and consummated, by a book emanating partly from man and partly from God?

But there is no need even of our having recourse to these powerful inferences in order to establish the prophetic inspiration of the Gospel; nay, its superiority to *Moses and the Prophets*.

## Section IV
## All the Scriptures of the New Testament Are Prophetic

The whole tenor of Scripture places the writers of the New Testament in the same rank with the prophets of the Old; and even when it establishes any difference between them, it is always in putting the last in date above the first, in so far as one of God's sayings is superior (not doubtless in divinity, not in dignity, but in authority) to the saying that preceded it.

Let the reader be so good as attend to the following passage of the Apostle Peter. It is very important, inasmuch as it lets us see that, in the lifetime of the apostles, the book of the New Testament was already almost entirely formed, in order to make one whole together with that of the Old. It was twenty or thirty years after the day of Pentecost that Peter felt gratified in referring to all the epistles of Paul, his beloved brother, and spoke of them as sacred writings which, even so early as his time, formed part of the Holy Letters (ἱερῶν γραμμάτων), and must of necessity be classed with the *other Scriptures* (ὡς καὶ τὰς λοιπὰς γραφὰς). He assigns them the same rank, and declares that "unlearned men can wrest them but to their own destruction." Mark this important passage: "Our beloved brother Paul also according to the wisdom given unto him has written unto you as also *in all his epistles*, speaking in them of these things; in which are some things hard to be understood, which they that are unlearned and unstable wrest, as they do also the *other Scriptures*, unto their own destruction."[39]

## SCRIPTURAL PROOF OF THE DIVINE INSPIRATION

The apostle, at the second verse of the same chapter, had already placed himself, along with the other apostles, on the same rank, and assumed the same authority, as the sacred writers of the Old Testament. Then he said, "That you may be mindful of the words which were spoken *before* by the holy prophets, and of the commandment of us the *apostles* of the Lord and Saviour."

The writings of the apostles, then, were that which those of the Old Testament were; and these being a *written prophecy* – that is to say, something spoken altogether by God – the latter are no less so.

But we have said the Scripture goes much further in the rank it assigns to the writers of the New Covenant. It teaches us to consider them as superior even to those of the Old, whether as respects the importance of their *mission*, or the glory of the *promises* made to them, or the greatness of the *gifts* conferred on them – or, in fine, the eminence of the *rank* assigned to them.

First, let us distinctly perceive what their mission was, compared with that of the ancient prophets; and it will at once be seen, from passages bearing on this point, that their inspiration could not be inferior to that of their predecessors.

When Jesus sent the apostles whom he had chosen, it is written, he said to them: "Go therefore, and teach all nations; teaching them to observe all things whatsoever I have commanded you; and, lo, I am with you alway, even unto the end of the world, Amen."[39] "But you shall receive power, after that the Holy Spirit is come upon you; and you shall be witnesses unto me both in Jerusalem, and in all Judea, and in Samaria, and unto the uttermost part of the Earth."[41] "Peace be unto you; as my Father has sent me, even so send I you."[42]

Such was their mission. They were the immediate *envoys* ($\dot{\alpha}\pi o\sigma\tau\acute{o}\lambda o\iota$) of the Son of God; they went to all nations; they had the assurance that their Master would be present with the testimony they were to bear to him in the Holy Scriptures. Did they require, then, less inspiration for their going to the ends of the Earth, and to make disciples of all nations, than the prophets required for going to Israel and teaching that one people, the Jews? Had they not to promulgate all the doctrines, all

---

39. *2 Peter* 3:15-16.
40. *Matthew* 28:19-20.
41. *Acts* 1:8.
42. *John* 20:21.

## GOD-BREATHED: THE DIVINE INSPIRATION OF THE BIBLE

the ordinances, all the mysteries of the kingdom of God? Had they not to bear "the keys of the kingdom of Heaven" in such sort, that whatsoever they should bind or loose on Earth should be bound or loosed in Heaven?[43] Had not Jesus Christ expressly conferred the Holy Spirit upon them for this end, that sins might be remitted or retained with regard to those to whom they should remit or retain them? Had he not breathed upon them, saying, "Receive the Holy Spirit?" Had he not deigned to reveal to them the wondrous character of the Word made flesh, and of the Creator so abased as to take upon him the form of a creature, and even to die upon the cross? Had they not to report his inimitable words? Had they not to perform on Earth the miraculous intransmissible functions of his representatives and of his ambassadors, as if it had been Christ that spoke by them?[44] Were they not called to such a glory "that, in the great final regeneration, when the Son of man shall sit on the throne of his glory, they also should sit upon twelve thrones judging the twelve tribes of Israel?"[45] If, then, the prophetic Spirit was necessary for the former men of God, in order to show the Messiah under the shadows, was it not much more necessary for them, in order to their bringing him out into the light, and to their evidently setting him forth as crucified amongst us,[46] in such a manner that he that despises them despises him, and he that hears them hears him?[47] Let one judge by all these traits what the inspiration of the New Testament must have been, compared with that of the Old; and let one say whether, while the latter was wholly and entirely prophetic, that of the New could be anything less.

But this is not all; listen further to the promises that were made to them for the performance of such a work. No human language can express with greatest force the most absolute inspiration. These promises were for the most part addressed to them on three great occasions: first, when sent out for the first time to preach the kingdom of God;[48] next, when Jesus himself delivered public discourses on the Gospel

---

43. *Matthew* 18:18; 16:19.
44. *2 Corinthians* 5:20.
45. *Matthew* 19:28.
46. *Galatians* 3:1.
47. *Luke* 10:16.
48. *Matthew* 10:19-20.

## SCRIPTURAL PROOF OF THE DIVINE INSPIRATION

before an immense multitude, gathered by tens of thousands around him;[49] third, when he uttered his last denunciation against Jerusalem and the Jewish nation.[50]

"But when they deliver you up, take no thought *how* or *what* you shall speak (πῶς ἢ τί), for *it shall be given you* in that same hour what you shall speak. For it is not you that speak, but the *Spirit of your Father which speaks in you.*"

"And when they bring you unto the synagogues, and unto magistrates and powers, *take you no thought how* or *what thing you shall answer, or what you shall say*; for *the Holy Spirit shall teach you* in the same hour *what you ought to say.*" "Take no thought beforehand what you shall speak, neither do you premeditate, but *whatsoever shall be given* you in that hour, that speak you; for *it is not you that speak, but the Holy Spirit.*"

On these different occasions, the Lord assured his disciples that the fullest inspiration would regulate their language in the most difficult and important moments of their ministry. When they should have to speak to princes, they would feel no disquietude; they were not even to premeditate, they were not even to take thought about it, because there would then be *immediately given to them by God, not only the things they were to say, but the words also* in which those things were to be expressed; not only τί, but πῶς λαλήσουσιν (*Matthew* 10:19-20). They were compelled to cast themselves entirely on him; it would be *given them entirely;* it would be given them by *Jesus;* it would be given them *in that same hour;* it would be given them in such a manner, and in such plenitude, that they should be able then to say that it was *no more they*, but the Holy Spirit, the *Spirit of their Father, which spoke in them*;[51] and that then also it was not only an irresistible wisdom that was given them, it was a *mouth*.[52]

"Settle it therefore in your hearts, not to meditate before what you shall answer; for I will give you a mouth and wisdom which all your adversaries shall not be able to gainsay or resist."

Then (as with the ancient prophets, Isaiah, Jeremiah, Ezekiel) it shall be the Holy Spirit that will speak by them, as God spoke by his holy

---

49. *Luke* 12:12.
50. *Mark* 13:11; *Luke* 21:14-15.
51. *Matthew* 10:20.
52. *Luke* 21:15.

prophets since the world began.[53] In one sense, indeed, it was *they* that were to speak; but it shall be the *Holy Spirit* who will teach them (*Luke* 12:12) in that same hour what they are to say; so that, in another sense, it was to be the *Holy Spirit* himself that was to speak by their lips.

We ask if it were possible, in any language, to express more absolutely the most entire inspiration, and to declare with more precision, that the very words were then vouched by God and given to the apostles?

No doubt, in these promises there is no direct reference to the support which the apostles were to receive as writers; and that they bear rather on what they were to expect when they had to appear before priests, before governors, and before kings. But is it not evident enough, that if the most entire inspiration were assured to them[54] for passing exigencies, to shut the mouths of some wicked men, to conjure the perils of a day, and to subserve interests of the narrowest range, if it were promised them, notwithstanding that the very words of their answers should then be given to them by means of a calm, mighty, but inexplicable operation of the Holy Spirit, is it not evident enough that the same assistance could not be refused to those same men, when, like the ancient prophets, they had to continue the book of God's oracles, and so to hand down to all succeeding ages the laws of the kingdom of Heaven, and describe the glories of Jesus Christ and the scenes of eternity? Can anyone suppose that the men who, before Ananias, or Festus, or Nero, were "the mouth of the Holy Spirit," that then it was no longer they that spoke, but that Spirit, should, when writing the everlasting Gospel, have returned to the condition of ordinary beings merely enlightened, denuded of their previous inspiration, no longer speaking by the Holy Spirit, and thenceforward employing only words dictated by human wisdom (θελήματι ἀνθρώτου καὶ ἐν διδαχτοῖς σοφίας λόγοις)? This is quite inadmissible.

See them, further, commencing their apostolic ministry on the day of Pentecost: See what gifts they received.

Tongues of fire descend on their heads; they are filled with the Holy Spirit; they leave their upper chamber, and a vast multitude hears them proclaim, in fifteen different languages, the wonderful works of God;

---

53. *Acts* 3:21.
54. *Luke* 12:12.

they speak *as the Spirit gives them utterance*;[55] they speak (it is said) *the Word of God* (ἐλάλουν τὸν λόγον τοῦ θεοῦ).[56] Assuredly, the words of those foreign languages must have been then supplied to them as well as the things, the expression as well as the thoughts, *the things* as well as the τί (*Matthew* 10:19; *Luke* 12:11). Now then, will it be believed that the Spirit could have taken care to dictate all that it was proper, necessary and advantageous for them to say, for preachings at the corners of the streets, for words which passed away with the sound of their voices, and which, after all, reached only some thousands of hearers; while those same men, when they came afterward to write for all Earth's nations, and for all ages of the church, "the lively oracles of God," were to be deprived of their first assistance? Will it be believed that after having been more than the ancient prophets as respects preaching in public, they were to be less than those prophets and were to become ordinary men when they took the pen to finish the Book of the prophets, to write their *Gospels*, their *Epistles*, and the *Book of the Revelation*? The unreasonableness and inadmissibility of such a supposition are felt at once.

But here we have to say something still more simple and more peremptory. We would speak of the rank that is assigned them; and indeed, after what we said of the prophets of the Old Testament, we might even have limited ourselves to this simple fact, that the apostles were all of them prophets, and more than prophets.

Their writings, therefore, are written prophecies (προφητεία γραφῆς), as much, and even more, than those of the Old Testament; and hence we are led to conclude, once more, that all Scripture in the New Testament, as well as in the Old, is inspired of God, even to its smallest particles.

I have said that the apostles were all prophets. They often declare this; but, not to multiply quotations unnecessarily, we content ourselves here with appealing to the two following passages of the Apostle Paul.

The first is addressed to the Ephesians (3:4-5) "Whereby," he tells them, "when you read *what I wrote* before in a few words, you may understand my knowledge in the mystery of Christ, which in other ages was not made known unto the sons of men as it is now revealed unto his holy *apostles and prophets* by the Spirit."

---

55. *Acts* 2:4.
56. *Acts* 4:31.

## GOD-BREATHED: THE DIVINE INSPIRATION OF THE BIBLE

One clearly sees, then, here the *apostle* and *prophet* Paul, the apostles and prophets Matthew, John, Jude, Peter, James, received by the Spirit the revelation of the mystery of Christ, and wrote about it as prophets.

Further, it is of the same mystery, and of the writings of the same prophets, that that same apostle speaks in the second of the passages we have indicated, that is, in the last chapter of his *Epistle to the Romans*.[57]

"Now to him that is of power to establish you according to my Gospel, and the preaching of Jesus Christ, according to the revelation of the mystery, which was kept secret since the world began, but now is made manifest, and by the *Scriptures of the prophets* (διά τε γραφῶν προφητικῶν), according to the commandment of the everlasting God, made known to all nations for the obedience of faith: To God only wise, be glory through Jesus Christ for ever. Amen!"

Here, then, we have the authors of the New Testament again called prophets; we have their writings called *prophetical writings* (γραφαὶ προφητικαί, the equivalent of the προφητεία γραφῆς of Peter). And since we have already seen that no prophecy ever came by the will of him that uttered it, but that it was as moved and impelled by the Holy Spirit that holy men of God spoke, the prophets of the New Testament spoke therefore like those of the Old, and according to the commandment of the everlasting God. They were all of them prophets.[58]

But we may advance a step farther; for, as we have said, they were *more than prophets*. Here again we have a remark of the learned Michaëlis.[59] Loose as are his principles on the inspiration of a part of the New Testament, this has not escaped his notice. It is clear, according to him, looking to the context, that, in the judgment pronounced by Jesus Christ on John the Baptist (*Matthew* 11:9, 11), the terms *great* and *little* of the eleventh verse apply only to the title of *prophet* which precedes them at the ninth verse; so that Jesus Christ there declares, that if John the Baptist is the *greatest of the prophets* – if he is even *more than a prophet* – still *the least of the prophets of the New Testament is greater than John the Baptist;* that is to say, greater than the greatest of the Old Testament prophets.[60]

---

57. *Romans* 16:25-27.
58. See further *Luke* 11:49; *Ephesians* 2:20; 3:5; 4:11; *Galatians* 1:12; 1 *Peter* 1:12; 1 *Corinthians* 12:28; 1 *Thessalonians* 2:15.
59. *Introduction*, Volume 1, page 118, French edition.
60. Michaëlis and *Luke* 7:28.

## SCRIPTURAL PROOF OF THE DIVINE INSPIRATION

Besides, this superiority of the *apostles and prophets* of the New Testament is more than once attested to us in the apostolical writings.

Everywhere, when mention is made of the different offices established in the churches, the apostles are placed above the prophets.

Take, for example, a very remarkable passage of the *First Epistle to the Corinthians*. The apostle's object is to make known to us the gradations of excellence and dignity among the several miraculous charges constituted by God in the primitive church, and he expresses himself as follows: "And God has set some in the church, *first apostles, secondarily prophets, thirdly teachers*, after that miracles, then gifts of healings, helps, governments, diversities of tongues."[61]

At the fourth chapter of his *Epistle to the Ephesians*, at verse 11, he again puts the apostles above the prophets.

At chapter 2, verse 20, he calls the apostles, *apostles* and *prophets*. And at chapter 14 of the *First Epistle to the Corinthians*, he places himself *above* the prophets whom God had raised up in that church. His wish is that every one of them, if he have really received the Holy Spirit, should employ the gifts he has received in acknowledging that the things that he wrote unto them were the commandments of the Lord; and so fully convinced is he that what he writes is dictated by inspiration of God, that, after having dictated orders to the churches, and concluded them with these words, which nothing short of the highest inspiration could sanction, *It is thus I ordain in all the churches*; he goes further; he proceeds to rank himself *above* the prophets; or rather, being himself a prophet, he calls upon the spirit of prophecy in them to acknowledge the words of Paul as the words of the Lord; and he ends with these remarkable expressions: "What? came the Word of God out from you? ...If any man think himself to be a *prophet*, or *spiritual*, let him acknowledge that the things that *I write unto you are the commandments of the Lord*."[62]

The writings of the apostles, then, are (like those of the ancient prophets) the commandments of the everlasting God; they are "written prophecies" ($\pi\rho o\phi\eta\tau\epsilon i\alpha\ \gamma\rho\alpha\phi\hat{\eta}s$), as much as the *Psalms*, and *Moses, and The Prophets* (*Luke* 24:44), and all their authors then could say with Paul, *Christ speaks in me* (2 *Corinthians* 13:3; 1 *Thessalonians* 2:13), what I say is the Word of God, and the things I speak are taught me by the

---

61. 1 *Corinthians* 12:28.
62. $\Pi\nu\epsilon\nu\mu\alpha\tau\iota\kappa\acute{o}s$, 1 *Corinthians* 14:36-37.

Holy Spirit (*1 Corinthians* 2:13); quite as David before them had said, "The spirit of the Lord spoke by me, and his word was in my tongue."[63]

Mark, besides, their own words, when they speak of what they are. Would it be possible to declare more clearly than they have done that words as well as subject have been given them by God? "As for us," they say, "*we have the mind of Christ*" (*1 Corinthians* 2:16). "For this cause also thank we God without ceasing, because, when you received the Word of God, which you heard of us, you received not the word of men, but (as it is in truth) the *Word of God*" (*1 Thessalonians* 2:13). "He therefore that despises, despises not man, but God, who has also given unto us his Holy Spirit" (*1 Thessalonians* 4:8).

Such then, in fine, is the word of the New Testament. It is like that of the Old, a word uttered by prophets, and by prophets greater even than those that preceded them; such, for example, as has been very well remarked by Michaëlis,[64] that an epistle commencing with these words, "Paul, an apostle of Jesus Christ,"[65] thereby gives us a higher attestation of his divine authority and his divine inspiration, than could have been given even by the writings of the most illustrious prophet of the Old Testament when they began with these words, "Thus says the Lord,"[66] "The vision of Isaiah," "The word that Isaiah saw,"[67] "the words of Jeremiah to whom the Word of the Lord came,"[68] "Hear the Word of the Lord," or such like analogous expressions. And if there be in the New Testament some books where such inscriptions are not to be found, their inspiration is no more compromised thereby than this or that book of the Old Testament (the second or the ninety-fifth *Psalm*, for example);[69] which, although they have not the names of the prophets that composed them, are not the less quoted as divine by Jesus Christ and his apostles.

The objection has sometimes been stated that Luke and Mark were not apostles, properly so called; and that consequently they did not receive the same inspiration as the other sacred writers of the New Testament. True, they were not apostles; but they were certainly prophets,

---

63. *2 Samuel* 23:2.
64. *Introduction*, Volume 1, pages 118-119, etc., French edition.
65. *Romans* 1:1; *Galatians* 1:1; *1 and 2 Corinthians* 1:1; *1 Peter* 1:1; *2 Peter* 1:1.
66. *Isaiah* 56:1; 43:1; and *passim*.
67. *Isaiah* 1:1; 2:7; and elsewhere.
68. *Jeremiah* 1:2.
69. *Acts* 4:25; 13:33; *Hebrews* 1:5; 3:7, 17; 4:3, 7; 5:5.

and they were even greater than the greatest of those of the Old Testament (*Luke* 7:26, 28).

Without insisting here on the ancient traditions,[70] which say that both were of the number of the seventy disciples whom Jesus sent at first to preach in Judea, or at least of those one hundred and twenty on whom the tongues of the Holy Spirit descended on the day of Pentecost; are such objectors not aware that the apostles had received the power of conferring, by the imposition of hands, miraculous gifts on all who believed, and that they exercised this power in all the countries and all the cities whither they directed their steps? And since Luke and Mark were, amid so many other prophets, the fellow-workers chosen by Paul and Peter, is it not clear enough that these two apostolic men must have bestowed upon such associates the gifts which they dispensed to so many besides who had believed? Do we not see Peter and John first go down to Samaria to confer these gifts on the believers of that city; this followed by Peter coming to Cesarea, there to shed them on all the Gentiles who had heard the word in the house of the centurion Cornelius?[71] Do we not see Paul bestow them abundantly on the believers of Corinth, on those of Ephesus, on those of Rome?[72] Do we not see him, before employing his dear son Timothy as his fellow laborer, causing spiritual powers to descend upon him?[73] And is it not evident that Peter must have done as much for his dear son Mark,[74] as Paul did for his companion Luke?[75] Silas, whom Paul had taken to accompany him (as he took Luke and John, whose surname was Mark), Silas was a prophet at Jerusalem.[76] Prophets abounded in all the primitive churches. Many were seen to come down from Jerusalem to Antioch;[77] a great many were to be found in Corinth;[78] Judas and Silas were prophets in Jerusalem. Agabus was such in Judea; further, four

---

70. Epiphanius, *Heeres.*, 51 and others – Origen, *De recta in Deum fide.* Doroth. in *Synopsi.* – Procopius, *Diacon.*, *Apud Bolland.*, 25th April.

71. *Acts* 8:15, 17.

72. *Acts* 19:6-7; *1 Corinthians* 12:28; 14; *Romans* 1:11; 15:19, 29.

73. *1 Timothy* 4:14; *2 Timothy* 1:6.

74. *1 Peter* 5:13.

75. *Acts* 13:1; 16:10; 27:1; *Romans* 16:21; *Colossians* 4:14; *2 Timothy* 4:11; *Philemon* 24; *2 Corinthians* 8:18.

76. *Acts* 15:32.

77. *Acts* 11:27.

78. *1 Corinthians* 12:19-20; 14:31, 38.

## GOD-BREATHED: THE DIVINE INSPIRATION OF THE BIBLE

daughters, still in their youth, of Philip the evangelist, were prophetesses in Cesarea;[79] and in the Church of Antioch, there were to be seen many believers who were prophets and doctors;[80] among others Barnabas (Paul's first companion), Simeon, Manaen, Saul of Tarsus himself; and, finally, that Lucius of Cyrene, who is thought to be the Lucius whom Paul (in his *Epistle to the Romans*) calls his kinsman,[81] and whom (in his *Epistle to the Colossians*) he calls *Luke the physician;*[82] in a word, the Luke whom the ancient fathers call indifferently Lucas, Lucius, and Lucanus.

From these facts, then, it becomes sufficiently evident that Luke and Mark ranked at least among the prophets whom the Lord had raised up in such numbers in all the churches of the Jews and the Gentiles, and that from among all the rest they were chosen by the Holy Spirit to be conjoined with the apostles in writing the sacred books of the New Testament.

But, moreover (and let this be specially noticed), the prophetical authority of Mark and Luke is far from resting solely on these inferences. It rests on the testimony even of the apostles of Jesus Christ. It ought not to be forgotten that it was under the long protracted government of those men of God that the divine canon of the Scriptures of the New Testament was collected and transmitted to all the churches. By a remarkable dispensation of God's providence, the lives of the greater number of the apostles were prolonged to a great many years. Peter and Paul lived to edify the church of God for above thirty-four years after the resurrection of their Master; nay, John continued his ministry, in the province of Asia, in the center of the Roman Empire, for more than thirty years longer, after their death. The book of the *Acts*, which was written by Luke subsequently to his *Gospel*,[83] had been already diffused through the church a long while (I mean to say, for ten years at least) before the martyrdom of Paul. But Paul, even long before going to Rome, had already diffused the Gospel abundantly from Jerusalem as far as Illyricum.[84] The apostles maintained a constant correspon-

---

79. *Acts* 11:28; 21:9-10.
80. *Acts* 13:1-2.
81. *Romans* 16:21.
82. *Colossians* 4:14.
83. *Acts* 1:1.
84. *Romans* 15:19.

## SCRIPTURAL PROOF OF THE DIVINE INSPIRATION

dence with the Christians of all countries; they were daily called to meet the cares they had to sustain with respect to all the churches.[85] Peter, in his second letter, addressed to the catholicity of God's churches, spoke to them even then of *all the epistles* of Paul as incorporated with the Old Testament. And for more than half a century, all the Christian churches were formed and conducted under the superintendence of these men of God. It was, accordingly, with the assent, and under the prophetic government of these apostles, called as they were to bind and to loose, and to become, next to Christ, the twelve foundations of the universal church, that the canon of the Scriptures was formed, and that the new people of God received its lively oracles to transmit them to us.[86] And it is thus that the *Gospel of Luke*, that of *Mark*, and the book of *Acts*, have been received by common consent on the same authoritative grounds, and with the same submission as the apostolical books of Matthew, of Paul, of Peter, and John. These books, then, have the same authority for us as all the rest; and we are called upon to receive them equally, "not as the word of men, but as it is in truth the Word of God, which works effectually in all that believe."[87]

We venture to believe that these reflections will suffice for enabling the reader to comprehend how little ground there is for the distinction which Michaëlis[88] and some other German doctors have made bold to establish with respect to inspiration, between the two evangelists and the other writers of the New Testament. It even appears to us, that it was in order to obviate any such supposition, that Luke took care to place at the head of his *Gospel* the four verses that serve as a preface to it. You see, in fact, that his object there is to contrast the certainty and divinity of his own account with the uncertainty and the human character of those narrations, which *many (πολλοί) had taken in hand to set forth (ἐπεχείρησαν ἀνατάξασθαι)* on the facts connected with the Gospel – facts, he adds, *most surely believed among us,* that is to say, among the apostles and prophets of the New Testament (τῶν πεπληροφορημένων ἐν ἡμῖν πραγμάτων, the word in the original signifying the highest degree of certainty, as may be seen, *Romans* 4:21; 14:5; *2 Timothy* 4:5, 17). And therefore, adds Luke, *it seemed good to me*

---

85. *2 Corinthians* 11:28.
86. *Acts* 7:38; *Romans* 3:2.
87. *1 Thessalonians* 2:13.
88. Introduction, Volume 1, pages 112-129, English edition.

also, *having had perfect understanding of all things*[89] *from above, to write of them unto you in order.*

Luke had obtained this knowledge *from above,* that is to say, by the wisdom which comes from above "and which had been given him." It is very true that the meaning ordinarily attached to this last expression, in this passage, is *from the very first,* as if instead of the word ἄνωθεν *(from above)* there were here the same words ἀπ' ἀρχῆς *(from the commencement),* which we find in the second verse. But it appears to us that the opinion of Erasmus, of Gomar, of Henry, of Lightfoot, and other commentators ought to be preferred as more natural, and that we must take the word ἄνωθεν here in the sense in which John and James have used it, when they say: "Every perfect gift comes from *above*" (*James 1:17*); "You could have no power against me, except it were given you from above" (*John* 19:11); "Except a man be born from above, he cannot see the kingdom of God" (*John* 3:3); "The wisdom that comes from above is first pure" (*James* 3:15, 17).

The prophet Luke, then, "had obtained from above a perfect understanding of all things that Jesus began both to do and teach, until the day in which he was taken up."

Meanwhile, whatever translation one may prefer giving to these words, it is by other arguments that we have shown how Luke and Mark were prophets, and how their writings, transmitted to the church by the authority of the apostles, are incorporated with those of the apostles, as well as with all the other books of the everlasting Word of God.

Such, then, is the extent to which our argument has conducted us, and this is, we have had to acknowledge, on the very authority of Holy Scripture. It is, first of all, that the inspiration of the words of the prophets was entire; that the Holy Spirit spoke by them, and that the Word of the Lord was upon their tongue. It is, next, that whatever was written in the Bible, having been so written by prophecy, all the sacred books are *holy letters* (ἱερὰ γράμματα), *written prophecies* (προπητεῖαι γραφῆς), and *Scriptures given by divine inspiration* (γραφαὶ θεόπνευστοι). Everything there is from God.

Nevertheless, the reader will be pleased to remember (we once more

---

89. Παρηκολουθηκότι – Thus Demosthenes de Corona, i. 55. Παρηκολουθηκὼς τοῖς πράγμασιν ἀπ ἀρχῆς. Theophrastus, *Char. Proem,* 4: Σὸν δὲ παρακολουθῆσαι καὶ εἰδῆσαι, εἰ ὀρθῶς λέγω, – Josephus, in the first lines of his book against Apion, opposes this same word παρακολουθηκότα (*diligenter assecutum*) to τῷ πυνθανομένῳ (*sciscitanti ab aliis*).

repeat it here, although we have had occasion more than once to say it already), that it does not necessarily follow that the prophets of the Old and New Testament were thrown into a state of excitation and enthusiasm, which took them out of themselves; we must, on the contrary, beware of entertaining any such idea. The ancient church attached so much importance even to this principle, that under the reign of the emperor Commodus, according to what Eusebius says, Miltiades (the illustrious author of a Christian *Apology*) "composed a book for the express purpose of establishing," against Montanus and the false prophets of Phrygia, "that true prophets ought to be masters of themselves, and ought not to speak in ecstasy."[90] The action of God was exerted upon them without their passing entirely out of their ordinary condition. "The spirits of the prophets," says Paul, "are subject to the prophets."[91] Their intellectual faculties were at the time directed, not suspended. They knew, they felt, they willed, they recollected, they understood, they approved. They could say, "It seemed good to me to write;" and, as apostles, "It seemed good to the Holy Spirit and to us."[92] And the words as well as the thoughts were given them; for, after all, words are themselves but second thoughts relating to language, and having recourse to it for the selection of expressions. In both cases, to explain the gift is equally easy and equally difficult.

Meanwhile, as respects inspiration, there is something in Holy Scripture that strikes us, if possible, still more than all those declarations of the apostles and of Jesus Christ himself, and that is the examples they present to us.

## Section V
### *The Examples of the Apostles and of Their Master Attest that, in Their View, All the Words of the Holy Books Are Given by God*

First of all, consider what use is made by the apostles themselves of the Word of God, and the terms in which they quote it. See how, in

---

90. *Hist. Eccles.*, Book V, chapter 17. – Ἐν ᾧ ἀποδείκνυσι περὶ τοῦ μηδένα Προφήτην ἐν ἐκστάσει λαλεῖν. See also Niceph., Book IV, chapter 24. See the same principles in Tertullian (*Against Marcion*, Book IV, chapter 22); in Epiphanius, (*Adv. Hæreses*, Book II, *Hæres.*, Book 48, chapter 5); in Jerome (*Præmium in Nahum*); in Basil the Great, (*Commentar. in Esaiam*, proem 5).
91. *1 Corinthians* 14:32.
92. *Luke* 1:3; *Acts* 15:28.

doing this, they not only think it enough to say, "God has said,"[93] "the Holy Spirit says;"[94] "God says in such a prophet;"[95] but observe, further, when they quote it, with what respect they speak of what are for them its smallest particles; how attentively they weigh every word; with what a religious assurance they often insist on a single word, in order to deduce from it the most serious consequences, and the most fundamental doctrines.

For ourselves, we confess nothing more strongly impresses us than this view of the subject; nothing has begot in us so deep and firm a confidence in the entire inspiration of the Scriptures.

The preceding reasonings and testimonies seem of themselves sufficient to carry conviction to every attentive mind; but if we felt conscious of any need on our own part of having our belief of this truth fortified, we feel that we should not go so far in search of reasons. It would be enough for us to inquire what Holy Scripture was in the view of God's apostles, and how far, according to their apprehension, its language was inspired. What, for example, were Paul's sentiments on the subject? For we make no pretension to be more enlightened divines than the twelve apostles. Cleaving to the dogmatical theology of Peter and the exegetical of Paul, among all the systems ever broached on the inspiration of the Scriptures, theirs is what we have decidedly resolved to prefer.

Hear, then, the Apostle Paul when he quotes them, and proceeds to comment upon them. On such occasions he discusses their minutest expressions; and often, when about to deduce the most important consequences from them, he employs arguments which, were it we that should employ them in discussions with the doctors of the Socinian school, would be treated as childish or absurd. For such a respect for the words of the text, we should be sent back to the sixteenth century with its "gross orthodoxy" and its "superannuated theology." Mark with what reverence the apostle dwells upon their most minute expressions; with what confidence he expects the submission of the church, while he notes the use of such a word rather than of such another; with what studiousness and affection he as it were presses every one of them in his hands till the last drop of meaning has been obtained from it.

93. *Ephesians* 4:8; *Hebrews* 1:8.
94. *Acts* 13:2; 28:25; *Hebrews* 3:7; 10:15; and elsewhere.
95. *Romans* 9:25.

Among so many examples which we might adduce, let us confine ourselves, for brevity's sake, to the *Epistle to the Hebrews*.

See how, at verse eight of chapter two, after quoting these words, "You have put all things under his feet," the sacred author argues from the authority of the word *all*.

See how, at the eleventh verse, in quoting the twenty-second *Psalm*, he argues from the expression *my brethren*, that the Son of God was compelled to put on the nature of man.

See how, at the twenty-seventh verse of chapter twelve, in quoting the prophet Haggai, he argues from the word *once more*, "Yet once more."

See at the fifth, sixth, seventh, eighth, and ninth verses, how largely he argues from these words, *my son*, of the third chapter of the *Proverbs*, "My son, despise not the chastening of the Lord."

See how, at the tenth chapter, in quoting the fortieth *Psalm* he argues from the words *Lo, I come,* set against the words, "You would not."

See how, at chapter eight, from the eighth to the thirteenth verses, in quoting *Jeremiah* 31:31, he argues from the word *new*.

See, at chapter 3:7-19, and 4:2-11, with urgency in quoting the ninety-fifth *Psalm*, he argues from the word "today," from the words "I have sworn," and, above all, from the words "my rest," illustrated by that other expression of *Genesis*, "And God *rested* on the seventh day."

See how, at chapter 3:2-6, he argues from these words *servant* and *my house*, taken from the book of *Numbers*: "My *servant* Moses, who is faithful in all *my house*."

See, especially at chapter seven, the use he makes successively of all the words of the one-hundred-tenth *Psalm*, mark how he takes up each of its expressions, one after another, in order to deduce from them the very highest doctrines: "The Lord has sworn;" "he has sworn by himself;" "You are a priest;" "You are a priest forever;" "You are a priest after the order of Melchizedec;" "of Melchizedec king of Sedec;" and "of Melchizedec king of Salem." The exposition of the doctrines contained in each of these words will be found to occupy three chapters, the fifth, the sixth, and the seventh.

But here I pause. Can we fail to conclude from such examples that, in the view of the Apostle Paul, the Scriptures were inspired by God, even to their most minute expressions? Let each of us, then, place himself in the school of the man to whom had been given by the Spirit

## GOD-BREATHED: THE DIVINE INSPIRATION OF THE BIBLE

of God the knowledge of the mystery of Christ, as to a holy apostle and prophet.[96] One must necessarily either account him an enthusiast, and reject in his person the testimonies of the Holy Bible, or receive with him the precious and fruitful doctrine of the plenary inspiration of the Scriptures.

O you who read these lines, to what school will you attach yourselves? To that of the apostles, or to that of the doctors of this age? "If any man take away from the words of this book" (this I testify, says John), "God shall take away his part out of the Book of Life, and out of the holy city, and from the things which are written in this Book."[97]

But, further, let us turn from the apostles, prophets as they are – men sent by God for the establishment of his kingdom, the pillars of the church, the mouths of the Holy Spirit, ambassadors of Jesus Christ; let us, for an instant, turn from them as men who had not yet quite thrown off their Jewish traditions and clownish prejudices, and let us go to the Master. Let us inquire of him what the Scriptures were in his view of them. Here is the grand question. The testimonies to which we have appealed are peremptory, no doubt; and the doctrine of a plenary and entire inspiration is taught as clearly in Scripture as that of the resurrection of the dead can be; that ought of itself to be enough for us; but we repeat, nevertheless, here is an argument which for us renders all else superfluous. How did Jesus Christ appeal to the Holy Bible? What were his views of the letter of the Scriptures? What use did he make of it, he who is its object and inspirer, beginning and end, first and last? He whose Holy Spirit, says Peter, animated all the prophets of the Old Testament (*2 Peter* 1:21), who was in Heaven in the bosom of the Father at the same time that he was seen here below, dwelling among us and preaching the Gospel to the poor? Among the most ardent defenders of their verbal inspiration, we know not one that ever expressed himself with more respect for the altogether divine authority and everlasting endurance of their most minute expressions than was done by the man Jesus. And we scruple not to say, that were any modern writer to quote the Bible, as Jesus Christ did, with the view of deducing from it any doctrine, he would forthwith have to be ranked among the most zealous partisans of the doctrine we defend. I am asked, What is your view of the Holy Letters? I answer, What thought

---

96. *Ephesians* 3:4-5.
97. *Revelation* 22:18-19.

my Master of them? How did he appeal to them? What use did he make of them? What were their smallest details in his eyes?

Ah! speak to them yourself, Eternal Wisdom, Uncreated Word, Judge of judges! And as we proceed to repeat to them here the declarations of your mouth, show them the majesty in which the Scriptures appeared to you — show them the perfection you did recognize in them, that everlasting endurance, above all, which you did assign to their smallest iota, and which will make them outlast the universe, after the very heavens and the Earth have passed away!

We are not afraid to say it: When we hear the Son of God quote the Scriptures, everything is said, in our view, on their divine inspiration — we need no further testimony. All the declarations of the Bible are, no doubt, equally divine; but this example of the Saviour of the world has settled the question for us at once. This proof requires neither long nor learned researches; it is grasped by the mind of a child as powerfully as by that of a doctor. Should any doubt, then, assail your soul, let it turn to the Lord of lords; let it behold him in presence of the Scriptures!

Follow Jesus in the days of his flesh. With what serious and tender respect does he constantly hold in his hands "the volume of the Book," to quote every part of it, and note its shortest verses. See how one word, one single word, whether of a *Psalm* or of an historical book, has for him the authority of a law. Mark with what confident submission he receives *the whole Scriptures*, without ever contesting its sacred canon; for he knows that "salvation comes of the Jews," and that, under the infallible providence of God, "To them were committed the oracles of God." Did I say, he receives them? From his childhood to the grave, and from his rising again from the grave to his disappearance in the clouds, what does he bear always about with him, in the desert, in the temple, in the synagogue? What does he continue to quote with his resuscitated voice, just as the heavens are about to exclaim, "Lift up your heads, you everlasting doors, and the king of glory shall come in?" It is the Bible, ever the Bible; it is *Moses*, the *Psalms*, and the *Prophets*: He quotes them, he explains them, but how? Why, verse by verse, and word by word.

In what alarming and melancholy contrast, after beholding all this, do we see those misguided men present themselves in our day, who dare to judge, contradict, cull, and mutilate the Scriptures. Who does not tremble, after following with his eyes the Son of Man as he commands the elements, stills the storms, and opens the graves, while, filled with so profound a respect for the sacred volume, he declares that he is one day to judge by that book the quick and the dead? Who does not shudder, whose heart does not bleed, when, after observing this, we venture to step into a Rationalist academy, and see the professor's chair occupied by a poor mortal, learned, miserable, a sinner, responsible yet handling God's Word irreverently; when we follow him as he goes through this deplorable task before a body of youths, destined to be the guides of a whole people – youths capable of doing so much good if guided to the height of the faith, and so much mischief if tutored in disrespect for those Scriptures which they are one day to preach? With what peremptory decision do such men display the phantasmagoria of their hypotheses; they retrench, they add, they praise, they blame, and pity the simplicity which, reading the Bible as it was read by Jesus Christ, like him clings to every syllable, and never dreams of finding error in the Word of God! They pronounce on the intercalations and retrenchments that Holy Scripture must have undergone – intercalations and retrenchments never suspected by Jesus Christ; they lop off the chapters they do not understand, and point out blunders, ill-sustained or ill-concluded reasonings, prejudices, imprudences, and instances of vulgar ignorance.

May God forgive my being compelled to put this frightful dilemma into words, but the alternative is inevitable! Either Jesus Christ exaggerated and spoke incoherently when he quoted the Scriptures thus, or these rash, wretched men unwittingly blaspheme their divine majesty. It pains us to write these lines. God is our witness that we could have wished to recall, and then to efface them; but we venture to say, with profound feeling, that it is in obedience, it is in charity, that they have been penned. Alas! in a few short years both the doctors and the disciples will be laid in the tomb, they shall wither like the grass; but not one jot or tittle of that divine book will then have passed away; and as certainly as the Bible is the truth, and that it has changed the face of the world, as certainly shall we see the Son come in the clouds of Heaven, and judge, by his eternal Word, the secret thoughts of all men![98] "All flesh is as grass, and all the glory of man as the flower of grass. The grass withers, and the flower thereof falls away: but the Word of the

---

98. *Romans* 2:16; *John* 12:48; *Matthew* 25:31.

## SCRIPTURAL PROOF OF THE DIVINE INSPIRATION

Lord endures forever. And this is the word which by the Gospel is preached unto you;"[99] this is the Word which will judge us.

Now, then, we proceed to close our proofs, by reviewing, under this aspect, the ministry of Jesus Christ. Let us follow him from the age of twelve to his descent into the grave, or rather, to his passing into the cloud, in which he went out of sight; and throughout the whole course of that incomparable career, let us see what the Scriptures were in the eyes of him who "upholds all things by the Word of his power."

First of all, let us contemplate him at the age of twelve years. He grew, like one of the children of men, in wisdom and in stature; he is in the midst of the doctors in the temple of Jerusalem; he ravishes with his answers those who hear him; for, said they, "he knows the Scriptures without having studied them."[100]

Behold him from the time he commenced his ministry. See him filled with the Holy Spirit; he is led into the wilderness, there to sustain, as the first Adam did in Eden, a mysterious contest with the powers of darkness. The impure spirit dares to approach him, bent on his overthrow; but how will the Son of God repel him, even he who had come to destroy the works of the Devil? Solely with the Bible. His only weapon, three successive times, in his divine hands, is the sword of the Spirit, the Bible. He quotes, thrice successively, the *Book of Deuteronomy*.[101] On every fresh temptation, he, the Word made flesh, defends himself by a sentence of the oracles of God, and by a sentence, too, the whole force of which lies in the use of a single word, or of two words; first of these words ($\mathring{\alpha}\rho\tau\omega\ \mu\acute{o}\nu\omega$), *bread alone;* then of those words, "You shall not tempt the Lord ($o\mathring{\upsilon}\kappa\ \mathring{\epsilon}\kappa\pi\epsilon\iota\rho\acute{\alpha}\sigma\epsilon\iota\varsigma\ K\acute{\upsilon}\rho\iota o\nu$);" then, finally, of these two words ($\theta\epsilon\grave{o}\nu\ \pi\rho o\sigma\kappa\upsilon\nu\acute{\eta}\sigma\epsilon\iota\varsigma$), *You shall worship God*.

What an example for us! His whole reply, his whole defence is this: "It is written;" "Get behind me, Satan, for it is written," and as soon as this terrible and mysterious contest closed, the angels drew near to minister to him.

But, mark this further, such was the respect of the Son of man for the authority of every word of the Scriptures, that the impure spirit himself, powerful as he was in evil, and who knew what all the words of the

---

99. *1 Peter* 1:24-25.
100. *John* 7:15.
101. *Deuteronomy* 8:3; 6:13; 10:20; *Matthew* 4:1-11.

## GOD-BREATHED: THE DIVINE INSPIRATION OF THE BIBLE

Bible were in his antagonist's eyes, could fancy no surer means of shaking his will than by quoting to him (but at the same time mutilating) a verse of the ninety-first *Psalm*; and forthwith Jesus Christ, to confound him, thinks it is enough to reply once more with, "It is written."

See how his priestly ministry commenced – with the use of the Scriptures; and see how his prophetic ministry commenced soon after – with the use of the Scriptures.

Once engaged in his work, let us follow him as he goes from place to place doing good, displaying in his poverty his creative power ever for the relief of others, never for his own. He speaks, and it is done, he casts out devils, he turns the storm into a calm, he raises the dead. Yet, amid all these tokens of greatness, observe what the Scriptures are to him. The Word is ever with him; not in his hands, for he knows it thoroughly, but in his memory and in his incomparable heart. Mark how he speaks of it! When he unrolls the sacred volume, it is as if an opening were made in Heaven, that we may hear Jehovah's voice. With what reverence, with what submission, does he expound the Scriptures, comment upon them, quote them word by word! See how it becomes his grand concern to heal men's diseases and to preach the Scriptures, as it was afterwards to die and to fulfil the Scriptures!

See who comes, "as his custom was," into the synagogue on the Sabbath-day; for we are told he taught in their synagogues.[102] He goes into that at Nazareth; and what do we find him doing there – he, the everlasting Wisdom, possessed by Jehovah in the beginning of his way, brought forth when there were no depths, before the mountains were settled, and before the hills?[103] He rises and takes the Bible, opens it at *Isaiah*, reads some words there – then having closed the book, he sits down, and while the eyes of all that are in the synagogue are fastened on him, he begins to say, "This day is this Scripture fulfilled in your ears."[104]

See him as he passes through Galilee, and mark how he employs himself there. "The volume of the book" is still in his hands; he explains it line by line, word by word; he points out to our respect its most minute expressions, as he would those of "the ten words" uttered on Sinai.

102. *Luke* 4:15-16.
103. *Proverbs* 8:22, 25.
104. *Luke* 4:21.

## SCRIPTURAL PROOF OF THE DIVINE INSPIRATION

See him once more in Jerusalem, before the pool of Bethesda; what do we find him saying to the people? "Search the Scriptures" (*John* 5:39).

See him in the holy place, in the midst of which he had dared to say aloud, "In this place is one greater than the holy place" (*Matthew* 12:6). Follow him into the presence of the Sadducees and the Pharisees, while he reprehends them successively with these words, "It is written," as he had done in the case of Satan.

Listen to his reply to the Sadducees who denied the resurrection of the body. How does he refute them? By one sole word of an historical passage of the Bible; by a single verb in the present tense, instead of that same verb in the past tense. "You greatly err," said he to them, "*not knowing the Scriptures. Have you not read* that which was spoken unto you by God, saying, I am the God of Abraham!" It is thus that he proves to them the doctrine of the resurrection. God, on Mount Sinai, four hundred years after the death of Abraham, says to Moses, not "I was," but "I am" the God of Abraham; I am that now (אנכי אלהי אברהם), which the Holy Spirit translates, Ἐγώ εἰμι ὁ Θεὸς Ἀβραάμ. There is a resurrection, then; for God is not the God of a few handfuls of dust, the God of the dead, the God of nothing: He is the God of the living. Those men therefore are, in the view of God, still alive.[105]

Next, behold him in the presence of the Pharisees. It is again by the letter of the Word that he proceeds to confound them.

Some had by this time followed him into the coasts of Judea beyond Jordan, and came to him asking to be informed what were his doctrines on the subject of marriage and divorce. Now, what followed on the part of Jesus Christ? He might certainly have given an authoritative reply, and announced his own laws on the subject. Is he not himself the King of kings and Lord of lords? But no; it was to the Bible that he made his appeal, still for the same purpose of making it the basis of doctrine, it was to these simple words taken from a purely historical passage in *Genesis*,[106] "*Have you not read*, that he which made them at the beginning made them male and female; so that they twain shall be one flesh? What therefore God has joined together, let not man put asunder."[107]

105. *Matthew* 22:31-32.
106. *Genesis* 1:27; 2:24.
107. *Matthew* 19:4-6.

## GOD-BREATHED: THE DIVINE INSPIRATION OF THE BIBLE

But listen to him, especially when in the temple he would prove to other Pharisees, by the Scriptures, the divinity of the expected Messiah. Here likewise, to demonstrate this, he still insists on the use of a single word, which he proceeds to take from the *Book of Psalms*: "If the Messiah be the son of David," said he, "how does David, *by the Spirit*, call him LORD; saying [at *Psalm* 110], The Lord said unto my Lord, Sit at my right hand? If David then calls him Lord, how is he his son?"

How happens it, that among those Pharisees none was found to say in reply, "What! do you mean to insist on a single word, and still more on a term borrowed from a poesy eminently lyrical, where the royal Psalmist might, without material consequence, have employed too lively a construction, high-flown expressions, and words which, doubtless, he had not theologically pondered before throwing them into his verses? Would you follow such a mode of minutely interpreting each expression as is at once fanatical and servile? Would you worship the letter of the Scriptures to such an extreme? Would you build a whole doctrine upon a word?"

Yes, I do, is Christ's reply; yes, I will throw myself on a single word, because that word is God's! And, to cut short all your objections, I tell you that it is by the Spirit that David wrote all the words of his hymns; and I ask you, "How, if the Messiah be his son, David, *by the Spirit*, can call him his Lord, when he says, The Lord said unto my Lord?"

Students of God's Word, and you especially who are to be his ministers, and who, as your preparation for preaching it, would desire first of all to have received it into a good and honest heart, behold what every saying, every single word of the Book of God, was in the regard of your Master. Go and do likewise!

But more than this. Again let us listen to him, even on the cross. There he poured out his soul as an offering for sin; all his bones were out of joint; he was poured out as water; his heart was like wax, melted in the midst of his bowels; his tongue cleaved to his jaws; he was about to give up his spirit to his Father. But, previous to this, what do we find him do? He desires to collect his remaining strength, in order to recite a *Psalm* which the church of Israel had sung on her religious festivals for a thousand years, and which told over, one after another, all his sorrows and all his prayers: "*Eli, Eli, lama sabachthani* (My God, my God, why have you forsaken me)?" He does even more than this: Listen to him. There remained in the Scriptures one word which had not yet been fulfilled. Vinegar had still to be given him on that cross (this the Holy Spirit had declared a thousand years before in the sixty-ninth *Psalm*). "After this," it is written, "Jesus knowing that all things were now accomplished, that the Scripture might be fulfilled, said, I thirst. When Jesus therefore had received the vinegar, he said, It is finished: And having bowed his head, he gave up the ghost."[108]

When David sang the sixty-ninth *Psalm* on Shoshannim and the twenty-second *Psalm* on Aijeleth, did he know the prophetic meanings of all these words, of those hands and feet that were pierced, of that gall poured out, of that vinegar, of those garments that were parted, of that vesture on which a lot was cast, of that mocking populace, wagging their heads and making mouths? It matters little to us his understanding of it; the Holy Spirit at least understood it, and David spoke *by the Spirit*, said Jesus Christ. The Heaven and the Earth shall pass away, but there was not in that book a jot or tittle that could pass away till all was fulfilled (*John* 10:35; *Matthew* 5:18).

Meanwhile, behold something, if possible, more striking still. Jesus Christ rises from the tomb; he has overcome death; he is about to return to the Father, there to resume that glory which he had with the Father before the world began. Let us follow him, then, during those fleeting moments with which he would still favor the Earth. What words are now about to proceed from that mouth, again restored to life? Why, words from Holy Scripture. Still he quotes it, explains it, preaches it. See him first of all, on the way to Emmaus, walking with Cleopas and his friend; afterwards in the upper chamber; and, later still, on the borders of the lake. How is he employed? In expounding the sacred books; he begins with *Moses*, he continues through all *The Prophets* and the *Psalms*; he shows them what had been said concerning him in all the Scriptures; he opens their minds to understand them; he makes their hearts burn within them as he speaks of them.[109]

But we have not yet done. All these quotations show us what the Holy Bible was in the eyes of him "in whom are hid all the treasures of wisdom and knowledge" (*Colossians* 2:3); and "by whom all things subsist" (*Colossians* 1:17). But on the letter of the Scriptures, listen further to two declarations, and a last example of our Lord.

---

108. *John* 19:28-30.
109. *Luke* 24:27, 44, 32.

## GOD-BREATHED: THE DIVINE INSPIRATION OF THE BIBLE

"It is easier," says he, "for Heaven and Earth to pass, than for one tittle (κεραία) of the law to fall;"[110] and by the law Jesus Christ understood the whole of the Scriptures, and even, more particularly, the *Book of Psalms*.[111] What terms could possibly be imagined capable of expressing, with greater force and precision, the principle which we defend; that is to say, the authority, the entire divine inspiration, and the perpetuity of all the parts, and of the very letter of the Scriptures? You who study God's Word, here behold the theology of your Master! Be theologians after his manner; be your Bible the same as that of the Son of God! Of that not a single tittle can fall.

"Till Heaven and Earth pass," said he, "one jot or one tittle shall in no wise pass from the law, till all be fulfilled" (*Matthew* 5:18). All the words of the Scriptures, accordingly, even to the smallest stroke of a letter, are no less than the words of Jesus Christ; for he has also said, "Heaven and Earth shall pass away; but my words shall not pass away" (*Luke* 21:33).

The impugners of these doctrines ask us if we are bold enough to maintain that Holy Scripture is a law of God even in its words, as hyssop, or as an oak, is a work of God even in its leaves. We reply, with all the fathers of the church, Yes, even in its "words, even to (ἰῶτα ἕν, ἢ μία κεραία) one jot or one tittle"!

But, passing from these two declarations, let us finally direct our attention to a last example given by our Lord which we have not yet adduced.

It is still Jesus Christ who is about to quote the Scriptures, but claiming for their smallest words such an authority, that one is compelled to rank him among the most ardent partisans of verbal inspiration, and that we do not think, that had we before us all the writings of theologians the most uncompromising in their orthodoxy, we should anywhere find an example of more profound respect for the letter of Scripture, and for the plenitude of their divine inspiration.

It was winter. Jesus walked in the temple in Solomon's (the eastern) Porch; the Jews came about him, upon which he said to them, "I give eternal life unto my sheep, and they shall never perish, neither shall any pluck them out of my hand: I and the Father are One." People were

---

110. *Luke* 16:17.
111. *John* 10:34, as did also the Jews, 12:34; *Romans* 3:19.

## SCRIPTURAL PROOF OF THE DIVINE INSPIRATION

astonished at such language; but he assumed a still bolder tone, until at last the Jews, exclaiming that it was blasphemy, took up stones to stone him, telling him they did so, "because you, being a man, make yourself God."[112]

Now then, let the reader carefully mark the several points involved in the answer made by Jesus Christ. He quotes a saying taken from one of the *Psalms*, and proceeds to rest the whole of his doctrine on that single saying: for "he made himself equal with God," says John elsewhere (5:18). In maintaining the most sublime and most mysterious of his doctrines, and, in order to legitimize the most extraordinary of his claims, he appeals to certain words in the eighty-second *Psalm*. But, mark well! Before pronouncing the words he takes care to interrupt himself; he pauses in a solemn parenthesis, and exclaims in a tone of authority, And the Scripture cannot be broken (καὶ οὐ δύναται λυθῆναι ἡ γραφή)!

Has sufficient attention been paid to this? Not only is our Lord's argument here founded entirely on the use made by the Psalmist of a single word, and not only does he proceed to establish the most astonishing of his doctrines on this expression; but further, in thus quoting the *Book of Psalms* in order to make us understand that in his eyes the whole book was dictated by the Holy Spirit, and that every word of it carried the authority of the law, Jesus calls it by the name of law, and says to the Jews, "Is it not written in your law, I have said you are gods?" These words are placed in the middle of a hymn; they might seem to have escaped from the unreflecting fervor of the prophet Asaph, or from the burning raptures of his poetry. And were we not to admit the full inspiration of all that is written, one might be tempted to tax them with indiscretion, since the imprudent use which the Psalmist may have made of them might have led the people to usages elsewhere censured by the Word of God, and to idolatrous imaginations. How then, once more we ask, was there no Rationalist scribe from the universities of Israel to be found there, under Solomon's Porch, to say to him, "You cannot, Lord, claim the authority of that expression. The use that Asaph makes of it can have been neither considerate nor becoming. Although inspired as respects the thoughts suggested by his piety, he no doubt did not maturely weigh every little word with a very

---

112. *John* 10:23, and following verses.

scrupulous regard to the use that might possibly be made of them a thousand years after his own day. It were rash, therefore, to insist upon them."

But now, let the reader mark, how our Lord anticipates the profane rashness of such an objection. Observe well: He solemnly reproves it; he proceeds to pronounce words concerning himself which would be blasphemy in the mouth of an archangel. "I and the Father are one;" but he interrupts himself, and immediately after saying, "Is it not written in your law, you are gods?" he stops, and, fixing his eyes with a look of authority on the doctors who surround him, he exclaims, "*And the Scripture cannot be broken!*" As if he had said, "Beware! There is not in the sacred books a single word to be found fault with, nor a single word that one can neglect. This which I cite in this eighty-second *Psalm* has been traced by the hand that made the heavens." If, then, he has been willing to give the name of gods to men, in so far as they were christs (anointed ones), and types of the true Christ, who is emphatically the Anointed One, and taking care nevertheless to call to mind "that they should die like men," how shall it not still more appertain to me to take that name to myself? I, "the everlasting Father," Emmanuel, the God-man, who do the works of my Father, and on whom the Father has put his seal?[113]

Here, then, we ask of every serious reader (and our argument, be it well observed, is altogether independent of the orthodox meaning or the Socinian meaning people may choose to give to the words of Jesus Christ); we ask, Is it possible to admit that the Being who makes such a use of the Scriptures does *not believe in their plenary verbal inspiration?* And if he could have imagined that the words of the Bible were left to the free choice and pious fancies of the sacred writers, would he ever have dreamed of founding such arguments on such a word? The Lord Jesus, our Saviour and our Judge, believed then in the most complete inspiration of the Scriptures; and for him the first rule of all hermeneutics, and the commencement of all exegesis, was this simple maxim applied to the most minute expressions of the written word, "*And the Scripture cannot be broken.*"

Let, then, the Prince of Life, the light of the world, reckon all of us as his scholars! What he believed let us receive. What he respected let us

---

113. *Isaiah* 9:6; 7:14; *John* 6:27.

revere. Let us press to our sickly hearts that Word to which he submitted his Saviour heart, and all the thoughts of his holy humanity, and to it let us subject all the thoughts of our fallen humanity. There let us look for God, even in its minutest passages; in it let us daily dip the roots of our being "like the tree planted by the rivers of waters, which brings forth his fruit in his season, and his leaf shall not wither."

Chapter 3
# Brief Didactic Abstract of the Doctrine of the Divine Inspiration

It has been our desire that this work should not bear so strictly theological a character, as that Christian women, or other persons not conversant with certain studies, and not acquainted with the sacred languages, should be deterred from the perusal of it. Nevertheless, we should be omitting part of our object if the doctrine were not, on some points, stated with more precision. We have to request, therefore, that in order to avoid being led off, under another form, into an excessive length of development, we may be allowed to exhibit it here in a more didactic shape, and to sum it up in a short catechetical sketch. We will do little more than indicate the proper place of the points already treated; and will enter somewhat at large into the consideration of those only that have not yet been mentioned.

*Section I*
*Catechetical Sketch of the Main Points of the Doctrine*

I. What, then, are we to understand by divine inspiration?

Divine inspiration is the divine power put forth by the Spirit of God on the authors of holy writ, to make them write it, to guide them even in the employment of the words they use, and thus to preserve them from all error.

II. What are we told of the spiritual power put forth on the men of God while they were writing their sacred books?

We are told that they were *led* or *moved* ($\phi\epsilon\rho\acute{o}\mu\epsilon\nu\sigma\iota$) "not by the will of man, but by the Holy Spirit; so that they set forth the things of God, not in words which man's wisdom teaches, but which the Holy Spirit teaches."[1] "God," says the apostle,[2] "Spoke by the prophets at sundry times, and in divers manners (πολυμερῶς και πολυτρόπως);" sometimes enabling them to understand what he made them say; sometimes without doing so; sometimes by dreams[3] and by visions which he afterwards made them relate; sometimes by giving them words internally (λόγῳ ἐδιάθετῳ), which he caused them immediately to utter; sometimes by words transmitted to them externally (λόγῳ προφόρικῳ), which he caused them to repeat.[4]

III. But what passed in their hearts and minds while they were writing?

This we cannot tell. It is a fact which, subject besides to great varieties, could not be for us an object either of scientific inquiry or of faith.

IV. Have not modern authors, however, who have written on this subject, often distinguished in the Scriptures three or four degrees of inspiration (*superintendence, elevation, direction, suggestion*)?

This is but idle conjecture; and the supposition, besides, is in contradiction with the Word of God, which knows but one kind of inspiration. Here, there is none true but suggestion.

V. Do we not see, however, that the men of God were profoundly acquainted, and often even profoundly affected, with the sacred things which they taught, with the future things which they predicted, with the past things which they related?

No doubt they might be so — nay, in most instances they were so — but they might not have been so; this happened in different measures, of which the degree remains to us unknown, and the knowledge of which is not required of us.

VI. What then must we think of those definitions of divine inspiration in which Scripture seems to be represented as the altogether hu-

---

1. *2 Peter* 1:21; *1 Corinthians* 2:13.
2. *Hebrews* 1:1.
3. *Numbers* 12:6; *Job* 33:15; *Daniel* 1:17; 2:6; 7:1; *Genesis* 20:6; 31:10; *1 Kings* 3:5; *Matthew* 1:20, 2:12, 22; *Acts* 2:17.
4. *Numbers* 20:6; 24:4; *Job* 7:14; *Genesis* 20:3; *Psalm* 89:19; *Matthew* 17:9; *Acts* 2:17; 9:10-12; 10:3, 17, 19; 11:5; 12:9; 16:9-10; *2 Corinthians* 12:1-2.

man expression of a revelation altogether divine – what, for example, must we think of that of Baumgarten,[5] who says that inspiration is but the means by which revelation, at first immediate, became mediate, and took the form of a book (*medium quo revelatio immediata, mediata facta, inque libros relata est*)?

These definitions are not exact, and may give rise to false notions of inspiration. I say they are not exact. They contradict facts. Immediate revelation does not necessarily precede inspiration; and when it precedes it, it is not its measure. The empty air prophesied;[6] a hand coming forth from a wall wrote the words of God;[7] a dumb animal reproved the madness of a prophet.[8] Balaam prophesied without any desire to do so, and the believers of Corinth did so without even knowing the meaning of the words put by the Holy Spirit on their lips.[9]

I would next observe that these definitions produce or conceal false notions of inspiration. In fact, they assume its being nothing more than the natural expression of a supernatural revelation; and that the men of God had merely of themselves, and in a human way, to put down in their books what the Holy Spirit made them see in a divine way, in their understandings. But inspiration is more than this. Scripture is not the mind of God elaborated by the understanding of man, to be promulgated in the words of man; it is at once the mind of God and the word of God.

VII. The Holy Spirit having in all ages illuminated God's elect, and having moreover distributed miraculous powers among them in ancient times, in which of these two orders of spiritual gifts ought we to rank inspiration?

We must rank it among the extraordinary and wholly miraculous gifts. The Holy Spirit in all ages enlightens the elect by his powerful inward virtue; he testifies to them of Christ;[10] gives them the unction of the Holy One; teaches them all things, and convinces them of all truth.[11] But, besides these *ordinary* gifts of illumination and faith, the

---

5. *De Discrimine Revelat. et Inspirationis.*
6. *Genesis* 3:14ff.; 4:6; *Exodus* 3:6ff.; 19:3ff.; *Deuteronomy* 4:12; *Matthew* 3:17; 17:5.
7. *Daniel* 5:5.
8. *2 Peter* 2:16.
9. *1 Corinthians* 14. (On the contrary, see footnote 23, page 71. – *Editor.*)
10. *John* 15:26.

same Spirit shed *extraordinary* ones on the men who were commissioned to promulgate and to write the oracles of God. Divine inspiration was one of those gifts.

VIII. Is the difference, then, between illumination and inspiration a difference of kind or only of degree?

It is a difference of kind, and not of degree only.

IX. Nevertheless, did not the apostles, besides *inspiriation,* receive from the Holy Spirit *illumination* in extraordinary measure, and in its most eminent degree?

In its most eminent degree, is what none can affirm, in an extraordinary degree, is what none can contradict.

The Apostle Paul, for example, did not receive the Gospel from any man, but by a revelation from Jesus Christ.[12]

He wrote "all his epistles" Peter tells us,[13] not only in words taught by the Holy Spirit,[14] as had been the *other Scriptures* (of the Old Testament), but according to a wisdom which had been given to him.[15] He had the knowledge of the mystery of Christ.[16] Jesus Christ had promised to give his disciples not only "a mouth, but wisdom to testify of him."[17] David, when he seemed to speak only of himself in the *Psalms,* knew that it was of the Messiah that his words were to be understood: "Being a prophet, and knowing that of the fruit of his loins, according to the flesh, God would raise up Christ to sit on his throne."[18]

X. Why then, should we not say that divine inspiration is but illumination in its most exalted and abundant measure?

We must beware of saying so; for thus we should have but a narrow, confused, contingent, and constantly fluctuating idea of inspiration. In fact,

---

11. *1 John* 2:20, 27; *John* 16:16-26; 7:38-39.
12. *Galatians* 1:12, 16; *1 Corinthians* 15:3.
13. *2 Peter* 3:15-16.
14. *1 Corinthians* 2:13.
15. *2 Peter* 3:15-16.
16. *Ephesians* 3:3.
17. *Luke* 21:15.
18. *Acts* 2:30.

1. God, who often conjoined those two gifts in one man, often also saw fit to disjoin them, in order that he might give us to understand that they essentially differ, the one from the other, and that, when united, they are independent. Every true Christian has the Holy Spirit,[19] but every Christian is not inspired, and such an one who utters the words of God may not have received either life-giving affections or life-giving light.

2. It may be demonstrated by a great many examples that the one of these gifts was not the measure of the other; and that the divine inspiration of the prophets did not observe the scope of their knowledge, any more than that of their holiness.

3. Far, indeed, from the one of those gifts being the measure of the other, one may even say that divine inspiration appeared all the more strikingly the more that the illumination of the sacred writer remained in arrear of his inspiration. When you behold the very prophets, who were most enlightened by God's Spirit, bending over their own pages after having written them, and endeavoring to comprehend the meaning which the Spirit in them had caused them to express, it should become manifest to you that their divine inspiration was independent of their illumination.

4. Even supposing the prophets' illumination raised to its utmost pitch, still it did not reach the altitude of the divine idea, and there might be much more meaning in the word dictated to them than the prophet was yet cognizant of. David, doubtless, in hymning his *Psalms*, knew[20] that they referred to "him who was to be born of his loins, to sit upon his throne for ever." Most of the prophets, like Abraham their father, saw the day of Christ, and when they saw it, were glad;[21] they searched what the Spirit of Christ, which was in them, did signify, when he testified beforehand of the sufferings of the Messiah, and the glory that should follow.[22] Yet notwithstanding all this, our Lord attests to us that the simplest Christian, the least (in knowledge) in the kingdom of God, knows more on that subject than the greatest of the prophets.[23]

---

19. *1 John* 2:20,27; *Jeremiah* 31:34; *John* 6:45.
20. *Acts* 2:30.
21. *John* 8:56.
22. *1 Peter* 1:11.
23. *Matthew* 11:11. Michaëlis, *Introduction*, Volume 1, pages 116-129, French translation. (That author thinks that in this passage *the least* means *the least prophet*.)

## DIDACTIC ABSTRACT OF THE DOCTRINE OF DIVINE INSPIRATION

5. These gifts differ from each other in essential characters, which we will presently describe.

6. Finally, it is always the inspiration of the book that is presented to us as an object of faith, never the inward state of him that writes it. His knowledge or ignorance nowise affects the confidence I owe to his words; and my soul ought ever to look not so much to the lights of his understanding as to the God of all holiness, who speaks to me by his mouth. The Saviour desired, it is true, that most of those who related his history should also have been witnesses of what they related. This was, no doubt, in order that the world might listen to them with the greater confidence, and might not start reasonable doubts as to the truth of their narratives. But the church, in her faith, looks much higher than this: to her the intelligence of the writers is imperfectly known, and a matter of comparative indifference – what she does know is their inspiration. It is never in the breast of the prophet that she goes to look for its source; it is in that of her God. "Christ speaks in me," says Paul, "and God has spoken to our fathers in the prophets."[24] "Why look you so earnestly on us," say to her all the sacred writers, "as though by our own power or holiness we had done this work?"[25] Look upwards.

XI. If there exist, then, between these two spiritual gifts of illumination and inspiration a specific difference, in what must we say that it consists?

Though you should find it impossible to say what that difference is, you would not the less be obliged by the preceding reasons to declare that it does exist. In order to be able fully to reply to this question, it were necessary that you should know the nature and the mode of both these gifts; whereas the Holy Spirit has never explained to us, either how he infuses God's thoughts into the understanding of a believer, or how he puts God's words into the mouth of a prophet. Nevertheless, we can here point out two essential characters by which these two operations of the Holy Spirit have always shown themselves to be distinct: the one of these characters relates to their duration, the other to their measure.

---

24. *2 Corinthians* 13:3; *Hebrews* 1:1 (ἐν).
25. *Acts* 3:12.

## GOD-BREATHED: THE DIVINE INSPIRATION OF THE BIBLE

In point of duration, illumination is continuous, whereas inspiration is intermittent. In point of measure, illumination admits of degrees, whereas inspiration does not admit of them.

XII. What are we to understand by saying that illumination is continuous and inspiration intermittent?

The illumination of a believer by the Holy Spirit is a permanent work. Having commenced for him on the day of his new birth, it goes on increasing, and attends him with its rays to the termination of his course. That light, no doubt, is but too much obscured by his acts of faithlessness and negligence, but never more will it leave him altogether. "His path," says the wise man, "is like the shining light, shining more and more unto the perfect day."[26] "When it pleased God, who separated me from my mother's womb, to reveal his Son in me,"[27] he preserves to the end the knowledge of the mystery of Jesus Christ, and can at all times set forth its truths and its glories. As it was not flesh and blood that had revealed these things to him, but the Father,[28] that unction which he received from the Holy One[29] abides in him, says John, and he needs not that any man teach him; but as the same anointing teaches him all things, and is truth, so, even as he has been taught by it, he will remain in it. Illumination, therefore, abides on the faithful; but it is not so with miraculous gifts, nor with the divine inspiration, which is one of those gifts.[30]

As for miraculous gifts, they were always intermittent with the men of God, if we except the only man who "received not the Spirit by measure."[31] The Apostle Paul, for example, who at one time restored Eutychus to life, and by whom God wrought such special miracles[32] (so as that it sufficed that handkerchiefs and aprons should touch his body and be laid upon the sick, in order to cures being effected); at other times could not relieve either his colleague Trophimus or his beloved Epaphroditus, or his son Timothy.[33] It is the same with inspi-

---

26. *Proverbs* 4:18.
27. *Galatians* 1:15.
28. *Matthew* 16:17.
29. *1 John* 2:20, 27.
30. *1 Corinthians* 14:1; *Acts* 19:6.
31. *John* 3:34.
32. *Acts* 19:11-12.
33. *2 Timothy* 4:20; *Philippians* 2:27; *1 Timothy* 5:23.

ration, which is only the most excellent of miraculous gifts. In the Lord's prophets, it was exerted only by intervals. The prophets, and even the apostles, who (as we shall show) were prophets, and more than prophets,[34] did not prophesy as often as they pleased. Inspiration was sent to them by intervals; it came upon them according as the Holy Spirit saw fit to give it to them (καθὼς τὸ πνεῦμα ἐδίδου ἀποφθέγγεσθαι αὐτοῖς);[35] for "never did prophecy come by the will of man," says Peter,[36] "but holy men of God spoke as they were moved by the Holy Spirit." God spoke in the prophets (ἐν τοῖς προφήταις), says Paul, when he wished to do so, at sundry times (πολυμερῶς), as well as in divers manners (πολυτρόπως). On such a day, and at such a time, it is often written, "the Word of Jehovah was upon such a man (ויהי דבר־יחוה אליו)." "In the tenth year, on the twelfth day of the tenth month, the Word of Jehovah came to me," said the prophet.[37] In the fifteenth year of the reign of Tiberius, the Word of the Lord came unto John, the son of Zacharias (ἐγένετο ῥῆμα Θεοῦ ἐπὶ ᾿Ιωάννην);[38] and on the eighth day, Zacharias, his father, was filled with the Holy Spirit and prophesied, saying, ....[39]

So then we ought not to imagine that the divine infallibility of the language of the prophets (and even of the apostles), lasted longer than the times in which they were engaged in their miraculous task, and in which the Spirit caused them to speak. Without divine inspiration, they were in most instances enlightened, sanctified, and preserved by God, as holy and faithful men in our own day may still be, but then they no more spoke as moved by the Holy Spirit; their language might still be worthy of the most respectful attention; but it was a holy man that spoke; it was no longer God: They again became fallible.

XIII. Can any examples be adduced of this fallibility being attached to their language, when unaccompanied with divine inspiration?

A multitude of instances occur. Men are often, after having been for a time the mouth of the Lord, seen to become false prophets, and

---

34. *Ephesians* 3:4-5; 4:11; *Romans* 16:25-27.
35. *Acts* 2:4.
36. *2 Peter* 1:21.
37. *Ezekiel* 29:1, and elsewhere.
38. *Luke* 3:1-2.
39. *Luke* 1:59, 67, 41, 42.

mendaciously to pretend to utter the words of Jehovah, after the Spirit had ceased to speak in them;"although the Lord sent them not, neither commanded them, neither spoke unto them." "They speak a vision of their own heart, not out of the mouth of the Lord."[40]

But without referring to those wicked men, or to the profane Saul, or to Balaam, who were for some time numbered among the prophets, shall it be thought that all the words of King David were infallible during the course of that long year which he passed in adultery? Yet "these," say the Scriptures, "be the last words of David, the sweet psalmist of Israel: *The Spirit of the Lord spoke by me, and his Word was in my tongue.*"[41] Shall it be thought that all the words of the prophet Solomon still continued infallible when he fell into idolatry in his old age, and the salvation of his soul became a problem for the church of God? And to come down to Christ's holy apostles and prophets (*Ephesians* 3:5), shall it be thought that all the words of Paul himself were infallible, and that he still could say that "Christ spoke by him"[42] when there was a sharp contention ($\pi\alpha\rho o\xi\upsilon\sigma\mu\grave{o}s$) between him and Barnabas;[43] or when, in the midst of the council, under a mistaken impression with regard to the person of the High Priest, he "spoke evil of the Ruler of his people," and cried, "God shall strike you, you whited wall;" or further (since there may remain some doubt as to the character of this reprimand), shall it be thought that all the words of the Apostle Peter were infallible, when, at Antioch, he showed himself "so much to be blamed" ($\kappa\alpha\tau\epsilon\gamma\nu\omega\sigma\mu\acute{e}\nu os$); when he feared those that came from James; when he dissembled; and when he forced the Apostle Paul "to withstand him to his face before them all, because he walked not uprightly according to the truth of the Gospel ($o\mathring{\upsilon}\kappa\ \mathring{\eta}\nu\ \mathring{o}\rho\theta o\pi o\delta\acute{\eta}\sigma\alpha s$)"?

XIV. What, then, are we to conclude from this first difference which we have recognized as existing between illumination and inspiration, with respect to the duration of those gifts?

We must conclude from it

1. That these two operations of the Holy Spirit differ in their essence, and not in their degree only.

40. *Jeremiah* 14:14; 23:11, 16; *Ezekiel* 8:2-3.
41. *2 Samuel* 23:1-2.
42. *2 Corinthians* 8:3.
43. *Acts* 15:39.

## DIDACTIC ABSTRACT OF THE DOCTRINE OF DIVINE INSPIRATION

2. That the infallibility of the sacred writers depended not on their illumination (which, although raised to an extraordinary measure in the case of some of them, they nevertheless enjoyed in common with all the saints), but solely on their divine inspiration.

3. That divinely inspired words, having been miraculous, are also all of them the words of God.

4. That as our faith in every part of the Bible rests no longer on the illumination of the writers, but on the inspiration of their writings, it may dispense henceforth with the perplexing study of their internal state, of the degree in which they were enlightened, or of that of their holiness; but must stay itself in all things on God, in nothing on man.

XV. If such have been the difference between illumination and inspiration in the prophets and the apostles, as respects the *duration* of those gifts, what has it been as respects their *measure*?

Illumination is susceptible of degrees; inspiration does not admit of them. A prophet is more or less enlightened by God; but what he says is not more or less inspired. It is so, or it is not so; it is from God, or it is not from God; here there is neither measure nor degree, neither increase nor diminution. David was enlightened by God; John the Baptist more than David; a simple Christian possibly more than John the Baptist; an apostle was more enlightened than that Christian and Jesus Christ more than that apostle. But of the inspired word of David, what do I say? The inspired word of Balaam himself is that of God, as was that of John the Baptist, as was that of Paul, as was that of Jesus Christ! *It is the Word of God*. The most enlightened of the saints cannot speak by inspiration, whilst the most wicked, the most ignorant, and the most impure of men may speak not of his own will (ἀφ' ἑαυτοῦ οὐκ εἰπεῖν), but by inspiration (ἀλλὰ προφητεῦσαι).[44]

In a man who is truly regenerated, there is always the divine spirit and the human spirit, which operate at once – the one enlightening, the other darkening; and the illumination will be so much the greater, the more that of the divine Spirit surpasses that of the human spirit. In the prophets, and, above all, in the apostles, these two elements also are to be found. But, thanks be to God, our faith in the words of Scripture nowise depends on the unknown issue of that combat which was waged

---

44. *John* 11:51.

between the Spirit and the flesh in the soul of the sacred writers. Our faith goes directly to the heart of God.

XVI. Can much harm result from the doctrine according to which the language of inspiration would be no more than the human expression of a superhuman revelation, and, so to speak, of a natural reflection of a supernatural illumination?

One or other of two evils will always result from it; either the oracles of God will be brought down to the level of the words of the saints, or these last will be raised to the level of the Scriptures.

This is a deplorable consequence, the alternative involved in which has been reproduced in all ages. It became unavoidable.

All truly regenerated men being enlightened by the Holy Spirit, it would follow, according to this doctrine, that they would all possess, though in different degrees, the element of inspiration; so that, according to the arbitrary idea that you would form to yourselves of their spiritual condition, you would be led inevitably sometimes to assimilate the sacred writers to them, sometimes to raise them to the rank of writers inspired from above.

XVII. Might religious societies be mentioned in which the former of these two evils is realized; I mean to say, where people have been led, by this path, to lower the Scriptures to the level of the sayings of saints?

All the systems of the Protestant doctors who assume that there is some mixture of error in the Holy Scriptures are based on this doctrine – from Semler and Ammon to Eichhorn, Paulus, Gabler, Schuster, and Restig; from M. De Wette to the more respectable systems of Michaëlis, Rosenmuller, Scaliger, Capellus, John LeClerc, or of Vossius. According to these theories, the divine light with which the intellects of the sacred writers was enlightened might suffer some partial eclipses, through the inevitable effect of their natural infirmities, of a defect of memory, of innocent ignorance, of popular prejudice; so that traces of these have remained in their writings, and so that we can perceive in these where their shadows have fallen.

XVIII. Might religious societies be mentioned also, where the latter of these evils has been consummated; I mean to say, where, in consequence of having been willing to confound inspiration with illumi-

## DIDACTIC ABSTRACT OF THE DOCTRINE OF DIVINE INSPIRATION

nation, saints and doctors have been elevated to the rank of divinely inspired men?

Of these, two in particular may be mentioned, the Jews and the Roman Catholics.

XIX. What have the Jews done?

They have considered the rabbins of the successive ages of the dispersion as endowed with an infallibility which put them on a level with (if not above) Moses and the prophets. They have, to be sure, attributed a kind of divine inspiration to Holy Scripture; but they have prohibited the explanation of its oracles otherwise than according to their traditions. They have called the immense body of those commandments of men the oral law (תורה שבעל פה), the *Doctrine,* or the *Talmud* (תלמוד), distinguishing it into the *Mishna,* or Second Law (משנה), and *Gemara, complement* or *perfection* (גמרא). They have said that it passed from God to Moses, from Moses to Joshua, from Joshua to the prophets, from the prophets to Esdras, from Esdras to the doctors of the great synagogues and from them to the Rabbins Antigone, Soccho, Shemaia, Hillel, Schammai, until at last Juda the saint deposited it in the *traditions* or *repetitions* of the law (משניות, δευτερώσεις), which afterward, with their commentary or complement (the *Gemara*), formed, first, the Talmud of *Jerusalem,* and afterward that of *Babylon.*

"One of the greatest obstacles that we have to encounter in dealing with the Jews," says the missionary MacCaul, "is their invincible prejudice in favor of their traditions and of their commentaries, so that we cannot prevail on them to buy our Bibles without notes or commentaries."[45]

"The law they say is salt; the mishna, pepper; the talmuds, aromatics;" "the Scripture is water; the mishna, wine; the gemara, spiced wine." "My son," says Rabbi Isaac, "learn to pay more attention to the words of the scribes than to the words of the law." "Turn away your children" (said Rabbi Eleazar, on his deathbed to his scholars, who asked him the way of life), "turn away your children from the study of the Bible, and place them at the feet of the wise." "Learn, my son," says the Rabbi Jacob, "that the words of the scribes are more agreeable than those of the prophets!"[46]

---

45. Letter from Warsaw, March 22, 1827.
46. In the Talmud of Jerusalem, *Encycl. Method.* at the word *Juifs.*

XX. And what has been the result of these monstrous principles?

It is that by this means millions and millions of immortal souls, although wandering upon the Earth, although weary and heavy laden, although everywhere despised and persecuted, have contrived to carry the book of the Old Testament, intact and complete, among all the nations of the whole world, without ceasing to read it in Hebrew every Sabbath, in thousands of synagogues, for the last eighteen hundred years...without, notwithstanding all this, recognizing there that Jewish Messiah whom we all adore, and the knowledge of whom would be at this day their deliverance, as it promises one day to be their happiness and their glory!

"Full well," said Jesus to them, "full well you reject the commandment of God, that you may keep your own tradition."[47]

XXI. And what have the Roman Catholics done?

They have considered the fathers, the popes, and the councils of the successive ages of the Roman Church as endowed with an infallibility which puts them on a level with Jesus, the prophets, and the apostles, if not above them. They have differed greatly, it is true, from each other on the doctrine of the inspiration of the Scriptures; and the faculties of Douay and Louvain, for example, have vigorously opposed[48] the opinion of the Jesuits, who would see nothing in the operation of the Holy Spirit but a direction preserving the sacred writers from error – but all have forbidden the explanation of the Scriptures otherwise than by their traditions.[49] They have thought themselves entitled to say, in all their councils, as did the apostles and prophets at Jerusalem, "It has seemed good to the Holy Spirit and to us." They have declared that it appertained to them to pronounce upon the true meaning of Holy Scripture. They have called the immense body of those commandments

---

47. *Mark* 7:9; see also 13 and *Matthew* 15:3-9. The mischief of those traditions begins at last to reveal itself to the Jews of our day: "The time is come," says the Israelite doctor Creissenach (*Entwickelungs Geschichte des Mosaischen Ritual Besetzes*, Preface), "the time is come when the Talmud will precipitate the Jewish religion into the most profound and humiliating downfall, if all the popular teachers of the Jews do not loudly declare that its statutes are of human origin, and may be changed."

48. Censure of 1588.

49. Council of Trent, session 4, second decree of April 28, 1546. Bellarmin, *De Eccl.*, Book 3, chapter 14; Book 4, chapters 3, 5, 6, 7, 8. Coton, *De Perron contre Tilenus*, Book 2, chapters 24, 34, 35.

## DIDACTIC ABSTRACT OF THE DOCTRINE OF DIVINE INSPIRATION

of men, the oral law, the unwritten traditions, the unwritten law. They have said that they have been transmitted by God, and dictated by the mouth of Jesus Christ, or of the Holy Spirit, by a continual succession.

"Seeing," says the Council of Trent,[50] "that the saving truth and discipline of manners are contained in the written books and the unwritten traditions, which, having been received by the apostles from the mouth of Jesus Christ, or from the inspiration of the Holy Spirit, by succession of time are come down to us, following the example of the apostolic fathers, the Council receives with the same affection and reverence (*pari pietatis et reverentiæ affectu*), and honors all the books of the Old and New Testament (seeing that God is their author), and *together with them the traditions* relating to faith as well as manners, as having been dictated by the mouth of Jesus Christ or of the Holy Spirit, and preserved in the Catholic Church by continual succession."

"If any one receive not the whole of the said books, with all their parts, as holy and canonical as they have been wont to be read in the Catholic Church, and in the old vulgate translation" (that of Jerome,[51] which, especially in *Job* and the *Psalms*, is crammed with very numerous, very serious, and very evident errors, and has even been corrected abundantly since by other popes),[52] "or knowingly despises the said traditions, let him be accursed!"

They have thus put the bulls of the bishops of Rome, and the decrees of their synods, above the Scriptures. "Holy Scripture," say they, "does not contain all that is necessary for salvation, and is not sufficient."[53] "It is obscure."[54] "It does not belong to the people to read Holy Scripture."[55] "We must receive with obedience of faith many things that are not contained in Scripture."[56] "We must serve God according to the tradition of the ancients."[57]

50. Council of Trent, First Decree, session 4.
51. It was in vain that the Abbot Isidore Clarius represented at the Council that there was temerity in ascribing inspiration to a writer who himself assures us that he had none (Father Paul, *History of the Council of Trent*, page 148 (London Edition, 1676).
52. See Thomas James, *Bellum Papale sive Concordia Discors Sexti V et Clementis VIII*.
53. Bellarmin, *De Verbo Dei*, Book 4.
54. *Idem*, Book 3. Charron, *Vérité* 3. Coton, Book 2, chapter 24. Bayle, *Traite*.
55. Bellarmin, *De Verbo Dei*, Book 2, chapter 19.
56. Bellarmin, Book 4, chapter 3, and Coton, *De Perron contre Tilenus*, Book 2, chapter 24.
57. Bellarmin, Book 4, chapter 5. Coton, Book 2, chapters 34-35. Council of Trent, session 4.

## GOD-BREATHED: THE DIVINE INSPIRATION OF THE BIBLE

The bull *Exsurge* of Leo X[58] places in the number of Luther's heresies his having said, "That it is not in the power of the church, or of the Pope, to establish articles of faith."

The bull *Unigenitus*[59] condemns to perpetuity, as being respectively false, captious, scandalous, pernicious, rash, suspected of heresy, savoring of heresy, heretical, impious, blasphemous, etc., the following propositions: "It is profitable at all times, in all places, and for all sorts of persons to study the Scriptures, and to become acquainted with their spirit, piety, and mysteries" (on *1 Corinthians* 16:5).[60] "The reading of Holy Scripture in the hands of a man of business, and a financier, shows that it is intended for everybody" (on *Acts* 8:28).[61] "The holy obscurity of the Word of God is no ground for the laity's being dispensed from reading it" (on *Acts* 8:30-31). "The Lord's Day ought to be sanctified by the reading of books of piety, and especially of the Scriptures. They are the milk which God himself, who knows our hearts, has supplied for them. It is dangerous to desire being weaned from it" (*Acts* 15:29). "It is a mistake to imagine that the knowledge of the mysteries of religion ought not to be communicated to that sex (women) by the reading of the holy books, after this example of confidence with which Jesus Christ manifests himself to this woman (the Samaritan)." "It is not from the simplicity of women, but from the proud learning of men, that abuse of the Scriptures has arisen, and heresies have been generated" (*John* 4:26). "It amounts to shutting the mouth of Christ to Christians, and to wresting from their hands the holy book, or to keep it shut to them by depriving them of the means of hearing it" (*1 Thessalonians* 5:2). "To interdict Christians from reading it is to interdict children from the use of light, and to subject them to a kind of excommunication" (on *Luke* 11:33).[62]

Still more lately, in 1824, the encyclical epistle of Pope Leo XII mournfully complains of the Bible Societies, "which," it says, "violate the traditions of the fathers and the Council of Trent, by circulating the Scriptures in the vernacular tongues of all nations." ("*Non vos latet, venerandi fratres, societatem quamdam, dictam vulgo Biblicam, per totum orbem*

---

58. 1520 Concil., Harduini, Volume 9, page 1893.
59. Clement XI of September 8, 1713.
60. Proposition 79.
61. Proposition 80.
62. *Exodus* 20:4-5.

*audacter vagari quae spretis S.S. Patrum traditionibus et contra notissimum Tridentini Concilii deretum in id collatis viribus ac modis omnibus intendit, ut in vulgares linguas nationum omnium sacra vertantur vel potius pervertantur Biblia.*") "In order to avert this pest," he says, "our predecessors have published several constitutions... tending to show how pernicious for the faith and for morals this perfidious institution [the Bible Society] is!" (*ut ostendatur quantopere fidei et moribus vaferrimum hocce inventum noxium sit!*).

XXII. And what has been the result of these monstrous principles?

It is this, that millions and millions of immortal souls in France, in Spain, in Italy, in Germany, in America, and even in the Indies, although they carry everywhere intact and complete the New Testament, although they have not ceased to read it in Latin, every Lord's Day, in thousands and thousands of churches, for twelve hundred years,... have been turned away from the fountain of life, have, like the Jews, "paid more attention to the words of the scribes than to those of the law;" have diverted their children, according to the counsel of Eleazar, "from the study of the Bible, to place them at the feet of the wise." They have found, like Rabbi Jacob, "the words of the scribes more agreeable than those of the prophets." It is thus that they have contrived, for twelve centuries, to maintain doctrines most contrary to the Word of God,[63]

on the worship of images;[64]
on the exaltation of the priests;
on their forced celibacy;
on their auricular confession;
on the absolution which they dare to give;
on the magical power which they attribute even to the most impure among them, of creating his god with Latin words, *opere operato*;
on an ecclesiastical priesthood, of which Scripture has never said a word;
on prayers to the dead;

---

63. *Exodus* 20:4-5.
64. Quisquis elanguerit erga venerabilium imaginum adorationem ($προσκύνησιν$), hunc anathemizat sancta nostra et universalis synodus! (was written to the Emperor, in the name of the whole Second Council of Nice). (Concil., Book 7, 585).

on the spiritual pre-eminence of the city which the Scripture has called Babylon;

on the use of an unknown tongue in worship;

on the celestial empire of the blessed but humble woman to whom Jesus himself said, "Woman, what have I to do with you?"

on the mass;

on the taking away of the cup;

on the interdiction of the Scriptures to the people;

on indulgences;

on purgatory;

on the universal episcopate of an Italian priest;

on the interdiction of meals;

so that just as people annul the sole priesthood of the Son of man by establishing other priesthoods by thousands, just as they annul his divinity by acknowledging thousands of demigods or dead men, present in all places, hearing throughout the whole Earth the most secret prayers of human beings, protecting cities and kingdoms, working miracles in favor of their worshipers; ... just so, also, they annul the inspiration of Scripture, by acknowledging by thousands other writings which share in its divine authority, and which surpass and swallow up its eternal infallibility!

It was in opposition to the very similar tenets maintained by the heretics of his time that Irenæus said, "For when convicted by the Scriptures, they turn about and accuse the Scriptures themselves, as if they were imperfect, and wanting in authority, and uncertain, and as if one could not find the truth in them, if ignorant of tradition; for that was given, not in writing, but by the living voice."[65]

"Full well," says Jesus to them too, "you reject the commandments of God, that you may keep your own traditions! *Bene irritum facitis praeceptum Dei, ut traditionem vestram servetis!*" (Mark 7:9).

XXIII. Without pretending to explain how the Holy Spirit could dictate the thoughts and the words of the Scriptures (for the knowl-

---

65. *Adv. Hæres.*, Book 3, chapter 2. "Cum enim ex Scripturis arguuntur, in accusationem convertuntur ipsarum Scripturarum, quasi non recte habeant, neque sint ex auctoritate, et quia varie sunt dictæ, et quia non possit ex his inveniri veritas ab his qui nesciant traditionem. Non enim per litteras traditam illam, sed per vivam vocem."

## DIDACTIC ABSTRACT OF THE DOCTRINE OF DIVINE INSPIRATION

edge of this mystery is neither given to us, nor asked of us), what is it that one can perceive in this divine action?

Why, two things; first, an *impulsion,* that is, an action on the *will* of the men of God, in order to make them speak and write; and, secondly, a *suggestion,* that is to say, an action on their understandings and on their organs, in order to their producing, first, within them more or less exalted notions of the truth they were about to utter, and, then, without them such human expressions as were most divinely suitable to the eternal thought of the Holy Spirit.

XXIV. Meanwhile, must it be admitted that the sacred writers were no more than merely the pens, hands, and secretaries of the Holy Spirit?

They were, no doubt, hands, secretaries, and pens; but they were, in almost every case, and in very different degrees, living pens, intelligent hands, secretaries docile, affected by what they wrote, and sanctified.

XXV. Was not the Word of God, however, often written as suggested by the occasion?

Yes, no doubt, and the occasion was prepared by God, just as the writer was. "The Holy Spirit," says Claude,[66] "employed the pen of the evangelists...and of the prophets. He supplied them with the occasions on which they wrote; he gave them the wish and the strength to do so; the matter, form, order, economy, expressions, are from his immediate inspiration and direction."

XXVI. But do we not clearly recognize, in the greater part of the sacred books, the individual character of the person who writes?

Far from disowning this, we, on the contrary, admire its being so. The individual character which comes from God, and not from sin and the fall, was prepared and sanctified by God for the work to which it had been destined by God.

XXVII. Ought we, then, to think that all has been equally inspired of God, in each of the books of Holy Scripture?

Scripture, in speaking of what it is, does not admit any distinction. All these sacred books, without exception, are the Word of the Lord. *All Scripture,* says Paul ($\pi\hat{\alpha}\sigma\alpha$ $\gamma\rho\alpha\phi\hat{\eta}$) *is inspired by God.*

---

66. Claude, *Œuvres Posthumes,* Volume 4, page 228.

## GOD-BREATHED: THE DIVINE INSPIRATION OF THE BIBLE

This declaration, as we have already said, is susceptible of two constructions, according as we place the verb, not expressed but understood, before or after the Greek word which we here translate *inspired by God;* both these constructions invincibly establish that in the apostle's idea all without exceptions in each and all of the books of the Scriptures, is dictated by the Spirit of God. In fact, in both the apostle equally attests that these *holy letters* (τὰ ἱερὰ γράμματα), of which he had been speaking to Timothy, are all *divinely inspired Scriptures.*

Now, we know that in the days of Jesus Christ, the whole church meant one sole and the same collection of books by the *Scripture, the Holy Scripture, the Scriptures,* the *Holy Letters,* or the *Law and the Prophets* (γραφὴ,[67] ἡ γραφη ἁγία,[68] αἱ γραφαὶ,[69] ὁ νόμος καὶ οἱ προφῆται,[70] or τὰ ἱερὰ γράμματα[71]). These were the twenty-two sacred books which the Jews held from their prophets, and on which they were all perfectly agreed.[72]

This entire and perfect divine inspiration of all the Scriptures of the Jews was so fully, in the days of Jesus Christ, the doctrine of the whole of that ancient people of God (as it was that of Jesus Christ, of Timothy, and of Paul), that we find the following testimony to it in the works of the Jewish general Josephus (who had reached his thirtieth year[73] at the time when the Apostle Paul wrote his *Second Epistle to Timothy*): "Never," says he in speaking of "the twenty-two books"[74] of the Old Testament, which he calls τὰ ἴδια γράμματα, as Paul calls them here τὰ ἴδια γράμματα, "never, although many ages have elapsed, has anyone dared either to *take away or to add, or to transpose* in these anything whatever;[75] for it is with all the Jews, as it were an inborn con-

---

67. 2 Peter 1:20; *John* 10:35; 17:12; 19:37.
68. *Romans* 1:2.
69. *John* 5:39; *Matthew* 21:42; 26:54; *Romans* 15:4; *1 Corinthians* 15:3.
70. *Acts* 24:14; *Luke* 16:16, 29, 31; *Matthew* 5:17-18; *John* 10:34.
71. *2 Timothy* 3:15.
72. See Krebs and Læsner on *2 Timothy* 3:15.
73. He was born in the year 37. See his *Life*, Edit. Aureliæ Allobr, page 999.
74. *Contra Apion*, Book 1, p. 1837. (δύο μόνα πρὸς τοῖς εἴκοσι βιβλία.) Our Bibles reckon thirty-nine books in the Old Testament; but Josephus and the ancient Jews, by making one book each of the two books of *Samuel, Kings,* and *Chronicles,* by throwing together *Ruth* and *Judges, Esdras* and *Nehemiah, Jeremiah* and *Lamentations,* and finally, *Hosea* and the eleven minor prophets that follow respectively, into one book, reduced our modern calculation of their sacred books by seventeen units.
75. Ούτε ΠΡΟΣΘΕΙΝΑΙ τις οὐδὲν οὔτε ΑΦΕΛΕΙΝ αὐτῶν, οὔτε ΜΕΤΑΘΕΙΝΑΙ τετόλμηκεν.

viction (*ΠΑΣΙ δὲ σύμφυτόν ἐστιν*), from their very earliest infancy,⁷⁶ to call them *God's teachings*, to abide in them, and, if necessary, to die joyfully in maintaining them."⁷⁷

"They are given to us," he says further, "by the inspiration that comes from God (*κατὰ τὴν ἐπίπνοιαν τὴν ἀπὸ τοῦ Θεοῦ*); but as for the other books, composed since the times of Artaxerxes, they are not thought worthy of a like faith."⁷⁸

These passages from Josephus are not quoted here as an authority for our faith, but as an historical testimony, showing the sense in which the Apostle Paul spoke, and attesting to us that, in mentioning the holy letters (*τὰ ἱερὰ γράμματα*), and in saying that they are all divinely inspired Scriptures, he meant to declare to us that, in his eyes, there was nothing in the sacred books which was not dictated by God.

Now, since the books of the New Testament are *ἱερὰ γράμματα, Holy Scriptures, the Scriptures, the Holy Letters,* as well as those of the Old; since the apostles have put their writings, and since Peter, for example, has put *all the letters of Paul* (*πάσας τὰς ἐπιστολας*) in the same rank with the *rest of the Scriptures* (*ὡς καὶ τὰς λοιπὰς ΓΠΑΦΑΣ*), hence we ought to conclude that all is inspired by God in all the books of the Old and New Testament.

XXVIII. But if all the sacred books (*τὰ ἱερὰ γράμματα*) are divinely inspired, how can we discover that such and such a book is a sacred book, and that such another is not one?

This, in a great measure, is a purely historical question.

XXIX. Yet, have not the Reformed churches maintained that it was by the Holy Spirit that they recognized the divinity of the sacred books; and, for example, has not the *Confession of Faith* of the churches of France said in its fourth article that we know these books to be canonical, and a very certain rule of our faith, not so much by the common accord and agreement of the church, as by the testimony and the persuasion of the Holy Spirit, which enables us to discern between them and the other ecclesiastical books?

---

76. *Εὐθὺς ἐκ τῆς πρώτης γενέσεως ὀνομάζειν αὐτὰ ΘΕΟΥ ΔΟΓΜΑΤΑ* (according to others: *from the first generation*)
77. *Ὑπὲρ εὐτὸν εἰ δίος θνήσκειν ἡδέως.*
78. *Πίστεως δὲ οὐχ ὁμοίας ἠξίωται.*

This maxim is perfectly true, if you apply it to the sacred books as a whole. In that sense the Bible is evidently an αὐτόπιστος book, which needs itself only in order to be believed. To the man, whoever he be, that studies it "with sincerity and as before God,"[79] it presents itself evidently, and of itself, as a miraculous book; it reveals all that is hidden in men's consciences; it discerns the thoughts and affections of the heart. It has foretold the future; it has changed the face of the world; it has converted souls; it has created the church. Thus it produces in men's hearts "an inward testimony and conviction of the Holy Spirit," which attests its inimitable divinity, independently of any testimony of men. But we do not think that our churches ever ventured to affirm that one might be content to abide by this mark for discerning such or such a book, or such or such a chapter, or such or such a verse of the Word of God, and for ascertaining its celestial origin. They think that for this detail one must look, as they did, "to the common accord and agreement of the church." We ought to admit as divine the entire code of the Scriptures, before each of its parts has enabled us to prove by itself that it is of God. It does not belong to us to judge this book; it is this book which will judge us.

XXX. Nevertheless, has not Luther,[80] starting from a principle laid down by Paul[81] and by John,[82] said that "the touchstone by which one might recognize certain Scriptures as divine, is this: Do they preach Christ or do they not preach him? [83] And among the moderns, has not Dr. Twesten also said "that the different parts of the Scriptures are more or less inspired, according as they are more or less preaching; and that inspiration does not extend to words and historical matters beyond what has a relation to the Christian conscience, beyond what proceeds from Christ, or serves to show us Christ"?[84]

Christ is, no doubt, the way, the truth, and the life; the spirit of prophecy, no doubt, is the testimony of Jesus;[85] but this touchstone

---

79. *2 Corinthians* 2:17.
80. In his preface to the *Epistles of James* and *Jude*.
81. *1 Corinthians* 3:9-10.
82. *1 John* 4:2.
83. Ob sie Christum treiben, oder nicht.
84. *Vorlesungen über die Dogmatik*, 1829, I:B, pages 421-429.
85. *John* 14:6; *Revelation* 19:10.

might in our hands prove fallacious: First, because many writings speak admirably of Christ without being inspired; second, although all that is to be found in the inspired Scriptures relates to Jesus Christ, possibly we might fail to perceive this divine character at a first glance; and third, in fine, because we ought to *believe before seeing* it, that all Scripture is profitable for doctrine, for reproof, for correction, and for instruction in righteousness: that the man of God may be perfect, thoroughly furnished unto all good works.

XXXI. What reasons have we, then, for recognizing as sacred each of the books which, at the present day, form for us the collection of the Scriptures?

For the Old Testament we have the testimony of the Jewish church; and for the New Testament the testimony of the universal church.

XXXII. What must here be understood by the testimony of the Jewish church?

We must understand by it the common opinion of all the Jews, Egyptian and Syrian, Asiatic and European, Sadducees and Pharisees,[86] ancient and modern, good and bad.

XXXIII. What reason have we to hold for divine the books of the Old Testament which the church of the Jews has given us as such?

It is written "that unto them were committed the oracles of God;"[87] which means that God in his wisdom chose them for being, under the Almighty government of his providence, sure depositories of his written word. Jesus Christ received their sacred code, and we accept it as he did.

XXXIV. Shall our faith then depend upon the Jews?

The Jews often fell into idolatry; they denied the faith; they slew their prophets; they crucified the King of kings; since that they have

---

86. See Josephus, *Against Apion*, Book 1, page 1037. Philo in Joseph Eichhorn, in November *Repert.*, page 239. "De Ægypticis Judæis"; compare Eichhorn, *Einleit ins A. T. R. I.*, § 21, pages 73, 89, 91, 113, 114, 116. *De Sadducceis*, §35, page 95. And Semler (*App. ad liberal.*, V.T. interpret., page 11). Eichhorn, *Alg. Bibl. der Bibl. Litterat,* Volume 4, pages 274, 276.

87. Romans 3:2.

hardened their hearts for nearly two-thousand years; they have filled up the measure of their sins, and wrath "is come upon them to the uttermost."[88] Nevertheless, to them were committed the oracles of God. And albeit that these oracles condemn them; albeit that the veil remains on their hearts when they read the Old Testament;[89] albeit they have for ages despised the Word of God, and worshiped their Talmud; they have not been able not to give us the book of the Scriptures, intact and complete; and the historian Josephus might still say of them what he wrote eighteen hundred years ago: "After the lapse of so many centuries (τοσούτου γὰρ αἰῶνος ἤδη ταρῳχηκότος), no one among the Jews has dared to add or to take away or to transpose anything in the sacred Scriptures."[90]

XXXV. What, then, have been the warranty, the cause, and the means of this fidelity on the part of the Jews?

We shall reply to this question in but a very few words. Its warranty is to be found in the promises of God; its cause in the providence of God; and its means in the concurrence of the five following circumstances:

1. The religion of the Jews, which has carried their respect for the very letter of Scriptures even to a superstitious length.

2. The indefatigable labors of the Massorethes, who so carefully guarded its purity, even to the slightest accents.

3. The rivalry of the Judaical sects, none of which would have sanctioned any want of faithfulness on the part of the others.

4. The extraordinary dispersion of that people in all countries long before the ruin of Jerusalem; for "of old time," says James,[91] "Moses has in every [pagan] city them that preach him, being read in the synagogues every Sabbath-day."

5. Finally, the innumerable copies of the sacred books diffused among all nations.

---

88. *1 Thessalonians* 2:16.
89. *2 Corinthians* 3:15.
90. See this quotation at question XXVII.
91. *Acts* 15:21. Josephus often attests the same fact.

## DIDACTIC ABSTRACT OF THE DOCTRINE OF DIVINE INSPIRATION

XXXVI. And with respect to the New Testament, what are we now to understand by the testimony of the universal church?

By this we are to understand the universal agreement of the ancient and modern churches, Asiatic and European, good and bad, which call on the name of Jesus Christ; that is to say, not only the faithful sects of the blessed Reformation, but the Greek sect, the Arminian sects, the Syrian sect, the Roman sect, and perhaps we might add the Unitarian sects.[92]

XXXVII. Should our faith then be founded on the universal church?

All churches have erred, or might have erred. Many have denied the faith, persecuted Jesus Christ in his members, denied his divinity, made his cross of none effect, restored the worship of statues and graven images, exalted the priests, shed the blood of the saints, interdicted the use of the Scriptures to the people, committed to the flames those of the faithful who desired to read them in the vernacular tongue, have set up in the temple of God him who sits there as a god, have trampled upon the Scriptures, worshiped traditions, warred against God, and cast down the truth. Nevertheless, the new oracles of God have been committed to them, as those of the Old Testament were to the Jews. And albeit these oracles condemn them; albeit for ages they have despised the Scriptures and almost adored their traditions; they have not been able not to give us the Book of the Scriptures of the New Testament intact and complete; and one may say of them, as Josephus said of Jews, "After the lapse of so many ages, never has anyone in the churches dared either to add or take away anything in the Holy Scriptures." They have been compelled, in spite of themselves, to transmit them to us in their integrity.

---

92. Following the example of the Scripture, we believe we may employ the word *church* as denoting, sometimes all that are enclosed in the nets of the Gospel, sometimes only all that in these is pure and living. And as for the word *sect* ($\alpha\H{\iota}\rho\varepsilon\sigma\iota\varsigma$, Acts 24:14; 26:5; 28:22), following the apostle's example, we employ it here neither in a good sense nor in a bad sense.

93. Josephus, *Against Apion*, Book 1, 8. Eusebius, *H. E.*, Book 3, chapters 9–10.

94. *Exposition of the Book of Job*. See Father Paul's *History of the Council of Trent*, Book 2, page 143 (London, 1676).

95. Origen (Eusebius, *H. E.*, Book 4, chapter 26). Athanasius (Pascal, *Epistles*). Hilary (Prolog, in *Psalmos*, page 9. Paris, 1693). Epiphanius (Lardner, Volume 4, page 312). Gregory Nazianzen (*Carm.* 33, *Opera*, Volume 2, page 98).

XXXVIII. Nevertheless, has there not been in Christendom one powerful sect, which for three hundred years has introduced into the canon of the Scriptures the apocryphal books, disavowed as they have been by the Jews[93] (as even Pope Gregory himself attests),[94] and rejected by the fathers of the ancient church[95] (as Jerome attests)?

This, it is true, is what was done for the Roman Catholic sect by the fifty-three persons who composed, on April 8, 1546, the famous Council of Trent, and who pretended to be the representatives of the church universal of Jesus Christ.[96] But they could do it for the Old Testament only, which was entrusted to the Jews and not to the Christians. Neither that Council, nor any even of the most corrupt and idolatrous churches, have been able to add a single apocryphal book to the New Testament. God has not permitted this, however mischievous may have been their intentions. It is thus that the Jews have been able to reject the New Testament, which was not committed to them; while they have never been able to introduce a single book of man into the Old Testament. God has never permitted them to do so; and, in particular, they have always excluded from it those which the fifty-three ecclesiastics of Trent were daring enough to cause to be inserted in it, in the name of the universal church.

XXXIX. And what have been the warranty, the cause, and the means of that fidelity, which the universal church has shown in transmitting to us the oracles of God in the New Testament?

To this question we shall reply but in a very few words.

The warranty has lain in the promises of God; the cause in the providence of God; and the means principally in the concurrence of the following circumstances:

1. The religion of the ancient Christians, and their extraordinary respect for the sacred texts; a respect shown on all occasions in their

---

96. *In præ. ad libr. Regum; sive Prologo-galeato.* (See Lard., Volume 5, pages 16-22.) "Judith, et Tobiæ et Macchabæorum libros legit quidem Ecclesia: sed eas inter canonicas Scripturas non recipit" (Præfat. in *Libros Salom.-Epist.*, 115). See also *Symbolum Ruffini*, Volume ix, page 186 (Paris, 1602). "Some thought it strange that five cardinals and forty-eight bishops should so easily define the most principal and important points of religion, never decided before, giving canonical authority to books held for uncertain and apocryphal," etc. Father Paul's *History of the Council of Trent*, Book 2, page 153 (London, 1676). Most were Italians.

## DIDACTIC ABSTRACT OF THE DOCTRINE OF DIVINE INSPIRATION

churches,[97] in their councils,[98] in their oaths,[99] and even in their domestic customs.[100]

2. The pains taken by learned men in different ages to preserve the purity of the sacred text.

3. The many quotations made from Scripture by the fathers of the church.

4. The mutual jealousy of the sects into which the Christian church has been subdivided.

5. The versions made from the first ages in many ancient tongues.

6. The number and abundant dissemination of manuscripts of the New Testament.

7. The dispersion of the new people of God as far as the extremities of Asia, and to the farthest limits of the west.

XL. Does it then result from these facts that the authority of the Scriptures is founded for us, as Bellarmin has said, on that of the church?

The doctors of Rome, it is true, have gone so far as to say that without the testimony of the church the Scripture has no more authority than Livy, the Alcoran, or Æsop's fables;[101] and Bellarmin, horrified no doubt at such impious opinions, would fain distinguish the authority of the church in itself, and with respect to us (*quoad se, et quoad nos*). In this last sense, he says, the Scripture has no authority except by the testimony of the church. Our answer will be very simple.

Every manifestation having three causes, an objective cause, a subjective cause, and an instrumental cause; one may say also that the

---

97. *Plotius contra Manich.*, Volume 1; apud Wolf., anecd., page 32, sq. I. *Ciampini Rom. vetera monum.*, 1, page 126 sq. All the Christian congregations in the East, even the poorest, kept a collection of the sacred books in their oratories. See Scholz, *Proleg.*

98. Cyrill. Alex. in *Apol. ad Theodos.*, imp. *Act. Concil.* ed. Mansi, Volume 6, column 579; Volume 7, column 6; Volume 9, column 187; Volume 12, column 1009, 1052, al. "Prohibition, under pain of excommunication, against selling the sacred book to druggists, or other merchants, who don't buy them to read" (Sixth Council, in Trullo. Canon 68).

99. *Corb. byz.*, i. page 422, al.

100. See Jerome, *Preface on Job*. Chrysostom, *Hom.* 19, "De Statuis." Women, says he, are wont to suspend copies of the *Gospels* from their children's necks. See Canon 68 of the VI. Council in Trullo.

101. *Hosius contra Brentium*, Book 3. Eckius, *De Auth. Ecclesiæ*. Bayli, *Tractat.* 1, *Catech.*, 9. 12. Andradius, Book 3. *Defens. Conc. Trident.* Stapleton, *Adv. Whittaker*, Book 3, chapter 17.

knowledge that we receive of the authority of the Scriptures has, first of all, for its objective cause, the Holy Bible itself, which proves its divinity by its own beauty, and by its own doings; in the second place, for subjective or efficient cause, the Holy Spirit,[102] who confirms and seals to our souls the testimony of God; and in fine, in the third place, for instrumental cause, the church, not the Roman, not the Greek, more ancient than the Roman, not even the Syriac, more ancient than either, but the universal church.

The pious Augustine expresses this triple cause in his book against the *Epistle of Manichaeus*, called *Fundamenti*. In speaking of the time at which he was still a Manichean, he says:[103] "I should not have believed in the Gospel had I not been drawn to it by the authority of the church;" but he takes care to add: "Let us follow those who invite us first to believe, when we are not yet in a state to see: in order that, being rendered more capable (*valentiores*) by faith itself, we may deserve to comprehend what we believe. Then it will no more be men, it will be God himself within us, who will confirm our souls and illuminate them."

In this affair, then, the church is a servant and not a mistress; a depositary and not a judge. She exercises the office of a minister, not of a magistrate, *ministerium non magisterium*.[104] She delivers a testimony, not a judicial sentence. She discerns the canon of the Scriptures, she does not make it; she has recognized their authenticity, she has not given it. And as the men of *Sichem* believed in Jesus Christ by means of the impure but penitent woman who called them to him, we say to the church: "Now we believe, not because of your saying; for we have heard him ourselves, and know that this is indeed the Christ, the Saviour of the world."[105] We have believed, then *per eam*, not *propter eam*, through her means, but not on her account. We found her on her

---

102. *Isaiah* 54:13; 59:21.

103. Evangelio non crederem [according to the African usage for *credidissem*, as confession, Book 2, chapter 8: *Si tunc amarem*, for *amavisem*] nisi me Ecclesiæ commoveret [commovisset] authoritas (ch. 5). [This, besides, is very classical Latin: Non ego hoc *ferrem*, says Horace, for *tulissem*, Book 3, ode 14]. Eos sequamur qui nos invitant prius credere, quum nondum valemus intueri, ut ipsâ fide valentiores facti, quod credimus intelligere mereamur, non jam hominibus, sed ipso Deo intrinsecus mentem nostram firmante et illuminante (chapter 14). *Opera August.*, Paris, Mabillon, Volume 8.

104. Turretin, *Theologia elenct.*, Volume 1, locus 2, question 6.

105. *John* 4:42.

knees; she showed us her Master; we recognized him, and we knelt down along with her. Were I to mingle in the rear of an imperial army, and should I ask those around me to show me their prince, they would do with respect to him, for me, what the church has done with regard to the Scriptures. They would not call their regiment the *ecumenical army*; above all, they would not say that the emperor has no authority but what is derived from its testimony, whether as it respected itself or with respect to us; whether *quoad se* or *quoad nos* (to use Bellarmin's language). The authority of the Scriptures is not founded, then, on the authority of the church; it is the church that is founded on the authority of the Scriptures.

XLI. If the authenticity of the Scriptures is proved in a great measure by history, how is their inspiration established?
Solely by the Scriptures.

XLII. But is such an argument rational? Does it not involve a begging of the question, and the proving of inspiration by inspiration?
There would be a begging of the question here, if, in order to prove that the Scriptures are inspired, we should invoke their testimony while assuming them to be inspired. But we are far from adopting this process. First of all, the Bible is viewed solely in the light of an historical document, deserving our respect from its authenticity, and by means of which one may know the doctrine of Jesus Christ, nearly as one would learn that of Socrates from the books of Plato, or that of Leibniz from the writings of Wolff. Now this document declares to us, in all its pages, that the whole system of the religion which it teaches, is founded on the grand fact of a miraculous intervention of God in the revelation of its history and its doctrines.

The learned Michaëlis, who held such loose principles on inspiration, himself declares that the inspiration of the apostolic writings necessarily results from their authenticity. There is no other alternative, says he; if what they relate is true, they are inspired; if they were not inspired, they would not be sincere; but they are sincere, therefore, they are inspired.

There is nothing in such reasoning that can be thought like a begging of the question.

XLIII. If it be by the Bible itself that we establish the dogma of a certain inspiration in the sacred books, by what can it be proved that that inspiration is universal, and that it extends to the minutest details of the instructions they convey?

If it be the Scriptures that tell us of their divine inspiration, it is they too that will be able to inform us in what divine inspiration consisted. In order to our admitting their inspiration on their own sole testimony, it should have sufficed for us to be assured that they were authentic; but, in order to our admitting their plenary inspiration, we shall have something more; for we shall then be able to invoke their testimony as writings already admitted to be divine. It will no longer be authentic books only that say to us, I am inspired; but books, both authentic and inspired, will say to us, I am so altogether. The Scriptures are *inspired*, we affirm, because, being authentic and true, they say of themselves that they are inspired; but the Scriptures are *plenarily inspired*, we also add, because, being inspired, they say that they are so entirely, and without any exception.

Here, then, there is neither more nor less than a doctrine which the Bible will teach us, as it teaches us all the rest. And just as we believe, because it tells us so, that Jesus Christ is God, and that he became man; so also we believe that the Holy Spirit is God, and that he dictated the whole of the Scriptures.

## Section II
### *On the Adversaries and Defenders of This Doctrine*

XLIV. Who are the theologians that have impugned the doctrine of the divine inspiration?

We have one general remark to make before enumerating them here, namely, that with the single exception of Theodore of Mopsuestia, that philosophical theologian whose numerous writings, so strongly tainted with Pelagianism, were condemned for their Nestorianism in the fifth ecumenical council (Constantinople, 553), and whose principles on the divine inspiration were very loose – with the exception, we say, of Theodore of Mopsuestia, it has been found impossible to produce, in the long course of the first eight centuries of Christianity, a single doctor who has disowned the plenary inspiration of the Scriptures, unless it be in the bosom of the most violent heresies that have tormented the Christian church; that is to say, among the Gnostics, the

Manicheans, the Anomeans, and the Mohammedans. Jerome himself, who sometimes permitted himself, while speaking of the style of certain parts of the sacred books, to use a language whose temerity will be censured by all pious persons,[106] nevertheless maintains, even for such passages, the entire inspiration of all the parts of the sacred Scripture;[107] and in that he further sees, under what he calls the grossness of the language and the seeming absurdity of the reasonings, intentions on the part of the Holy Spirit full of profound art and wisdom. And if, transporting ourselves from the days of Jerome to four hundred years further down, we come to the celebrated Agobard, who is alleged by Dr. Du Pin to have been the first of the fathers of the church that abandoned the doctrine of a verbal inspiration,[108] it is most unjustly, says Dr. Rudelbach, that such a charge has been brought against that bishop. It is true, that in disputing with the Abbot Fredigise,[109] touching the latitude to be allowed to Latin translators of the sacred text, he maintains that the dignity of the Word of God consists in the force of meaning, not in the pomp of words; but he took care to add that the authority of the apostles and the prophets remains intact, and that no one is permitted to believe that they could have placed a letter otherwise than they have done; for their authority is stronger than Heaven and Earth.[110]

If, then, we would class, in the order of time, the men who controverted the entire divine inspiration of our sacred books, we must place:

In the second century, the Gnostics (Valentine, Cerdo, Marcion, his disciples, etc.). They believed in two equal principles, independent, contrary, and co-eternal; the one good and the other bad; the one the father of Jesus Christ, and the other the author of the law; and, entertaining this idea, they rejected the Pentateuch, at the same time admitting no more of the New Testament than the *Gospel of Luke*, and part of Paul's epistles.

In the third century, Manes or Manichaeus, who, calling himself the Paraclete promised by Jesus Christ, corrected the books of the Christians, and added his own.

---

106. Qui solœcismos in verbis facit, qui non potest hyperbaton reddere, sententiamque concludere. (*Comment. in Epist. ad Titum*, Book 1 [ad chapter 1, 1.] *Et ad Ephes.*, Book 2 [ad chapter iii. 1.] See also his *Comment on the Epistle to the Galatians*).
107. *Proem. in Ep. ad Galat.*, Book 2.
108. Du Pin, doctor of the Sorbonne. *Prolegom. on the Bible,* Book 5, page 256.
109. Agobard, *Adv. Fredeg.*, chapters 9-12.
110. Rudelbach, *Zeitschrift*, first part, 1840, page 48.

In the fourth century, the Anomeans or Ultra-Arians (for Arius himself held a more reserved language), who maintained, with their leader Ætius, that the Son, a created intelligence, unlike[111] to the Father, took to himself a human body without a human soul. They spoke of the Scriptures with an irreverence tantamount to the denial of their entire inspiration. "When pressed with Scriptural reasons," says Epiphanius, "they escape by saying: That it was as a man that the apostle said those things;" or, "Why do you bring the Old Testament against me?" And what does the holy bishop add? "It was to be expected that those who denied the glory of Christ should deny still more that of the apostles."[112]

In the fifth century, Theodore of Mopsuestia, chief of the Antioch school, an able philosopher, and a learned but rash theologian. All that remains to us of his numerous works are some fragments only, preserved to us by other authors. His books, as we have said, were condemned (two hundred years after his death) at the Council of Constantinople. There were quoted there, for example, his writings against Appollinarius, in which he had said that the book of *Job* is merely a poem derived from a pagan source; that Solomon had no doubt received λόγον γνώσεως, but not λόγον σοφίας; that the *Song of Songs* is but a long and insignificant epithalamium, without any character prophetical, historical, or scientific, and in the manner of the *Symposium* of Plato, *etc.* [113]

In the seventh century, Mohammed (whose false religion is nothing more than a heresy of Christianity and who speaks of Christ at least as honorably as most of the Socinians have done) – Mohammed acknowledged, and often quoted as inspired, the books of the Old and New Testament; but he said they had been corrupted, and, like Manes, he added his own.

In the twelfth and thirteenth centuries, as it would appear, there sprang up and took a regular shape, first among the Talmudist Jews,[114] the system of those modern doctors who have thought fit to class the various passages of Holy Scripture under various orders of inspiration, and to reduce the divine inspiration to more or less natural proportions.

---

111. 'Ανόμειος: hence their name.
112. Epiphanius, *Advers. Hær.*, 70, 6. *Ætii salutat, Confut.*, 6.
113. *Acta concilii Constantinop.*, ii, 65, 71, apud Harduin., *Acta Concil.*, Volume 3, pages 87-89.
114. See Josephus *Against Apion*, Book 1, chapters 7-8; and Philo, ed. Hæschel, pages 515 and 918.

## DIDACTIC ABSTRACT OF THE DOCTRINE OF DIVINE INSPIRATION

It was under the double influence of the Aristotelian philosophy, and of the theology of the Talmud, that the Jews of the Middle Ages, differing much in this from the ancient Jews,[115] imagined this theory. That was the time of the Solomon Jarchis, the David Kimchis, the Averroëses, the Aben-Ezras, the Joseph Albos; and above all, of Moses Maimonides, that Spanish Jew who has been called the *eagle of the doctors*. Maimonides, borrowing the vague terms of the peripatetic philosophy, taught that prophecy is not an exclusive product of the action of the Holy Spirit. Just, says he, as if the *intellectus agens* (the intellectual influence that is in man) associate itself more intimately with reason, there results from it the *secta sapientum speculatorum,* and as, if that agent operates more on the imagination, there results from it the *secta politicorum, legislatorum, divinatorum, et præstigiatorum;* so also, when this superior principle exercises its action in a more perfect manner on those two faculties of the soul at once, the result is the *secta prophetarum*. Almost all the modern Jewish doctors have adopted the ideas of Maimonides; and there, also, seems to have originated Schleiermacher's modern system of inspiration. It is in starting from these principles that the doctors have admitted several degrees of inspiration in the prophets. Of these, Maimonides reckoned sometimes eight, sometimes eleven. Joseph Albo reduced them to four, and Abarbanel to three. They applied these distinctions of different degrees of inspiration to the division of the Old Testament into *Law, Prophets,* and *Hagiographa* (תורה נביאים וכתובים). The *kethubim,* according to him, had not received the prophetic spirit (רוח נבואה), but only the Holy Spirit (רוח הקדש), which, according to him, was no more than a human faculty, by means of which a man pronounced words of wisdom and holiness.[116]

The modern German school of the adversaries of inspiration, seems accordingly to be a mere reproduction of the theory of the rabbins of the thirteenth century, or a borrowing from the Talmudist doctors of our own days.

In the sixteenth century, Socinus[117] and Castellio[118] maintained that the sacred writers sometimes show a failure of memory, and might err on subjects of slight importance.

---

115. Ibid.
116. Moses Maimonides, *More Nebuchim,* part 2, chapter 37, *et* 45. Rudelbach (*ut supra*), page 53.
117. *De Author. Script.*
118. *In Dialogis.*

## GOD-BREATHED: THE DIVINE INSPIRATION OF THE BIBLE

In the seventeenth century, three orders of adversaries, according to the celebrated Turretin,[119] opposed inspiration. These were, besides the infidels properly so-called (*atheos et gentiles*): 1. the fanatics (*enthusiasts*), who charged Scripture with imperfection in order to exalt their own particular revelations; 2. those of the pope's sect (*pontificii*) who scrupled not, says he, to betray the cause of Christianity by alleging the corruption of the original text (*fontium*), in order to exalt their Vulgate translation; 3. the Rationalists of different classes (*libertini*), who, without going out of the church, unceasingly attempted to shake the authority of the Scriptures by pointing to difficult passages and apparent contradictions (ἄπορα καὶ ἐναντιοφανῆ).

In the latter half of the eighteenth century, this last class of adversaries became very numerous in Germany. Semler gave the first impulsion to what he called the liberal interpretation of the Scriptures; he rejected all inspiration, denied all prophecy, and treated all miracle as allegory and exaggeration.[120] Ammon, more lately, laid down positive rules for this impious manner of explaining the miraculous facts.[121] The writings of a legion of doctors no less daring, Paulus, Gabler, Schuster, Restig, and many others, abound in practical applications of these principles. Eichhorn, more recently still, has reduced into system the Rationalist doctrine of prophecy.[122] De Wette, in his *Preliminary Manuals*, appears not to see any true prediction in the prophets, and not to find any difference between those of Israel and those of the pagan nations, beyond the spirit of morality and sincerity which characterizes monotheism, and which, says he, purified Hebrew prophecy, while it was wanting to the seers among the pagans.[123] Hug, in his *Introduction to the New Testament Scriptures*,[124] nowhere speaks of inspiration. Michaëlis admits it for a part of the Scriptures, and rejects it for the other. So did John LeClerc in the last century.[125] Rosenmuller is still more wavering in his sentiments.

---

119. *Theol. Elenct.*, locus 2, question 5.
120. Preface to *Schultens' Compendium on the Proverbs*, by Vogel. Halle, 1769, page 5.
121. *De interpret. narrationum mirabil.* N.N. (at the beginning of his Ernesti).
122. *Einleitung in das alte Testament*; fourth edition, Gœttinger, 1824, Volume 4, page 45.
123. *Zweite Verbesserte Auflage.* Berlin 1822, page 276. *Lehrbuch, Anmerkungen.*
124. *Einleitung, etc.*, second edition, 1821.
125. *Sentiments de quelques theologiens de Holland*, Letters 11-12. La Chamb., *Traité de la Religion*, Volume 4, page 159 and the following.

## DIDACTIC ABSTRACT OF THE DOCTRINE OF DIVINE INSPIRATION

Of late years, however, there have been German theologians more reverentially inclined, who have admitted different degrees of inspiration in the different parts of the Scriptures by distinguishing the passages which do not relate, say they, to salvation, and making bold to see in them, as Socinus and Castellio did of old, slips of memory, and errors, on subjects which, in their eyes, seemed of little importance.

Among the English, too, there have been seen, of late years, persons otherwise respectable, who have allowed themselves to range the sentences of God's Word under different classes of inspiration.

XLV. Can many illustrious doctors of the church be mentioned as maintaining the plenary inspiration of the Scriptures?

It is the uniform doctrine of the whole church down to the days of the Reformation.

"Hardly," says Rudelbach, "is there a single point with regard to which there reigned, in the eight first ages of the church, a greater or more cordial unanimity."[126]

To the reader who wishes to consult these testimonies of history, we recommend the dissertation lately published on this subject by the learned doctor of Glogau, already mentioned. The author, commencing with a review of the first eight hundred years of the Christian era, establishes the following principles there, by very numerous quotations from the Greek and Latin fathers:

1. The ancient church, with one unanimous voice, teaches that all the canonical writings of the Old and New Testaments are given by the Holy Spirit of God; and it is on this sole foundation (and independently of the fragmentary information that human imperfection may acquire from them) that the church founded her faith on the perfection of the Scriptures.

2. The ancient church, following out this first principle, no less firmly maintains the infallibility of the Scriptures as their sufficiency ($αὐτάρκειαν$) and their plenitude. She attributes to their sacred authors not only *axiopistia,* to wit, a fully deserved credibility, but also *autopistia,* to wit, a right to be believed, independently of their circumstances or

---

126. *Kaum ist irgend ein Punct, worüber im Alterthume eine grössere und freudigere Einstimmigkeit herrschte.* (*Zeitschrift* von Rudelback und Guerike, 1840, Volume 1, pages 1-47. *Die lehre von der Inspiration der heiligen Schrift, mit Bierücksichtigung der neuester Untersuchungen darüber, von Schleiermacher, Twesten, und Steudel.*

of their personal qualities, and on account of the infallible and celestial authority which caused them to speak.

3. The ancient church, viewing the whole Scripture as an utterance on the part of God addressed to man and dictated by the Holy Spirit, has ever maintained that there is nothing erroneous, nothing useless, nothing superfluous there; and that in this divine work as in that of creation, one may always recognize, amid the richest plenty, the greatest and the wisest economy. Every word there will be found to have its object, its point of view, its sphere of efficacy. "*Nihil otiosum, nec sine signo, neque sine argumento apud eum*" (Irenæus); τᾶν ῥῆμα ... ἐργαξόμενον τὸ ἑαυτοῦ ἔργον (Origen). It is in vigorously establishing and defending both these characters of the Scriptures, that the ancient church has shown the elevated and profound idea she entertained of their divine inspiration.

4. The ancient church has always maintained that the doctrine of Holy Scripture is the same throughout, and that the Spirit of the Lord gives utterance in every part of it to one and the same testimony. She vigorously opposed that science, falsely so called (*1 Timothy* 6:20), which even in the first ages of her history had taken a regular shape in the doctrines of the Gnostics, and which, daring to impute imperfection to the Old Testament, made it appear that there were contradictions between one apostle and another apostle, where there was really none.

5. The ancient church thought that inspiration ought chiefly to be viewed, it is true, as a passive state, but as a state in which the human faculties, far from being extinguished or set aside by the action of the Holy Spirit, were exalted by his virtue, and filled with his light. She has often compared the soul of the prophets and of the apostles to "a stringed instrument, which the Holy Spirit put in motion, in order to draw out of it the divine harmonies of life" (*Athenagoras*).[127] What they had to do, was simply to submit themselves to the powerful action of the Holy Spirit, so that, touched by his celestial influence, the harp, though human, might reveal to us the knowledge of the mysteries of Heaven" (*Justin Martyr*).[128] But in their view, this harp, entirely passive as it was, as respects the action of God, was the heart of a man, the soul of a man,

---

127. *Legatio pro Christianis*, chapter 9.
128. *Ad Græcos cohortatio*, chapter 8.

# DIDACTIC ABSTRACT OF THE DOCTRINE OF DIVINE INSPIRATION

the understanding of a man, renewed by the Holy Spirit, and filled with divine life.

6. The ancient church, while it maintained that there was this continued action on the part of the Holy Spirit in the composition of the Scriptures, strenuously repelled the false notions that certain doctors, particularly among the Montanists, sought to propagate respecting the activity of the Spirit of God, and the passiveness of the spirit of man in divine inspiration; as if the prophet, ceasing to have the mastery of his senses, had been in the state which the pagans attributed to their sibyls ($μανίᾳ$ or $ἐκστάσει$). While the Cataphrygians held that an inspired man, under the powerful influence of the divine virtue, loses his senses (*excidit sensu, adumbratus, silicet, virtute divina*),[129] the ancient church maintained, on the contrary, that the prophet does not speak in a state of ecstasy (*non loquitur in* $ἐκστάσει$)[130] and that one may distinguish by this trait false prophets from the true. This was the doctrine held by Origen against Celsus (Book 7, chapter 4); as also of Miltiades, of Tertullian, of Epiphanius, of Chrysostom, of Basil, and of Jerome, against the Montanists.

7. The ancient church in her endeavors, by means of other definitions, which we shall not indicate here, to give greater clearness to the idea of divine inspiration, and to disentangle it from the difficulties with which it was sometimes obscured, still further showed how much she cherished this doctrine.

8. The ancient church thought that if the name of action on the part of God is to be applied to inspiration, it must be understood to extend to words as well as to things.

9. The ancient church, by her constant mode of quoting the Scriptures, in order to the establishment and defense of her doctrines; by her manner, too, of expounding and commenting on them; and, in fine, by the use which she recommends all Christians, without exception, to make of them as a privilege and a duty; the ancient church, by these three habitual practices, shows, still more strongly, if it be possible, than she could have done by direct declarations, how profoundly attached she was to the doctrine of a verbal inspiration.

And it is not only by her exposition of the Word that the ancient church shows us to what point she held the entire inspiration of the

---

129. Tertullian, *Adv. Marcion*, Book 4, chapter 22.
130. Hieronymus, *Proem. in Jahum. Præfat. in Habak. in Esaiam.* Epiphanius, *Adv. Hæreses*, Book 2. *Hæres.*, 48, chapter 3.

Scriptures as an incontrovertible axiom; she will show you this still more strongly, if you will follow her while she is engaged in reconciling the apparent contradictions sometimes presented by the *Gospel* narratives. After having made an essay of some explanation, she does not insist upon it; but hastens to conclude that whatever be its validity, there necessarily exists some method of reconciling those passages, and that the difficulty is only apparent, because the cause of that difficulty lies in our ignorance, and not in Scripture. "Whether it be so, or otherwise [she says with Julius Africanus], it matters not, the Gospel remains entirely true (τὸ μέντοι εὐαγγέλιον πάντως ἀληθεύει).[131] This is her invariable conclusion as to the perfect solubility of all the difficulties that one can present to her in the Word of God.

10. The ancient church was so strongly attached to the doctrine of the personality of the Holy Spirit, and of his sovereign action in the composition of the whole Scriptures, that she made no difficulty in admitting at one and the same time the greatest variety and the greatest liberty in the phenomena, in the occasions, in the persons, in the characters, and in all the external circumstances, under the concurrence of which that work of God was accomplished. At the same time that she owned with Paul, that in all the operations of this Spirit, it is one and the self-same Spirit that divides to every man severally as he will (*1 Corinthians* 12:11), she equally admitted that in the work of divine inspiration, the divine causation was exercised amid a large amount of liberty, as respects human manifestations. And, be it carefully remarked, you will nowhere find in the ancient church a certain class of doctors adopting one of these points of view (that of the divine causation and sovereignty), and another class of doctors attaching themselves exclusively to another (that of human personality, and of the diversity of the writers' occasions, affections, intelligence, style, and other circumstances). "If this were so," says Rudelbach, "one might justly accuse us of having ourselves forced the solution of the problem, instead of faithfully exhibiting the views of the ancient church." But no; on the contrary, you will often see one and the same author exhibit, at once and without scruple, both of these points of view: the action of God and the personality of man. This is what we see, for example, abundantly in Jerome,

---

131. In his letter to Aristides on the agreement of the *Gospels* that relate the two genealogies of Jesus Christ (Eusebius, *Hist. Eccl.*, Book 1, chapter 7).

## DIDACTIC ABSTRACT OF THE DOCTRINE OF DIVINE INSPIRATION

who, even when speaking of the specialties of the sacred writers, never abandons the idea of a word introduced by God into their minds.

This we further remark in Irenæus, who, while he insists more than anyone else on the action of God in the inspiration of the Scriptures, is the first of the fathers of the church that relates in detail the personal circumstances of the Evangelists. This is what you will find again in Augustine; this is what you will see even in the father of ecclesiastical history, Eusebius of Cæsarea, who gives so many details on the four authors of the *Gospels*, and who, nevertheless, professes the most rigorous principles on the plenary inspiration of the canonical Scriptures.

11. The ancient church shows us more completely still, by two other traits, the idea she had formed of divine inspiration, by the care she took, on the one hand, to fix the relations which the doctrine of divine inspiration bore to the doctrine of the gifts of grace; and, on the other, to exhibit the proofs of inspiration.

In fine, although the ancient church presents this spontaneous (*ungesüchte*) and universal agreement in the doctrine of inspiration, we must not imagine that this great phenomenon is attached, as some have said, to some particular system of theology, or may be explained by that system. No more must we regard this wonderful agreement as the germ of a theory that was to establish it at a later period in the church. No. The very assertions of an opposite opinion which, from time to time, made themselves heard on the part of the heretics of the first centuries, and the nature of the replies that were put forth by the ancient church, clearly demonstrate, on the contrary, that this doctrine was deeply rooted in the church's conscience. Every time that the fathers, in defending any truth by passages from Scripture, succeeded so far as to drive their adversaries into the impossibility of defending themselves, otherwise than by denying the full inspiration of the divine testimonies, the church thought the question was decided. The adversary was tried; he had no more to say for himself; he denied the Scripture to be the Word of God! What more remained to be done, but to compel him to look his own ill-favored argument in the face, and to say to him, See what you have come to as one would bid a man who has disfigured himself, look at himself in a glass? And this the fathers did.

Such are facts of the case; such is the voice of the church.

GOD-BREATHED: THE DIVINE INSPIRATION OF THE BIBLE

We had at first brought together, with the design of giving them here, a long series of passages, taken first from Irenæus,[132] Tertullian,[133] Cyprian,[134] Origen,[135] Chrysostom,[136] Justin Martyr,[137] Epiphanius,[138] Augustine,[139] Athanasius,[140] Hilary,[141] Basil the Great,[142] and Gregory the Great,[143] Gregory of Nyssa,[144] Theodoret,[145] Cyril of Alexandria;[146] then, the most revered fathers of after centuries; and, finally, the most holy doctors of the Reformation.[147] But we soon perceived that all these names, were we to give them by themselves, would seem nothing better than an idle appeal to the authority of men; and were we to give them along with the passages referred to, in full, we should run into an excessive multiplication of words.

We shall proceed, therefore, with a careful examination of the difficulties and the systems that are opposed to the doctrine of a plenary inspiration. Those difficulties constitute what are objections, and those systems what are rather evasions. The two next chapters we shall devote to the study of both.

---

132. *Advers. Hæreses*, Book 2, chapter 47; Book 3, chapter 11; Book 4, chapter 34.

133. *De Anima*, chapter 28. *Advers. Marcion*, Book 4, chapter 22. *De Præscript. advers. hæret.*, chapter 25. *Advers. Hermog.*, chapter 22.

134. *De Opere et Eleemos*, pages 197-201, *Adv. Quirin.*, *Adv. Judæos*, præfat.

135. *Hom.* 39 in *Jerem.* (quoted here chapter VI. section 1). Homil., 2 *in eumd.* (chapters 19 & 50). Homil., 25 in *Matth. Ejusdem Philocalia*, Book 4. *Commentar. in Matth.*, pages 227-428 (edit. Huet.). Homil., 27 in *Numer.* In *Levit.*, homil. 5.

136. Homil., 49 in *Joan.* Homil., 40, in *Joan.* 5. Homil., 9 in *2 Tim.* 4. Serm. 53, *de utilit. lect. Script.* Serm. 3, de Lazaro.

137. *Apol.* 1, chapters 53, and 35, 50, 51. *Dial. cont. Tryph.*, chapter 7. *Ad Græcos cohort.*, chapter 8.

138. Σύντομος λόγος περὶ πίστεως. *De doctrin. Christi.*, Book 2, chapter 9. *De Pastor.*, chapter 2. *Epist.* 42.

139. *Epist.* 97 (ad Hieronymus). *De unitate Ecclesiæ.*, chapter 3, Volume 9, page 341 (Paris, 1694).

140. *Contra Gentes*, Volume 1, page 1. *De Incarnat. Christi* (Paris, 1627).

141. *Ad Constant. Aug.*, page 244. *De Trinit.*, Book 8 (Paris, 1652).

142. *Comment. in Isaiam*, Volume 1, page 379. (Ed. Bened.). Homil. 29. *Advers. calumniantes S. Trinit.* In *Ethicis regni*, 16, 18, chapter 22.

143. *Moralia in Job*, præfat., chapter 1.

144. *Dialog. De Anima et Resurrectione*, Volume 1, edit. Græcolat, page 639. *De cognit. Dei* cit. ab. *Euthymio in Panoplia*, Volume 8.

145. *Dial.* 1. Ἄτρεπτ. Dial. ii. Ἀσύγχυτ in *Exod.*, question 26. *In Gen.*, question 45.

146. Book 7, cont. Jul. *Glaphyrorum in Gen.*, Book 2.

147. See Lardner, Volume 2, pages 172, 488, 475. Haldane, *The Inspiration of the Holy Scriptures*, pages 167 to 176.

Chapter 4
# Examination of Objections

IT IS OBJECTED that the fallibility of the translators of the Bible renders the infallibility of the original text illusory; that the fact of the apostles having availed themselves of the merely human version made by the Seventy renders their divine inspiration more than questionable. Objections are grounded on the various readings presented by different manuscripts, on the imperfections observed in the reasonings and in the doctrines, and on errors discovered in matters of fact. Objectors tell us that the laws of nature, now better understood than formerly, give the lie to certain representations of the sacred authors. Finally, we are told to look to what objectors are pleased to call the admissions made by Paul. To these difficulties we proceed to reply, taking them one after another; and we can afterward examine some of the theories by the help of which some have sought to rid themselves of the doctrine of a plenary inspiration.

*Section I*
*The Translations*

The first objection may be stated thus: It is sometimes said to us, You assert that the inspiration of the Scriptures extended to the very words of the original text; but wherefore all this verbal exactness of the Holy Words seeing that, after all, the greater number of Christians can make use of such versions only as are more or less inexact? Thus, then, the privilege of such an inspiration is lost to the church of modern times; for you will not venture to say that any translation is inspired.

This is a difficulty which, on account of its insignificance, we felt at first averse to noticing; but we cannot avoid doing so, being assured that it has obtained some currency among us, and some credit also.

Our first remark on this objection must be that it is not one at all. It does not bear against the *fact* of the verbal inspiration of the Scriptures;

it only contests the advantages of that inspiration. With regard to the greater number of readers, it says, the benefit of such an intervention on the part of God would be lost; because, instead of the infallible words of the original, they never can have better than the fallible words of a translation. But no man is entitled to deny a fact, because he does not at first perceive all the use that may be made of it, and no man is entitled to reject a doctrine for no better reason than that he has not perceived its utility. All the expressions, for example, and all the letters of the Ten Commandments were certainly written by the finger of God, from the *aleph* with which they commence, to the *caph* with which they end; yet, would anyone venture to say that the credibility of this miraculous fact is weakened by most unlettered readers, at the present day, being under the necessity of reading the Decalogue in some translation? No one would dare to say so. It must be acknowledged, then, that this objection, without directly attacking the dogma which we defend, only questions its advantages: These, it tells us, are lost to us in the operation of translating from the original, and in that metamorphosis disappear.

We proceed, then, to show how even this assertion, when reduced to these last terms, rests on no good foundation.

The divine word, which the Bible reveals to us, passes through four successive forms before reaching us in a translation. First, it was from all eternity in the mind of God. Next, it was passed by him into the mind of man. In the third place, under the operation of the Holy Spirit, and by a mysterious process, it passed from the prophets' thoughts into the types and symbols of an articulate language; it took shape in words. Finally, after having undergone this first translation, alike important and inexplicable, men have reproduced it, by a new translation, in passing it from one human language into another human language. Of these four operations, the first three are divine; the fourth alone is human and fallible. Shall it be said that because the last is human, the divinity of the three former should be a matter of indifference to us? Mark, however, that between the third and the fourth – I mean to say, between the first translation of the thought by the sensible signs of a human language, and the second translation of the words by other words – the difference is enormous. Between the doubts that may cleave to us respecting the exactness of the versions, and those with which we should be racked with respect to the correctness of the original text (if not inspired even in its language), the distance is infinite. It is said: Of what consequence is it to me that the third operation is effected by the Spirit of God, if the last be accomplished only by the spirit of man? In other words, what avails it to me that the primitive language be inspired, if the translated version be not so? But people forget, in speaking thus, that we are infinitely more assured of the exactness of the translators than we could be of that of the original text, in the case of all the expressions not being given by God.

Of this, however, we may become perfectly convinced by attending to the five following considerations:

The operation by which the sacred writers express with words the mind of the Holy Spirit, is, we have said, itself a rendering not of words by other words, but of divine thoughts by sensible symbols. Now this first translation is an infinitely more important matter, more mysterious and more liable to error (if God puts not his hand to it) than the operation can be afterward by which we should render a Greek word of that primitive text by its equivalent in another tongue. In order to a man's expressing exactly the thought of God, it is necessary, if he be not guided in his language from above, that he have thoroughly comprehended it in its just measure, and in the whole extent and depth of its meaning. But this is by no means necessary in the case of a mere translation. The divine thought being already incarnated, as it were, in the language of the sacred text, what remains to be done in translation is no longer the giving of it a body, but only the changing of its dress, making it say in French what it had already said in Greek, and modestly substituting for each of its words an equivalent word. Such an operation is comparatively very inferior, very immaterial, without mystery, and infinitely less subject to error than the preceding. It even requires so little spirituality that it may be performed to perfection by a trustworthy pagan who should possess in perfection a knowledge of both languages. The version of an accomplished Rationalist who desires to be no more than a translator, I could better trust than that of an orthodox person and a saint who should paraphrase the text and undertake to present it to me more complete or more clear in his French than he found it in the Greek or in the Hebrew of the original. And let no one be surprised at this assertion; it is justified by facts. Thus, is not De Wette's translation, among the Germans, preferred at the present day to that even of the great Luther? At least, is there not greater confidence felt in having the mind of the Holy Spirit in the lines of the Basel professor than in those of the great Reformer; because the former has always kept very close to the expressions of his text, as a man of learning subject to the rules of philology alone; while the latter seems at times to have momentarily endeavored after something more, and sought to make himself interpreter as well as translator? The more then, one reflects on this first consideration, the more immeasurable ought the difference to appear between these two orders of operations; to wit, between the translation of the divine thoughts into the words of a human language, and the translation of the same thoughts into the equivalent terms of another language. No longer, therefore, be it said, "What avails it to me, if the one be human, that the other is divine?"

A second character by which we perceive how different these two operations must be, and by which the making of our versions will be seen to be infinitely less subject to the chances of error than the original text (assuming that to be uninspired), is, that while the work required by our translations is done by a great many men of every tongue and country, capable of devoting their whole time and care to it – by men who have from age to age controlled and checked each other, and who have mutually instructed and perfected each other – the original text, on the contrary, was necessarily written at a given moment, and by a single man. With that man there was none but his God to put him right if he made a mistake, and to supply him with better expressions if he had chosen imperfect ones. If God, therefore, did not do this, no one could have done it. And if that man gave a bad rendering of the mind of the Holy Spirit, he had not, like our translators, friends to warn, predecessors to guide, successors to correct, nor months, years, and ages in which to review and consummate his work. It was done by one man, and done once for all. This consideration, then, further shows how much more necessary the intervention of the Holy Spirit was to the sacred authors than to their translators.

A third consideration, which ought also to lead us to the same conclusion, is, that while all the translators of the Scriptures were literate and laborious persons, and versed in the study of language, the sacred authors on the contrary, were, for the most part ignorant men, without literary cultivation, without the habit of writing their own tongue, and liable, from that very circumstance, if they expressed fallibly the divine revelation, to give us an infallible thought in a faulty way.

A fourth very powerful consideration, which will make one feel still more sensibly the immense difference existing between the sacred writers and their translators, is, that whereas the thought from God passed like a flash of lightning before the soul of the prophet – this thought could nowhere be found again upon Earth, except in the rapid expression which was then given to it by the sacred writer; whereas, if he have expressed it ill, you know not where to go in search of its prototype in order to recover the thought meant to be conveyed by God in its purity; whereas, if he have made a mistake, his blunder is forever irreparable; it must last longer than Heaven and Earth; it has blemished the eternal book remedilessly; and nobody on Earth can correct it; it is quite otherwise with translators. These, on the contrary, have always the divine text at hand, so as to be corrected and re-corrected, according to the eternal type, until they have become an exact counterpart of it. The inspired word leaves us not; we need not go in search of it to the third Heaven; it is still upon the Earth, just as God himself first dictated it to us. You may thus devote ages to its study, in order that the human process of our translation may be subjected to its immutable truth. You can now, after the lapse of a hundred and thirty years, correct Osterwald and Martin, by means of a closer comparison of them with their infallible standard; after the lapse of three hundred and seventeen years, you can correct the work of Luther; after that, of fourteen hundred and forty years, that of Jerome. God's phraseology is still before us, with which to confront our modem versions, as dictated by God himself, in Hebrew or in Greek, on the day of its being revealed; and, with our dictionaries in your hand, you may, age after age, return to the examination of the infallible expression which it has been his good pleasure to give to the divine thought, until you become assured that the language of the modern ones has truly received the counter impression and given you the most faithful facsimile of it for your own use. Say no more then, What avails it to me, that the one is divine since the other is human? If you would have a bust of Napoleon, would you say to the sculptor, What avails it to me that your model has been molded at St. Helena on the very face of Bonaparte, seeing that, after all, your copy cannot have been so?

In fine, what further distinguishes the first expression that the mind of God has received in the individual words of the sacred book, from its new expression in one of our translations, is that, if you assume the words of the one to be as little inspired as those of the other, nevertheless, the range of conjectures that you might make on their possible faults would be, as respects the original text, a space without bounds and ever enlarging itself; while that same range, as respects the translations, is a very limited space, which is constantly diminishing the longer you remain in it.

If some friend, returning from the East Indies, where your father has, at a great distance from you, breathed his last, were to bring you from him a last letter, written with his own hand, or dictated by him, word for word, in Bengalee, would that letter's being entirely from him be a matter of indifference to you, because you are not acquainted with the Bengalee language, and can read it only in a translation? Don't you know that you can cause translations of it to be multiplied, until they leave you no more doubt of the original meaning than if you had been a Hindu? Will you not allow, that after each of these new translations your uncertainties will be always growing less and less, until they cease to be appreciable, as is the case in arithmetic with those fractionary and convergent progressions, the last terms of which are equivalent to zero; while, on the contrary, if the letter were not from your father himself, but from some stranger, who says he has only reproduced his thoughts, then you would find no limits to possible suppositions; and your uncertainties, transported into spheres new and boundless, would go on increasing the more you allowed your mind to dwell upon them; as is the case in arithmetic with those ascending progressions, the last terms of which represent infinity. It is the same with the Bible. If I believe that God has dictated the whole of it, my uncertainties with respect to its translations are confined within a very narrow range; and even in this range, in proportion as it is re-translated, the limits of doubt are constantly drawn in more closely. But if left to think, on the contrary, that God has not entirely dictated it, and that human infirmity may have had its share in it, where shall I stop in assuming that there may be errors? I know not. The apostles were ignorant – shall I say, they were illiterate; they were Jews; they had popular prejudices; they judaized; they platonized;... I know not where to stop. I will begin like Locke, and end like Strauss. I will first deny the personality of Satan, as a rabbinical prejudice; I will end with denying that of Jesus Christ, as another prejudice. Between these two terms, in consequence, moreover, of the ignorance, on many points, to which the apostles were subject, I will proceed, as so many others have done, to admit, in spite of the letter of the

Bible, and with the Bible in my hand, that there is no corruption in men, no personality in the Holy Spirit, no divinity in Jesus Christ, no expiation in his blood, no resurrection of the body in the grave, no eternity in future punishments, no anger in God, no devil, no miracle, no damned souls, no Hell. Paul was orthodox, shall I say? as others have done – but he misunderstood his Master. Whereas, on the contrary, if all have been dictated by God in the original, and even to the smallest expression, "to the least iota and tittle," who is the translator that could seduce me, by his labors, into any one of these negations, and make even the least of these truths disappear from my Bible?

Accordingly, who now can fail to perceive the enormous distance interposed by all these considerations between those two texts (that of the Bible and that of the translations), as respects the importance of verbal inspiration? Between the passing of the thoughts of God into human words, and the simple turning of these words into other words, the distance is as wide as from Heaven to Earth. God was required for the one; man sufficed for the other. Let it no longer be said, then, What would it avail to us that we have verbal inspiration in the one case, if we have not that inspiration in the other case? for between these two terms, which some would put on an equality, the difference is almost infinite.

## Section II
## Use of the Septuagint Translation

People insist and say, We agree that the fact of these modern translations does not at all affect the question of the first inspiration of the Scriptures; but we have much more to urge. The sacred authors of the New Testament, when they themselves quote the old Hebrew Scriptures in Greek, employ for that purpose the Greek translation, called that of the Seventy, executed at Alexandria two centuries and a half before Jesus Christ. Now, no one among the moderns will dare to affirm (as was done in former times) that the Alexandrine interpreters were inspired. Would a man any more dare to contend that that version, still human at the time of Jesus Christ, acquired, by the sole fact of the apostolic quotations, a divinity which it did not previously possess? Would not this strange allegation resemble that of the Council of Trent, when it pronounced to be divine apocryphal writings, which the ancient church rejected from the canon, and which Jerome called fables,

GOD-BREATHED: THE DIVINE INSPIRATION OF THE BIBLE

and a "medley of gold and clay;"[1] or when it pronounced that translation by Jerome to be authentic, which, at first, in the opinion of Jerome himself, and thereafter in that of the church for above a thousand years, was no more than a human work, respectable, no doubt, but imperfect? Would it not further resemble the silly infallibility of Sixtus V, who declared his edition of 1590 to be authentic; or that of his successor, Clement VIII, who, finding the edition of Sixtus V intolerably incorrect, suppressed it in 1592, in order to substitute in its place another very different, and yet still more "authentic"?[2]

Here we gladly recall this difficulty; because, like many others, when more closely examined, it converts the objections into arguments.

No more is required, in fact, than to study the manner in which the apostles employ the Septuagint, in order to see in it a striking sign of the verbal inspiration under which they wrote.

Were a prophet to be sent by God in our day to the churches speaking the French tongue, how shall it be thought he would act in quoting the Scriptures? He would do so in French no doubt; but according to what version? As Osterwald and Martin's are those most extensively circulated, he would probably make his quotations in the words of one or other of them, in all cases where their translation should seem to him sufficiently exact. But also, notwithstanding our habitual practice and his, he would take care to abandon both those versions, and translate in his own way, as often as the thought intended to be conveyed by the original did not seem to him to be rendered with sufficient fidelity. Nay, he would sometimes even do more. In order to our being enabled to comprehend more fully in what sense he meant to make for us the application of such or such a Scripture, he would paraphrase the passage quoted, and in citing it, follow neither the letter of the original text nor that of the translations.

This is precisely what has been done by the sacred writers of the New Testament with respect to the Septuagint.

---

1. Caveat omnia apocrypha.... Sciat multa his admixta vitiosa et grandis esse prudentiæ aurum in luto quærere. See *Epist. ad Lætam. Prolog. Galeat. sive Præfat. ad. lib. Regum.* Symbol. Ruffini, Volume 9, page 186. See Lardner, Volume 5, pages 18-22.

2. See Korholt, *De Variis S. Scripturæ editionibus*, pages 110-251. Thomas James, *Bellum Papale, sive Concordia Discors Sixti V, etc.*, London, 1600. Hamilton's *Introduction to the Reading of the Hebrew Scriptures*, pages 163, 166.

## EXAMINATION OF OBJECTIONS

Although it was the universal practice of the Hellenistic Jews, throughout the whole of the East, to read in their synagogues and to quote in their discussions the Old Testament according to that ancient version,[3] the apostles show us the independence of the Spirit that guided them, by the three several methods they follow in their quotations.

First, when the Alexandrine translators seem to them correct, they do not hesitate to conform to the recollections of their Hellenist auditors, and to quote the Septuagint version *literatim* and *verbatim*.

Second, and this often occurs when dissatisfied with the work of the Seventy, they amend it, and make their quotations according to the original Hebrew, translating it more correctly.

Third, in fine, when they would point out more clearly in what sense they adduce such or such a declaration of the holy books, they paraphrase it in quoting it. It is then the Holy Spirit who, by their mouth, quotes himself, modifying at the same time the expressions which he had previously dictated to the prophets of his ancient people. One may compare, for example, *Micah* 5:2 with *Matthew* 2:6; *Malachi* 3:1 with *Matthew* 10:10, *Mark* 1:2, and *Luke* 7:27, etc.

The learned Horne, in his *Introduction to the Critical Study of the Bible* (volume 1, page 503) has ranged under five distinct classes, relative to the Septuagint version, the quotations made in the New Testament from the Old. We do not here warrant all his distinctions, nor all his figures; but our readers will comprehend the force of our argument, on our informing them that that learned author reckons eighty-eight verbal quotations that agree with the Alexandrine translations; sixty-four more that are borrowed from them, but with some variations; thirty-seven that adopt the same meaning with them without employing their words; sixteen that differ from them in order to agree more nearly with the Hebrew; and, finally, twenty that differ from both the Hebrew and the Septuagint, but in which the sacred authors have paraphrased the Old Testament, in order that the sense in which they quote it may be better understood.

These numerical data will sufficiently enable the reader to form a just idea of the independence claimed by the Holy Spirit with regard to human versions, when he desired to quote, in the New Testament, that

---

3. The Talmud even forbids the translations of the Scriptures, except into Greek (Talmud Megillah, folio 86).

which he had previously caused to be written in the Old. Accordingly, they not only answer the objection – they convert it into a testimony.

## Section III
## The Various Readings

We must give up the translations, then, other opponents will say, and admit that they nowise affect the question of the primary inspiration of the original text. But in that very text there are numerous differences among the ancient manuscripts which our churches consult, and on which our printed editions are based. Confronted with proofs of such a fact, what becomes of the doctrine of verbal inspiration, and what purpose can it serve?

Here, too, the answer is easy. We might say at once of the various readings of the manuscripts what we have said of the translations: Why confound two orders of facts that are absolutely distinct: that of the first inspiration of the Scriptures, and that of the present integrity of the copies that have been made of them? If it was God himself that dictated the letter of the sacred oracles, that is a fact past recall, and no more can the copies made of them, than the translations given to us of them, undo that first act.

When a fact is once consummated, nothing that happens subsequently can efface it from the history of the past. There are here, then, two questions which we must carefully distinguish. Was the whole of Scripture divinely inspired? This is the first question; it is that with which we have now to do. Are the copies made of it many centuries afterward by doctors and monks correct? Or are they not correct? That is the second question. This last can nowise affect the other. Don't proceed, then, to subject the former, by a strange piece of inattention, to the latter; they are independent of each other. A book is from God, or it is not from God. In the latter case, it were idle for me to transcribe it a thousand times exactly – I should not thereby render it divine; and in the former case, I should in vain take a thousand incorrect copies – neither folly nor unfaithfulness on my part can undo the fact of its having been given by God. The Decalogue, yet once more we repeat, was entirely written by the finger of Jehovah on two tables of stone; but if the manuscripts that give it to me at the present day present some various readings, this second fact would not prevent the first. The sentences, words, and letters of the Ten Commandments, would not the less have been all engraven by God. Inspiration of the first text, integrity of the subsequent copies – these are two orders of facts absolutely different and separated from each other by thousands of stadia, and thousands of years. Beware, then, of confounding what logic, time, and place compel you to distinguish.

It is by precisely a similar process of reasoning that we reprove the indiscreet lovers of the apocryphal writings. The ancient oracles of God, we tell them, were committed to the Jewish people, as the new oracles were committed afterward to the Christian people. If, then, the *Book of Maccabees* was a merely human book in the days of Jesus Christ, a thousand decrees of the Christian church could not have any such effect thereafter as that, in 1560, becoming what it had never been till then, it should be transubstantiated into a divine book. Did the prophets write the Bible with the words which human wisdom dictated, or with words given them by God? Such is our question. But have they been faithfully copied from age to age, from manuscripts into manuscripts? This is yours, perhaps. It is very important no doubt; but it is entirely different from the first. Do not, then, confound what God has separated.

It is true, no doubt, people will say that the fidelity of one copy does not make the original divine, when it is not so; and the incorrectness of another copy will not make it human, if it was not so. Accordingly, this is not what we maintain. The fact of the inspiration of the sacred text in the days of Moses, or the days of John, cannot depend upon the copies which we shall have made of it in Europe and Africa, two or three thousand years after them; but though the second of these facts does not destroy the first, it at least renders it illusory by depriving it of its whole worth and utility.

Now, then, mark to what the objection is confined. The question is no longer about the inspiration of the original text – the whole attack here is directed against its present integrity. It was first a question of doctrine: "Is it declared in the Bible that the Bible is inspired even in its language?" But it is no more now than a question of history, or of criticism: "Have the copyists copied faithfully? Are the manuscripts faithful?" Accordingly, we might say nothing now on a position of which we are not here called upon to undertake the defense, but the answer is easy; I will say more – God has rendered it so triumphant that we will not restrain ourselves from giving it. Besides, the faith of simple minds has been so often disquieted on this subject by a phantasmagoria of learning that we consider it useful here to expose its hollowness. And, although this objection in some sort withdraws us from the field which we had traced out for our ourselves, we will follow it for the purpose of answering it.

No doubt, had this difficulty been presented to us in the days of Anthony Collins and the Free Thinkers we should not have been left without reply, but we should have felt perhaps some embarrassment, because full light had not then been thrown upon the facts, and because the field of conjectures, as yet unexplored, remained undefined. We know the perplexities of the excellent Bengel on this question; and we know that these led, first, to his laborious researches on the sacred text, and, next, to his pious wonder and gratitude at the preservation of that text. Of what use, one might have said, is the assurance that the original text was dictated by God eighteen hundred years ago, if I have no longer the certainty that the manuscripts of our libraries still present it to me in its purity, and if it be true (as we are assured) that the various readings of these rolls are at least thirty thousand in number?

Such is the old objection: It was specious; but nowadays it is known by all who have studied it to be a mere illusion. The Rationalists themselves have admitted that it can no longer be made and must be given up.

The Lord has watched miraculously over his Word. This the facts of the case have demonstrated.

In constituting as its depositaries, first, the churches of the Jewish people, and then those of the Christian people, his providence had by this means to see to the faithful transmission of the oracles of God to us. It has done this; and in order to the attainment of this result, it has put different causes in operation, of which we shall have again to speak afterward. Late learned researches have thrown the clearest light on this great fact. Herculean labors have been bestowed during the whole of the last century (particularly in its last half) and the first part of this on the task of bringing together all the various readings that either the detailed examination of the manuscripts of Holy Scripture preserved in the different libraries of Europe, or the study of the most ancient versions, or the searching out of the innumerable quotations made from our sacred books in all the writings of the fathers of the church could furnish; and this immense toil has ended in a result wonderful by its insignificance, and (shall I say?) imposing by its nullity.

As respects the Old Testament, the indefatigable investigations and the four folios of Father Houbigant; the thirty years' labors of John Henry Michaëlis; above all, the great *Critical Bible* and the ten years' study of the famous Kennicott (who consulted five hundred eighty-one Hebrew manuscripts); and, in fine, Professor Rossi's collection of six hundred eighty manuscripts; as respects the New Testament, the no less gigantic investigations of Mill, Bengel, Wetstein, and Griesbach (who consulted three hundred thirty-five manuscripts for the *Gospels* alone); the latest researches of Nolan, Matthæi, Lawrence, and Hug; above all, those of Scholz (with his six hundred seventy-four manuscripts for the *Gospels*, his two hundred for the *Acts*, his two hundred fifty-six for the *Epistles of Paul*, his ninety-three for the *Apocalypse* (without reckoning his fifty-three *Lectionaria*): All these vast labors have so convincingly established the astonishing preservation of that text, copied nevertheless so many thousands of times (in Hebrew during thirty-three centuries, and in Greek during eighteen hundred years), that the hopes of the enemies of religion, in this quarter, have been subverted, and as Michaëlis has said, "They have ceased henceforth to look for anything from those critical researches which they at first so warmly recommended, because they expected discoveries from them that have never been made."[4] The learned Rationalist Eichhorn himself also owns that the different readings of the Hebrew manuscripts collected by Kennicott hardly offer sufficient interest to compensate for the trouble they cost!

But these very misreckonings, and the absence of those discoveries have proved a precious discovery for the church of God. She expected as much; but she is delighted to owe it to the labor of her very adversaries. "In truth," says a learned man of our day, "but for those precious negative conclusions that people have come to, the direct result obtained from the consumption of so many men's lives in these immense researches may seem to amount to nothing and one may say that in order to come to it, time, talent, and learning have all been foolishly thrown away."[5] But, as we have said, this result is immense in virtue of its nothingness and all-powerful in virtue of its insignificance.

---

4. Michaëlis, Volume 2, page 266.
5. Wiseman's *Discourses on the Relations, etc.*, 2, Discourse 10.

## GOD-BREATHED: THE DIVINE INSPIRATION OF THE BIBLE

When one thinks that the Bible has been copied during thirty centuries, as no book of man has ever been, or ever will be; that it was subjected to all the catastrophes and all the captivities of Israel; that it was transported seventy years to Babylon; that it has seen itself so often persecuted, or forgotten, or interdicted, or burnt, from the days of the Philistines to those of the Seleucidæ – when one thinks that since the time of Jesus Christ, it has had to traverse the first three centuries of the imperial persecutions, when persons found in possession of the holy books were thrown to the wild beasts; next, the seventh, eighth, and ninth centuries, when false books, false legends, and false decretals were everywhere multiplied; the tenth century, when so few could read, even among princes; the twelfth, thirteenth, and fourteenth centuries, when the use of the Scriptures in the vulgar tongue was punished with death, and when the books of the ancient fathers were mutilated, when so many ancient traditions were garbled and falsified, even to the very acts of the emperors, and to those of the councils – then we can perceive how necessary it was that the providence of God should have always put forth its mighty power in order that, on the one hand, the church of the Jews should give us, in its integrity, that Word which records its revolts, which predicts its ruin, which describes Jesus Christ; and, on the other, that the Christian churches (the most powerful of which, and the Roman sect in particular, interdicted the people from reading the sacred books, and substituted in so many ways the traditions of the Middle Ages for the Word of God) should nevertheless transmit to us, in all their purity, those Scriptures – which condemn all their traditions, their images, their dead languages, their absolutions, their celibacy – which say, that Rome would be the seat of a terrible apostasy where "the Man of Sin would be seen sitting as God in the temple of God, waging war on the saints, forbidding to marry, and to use meats which God had created"; which say of images, "You shall not bow down to them"; of unknown tongues, "You shall not use them"; of the cup, "Drink all of you of it"; of the Virgin, "Woman, what have I to do with you?" and of marriage, "It is honorable in all."

Now, although all the libraries in which ancient copies of the sacred books may be found have been called upon to give their testimony; although the elucidations given by the fathers of all ages have been studied; although the Arabic, Syriac, Latin, Armenian, and Ethiopian versions have been collated; although all the manuscripts of all coun-

## EXAMINATION OF OBJECTIONS

tries and ages, from the third to the sixteenth century, have been collected and examined a thousand times over by countless critics who have eagerly sought out some new text, as the recompense and the glory of their wearisome watchings; although learned men, not content with the libraries of the West, have visited those of Russia, and carried their researches into the monasteries of Mont Athos, Turkish Asia, and Egypt, there to look for new instruments of the sacred text; "Nothing has been discovered," says a learned person, already quoted, "not even a single reading, that could throw doubt on any one of the passages before considered as certain. All the *variantes,* almost without exception, leave untouched the essential ideas of each phrase, and bear only on points of secondary importance," such as the insertion or the omission of an article or a conjunction, the position of an adjective before or after its substantive, the greater or less exactness of a grammatical construction.

And would we be less rigorous in our demands with respect to the Old Testament? The famous Indian manuscript, recently deposited in the Cambridge library, will furnish an example.

It is thirty-three years since the pious and learned Claudius Buchanan, while visiting, in the Indian peninsula, the black Jews of Malabar (who are supposed to be the remains of the first dispersion under Nebuchadnezzar), saw in their possession an immense roll, composed of thirty-seven skins, tinged with red, forty-eight feet long, twenty-two inches wide, and which in its originally entire state, must have had ninety English feet of development. The Holy Scriptures had been traced on it by different hands. There remained one hundred seventeen columns of beautiful writing, and there was wanting only *Leviticus* and part of *Deuteronomy.* Buchanan succeeded in having this ancient and precious monument, which served for the worship of the synagogue, committed to his care, and he afterward deposited it in the Cambridge library.

The impossibility of supposing that this roll had been taken from a copy brought by European Jews was perceived from certain evident marks. Now, Mr. Yeates lately submitted it to the most attentive examination; and took the trouble to collate it, word by word, letter by letter, with our Hebrew edition of Van der Hooght. He has published the results of his researches. And what have they been? Why, this: That there do not exist, between the text of India and that of the West above forty small differences, not one of which is of sufficient importance to lead to even a slight change in the meaning and interpretation of our ancient text; and that these are but the additions or retrenchments of an ׳ or a ו – letters the presence or absence of which, in Hebrew, cannot alter the import of the word.[6]

We know the peculiar character, among the Jews, of those Massorethes, or doctors of tradition, whose whole profession consisted in transcribing the Scriptures – we know to what a pitch these learned men carried respect for the letter; and when we read the rules that regulated their labors, we can comprehend what use the providence of the Lord, who had "committed his oracles to the Jewish people," knew to make of their reverential respect, their strictness, and even their superstition. In each of the books they counted the number of verses, of words, of letters: They could have told you, for example, that the letter א appears forty-two thousand three hundred seventy-seven times in the Bible; the letter ב thirty-eight thousand two hundred eighteen times, and so on: They would have scrupled at changing the position of a single letter evidently displaced; they would only have called your attention to it on the margin, and would have supposed some mystery involved in it; they would have told you the middle letter in the Pentateuch, and that which is in the middle of each of the particular books of which it is composed: They never would permit themselves to retouch their manuscript; and if any mistake had escaped from them, they would have rejected the papyrus or the parchment which it had spoiled, and would have begun anew; for they were equally interdicted from ever correcting any of their blunders, and from preserving for their sacred volume a parchment or skin that had suffered any erasure.

This intervention of God's providence in the preservation of the Old Testament becomes still more striking in our eyes if we compare the astonishing integrity of the original Hebrew (at the close of so many centuries) with the rapid and profound alteration which the Greek version of the Septuagint had undergone in the days of Jesus Christ (after the lapse of only two hundred years). Notwithstanding that that book had acquired throughout the whole East, after the almost universal propagation of the Greek language, a semi-canonical author-

---

6. See *Christian Observer*, Volume 12, page 170. "Examen d'un exemplaire Indien du Pentateuque," page 8. Horne's *Introduction* and Appendix, page 95, edition 1818.

ity, first among the Jews and then among the Christians; notwithstanding its being afterward the only text to which the fathers of the East and of the West (with the exception of Origen and of Jerome) had recourse for what they knew of the Old Testament, the only one that was commented on by the Chrysostoms and the Theodorets – the only one whence such men as Athanasius, Basil, and Gregory of Nazianzus drew their arguments; notwithstanding that the Western no more than the Eastern world had any better source of illumination, during so many ages, than that borrowed light (seeing that the ancient Latin Vulgate, which was in universal use, had been translated from the Greek of the Septuagint, and not from the Hebrew of the original); yet hear what the learned tell us of the alteration of that important monument – of the additions, changes, and interpolations to which it had been subjected, first through the doings of the ancient Jews before the days of Jesus Christ, after that by the unbelieving Jews, and later still through the heedlessness of Christian copyists. "The evil was such (*mirum in modum*)," says Dr. Lee, "that in certain books the ancient version could hardly be recognized; and when Origen, in the year 231, had devoted twenty-eight years of his noble life in searching for different manuscripts of it, with the view of doing for that text (in his Tetrapla and his Hexapla) what modern critics have done for that of the Old and New Testaments, not only could he not find any copy that was correct, but he further made matters worse. Through the unskillfulness of the copyists (who neglected the transcriptions of his obelisks, asterisks, and other marks), the greater number of his marginal corrections found their way into the text; so that new errors having spread there, one could no longer, in the time of Jerome, distinguish between his annotations and the primitive text."[7] We repeat, these facts, placed in contrast with the astonishing preservation of the Hebrew text (older than that of the LXX by more than twelve hundred years), proclaim loudly enough how necessary it was that the mighty hand of God should intervene in the destinies of the sacred book.

So much for the Old Testament. But let it not be thought that the providence that watched over that sacred book, and which committed it to the Jews (*Romans* 3:1-2), has done less for the protection of the oracles of the New Testament, committed by it to the new people of

---

7. *Proleg. in Bibl. Polyglott.* Bagsteriana (4, section 2).

God. It has not left to the latter less cogent motives to gratitude and feelings of security.

Here we would appeal, by way of testimony, to the late experience of the authors of a version of the New Testament which has just been published in Switzerland, and in the long labors of which we ourselves had a part. A single trait may enable all classes of readers to understand how very insignificant are the different readings presented by the manuscripts. The translators to whom we refer followed, without the smallest deviation, what is called the received edition, that is to say, the Greek text of Elzevir, 1624, so long adopted by all our churches – but as, in conformity with the original plan of the work they had undertaken, they had first of all to introduce into their original text the various readings that have been most approved by the criticism of the last century, they very often found themselves embarrassed, from perceiving the impossibility of expressing, even in the most literal French, the new shade of meaning introduced by that correction into their Greek. The French language, in the most scrupulous version, has not flexibility enough to enable it to assume these differences of manner so as to put them in proper relief; just as the casts taken from the face of a king reproduce in brass his noble features, yet without being capable of marking every vein and wrinkle. We desire, however, to give such of our readers as are strangers to sacred criticism two or three other and still more intelligible means of estimating that providence which has for thirty centuries watched over our sacred texts.

The first is as follows: We would bid them compare the two Protestant translations by Osterwald and Martin. There are few modern versions that come so close to each other. The old version of the Geneva pastors having been taken as the basis of both – both having been written at nearly the same time and in the same spirit – they differ so little, especially in the New Testament, that our Bible Societies distribute them indifferently, and that one finds it hard to say which of the two ought to be preferred. Nevertheless, if you take the trouble to note their differences, taking all things into account, as has been done on comparing our four hundred manuscripts of the New Testament, the one with the other, we affirm beforehand (and rather think that in this we understate the truth), that these two French texts are three-times, and in many chapters ten-times wider from each other than the Greek text of our printed editions is – we will not say only from the least esteemed

## EXAMINATION OF OBJECTIONS

of the Greek manuscripts of our libraries) – but *from all their manuscripts put together*. Hence we will venture to say that were some able and ill-meaning person (such as we may suppose the wretched Voltaire or the too celebrated Anthony Collins to have been in the last century) to study to select at will, out of all the manuscripts of the East and the West, when placed before him, the worst readings and the variations most remote from our received text, with the perfidious intention of composing at pleasure the most faulty text – such a man, we say (even were he to adopt such various readings as should have in their favor no more than *one sole* manuscript out of the four or five hundred of our libraries), could not, in spite of all his mischievous inclination, produce a Testament, as the result of his labors, that would be less close to that of our churches than Martin is to Osterwald. Further, you might send it abroad instead of the true text, with as little inconvenience as you would find in giving French Protestants Martin rather than Osterwald, or Osterwald rather than Martin; and with far less scruple than you would feel in circulating De Sacy's version among the followers of the Church of Rome.

No doubt these last books are only translations, whereas all the Greek manuscripts profess to be original texts; and it must be admitted that, in this respect, our comparison is very imperfect; but it is not less fitted to reassure the friends of the Word of God by enabling them to understand the extreme insignificance of the various readings.

Meanwhile, what follows is something more direct and more precise.

In order to give all our readers some measure at once of the number and of the harmlessness of the readings that have been collected together in the manuscripts of our libraries, we proceed to present two specimens of these. It will consist, first, of a schedule containing the first eight verses of the *Epistle to the Romans*, with all the various readings relating to these in all the manuscripts of the East and of the West. This will be followed by a schedule of the whole epistle, with all the corrections that the celebrated Griesbach, the oracle of modern criticism, thought he ought to introduce into it.

We have taken these passages at random and declare that we have not been led to make choice of them in preference to others by any reason bearing upon our argument.

## GOD-BREATHED: THE DIVINE INSPIRATION OF THE BIBLE

We feel gratified at placing these short documents before the eyes of persons who are not called by their position to follow out, of themselves, the investigations of sacred criticism, and whose minds, nevertheless, may have been somewhat discomposed by the language, at once mysterious and imposing, which the Rationalists of the last century have so often employed on the subject. To hear them speak, would you not have said that modern science was about to give us a new Bible, to bring down Jesus Christ from the throne of God, to restore to man, when calumniated by our theology, all his titles to innocence, and to set to rights all the dogmas of our old orthodoxy?

As a first term of comparison, our columns will present first of all, in the first eight verses of the *Epistle to the Romans*, the differences between the one text of Martin (1707) and the one text of Osterwald (Bagster's edition), while the following columns, instead of comparing any one sole manuscript with any other sole manuscript whatsoever, will present the differences between our received text and all the manuscripts that one has been able to collect down to Griesbach. That learned and indefatigable person, for the *Epistle to the Romans*, scrutinized first of all seven manuscripts written with uncial letters (or Greek capitals), and it is thought, from thirteen to fourteen centuries old (the Alexandrine, in the British Museum; that of the Vatican, and that of Cardinal Passionei at Rome; that of Ephrem at Paris; that of Germain; that of Dresden; and that of Cardinal Coislin); and after that, a hundred and ten manuscripts in small letters, and thirty others, brought for the most part from Mount Athos, and consulted by the learned Matthæi, who travelled long for that purpose in Russia and the East.

For the four *Gospels,* the same Griesbach had opportunities of consulting as many as three hundred thirty-five manuscripts.

## EXAMINATION OF OBJECTIONS

## VARIOUS READINGS

### FIRST TABLE

| | *Ostenvald's Text* | *Martin's Text* (1707) |
|---|---|---|
| Verse 2. | qu'il | lequel |
| | promis auparavant | auparavant promis |
| 3. | de la race | de la semence |
| 4. | et qui selon l'Esprit … a été | et qui a été selon, … l'Esprit |
| | a été declaré | a été pleinement declaré |
| | avec puissance | en puissance |
| | par sa resurrection | par la resurrection |
| | l'Esprit de sainteté | l'Espirit de sanctification |
| | *savoir* | c'est a dire |
| | J. C. notre Seigneur | notre Seigneur J. C. |
| 5. | afin d'amener tous les Gentils à l'obeissance de la foi | afin qu'il y ait obeissance de foi parmi tous les Gentils |
| 6. | du nombre desquels vous êtes aussi, vous qui avez été appelés | entre lesquels aussi vous êtes, vous qui êtes appelés |
| 7. | appelés et saints. | appelés *á etre* saints. |
| | la grace et la paix vous *soièent données* | grace vous soit et paix vous soìent données |
| | de la part de Dieu notre père | de par Dieu notre père |
| | et de | et *de par* |
| | notre Seigneur J. C. | le Seigneur J.C. |
| 8. | Avant toutes choses | Premierement |
| | au sujet de vous tous | touchant vous tous |
| | est celebre | est renommée |

These differences between the two French texts are sufficiently insignificant; and were one to tell us that, in all these verses, one or other of the two is inspired of God, our faith would receive great aid from this. Now it will be seen that the various readings of the Greek manuscripts are still more insignificant.

Let us now examine, on the same verses, the table containing the received text, compared with all the different readings that could be presented by the hundred fifty Greek manuscripts collected and consulted for the *Epistle to the Romans*.

## GOD-BREATHED: THE DIVINE INSPIRATION OF THE BIBLE

Here we shall not point out either the differences presented by the ancient translations, or those that belong only to the punctuation (that element being almost null in the most ancient manuscripts).

We shall translate the first column (that of the received text) according to the old version, which is more literal than Osterwald's; and we shall also endeavor to render the Greek readings of the second column as exactly as possible.

### SECOND TABLE

| | *The Received Text* *(that of Elzevir, 1624)* | *Various Readings* *collected from among all the Greek manuscripts united* |
|---|---|---|
| Verse 1. | No difference | |
| 2. | by his prophets | by the prophets (*In a single Parisian manuscript*) |
| 3. | who was made | who was begotten (*In a single Upsala manuscript, and by the mere change of two letters*) |
| 4. | and declared | and predeclared (*In only one of the twenty-two manuscripts of the Barberini Library*) |
| 5. | No difference | |
| 6. | No difference | |
| 7. | that be in Rome, beloved of God, called | who are in the love of God, called (*A single manuscript – that of Dresden, in uncial letters*) |
| | | that be in Rome, called (*Only in two manuscripts – that of St. Germain, in uncial letters, and a Roman one, in small letters*) |
| | from God our Father. | from God the Father (*A single Upsala manuscript*) |
| 8. | First | First (*The difference is untranslatable. It is to be found in only one manuscript*) |
| | for you all | with respect to you all (*Two manuscripts*) |

Here we have nine or ten different readings, of no importance in themselves; and, moreover, they have in their favor only one or two manuscripts of the hundred fifty open to consultation on those eight verses, with the exception of the last ("for you all," instead of "with respect to you all"), which reckons in its favor twelve manuscripts, four of which are in uncial letters.

The differences between Osterwald's and Martin's translations are three times as numerous; and, generally speaking, these differences are far more important in point of meaning. This comparison, were we to continue it through the whole New Testament, would bear the same character, and become even still more insignificant.

Nevertheless, those of our readers who have hitherto been strangers to such researches will not be displeased, we believe, at our offering, in a third table, a fresh method of estimating the harmlessness of the variations, and the nullity of the objection that has been drawn from them.

This last table will present the totality of the corrections which, according to the learned Griesbach, the father of sacred criticism, ought to be introduced into the text of the *Epistle to the Romans*, after the prolonged study of the extant manuscripts to which he had devoted himself, and after all that had been done by his predecessors in the same field of research.

No one who has not entered on these researches, can form a just idea of the immensity of those labors.

Before perusing this third table, however, we would have the reader to know:

*First,* that Griesbach is, in general, charged by the learned (such as Matthæi, Nolan, Lawrence, Scholz, and others) with an excessive eagerness for the admission of new readings into the ancient text. This tendency is explained by the habits of the human heart. The learned Whitby had, before that, charged Dr. Mill, not without some foundation, with the same fault, although he had never ventured on so many corrections as Griesbach.

*Second*, observe, further, that in this table we give not only those corrections which the learned critic was fully persuaded people ought to adopt, but those also which he has said were as yet only doubtful in his eyes, and not to be confidently preferred to the generally received text.

## THIRD TABLE
### Griesbach's corrections, extending to the whole of the *Epistle to the Romans*

| *The Received Text*<br>*Substantially our English Version* | *New Text*<br>*Corrected by Griesbach* |
|---|---|
| **CHAPTER 1** | |
| Verse 13. that I might have some fruit | that I might have some fruit<br>(*There is a mere inversion of the words*) |
| 16. I am not ashamed | I am not ashamed<br>(*Difference not translatable*) |
| the gospel of Christ | the gospel |
| 19. for God | for God<br>(*Difference cannot be explained.*) |
| 21. glorified him not | glorified him not<br>(*Difference one of orthography*) |
| 24. Wherefore God also | Wherefore God |
| 27. And likewise | And likewise<br>(*Difference not translatable*) |
| 29. with all unrighteousness, fornication, wickedness | with all unrighteousness, wickedness |
| 31. without natural affection, implacable, unmerciful | without natural affection, unmerciful |
| **CHAPTER 2** | |
| Verse 3. indignation and wrath | wrath and indignation |
| 13. the hearers of the law | the hearers of the law<br>(*The mere absence of the article*) |
| **CHAPTER 3** | |
| Verse 22. unto all and upon all them that believe | unto all them who believe |
| 25. through the faith | through faith |
| 28. Therefore we conclude, that a man is justified by the faith | In fact we conclude, that a man is justified by faith |

# EXAMINATION OF OBJECTIONS

|  |  |  |
|---|---|---|
| 29. | is he not | is he not *(Difference not translatable)* |

### CHAPTER 4

|  |  |  |
|---|---|---|
| Verse 1. | What shall we then say, that Abraham hath found | What shall we then say, that hath found Abraham |
|  | Abraham our father | Abraham our ancestor |
| 4. | as a debt | as debt |
| 12. | in the circumcision | in circumcision |
| 15. | heir of the world | heir of the world *(Difference not translatable)* |
| 19. | And being not weak in faith, he considered not | and did not, weak in the faith, consider |

### CHAPTER 5

|  |  |  |
|---|---|---|
| Verse 1. | to Moses | To Moses *(Difference in spelling)* |

### CHAPTER 6

|  |  |  |
|---|---|---|
| Verse 1. | Shall we continue | Shall *we* continue. *(Pronoun understood – not expressed)* |
| 11. | yourselves to be dead | yourselves dead |
|  | through Jesus Christ, our Lord | through Jesus Christ |
| 12. | that you should obey it in the lusts thereof | that he should obey *it* |
| 16. | whether of sin unto death, or of obedience unto righteousness | whether of sin, or of obedience unto righteousness |

### CHAPTER 7

|  |  |  |
|---|---|---|
| Verse 6. | The law by which ... being dead | being dead to the *law* by which |
| 10. | the commandment which | the commandment which *(Difference of a simple accent)* |
| 14. | carnal | carnal *(Difference of a letter)* |

|     |     |     |
| --- | --- | --- |
| 18. | I find not. | I find not<br>(*Difference of orthography*) |

### CHAPTER 8

|     |     |     |
| --- | --- | --- |
| Verse 1. | to them which are in Jesus Christ, who walk not after the flesh but after the Spirit | To them which are in Christ Jesus<br>(*The words left out here recur at verse 4.*) |
| 11. | by his Spirit that dwells in you | on account of his Spirit that dwells in you |
| 26. | our infirmities | our infirmity |
|  | what we should pray for | what we should pray for<br>(*Difference not translatable*) |
|  | makes intercession for for us with groanings | makes intercession with groanings |
| 36. | For your sake | for your sake<br>(*Difference not translatable*) |
| 38. | nor angels, nor principalities, nor powers, nor things present, nor things to come | nor angels, nor principalities, nor things present, nor things to come, nor powers |

### CHAPTER 9

|     |     |     |
| --- | --- | --- |
| Verse 1. | neither good nor evil that the purpose, according to the election of God | neither good nor evil that the purpose of God according to the election<br>(*Difference not easily rendered*) |
| 15. | He says to Moses | he says to Moses<br>(*Difference in spelling*) |
| 32. | as it were by the works of the law | as it were by works |
|  | for they stumbled | they stumbled |
| 33. | whosoever believes on him | he that believes on him |

### CHAPTER 10

|     |     |     |
| --- | --- | --- |
| Verse 1. | prayer to God for Israel, that they might be saved | prayer to God for them, that they might be saved<br>(*Difference cannot be expressed*) |

## EXAMINATION OF OBJECTIONS

| | | |
|---|---|---|
| 5. | Moses | Moses *(Different spelling)* |
| 15. | bring glad tidings | bring glad tidings *(Difference not translatable)* |
| 19. | Did not Israel know? | Did it not know, Israel? |
| | Moses | Moses *(Difference in spelling)* |

### CHAPTER 11

| | | |
|---|---|---|
| Verse 2. | against Israel, saying: Lord | against Israel: Lord |
| 5. | and they have digged down the altars | they have digged down the altars |
| 6. | And if by grace, then it is no more of works; otherwise grace is no more grace. But if it be of works, then it is no more grace; otherwise work is no more work | And if by grace, then it is no more of works; otherwise grace is no more grace |
| 7. | he has not obtained | he has not obtained *(Difference not translatable)* |
| 19. | The branches were broken off | branches were broken off |
| 21. | spare not you | spare not you *(Difference cannot be rendered.)* |
| 23. | And they also | and they also *(Difference in spelling)* |
| 30. | and as you have been yourselves in times past | and as you have been in times past |

### CHAPTER 12

| | | |
|---|---|---|
| Verse 2. | And be not conformed, ... but be you transformed | And that you be not conformed,... but that you be transformed |
| | by the renewing of your mind | by the renewing of the mind |

|     |                                                                                   |                                                                                                   |
| --- | --------------------------------------------------------------------------------- | ------------------------------------------------------------------------------------------------- |
| 11. | serving the Lord                                                                  | serving the occasion<br>(*The difference lies but in two letters, the one changed, the other transposed.*) |
| 20. | Therefore if your enemy hunger                                                    | if your enemy hunger                                                                              |

### CHAPTER 13

|            |                                                                                   |                                                                                                   |
| ---------- | --------------------------------------------------------------------------------- | ------------------------------------------------------------------------------------------------- |
| Verse 1.   | but of God; and the powers that be                                                | but from God, and those that be                                                                   |
|            | are ordained of God                                                               | are ordained of God<br>(*Difference not translatable*)                                            |
| 8.         | but that you love one another                                                     | but that you one another love                                                                     |
| 9.         | You shall not steal, you shall not bear false witness, you shall not covet        | You shall not steal, you shall not covet                                                          |

### CHAPTER 14

|            |                                                                                   |                                                                                                   |
| ---------- | --------------------------------------------------------------------------------- | ------------------------------------------------------------------------------------------------- |
| Verse 9.   | Christ both died, and rose, and revived that                                      | Christ both died and lived that<br>(*The difference lies only in adding two letters.*)            |
| 14.        | Nothing is unclean of itself                                                      | Nothing is unclean of itself<br>(*Difference not translatable*)                                   |

### CHAPTER 15

|            |                                                                                   |                                                                                                   |
| ---------- | --------------------------------------------------------------------------------- | ------------------------------------------------------------------------------------------------- |
| Verse 1.   | We then that are strong ought to                                                  | (*Griesbach thinks that probably here ought to be placed the three verses at the end of the Epistle:*) Now, to him.... We then that are strong ought to<br>(*The question is merely about a transposition; one which Scholz has adopted.*) |
| 2.         | Let every one of us please                                                        | (*A difference that cannot be rendered*)                                                          |
| 4.         | For whatsoever things were written aforetime ... were written                     | (*A difference that cannot be rendered*)                                                          |
| 8.         | Now I say                                                                         | for I say                                                                                         |

## EXAMINATION OF OBJECTIONS

| | | |
|---|---|---|
| 19. | by the power of the Spirit of God | by the power of the Spirit |
| 24. | I will come to you whensoever I take my journey into Spain, and I hope that I shall see you | whensoever I take my journey into Spain, I hope that I shall see you |
| 29. | in the fulness of the blessing of the gospel of Christ | in the fulness of the blessing of Christ |

### CHAPTER 16

| | | |
|---|---|---|
| Verse 2. | for she has been a succourer | (*The difference cannot be rendered.*) |
| 3. | Priscilla | Prisca |
| 5. | Who is the first fruits of Achaia | Who is the first fruits of Asia |
| 6. | Who bestowed much labour on us | Who bestowed much labour on you |
| 18. | serve not our Lord Jesus Christ | Serve not our Lord Christ |
| 20. | The grace of our Lord Jesus Christ be with you! Amen | the grace of our Lord Jesus Christ be with you |
| 25. | Now to him that is of power.... | (*These words, according to Griesbach, ought rather to be placed at the beginning of chapter 15.*) |

Here, then, the thing is evident: Such is the real insignificance of the various readings about which so much noise was made at first. Such has been the astonishing preservation of the Greek manuscripts of the New Testament that have been transmitted to us.

After the copying and recopying of the sacred text, whether in Europe, in Asia, or in Africa, whether in monasteries, or in colleges, or in palaces, or in the houses of the clergy (and this, too, almost without interruption, during the long course of fifteen hundred years); after that, during the three last centuries, and, above all, in the hundred thirty years that have just elapsed, so many noble characters, so many ingenious minds, so many learned lives have been consumed in labors hitherto unheard of for their extent, admirable for their sagacity, and scrupulous as those of the Massorethes; after having scrutinized all the Greek manuscripts of the New Testament that are buried in the private, monastic, or national libraries of the East and of the West; after these have been compared not only with all the old translations, Latin, Armenian, Sahidic, Ethiopic, Arabic, Sclavonian, Persian, Coptic, Syrian, and Gothic, of the Scriptures, but further, with all the ancient fathers of the church, who have quoted them in their innumerable writings, in Greek and in Latin – after so many researches, take this single example as a specimen of what people have been able to find!

Judge of the matter by this one epistle which you have before you. It is the longest and most important of the epistles of the New Testament, "the golden key of the Scriptures" (as it has been called), "the ocean of Christian doctrine." It contains four hundred thirty-three verses, and in these four hundred thirty-three verses, ninety-six Greek words that are met with nowhere else in the New Testament. And how many (admitting even all the corrections that have been adopted or only preferred by Griesbach), how many have you found, in these, of readings that go to change, even slightly, the meaning of some phrase? You have seen five such! And, further, what are these? We shall repeat them; they are as follows:

The first, chapter 5:6, instead of , "That in which... being dead," Griesbach reads, "Being dead to that in which." And note well that here in the Greek, the difference depends only on the change of a single letter (an *o* instead of an *e*); and besides that, the greater number of manuscripts were so much in favor of the old text that, since Griesbach's time, Mr. Tittman, in his edition of 1824, has rejected this correction, and Mr. Lachman has done so also, in his edition of 1831 (Scholz, however, has retained it).

The second is as follows, chapter 11:6: Instead of, "And if by grace, then is it no more of works; otherwise grace is no more grace; but if it be of works, then is it no more grace: otherwise work is no more work," Griesbach takes away the latter half of this phrase.

The third is as follows, chapter 12:11: Instead of, "Serving the Lord," Griesbach reads, "Serving the occasion." Note that the correction depends only on the change of *two letters* in one of the Greek words and that, moreover, it does not appear to be justified by the number of the manuscripts. Further here, Whitby told Mill that more than thirty manuscripts, that all the ancient translations, that Clement of Alexandria, Basil, Jerome, all the scholiasts of the Greeks, and all those of the Latins with the exception of Ambrose followed the old text; and the two learned men whom we have just named (Lachman and Tittman), the one laboring at Berlin, the other a professor at Leipsic, have restored the old text, in their respective editions of the New Testament. This has been done also by Scholz, in his edition of 1836, which the learned world seems to prefer to all that have preceded it.

The fourth is as follows, chapter 6:16: Instead of, "Whether of sin unto death or of righteousness," Griesbach reads, "Whether of sin or of righteousness;" but he himself puts at the place the simple sign of a feeble probability; and Tittman and Lachman, in their respective editions, have further rejected this correction. Scholz, following their example, has equally rejected it.

The fifth is as follows, chapter 16:5: Instead of, "The first fruits of Achaia," Griesbach reads, "The first fruits of Asia."

Here we have taken no notice of the words that are taken away from the first paragraph of chapter eight, because we find them again at the fourth verse.

We see, then, the amount of the whole: such is the admirable integrity of the *Epistle to the Romans*. According to Griesbach five insignificant corrections, in the whole epistle – according to more modern critics only two, and these the most insignificant of the five; and according to Scholz three!

We repeat, that we have chosen the *Epistle to the Romans*, as a specimen, only because of its length and its importance. We have not given ourselves the time to examine whether it presents more or fewer various readings than any other part of the New Testament. We have run over, for example, in Griesbach, while reviewing these last pages, the *Epistle to the Galatians*, written at the same time and on the same subject with the *Epistle to the Romans*, and there we have been unable to find more than the three following corrections that can affect the sense, or, to speak more correctly, the form of the sense:

Chapter 4:17. "They would exclude us" – say, "They would exclude you."

Chapter 4:26. "She is the mother of us all – say, "She is the mother of us."

Chapter 5:19. "Adultery, fornication, uncleanness" — say, "Fornication, uncleanness."

These simple schedules, in our opinion, will speak more loudly to our readers than all our general assertions could do. Of this we ourselves have felt the happy experience. We had read, no doubt, what others before us have been able to say on the insignificance of the different readings presented by the manuscripts; and we had often studied the various readings of Mill and the severe reproaches of his adversary Whitby;[8] we had examined the writings of Wetstein, of Griesbach, of Lachman, and of Tittman; but when, on two occasions, while taking part in the work of a new translation of the New Testament, we have been called upon to correct the French text according to the most esteemed various readings, first to introduce these into it, and afterward to remove them out of it again, and to replace there in French the sense conveyed by the old reading; then we have had on two occasions, as it were, an intuition of that astonishing preservation of the Scriptures, and we have felt ourselves penetrated with gratitude toward that wonderful providence which has not ceased to watch over the oracles of God, in order to preserve their integrity to this point.

Let its true value be then assigned to the objection that has been made to us.

Let it be shown us, for example, how three or four various readings that we have passed under review in the *Epistle to the Romans*, and which, in the opinion of the most modern critics, are reduced to two or to three, could render the fact of its original inspiration illusory for us.

No doubt, in these three or four passages, as well as in those of the other sacred books where the true word of the text might be contested, no doubt there, and there alone, of the two different readings of the manuscripts, one is the inspired word, and not the other; no doubt people must in this small number of cases divide or suspend their confidence between two expressions; but such is the extent that uncertainty reaches; such the point beyond which it must not go.

It is reckoned, that of the seven thousand nine hundred fifty-nine verses of the New Testament, there hardly exist ten or twelve in which the corrections that have been introduced by the new readings of

---

8. *Examen variantium lectionum*, J. Millii. London, 1710.

Griesbach and Scholz, as the result of their immense researches, have any weight at all. Further, in most instances they consist but in the difference of a single word, and sometimes even of a single letter.

We should be doing well, perhaps, to point these out here also, as an addition to those to which we have directed the reader's attention in the *Epistle to the Romans*.

The twelve or thirteen following have usually been regarded as the most important among the various readings collected by Griesbach, and more recently by Scholz. The first four even have appeared the most serious, only because they strike at the divinity of Jesus Christ.

First, *Acts* 20:28, instead of "Feed the church of God, which he has bought with his own blood," the text of Griesbach bears: "Feed the church of the Lord, which he has bought with his own blood."

Here the difference of the reading preferred by Griesbach consists in a single letter ($\overline{KY}$ instead of $\overline{\Theta Y}$). Scholz even preserves the old text.

Second, *1 Timothy* 3:16), instead of "And without controversy great is the mystery of godliness, God was manifested in the flesh, justified in the Spirit," some manuscripts bear: "Without controversy, great is the mystery of godliness, which was manifest in the flesh, justified in the Spirit." But some other manuscripts adopted by Griesbach bear: "Great is the mystery of godliness, he who was manifest in the flesh was justified in the Spirit." Here the difference is still no more than that of a single letter, or even only that of two strokes of a letter (some manuscripts instead of $\overline{\Theta \Sigma}$ having $O\Sigma$ and others $O$).

Scholz has not admitted Griesbach's correction. Almost all the Greek manuscripts, says he, bear Θεὸς (God). He assures us he has found it in eighty-six manuscripts, examined by himself.

Third, *Jude* 4, instead of "Who deny our only ruler, God and Saviour, Jesus Christ," the text of Griesbach and that of Scholz bear: "Who deny our only master and Lord Jesus Christ." Here the difference is only in these two letters ($\Theta N$, God), omitted in the manuscripts that Griesbach has preferred.

We approve of the adversaries of the divinity of Jesus Christ attaching importance to these first three corrections, in respect of criticism (for everything is of importance in the Scripture), but in respect of doctrine, we cannot comprehend how they should do so; inasmuch as, by their own admission, there are many other passages without various readings, in which our Lord is called by the name of God, of true God, of the great God. No manuscript, for example, presents variations on the first verse of the *Gospel of John:* "In the beginning was the Word, and the Word was with God, and the Word was God."[9] So, too, no Greek manuscript whatsoever presents a variation in the reading of that verse of the *Epistle to Titus* (2:13), "Looking for the glorious appearance of our great God, and Saviour Jesus Christ."[10]

Fourth, *1 John* 5: 7, 8, instead of "There are three that bear witness [in Heaven: the Father, the Word, and the Holy Spirit: and these three are ONE ('EN); and there are three that bear witness] in the Earth, the Spirit, and the water, and the blood; and these three agree in that one" (τὸ 'EN), Griesbach's text bears: "There are three that bear witness on the Earth: the Spirit, the water, and the blood, and the three agree in that one" (τὸ 'EN).

Here, without doubt, there is the most serious variation, and, at the same time, that which is the most justified by the testimony of the manuscripts that have been preserved down to the present day (more than a hundred forty against three), as well as by the universal silence of the Greek fathers. We should be traveling out of our subject were we to undertake to discuss here the historical testimonies[11] and the grammatical considerations that plead, on the contrary, for retaining the old

---

9. One sole manuscript among three hundred fifty, that of Stephanus of the eighth or ninth century, puts an article before the name of *God,* which would not even change the meaning here.

10. We know that Mr. Wordsworth, to ascertain the meaning that was given to that passage and the following (*Ephesians* 5:5; *2 Thessalonians* 1:12; *2 Timothy* 4:1; *Jude* 4; *2 Peter* 1:1; *James* 1:1; *1 Timothy* 1:1), at the time when the Greek was a living tongue, was not afraid to consult the voluminous writings of seventy Greek and sixty Latin contemporary fathers, and that he saw that they invariably put the same sense on these constructions, as designating one and the same person. In the space of a thousand years (from the second to the twelfth century) he found fifty-four authorities of Greek fathers and sixty of Latin fathers, unanimously giving the same meaning to those words of Paul (*Titus* 2:13): *Our great God and Saviour.* The heretics themselves, says he, during the long triumph of Arianism, never once imagined translating this passage otherwise than as we do. "No doubt [said the Arian bishop Maximin in the fifth century] the Son, according to the apostle, is not a petty God [*non pusillus sed magnus Deus*] but a great God, according to these words of Paul: Looking for" (See Wordsworth's *Six Letters to Granville Sharpe*).

11. That of several Latin fathers of the second, third, fourth, and fifth centuries; that the Latin Vulgate, more ancient than the most ancient manuscripts of our libraries (supposed to date from the fifth or the close of the fourth century): and, above all, that of the Confession of Faith publicly presented in 484 by four hundred bishops of Africa to the king of the Vandals, who, as an Arian, persecuted them, and called on them to

reading. We shall confine ourselves to these two remarks by Bishop Middleton:

> Why is the word *three, the three*, in the masculine in the Greek (τρεῖς οἱ μαρτυροῦντες, καὶ οἱ τρεῖς), while the words *spirit, water,* and *blood,* to which it relates, are all neuter (for it would have been necessary to say τρία τὰ μαρτυροῦντα)? This irregularity, which is fully justified by what is called in grammar the *principle of attraction,* if the passage remains entire, becomes inexplicable when you would deprive it of the contested words.

> Wherefore, above all, this word, *that one* (τὸ ἕν, the one), if some certain one have not been spoken of in the preceding words? That expression (*to; e{n}*), in that case, would be without example.

To this Bishop Middleton devotes eighteen pages in his beautiful work on the *Doctrine of the Greek Article* (in octavo, Cambridge, 1828, pages 606 to 624). "I cannot conceive," says he in conclusion, "how this word, *that* one (τὸ ἕν) can be reconciled with the taking away of the preceding words. I am aware that the greater number of the learned are favorable to these retrenchments; but, taking all things into view, I am led to suspect that, notwithstanding the immense labour bestowed on this celebrated passage, something more yet remains to be done in order to clear away the mystery in which it is still involved." The learned Bengel, for still further reasons, said that the two verses of this passage remain united *adamantinâ adhærentiâ.*

Scholz has, like Griesbach, taken away the three heavenly witnesses.

Fifth, *Revelation* 8:13, instead of "And I beheld and heard an angel flying," Griesbach's text and that of Scholz bear: "And I beheld and heard an eagle flying."

Sixth, *James* 2:18, instead of "Show me your faith by works," Griesbach's text and that of Scholz bear: "Show me your faith without works."

Seventh, *Acts* 16:7, instead of "But the Spirit suffered them not," Griesbach's text and that of Scholz bear, "But the Spirit of Jesus suffered them not."

Eighth, *Ephesians* 5:21, instead of "Submitting yourselves one to

---

give an account of their doctrines. (See the dissertations of Mill, Griesbach, Bengel, Wetstein, and Lee.)

another in the fear of God," Griesbach's text and that of Scholz bear: "Submitting yourselves one to another in the fear of Christ."

Ninth, *Revelation* 1:11, instead of "I am Alpha and Omega, the first and the last," the text of Griesbach suppresses these words, which it has retained, however, at the eighth verse, as well as at chapter 22:13. Scholz has made the same correction.

Tenth, *Matthew* 19:17, instead of "Why do you call me good?" Griesbach's text bears: "Why do you ask me about the good (or about happiness)?" But Scholz does not admit this correction, and retains the old text.

Eleventh, *Philippians* 4:13, instead of "I can do all things through Christ strengthening me," Griesbach's text and that of Scholz bear: "I can do all things through him who strengthens me."

Twelfth, finally, *Acts* 8:37; 9:5, 6; 10: 6, Griesbach's text and that of Scholz suppress the thirty-seventh verse and these words: "It is hard for you to kick against the pricks; and he, trembling and astonished, said, Lord, what will you have me to do?" and, "He shall tell you what you ought to do."

No doubt, in these passages (I repeat), among the different readings which the manuscripts present, it will not be possible to know infallibly which is the one that ought to be regarded as the primitive text, or the very word given by God; but, as to the meaning of the sentence, our uncertainties will always be circumscribed within a very narrow and very clearly defined field. It is true that I must choose between one word and another word – between one letter and another letter; but there all my doubts are limited, there they stop: They are not allowed to go any further. Not only, in fact, have I the assurance that the rest of the text is entirely from God; but I further know that of the two different readings which the manuscripts present to me, one is certainly the inspired word. Thus you see how it stands: Here my uncertainties can bear only on the alternative of two readings, almost always very much alike; while, on the contrary, under the system of partial inspiration, the field of our doubts and of our perplexities will have no bounds. If the language of the sacred books had been so far left to the ever fallible choice of human wisdom – and if divine wisdom, which alone is infallible, have not controlled and guaranteed it – I am exposed incessantly to the temptation of abstracting something from it, modifying something in it, or adding something to it.

## EXAMINATION OF OBJECTIONS

Thus, then, have all the efforts of the adversaries of inspiration to shake our faith by attacks on this side only served, as a last result, to confirm it. They have obliged the church to follow them in their investigations, and soon thereafter to precede them in these; and what has she found in this pursuit? Why this: that the text is still purer than the most godly men had ventured to hope; that the adversaries of inspiration, and those of the orthodox dogmas, at least in Germany, have been compelled to admit it. After the labors of Erasmus, of Stephanus, and of Mill, they hoped to find, among all the manuscripts of our libraries, readings more favorable to the Socinian doctrines than those adopted by the Bezas and the Elzevirs. Many even thought that the uncertainties would become such, and the differences so serious, that all the positive evangelical doctrines – exclusive, as they call them – would be shaken. But it has not been so. The process has now been brought to a close – the complainants have lost their cause; the trial having been conducted at their demand by modern criticism, all the judges on the benches of the Rationalists,[12] have with one voice pronounced it a lost case, and that the objectors must go elsewhere to look for arguments and complaints.

When this question, respecting the integrity of the original text, presented itself for the first time to the excellent and learned Bengel, more than a hundred and twenty years ago, he was dismayed at the thought of it; it gave his upright and godly soul profound distress. Then did there commence on his part those labors of sacred criticism that gave a new direction to that science among the Germans. The English had preceded the Germans in it; but the latter soon got before them. At last, after long researches, Bengel, in 1721, happy and reassured, wrote to his disciple Reus: "Eat simply the bread of the Scriptures as it presents itself to you; and do not distress yourself at finding here and there a small particle of sand which the millstone may have left in it. You may, then, dismiss all those doubts which at one time so horribly tormented myself. If the Holy Scriptures – which have been so often copied, and which have passed so often through the faulty hands of ever fallible men – were absolutely without variations, the miracle would be so great that faith in them would no longer be faith. I am astonished, on

---

12. Read Michaëlis, Volume 2, page 266. Eichhorn, *Einleitung,* 2nd s. 700, edit. Lips., 1824.

the contrary, that the result of all those transcriptions has not been a much greater number of different readings." The comedies of Terence alone have presented thirty thousand; and yet these are only six in number,[13] and they have been copied a thousand times less often than the New Testament.

How shall we not recognize the mighty intervention of God in this unanimous accord of all the religious societies of the East and of the West! Everywhere the same Scriptures! What distances separate Christians from Jews in their worship! And yet, walk into our schools of learning, examine our Hebrew Testaments; then go into their synagogues, ask their rabbis to show you their sacred rolls – you will there find the same books, without the difference of a letter! What distances separate, in their worship, the Reformed Christians from the members of the Roman sect! And yet, pursue your search, you will find in our respective schools the same Greek Testament, without the difference of an iota! We take theirs as they take ours – Erasmus or Beza, Ximenes or Mill, Scholz or Griesbach! What distances, further, separate the Latin Church from the Greek Church – which also calls itself catholic, but orthodox, apostolic daughter of Antioch, and condemning the Romans as rebellious and schismatical sons! And yet, ask both for their sacred texts, no more will you find here any difference; here the various readings will not at all make two schools that distinguish them – here the same manuscript will be consulted – the priests and the pope, Munich and Moscow, will make you hear one and the same testimony. The necessary result, then, has been, that we all – Greeks, Latins, and Protestants – should have among us the same sacred book of the New Testament, without the difference of a single iota!

We have said enough on this great fact. We have felt it right merely to glance at it for the purpose of repelling an objection, since it took us away from our subject. What we had undertaken was to prove a doctrine – to wit, the *plenary inspiration* of Holy Scripture; and some have thought they could oppose us by urging that, even were this doctrine true, it would be deprived of all effect by the alterations which Holy Scripture must have undergone. We were compelled to show that these alterations are a vain and harmless phantom. While engaged in estab-

---

13. *Archives du Christianisme*, Volume 7, No. 17. *Wiseman's Discourses on the Relations of Science, etc.*, Volume 2, page 189.

lishing a doctrine, we have already said, we have been led to write a history. We would now, then, return to the doctrine. Nevertheless, before returning to it, we must once more conclude that not only was the Scripture inspired on the day when God caused it to be written, but that we possess this word inspired eighteen hundred years ago; and that we may still, while holding our sacred text in one hand, and in the other all the readings collected by the learned in seven hundred manuscripts,[14] exclaim, with thankfulness, I hold in my hands my Father's testament, the eternal Word of my God!

## Section IV
### Errors of Reasoning or of Doctrine

We abandon the various readings, other opponents will say; and we own that one may regard the sacred text as the original language of the prophets and the apostles. But this very text, intact as it is, we cannot study without being compelled to recognize in it the part that has been taken in it by human weakness. We find there reasonings ill conducted or ill wound up, quotations ill applied, popular superstitions, prejudices, and other infirmities – all this being the unavoidable tax which the simplicity of the men of God had to pay to the ignorance, on various points, of their times and of their condition. "Paul," Jerome himself has said,[15] "does not know how to develop a hyperbaton,[16] or how to conclude a sentence; and as he had to do with rude, uncultivated persons, he has availed himself of conceptions which (if he had not taken care to let us know beforehand that he spoke after the manner of men) might have given umbrage to persons of good sense." Such, then, being the marks of human infirmity which we can trace in the Scriptures, it remains an impossibility to recognize in such a book an inspiration that has descended even to the smallest details of their language.

To these charges brought against the Scriptures our reply is fourfold.

First of all, we protest, with the utmost force of our convictions, against such reproaches. We maintain that a more attentive and a more

---

14. Scholz has quoted 674 for the Gospel alone.
15. *Comment. on the Epistle to the Galatians* (Book 2), *to Titus* (Book 1 on 1:1), and *to the Ephesians* (Book 2 on 3:1).
16. A hyperbaton is a figure of speech in which the customary or logical order of words or phrases is inverted, especially for the sake of emphasis. – *Editor.*

serious study of the Word of God would reduce them to nothing; and we protest that they have no foundation but in the errors and the precipitation of those who advance them. This we could demonstrate, by repelling, one by one, all these charges, in each of the cases in which they have been sought to be renewed. It would prove a task more long than difficult, and we cannot find room for it here, for its details would be endless. There is not, in fact, a line of argument – there is not a quotation – there is not a doctrine – which the adversaries of the inspiration of the Scriptures have not at various times made a subject for reproaches; and it is well enough known that the greater part of objections that can be stated clearly in three words require three pages for a clear refutation. It is necessary, therefore, that in proportion as the men of the world recommence their attacks, the church should renew her replies; and that, like those respectful and indefatigable servants who, among the Eastern nations, watch day and night near the face of their king, she stand constantly by the side of the Word of her God, to repel those swarms of objections, which are no sooner seen to be driven off than they reappear by another way, and incessantly return to plant some sting in it anew. Before inquiry – and this the experience of all ages, and in particular that of these last times, has sufficiently shown – before inquiry, those difficulties which some would object to the Scriptures are smoothed away; those obscurities burst into light; and before long unexpected harmonies, beauties which no human eye had till then suspected, reveal themselves in the Word of God by means of those very objections. Though today objects of doubt, tomorrow, when better studied, they would become to you motives to faith: today, subjects that distract and perplex you; tomorrow they would become proofs to convince and assure you.

Meanwhile, we have no wish to evade any one of these charges brought against the Scriptures by the adversaries of the full inspiration of that sacred book, for it is an advantage which they give us. Yes, and we are not afraid to say it: on hearing such objections, we feel ourselves at one and the same time under the too opposite impressions of satisfaction and of sadness; of sadness at seeing persons who acknowledge the Bible to be a revelation from God, not afraid, notwithstanding, to bring so hastily the most serious accusations against it; and of satisfaction, from considering with what force such language confirms the doctrine which we defend.

In the mouth of a Deist, they would be objections, and we were compelled to reply; but in that of the Christians who advance them, they involve a flagrant abandonment of their own proper principle, and an admission of all the evil to be found in that abandonment.

Let us not be misunderstood: It is not at the bar of professed infidels that we here maintain the plenary inspiration of the Scriptures; it is before men who say that they hold the Bible to be a revelation from God. Inspiration, we have told them, is a doctrine written down in that sacred book; according to its own testimony, all Scripture is given by inspiration of God; it is perfect, it is pure; it is silver seven times refined. What has been their reply? They do not reject, they say, such an inspiration, except with regard to the language, the forms of discourse, and unimportant details; they believe, moreover, that a continual providence directed the minds of the sacred writers to preserve them from all serious error. But how do they prove this position? Is it to the language only, is it to the forms of discourse, is it to insignificant details, that they object? Alas! let us hear their own words: In the doctrines there are superstitions; in the quotations there are things misapprehended; in the reasonings there are weak points! You see, then, it is thus that, in order to attack the plenary inspiration of the Scriptures, they descend into the ranks of the unbelievers who cast stones at the Word of God; and if they will not venture, like them, to take away God from the Holy Bible, they are obliged at least to rectify God's errors in the Holy Bible. Which of these two attempts would be the most outrageous, it were hard to say.

We conclude, therefore, that since it is impossible to combat plenary inspiration without charging the Word of God with error, we must necessarily cleave ever more and more to this sentence of Scripture, that "all Scripture is given by inspiration of God."

But we have to call attention to a still more serious view of the matter. We ask, Where do they mean to stop in the course they have begun? And by what reasons would they stop those, in their turn, who are compelled to advance further than they are willing to go? They make bold to correct one saying of God's Word; what right, then, have they to censure those who would rectify all the rest? Creatures of a day, during which they fly swiftly through this world with the everlasting book of God in their hands, they are foolhardy enough to say to him: This, Lord, is worthy of you; this is not worthy of you! They make bold of themselves to sift God's oracles, to assign a share in them to the folly of man, to separate in them from the thought of the divine mind, proofs of ignorance shown by Isaiah and Moses, the prejudices of Peter and Jude, the paralogisms of Paul, the superstitions of John! Lamentable temerity! We repeat: Where will they stop in this fatal task? for they proceed to take their seats at the same table where the Socinuses, the Grimaldis, and the Priestleys occupy one side, and the Rousseaus, the Volneys, and the Dupuis the other. Between them and Eichhorn, between them and William Cobbet, between them and Strauss, where will you find the difference? It is in the species, not in the genus. It is in the quantity, and no longer in the quality, of imputations of error and tokens of irreverence. There is a difference in point of hardihood, none at all in point of profanation. Both pretend to have found errors in the Word of God; both take it upon them to rectify it. But will they tell us, is it less absurd on the part of a creature to set about correcting in the works of God the creation of the hyssop that springs from the wall than that of the cedar that grows in Lebanon; to pretend to rectify the organism of a glow-worm than to send a supply of light to the Sun? What right have ministers who say they see only the language of Jewish prejudices in what the Evangelists relate about the demoniacs and the miracles of Jesus Christ in casting out unclean spirits – what right have they to think it strange that such or such another person should see in the miracles of the conversion of Paul, of the resurrection, of the multiplication of the loaves, or of the day of Pentecost, no more than an useful and sage complaisance for the ignorant minds of a people that were fond of the marvelous? What right would a professor, who should deny the inspiration of the reasonings of Paul, have to blame M. DeWette for rejecting that of the prophecies of the Old Testament,[17] or M. Wirgmann for proceeding to his *Divarication of the New Testament*[18] or M. Strauss, for changing into myths the miracles, and even the person of Jesus Christ?

---

17. This was his opinion some years ago. We know not whether this professor, whose learning and candor we have admired in his translation of the New Testament, has not withdrawn such assertions.

18. This is the title of his book (translated from the English by Lambert, Paris, 1838). "He says he understands by it, the separation of the New Testament into *Word of God* or moral precepts, and *word of man* or facts of the sensible world."

## EXAMINATION OF OBJECTIONS

Three or four years ago, a young Bernese minister gave us a reading of a manual of theology which, he said, had been put into his hands in one of the academies of Eastern Switzerland. We have forgotten the name of the author, together with that of his residence; but having at the time taken a note of his principal arguments against the plenary inspiration of the Scriptures, we can reproduce here the quotations by which he sought to prove that the sacred books, as they contained evident errors, could not be altogether the Word of God. The reader will understand that we cannot stop here to reply to him. All we wish to do is merely to give one an idea of the measure of these temerities.

"St. Paul speaks of 'having delivered an incestuous person over to Satan' (*1 Corinthians* 5:5). Could this passage (fanatical no doubt) have been inspired?"

"He tells them that 'we shall judge the angels' (*1 Corinthians* 6:3). A Gnostic reverie, no doubt. Could such a passage be inspired?"

"He even goes so far as to tell them that, 'in consequence of their unworthy communions, many among them are sick, and some are dead' (*1 Corinthians* 11:30). This passage cannot be inspired!"

"He tells them, further, 'that in Adam all die' (*1 Corinthians* 15:22). Judaical superstition! It is impossible that such a passage can be inspired!"

"And when Paul assures the Thessalonians (*1 Thessalonians* 4:15), which James repeats (*James* 5:8), 'that the coming of the Lord draws nigh,' could so manifest an error be inspired?"[19]

It is thus, then, that men dare to sit in judgment on the eternal God! We still remain unaware, we have said, if these doctrines, professed in Switzerland ten or twelve years ago, were so professed at Zurich more than elsewhere. But if they were actually in vogue there, then one must excuse, alas! the magistrates of that city, if we would not deal unfairly by them. It was not they who called Strauss into their country, in order to subvert the faith of a whole people there; for Strauss was already in their professors' chairs, if such teachers delivered their opinions from them.

---

19. We have not felt ourselves called upon to answer such charges. It would be going out of our subject. The Lord's coming is nigh to each of us: From one instant to another, three sighs separate us from it. When a man dies he is immediately transported to the day of Jesus Christ. As for the distance of that day relatively to this world, see in the second chapter of the *Second Epistle to the Thessalonians* if the apostle Paul deceived himself about it.

They had seen them with ample scissors in hand, cutting out from the Scriptures the errors of the apostles. What difference could they perceive between such men and the man they called? A little more learning, boldness, consistency in following out his principles; and in his more practiced hand, a longer and sharper instrument; but hardly more heartfelt contempt for the Scriptures of God! Among the judges of the Sanhedrin who smote Jesus on the face we should make little difference as to the number of blows they severally dealt; and when sixty conspirators in the palace of Pompey threw down Caesar from his throne of gold in the midst of the senate, Casca, who first grazed him with his sword, was no less his murderer than Cassius, who clove his head, or than the sixty conspirators, who on all sides drew their swords on him, and pierced him with twenty-three wounds. Is the doctor, then, who denies the inspiration of an argument or of a doctrine of the Scriptures less in revolt against the God of the Scriptures than the man who rejects the inspiration of a whole book? We think not.

We conclude that since the man who denies the plenary inspiration of the Scriptures necessarily enters on the career of daring temerities, and gives the signal, by the first thrust of his sword, for all the revolts that may follow against the Word of God, we must, once more, look more narrowly to that saying of the Holy Spirit: "All Scripture is given by inspiration of God."

But we have one last reflection further to make.

You do not, it seems, comprehend the divinity, the propriety, the wisdom, the utility of such or such a passage of the Scriptures; and, on that account you deny their inspiration! – Is this an argument that can have any real value, we do not say in our eyes, but in yours? Who are you? "Keep your foot when you go into the house of God," feeble child of man, "and be more ready to hear than to give the sacrifice of fools; for they consider not the evil that they do. Be not rash with your mouth: God is in Heaven, and you upon Earth."[20] Who are you, then, who would judge the oracles of God? Has not the Scripture itself told us beforehand that it would be to some a stumbling-block, and to others foolishness;[21] that the natural man receives not the things of the Spirit of God, and that he cannot even do so, and that they are spiritu-

---

20. *Ecclesiastes* 5:1-2.
21. *1 Corinthians* 1:23.

ally discerned?[22] Ought you not, therefore, to expect to feel at first some repugnance in mind, in heart, in conscience, even to its first teachings? Man must first return to his place as a weak, ignorant, and demoralized creature! He cannot comprehend God until he has humbled himself. Let him go and cast himself upon his knees in his closet; let him pray, and he will comprehend what it means! An argument is ill-grounded, because you do not seize its scope! A doctrine is a prejudice, because you do not admit it! A quotation is not to the point, because its true meaning has escaped you! What would remain in the world, were God to leave nothing there but what you could explain? The emperors of Rome, incapable of understanding either the lives or the faith of our martyrs, threw them to the wild beasts in the amphitheater, and had their bodies dragged to the Tiber. It is thus that people strike their own defective knowledge, like an impure hook, into the Word of God, and drag to the public dunghill whatever they have been unable to understand and have condemned!

While tracing these lines, we are reminded of a teacher of divinity, in other respects an honorable man, but imbued with the wisdom of his own age, who set himself to prove that the reasonings of Paul are not inspired. Now, how went he about to demonstrate this? Why, he quoted as a convincing example a passage (*Galatians* 3:16) in which Paul proposes, not to prove (mark this well – the whole solution lies here), not to prove, but to *affirm* that the promise made by God to Abraham and his posterity, regarded not all his posterities (since it was evident enough that his posterities by Agar, by Keturah, by Esau, were rejected), but one special, elected, and personal posterity. And what think you the professor did to establish his thesis on this passage? Why, he palmed on the apostle an argument so puerile that the merest child among the Galatians might have reproved him for it! Paul, according to him, instead of doing no more than *affirm* a fact, meant to argue from the singular of a collective noun that such a word could designate no more than a single person! Absurd as it is for us, said he, this argument might be good for the Jews, or for the gross-minded Gauls of Asia Minor. We give this example; a hundred more of the same value might easily be produced.

May the author venture here to refer to his own experience? He recollects, with no less humiliation than gratitude, his earliest and his

---

22. *1 Corinthians* 2:14.

latest impressions on the epistles of Paul. He was enabled, from his earliest years, to come to the conviction that the Bible is from God; but he did not yet understand the doctrines which it teaches. He wished to respect the apostle's pages, because he saw, through other marks, that the not-to-be-counterfeited seals of the most high God are suspended there; but in reading them he was agitated with a secret uneasiness, which drove him to other books. Paul appeared to him to reason wrong – not to go straight to his point; to discourse in a round-about and embarrassed manner – to wind about his subject in long spiral turnings, and to say the things that were attributed to him quite differently from what one himself would have wished to have done. In a word, he felt, in reading them, somewhat of the painful discomfort of a tenderly affectionate son as he waits on a declining parent whose memory is beginning to fail, and who stammers in his attempts to speak. O how anxiously would he conceal from others, and dissemble to himself, that his venerated father totters, and seems no longer to be himself! But no sooner had divine grace revealed to us that doctrine of the righteousness of faith, which is the burning and shining flame of the Scriptures, than every word became light, harmony, and life; the apostle's reasonings seemed limpid as the water that flows from the rock – his thoughts profound and practical – all his epistles a power of God unto salvation for those who believe. We saw abundant proofs of divinity shine forth from those very parts of the Scriptures which had long given us such uneasiness; and we could say, with the joy of one who has made a discovery, and with the gratitude of a tender adoration, as we felt inimitable, and until then silent, chords vibrate within us, in unison with the Word of God, "Yes, my God, all the Scriptures are divinely inspired!"...But people insist.

## Section V
### Errors in Narratives; Contradictions in the Facts

All these just repugnances felt to the reasonings or the doctrines of the sacred writers will be abandoned, we are told, if it must be so, by admitting that, on these matters, what is a difficulty for some may be none at all for others. But, if an appeal be now made to facts, if it be shown that there are manifest contradictions in the narratives of the Bible, in its dates, in its allusions to contemporary history, in its Scriptural quotations – we might further, perhaps, reproach those who ob-

## EXAMINATION OF OBJECTIONS

ject on the ground of having seen these, with not being consistent with themselves, and with going further in this respect than their own thesis will admit. This, however, matters not; these, if facts at all, are facts that cannot be thrown out on any such preliminary plea, and that no reasoning can destroy. Reasoning no more destroys facts than it creates them. If, then, it is added, these contradictions exist, they may, indeed, convict their thesis of not going far enough; but they are three times more relevant against ours, in charging it with error.

First of all, we acknowledge that, were it true that there were, as they tell us, erroneous facts and contradictory narratives in the Holy Scriptures, one must renounce any attempt to maintain their plenary inspiration. But we are not reduced to this: These alleged errors do not exist.

We admit, no doubt, that, among the numerous attacks made on the smallest details of the narratives of our sacred books, there are some, which, at first sight, may give some embarrassment; but no sooner do we look at them more closely than these difficulties are cleared up and vanish. We proceed to give some examples of this, and will be careful to select them from among those which the adversaries of a plenary inspiration have seemed to regard as the most insurmountable.

These we shall preface with some observations.

The Scriptures have in all ages had their adversaries and their defenders – their Celsuses as well as their Origens, their Porphyry as well as their Eusebiuses, their Castellios and their Calvins, their Strausses and their Hengstenbergs. It is now sixteen hundred years since Malchus Porphyry, that learned and spiteful Syrian, who lived in Sicily under the reign of Diocletian, and whom Jerome calls *rabidum adversus Christum canem*[23] wrote fifteen books against Christianity. In these fifteen books – the fourth of which was directed against the Pentateuch, the twelfth and the thirteenth against Daniel – there was one (the first) entirely devoted to the bringing together of all the contradictions which, he maintained, he had found in the Scriptures.[24] From Celsus and Porphyry down to the English unbelievers of the eighteenth century, and from these down to Strauss, who has had hardly more to do than copy

---

23. A rabid dog against Christ. Preface to his *Eccles. Writers*.
24. Τὸν καθ' ἡμῶν συσκευὴν ὑπερβολῇ μισοῦς προβεβλημένον, says Eusebius, in speaking of him. Eusebius, *Prepar. Evangel.*, Book 10, chapter 9, and Eusebius' *Ecclesiastical History*, Book 6, chapter 19.

them,[25] unceasing endeavors have been made to discover more, by comparing Scripture with Scripture, line with line, word with word, detail with detail. It was easy, therefore, to multiply them, and even to find some that were specious, in a book eminently anecdotic – where narratives of the same events are often repeated under different forms, by different historians, in different circumstances, with manifold objects, and with more or less extensive developments. After this, the reader must see that this fifth objection, which is composed altogether of detached observations, and resolves itself into an infinity of minute details, can only be refuted in detail, and by detached answers. The matter, accordingly, is inexhaustible. Every passage has its objection, and every objection its reply. Our sole general response, then, can only be this: Examine, and the obscurity will vanish.

It is acknowledged, besides, by all parties that the alleged contradictions, adduced by the adversaries of inspiration, have not in themselves any religious importance, and bear only on dates, numbers, and other very minute circumstances. But though incapable of directly affecting Christian doctrine, they would tend, nevertheless, not less directly to subvert the plenary inspiration of the Scriptures. It is necessary, therefore, that they should be met. This is what the friends of religion have done in all ages; and this is what Mr. Hengstenberg at Berlin has lately accomplished with such honorable success; it is this, too, which has been done, in these last times, by Messrs. Barrett, Hales, Gerard, Dick, Horne, and others in England.

It is very easy to say, in a general manner, and in a peremptory tone, that there are contradictions in the Bible; and it has often happened that unreflecting though pious Christians have not taken the pains to look narrowly into the matter, and have suffered themselves to be led away into loose maxims on inspiration before having sufficiently studied, on one hand, the general testimonies of the Scriptures on that doctrine, and, on the other, the nature of the objections that have been opposed to them. Then it is that they have been seen to seek in their own minds, rather than in the Bible, for a mitigated system of inspiration, such as can be reconciled with the alleged existence of some errors in the Word of God. Here, in the sixteenth century, lay the doctrine of Socinus,[26] of

---

25. He says himself that on the criticism of the *Gospels* he had studied and collected from Celsus to Paulus, and even to the fragments of Wolfenbüttel.
26. *De Autor. Script.*

EXAMINATION OF OBJECTIONS

Castellio,[27] and some others; but it was then loudly rejected by all pious men. *"Hoc non est causam tueri adversus atheos,"* said Francis Turretin,[28] *"sed illam turpiter prodere."* *"Non est eo concedendum, ad ea concilianda, ut dicamus codicem sacrum mendosum,"*[29] said the learned and pious Peter Martyr, "the wonder of Italy," as Calvin called him. In our days, the estimable Dr. Pye Smith[30] in England, and the worthy bishop of Calcutta,[31] have allowed themselves to run into statements of opinion which we deplore, and which they would probably correct had they to make them again. And at Berlin, the learned rector of the university, M. Twesten, whom, for his labors and reputation in other respects, we honor, has not been afraid to say, in his work on dogmatic theology,[32] that all is not equally inspired in the Holy Bible; and that if we refuse to admit that there are errors in the details of the evangelical narratives, we throw ourselves into inextricable difficulties in our endeavors to explain them. And what examples does he give, in passing, in justification of such maxims? Why, he quotes two of the passages which we are about to expound (the first, that of the blind man of Jericho; the second, that of the census taken under Cyrenius). The reader may judge of the ease with which some can abandon the testimony that the Scriptures themselves render to their entire inspiration.

We proceed, then, to give some examples both of the contradictions which objectors have fancied they could oppose to us, and of the causes of the precipitation with which some allow themselves to call certain passages contradictory; which, however, only require a little reflection in order to their being reconciled.

We have said, and we repeat, that as it is out of our power to adduce more than a small number here, we have been at pains to select such as our adversaries have apparently regarded as the most embarrassing.

(In the interval between the first and second edition of this book, several pious persons have blamed us for having resolved difficulties which were not such to them, while we had neglected others which seemed to them of greater weight. Other readers will, no doubt, pass a

27. *In Dialogis.*
28. *Théol. elencht.*, Volume 1, page 74.
29. *In Reg.* 8:17.
30. *Defense of Dr. Haffner's Preface to the Bible.*
31. *Lectures on the Evidences of Christianity.*
32. *Vorlesungen über die Dogmatik*, Volume 1, pages 421-429, Hamburg, 1829.

directly contrary judgment on these relative values. Such appreciations are altogether subjective. None is judge of the importance that may be attached elsewhere to his objections on such matters; so that they present a boundless field. Still, however, we think it right to bring under consideration, in this volume, the new difficulties that have been pointed out to us.)

*First Cause of Precipitate Judgment.* The complement of the circumstances of two facts that happened in the East, eighteen hundred years ago, remains unknown, because the sacred historians relate them to us with signal brevity. Some persons, nevertheless, should the narrative not explain to us in what manner some of their traits may be reconciled, are in haste to declare them contradictory. Nothing is more irrational. Suppose (to give an instance not from the Scriptures) that a Hindu pundit happened to read three succinct histories, all three veridical, of the illustrious Napoleon. The first will tell him that the capture of Paris, preceded by much bloodshed at the gates of that capital, compelled him to abdicate; and that an English frigate was commissioned to transport him to an island in the Mediterranean. A second will relate that this great captain, vanquished by the English, who made themselves masters of Paris without opposition, was transported by them to St. Helena, whither General Bertrand desired to follow him, and where he breathed his last in the arms of that faithful servant. A third will relate that the fallen emperor was accompanied in his exile by Generals Gourgaud, Bertrand, and Montholon. All these narratives would be true, and yet, how many palpable contradictions in these few words! The learned man of Benares might say. St. Helena in the Mediterranean! Who knows not that it rises like a rock in the great ocean? So much for a first contradiction: One of these books must be false; we must reject it. But again: Paris taken without a blow being struck! and Paris taken after a bloody battle at the gates! There is a second. Once more: Here we find one general; there three generals – showing a third contradiction.

Now, compare these supposed precipitate judgments with many of the objections that have been started against the narratives of our *Gospels*.

First example: *Mark* (16:5) relates to us that the women "saw a young man [only one] sitting on the right side... who said to them, Be not affrighted. You seek Jesus of Nazareth, who was crucified: He is risen."

And *Luke* relates (24:4), that "two men stood by them each said to them, Why seek you the living among the dead? He is not here, but is risen."

These passages are objected to as irreconcilable with each other, but on what good grounds? No doubt there is a difference; but there is neither contradiction nor disagreement between the two narratives. If they are both true, wherefore would you insist on their being identical? It is enough that they be true, particularly in histories so admirably succinct. Does it not often happen with us, that, without ceasing to be exactly accordant with truth, we tell, twice in succession to different persons, the same adventure in two very different manners? Now, why should the apostles not do as much? Luke relates that two personages presented themselves to the women; while Mark speaks only of that one of the two who at first had alone rolled away the stone, who sat on the right side of the sepulchre, and who addressed himself to them. It was thus that one of our (supposed) historians of the life of Bonaparte spoke of three generals; while the other, without ceasing to be true, spoke only of Bertrand. It is thus that Moses, after having spoken of three men as appearing to Abraham at Mamre (*Genesis* 18), forthwith confines himself to speaking of one (verses 2, 10, 17), as if he had been alone. It is thus that, twice in succession, and in a different manner, I may relate the same circumstance, without ceasing to be true: "I met three men, who told me the right way. I met a man, who put me on the proper road." Thus, though there be in the passages adduced a marked difference, still there is not even the semblance of a contradiction.

Second example: *Matthew* (20:30) says that "as Jesus departed from Jericho, a great multitude followed him. And, behold, two blind men, sitting by the wayside, when they heard that Jesus passed by, cried out, saying, Have mercy on us!"

And *Mark* (10:46) tells us that "as Jesus went out of Jericho with his disciples, and a great number of people, blind Bartimeus, the son of Timeus, sat by the highway-side begging. And when he heard that it was Jesus of Nazareth, he began to cry out, and say, Jesus, son of David, have mercy on me."

Luke likewise (18:35) speaks of one blind man only.

What is there here, we again ask, contradictory or incorrect? Of those two blind men whom Jesus, amid so many other works, healed at Jericho, there was one more remarkable than the other, better known perhaps in the country, and who spoke for both. Mark speaks of him only; he even goes on to tell us his name: He does not assure us that he was alone. Matthew, accordingly, might speak of two. The narratives of the three evangelists are equally true, without being like each other throughout. What, then, is there extraordinary in this?

But, in this same narrative we are told there is a still greater difficulty; let us hear it.

This forms a third example. Matthew and Mark relate that the occurrence took place as Jesus departed from Jericho. Whereas Luke tells us that it happened as Jesus drew near to Jericho. Here, once more, people have been found to exclaim, What a palpable contradiction!

We must reply, How would you prove this? What know you about it? The details of this fact being unknown to you, how could you possibly demonstrate that they are irreconcilable? While it is very easy, on the contrary, by the simplest supposition, to make them agree?

Luke, as he does so often in every part of his *Gospel*, has united in his narrative two successive circumstances of the same event. Mark well that he is the only one of the three historians who makes mention of the first question put by Bartimeus: "And hearing the multitude pass by, he asked what it meant." This question the blind man put before the entrance of Jesus into Jericho. Being then made aware who this great prophet was, whom hitherto he had not known, he followed him, and during our Lord's repast in the house of Zaccheus, took his place in the crowd that waited for his coming out. It was then that there was announced to him that "Jesus of Nazareth passed by" (these words are in *Luke*). He followed him long thus; he was joined by the other blind man; and their cure was performed only when Jesus, on his way to Jerusalem, left Jericho, where he had stopped only for the purpose of being the guest of the happy Zaccheus. This very simple explanation instantly removes the alleged discrepancy of the three texts.

Fourth example: Matthew (in his twenty-seventh chapter, verse 5) says that Judas "hanged himself;" Peter, in *Acts* (1:18), says that "falling headlong he burst asunder in the midst, and all his bowels gushed out."

Here, again, we have been told, there is a contradiction.

We remember that once, at a public conference at Geneva where we defended this same thesis, our much valued friend, Professor Monod, at that time pastor at Lyons, adduced the analogous traits of a lamentable

## EXAMINATION OF OBJECTIONS

death of which he had almost been witness. An unhappy inhabitant of that city, in order to make the surer of committing suicide, and to give himself a double death, having seated himself outside of a fourth-storey window, fired a pistol into his mouth. The same relater of that sad event, said he might have given three different accounts of it, and all three correct. In the first he might have reported the whole that had happened; in the second, he might have said the man shot himself; and, in the third, he threw himself from a window and was killed.

Such, also, was the self-inflicted punishment by which the unhappy Judas departed into his own place. He hanged himself, and fell headlong; he burst asunder in the midst, and all his bowels gushed out. One single particular more on the frightful circumstances of one same death would have showed us the connection. It has not been given to us; but who will venture, on that account, to maintain that here there is a contradiction?

Fifth example: Here ought to be placed the greater number of those cases where different numerical calculations may seem to disagree, such as that of the talents of gold brought from Ophir to King Solomon (*1 Kings* 9:28; *2 Chronicles* 8:18); that of the census taken of the Israelites in the days of David (*2 Samuel* 29:9; *1 Chronicles* 21:5); that of the children of the patriarch Jacob, transported into Egypt (*Genesis* 46:27; *Deuteronomy* 10:22; *Acts* 7:14), etc.

One single additional circumstance in these rapid narratives would have instantly furnished the reconciliation required. King Solomon might, in the one case, reckon his gross revenues; and, in the other, deduct thirty talents for the expenses of the fleet. David's census might present two results, according as the ordinary and already numbered militia of the kingdom was included or left out (288,000 men with their officers of all ranks; *2 Chronicles* 27:1; *2 Samuel* 28:8). Finally, you might have sixty-six, seventy, or seventy-five persons as the patriarch's family, according as you reckon in it, or do not reckon, on the one hand, Jacob with Joseph and his two sons; on the other, Er, Onan, and Dinah; or again, the wives of the eleven patriarchs. We enter not into the combination of these details, we need only to point them out.

Sixth example: Matthew, in his twenty-seventh chapter (verses 9, 10), quotes as those of Jeremiah words not to be found in the book of that prophet. "Then," says he, "was fulfilled that which was spoken by Jeremy the prophet, saying, And they took the thirty pieces of silver, the price of him that was valued, whom they of the children of Israel did value."

Here, it has been said, what an evident error — these words are met with only in the book of *Zechariah* (11:13).

We do not answer, with Augustine, that as several Greek manuscripts have only these words, "Then was fulfilled that which was spoken by the prophet,""one might say that the reference is to one of those who did not bear the name of Jeremiah."[33] It is true, that even at this day, among the Greek manuscripts of our libraries, there are two which have not the name of that prophet; and that, among the most ancient versions, the Syrian and the Persian have it not. This solution however, does not appear to us conformable to the ordinary rules of sacred criticism; and Augustine himself candidly admits that it does not satisfy him, seeing that, even in his time, the greater number of Latin copies, and of Greek copies, bore in this sentence the name of Jeremiah.

Some learned men, consequently, presume that this name may have easily slipped into the text by some mistake; and that the copyists, having noticed on the margin the letters *Zου* (signifying in abridgment the name of Zechariah), and having mistaken them for *'Ιου*, had slipped it into the text, thinking what they saw was the name *Jeremiah*. Meanwhile, even this explanation does not satisfy us any better, for it rests on a mere hypothesis gratuitously opposed to the testimony of the manuscripts, and opens a door for the admission of rash alterations. Our safety must ever lie in having the manuscripts respected.

I prefer, therefore, Whitby's explanation, which is as follows: "We know," says he, "from Jerome, that there was still extant in his time an apocryphal book of the prophet Jeremiah, in which was found every letter of the words quoted by Matthew."[34] We know also that the *Second Book of Maccabees* (2:1-9) relates many of the actions and words of Jeremiah, which are taken from another book than that of his canonical prophecies. Why, then, might not the words quoted by the evangelist have been pronounced really by Jeremiah, and have remained in the memory of the church to the days of Zechariah, who might then have again given them a place theopneustically in holy Scripture (as is

---

33. Possumus ergo dicere his potius codicibus esse credendum qui Jeremiæ nomen non habent (*De consensu Evang.*, Book 3, chapter 7).

34. Legi nuper, in quodam Hebraico volumine quod Nazarenæ sectæ Hebræus mihi obtulit, Hieremiæ apocryphum, in quo hæc ad verbum scripta reperi (Hieronymus on *Matthew* 27).

the case with the unwritten words of Enoch, quoted in the *Epistle of Jude*,[35] or the unwritten words of Jesus Christ, quoted by Paul in the *Book of the Acts?*)[36] What confirms this supposition is that part only of the words quoted by Matthew are found in *Zechariah*. Besides, it is known that this prophet was fond of recalling the words of Jeremiah.[37] The Jews used to say that the spirit of Jeremiah was in Zechariah, and that the two prophets made only one. Mede thought it very probable that the ninth, tenth and eleventh chapters of *Zechariah* were written in the first instance by Jeremiah. Now, it is in the last of these chapters that we find the words quoted by Matthew. That evangelist, therefore, could quote them as those of Jeremiah, in like manner as the apostle Jude has quoted as those of Enoch the words of his fourteenth and fifteenth verses.

Seventh example: Many difficulties have been started of late, especially in Germany, on the fourfold narrative given us of our Lord's resurrection. For the sake of briefness we shall treat of the whole four accounts at once, taking care to distinguish them, in both objection and reply, by corresponding letters.

A. According to Luke (it has been said), the women of Galilee, on their return from the sepulchre, had prepared their spices before the Sabbath (*Luke* 23:56); while according to Mark (16:1-2), they bought them only on the Saturday evening, after the expiration of that sacred repose.

B. The reading of *Matthew* gives us to understand that these women were Mary of Magdala and the other Mary; while there must have been, besides, Salome, according to Mark (16:1); and even, according to Luke (24:10), there must further have been Joanna, and others with them.

C. According to Mark (16:2) they went to the sepulchre "at the rising of the Sun;" according to John (20:1), "it was yet dark."

---

35. Verses 14 and 15.
36. *Acts* 20:35.
37. See *Zechariah* 1:4, and *Jeremiah* 18:11; *Zechariah* 3:8, and *Jeremiah* 23:2.

D. If (according to Matthew alone) the Jews had set men to guard the sepulchre, one can hardly comprehend how these women should risk visiting it, and think of opening it.

E. According to Matthew (28:5) and Mark (16:5), the women saw only one angel at the sepulchre; they saw two according to Luke (24:4).

F. According to Matthew (28:8) and Luke (24:9-10), the women, on departing from the sepulchre, "with fear and great joy," ran to tell the disciples what they had seen; whereas, according to Mark (16:8), they fled; "they trembled and were amazed; neither said they anything to any man, for they were afraid."

G. If, according to the first and the third *Gospels*, the women informed the disciples of what had passed (*Matthew* 28:8; *Luke* 24:9), according to the fourth, Simon Peter and John alone were informed.

H. According to the first three *Gospels,* Mary of Magdala, on reaching the sepulchre, saw two angels, who informed her of the resurrection of Jesus; while according to John (20:2), she had contented herself with saying to the disciples, "They have taken away the Lord out of the sepulchre!" and said nothing either about his resurrection or even about the angels. "We know not where they have laid him!" she adds.

I. According to Luke (24:12), it would appear that Peter, on being told, ran alone to the sepulchre; according to *John*, there was with Peter "that other disciple whom the Lord loved" (20:2).

J. If you attend to the three first evangelists only, several women seem to have witnessed the appearance of the angels and the resurrection of Jesus; while from reading John, you would believe that Mary of Magdala alone was honored with these revelations.

K. According to Luke (24:23-24), and even according to John (20:2), Mary and the women, on returning from the sepulchre, merely told the disciples of the removal of the body of Jesus, and of their having seen the angels; they had not seen the Lord himself; while according to Matthew (28:9), Jesus had appeared to them "while they were yet in the way."

## EXAMINATION OF OBJECTIONS

Here, then, we are told, there are *eleven contradictions* which do not, it is true, affect the essence of the sacred narrative, and which ought not by any means to affect our faith, but which rise irresistibly to testify against the alleged fact of an entire divine inspiration. (This objection, we will avow it, appeared to us too ill-founded, and to have been too often solved already to find a place in the first edition of this work. Nevertheless, it has been reproduced against us, and we have thought proper to make a reply.)

The day of the resurrection of Jesus Christ, for the disciples, began with the first dawnings of morning (*John* 20:1), and was lengthened out to midnight (*Luke* 24:29, 33, 36). The sepulchre where their Lord had been laid was not far from where they dwelt, seeing that at this day it is placed within the circuit of modern Jerusalem. Thus the disciples and the women may have repaired thither often, and in various ways, during the course of that incomparable Sunday. But as each of the four evangelists imposed on himself a marvelous brevity in relating that event, it is quite natural that at the first aspect their narratives should present, on the innumerable incidents of the day, an apparent confusion. Each was called upon to relate the truth, and nothing but the truth; but none of them was bound to tell the whole; and owing to this conciseness, you may not at once perceive their perfect agreement. They relate, each for himself, according to one special point of view, and without embarrassing himself about a reconciliation which they knew lay in the reality of the facts. What more would you have? One speaks specially of Mary Magdalene, for to her Jesus desired to make his first appearance; the other of Peter, because Jesus made himself appear to him notwithstanding his crime, and because he was called to occupy a leading place in the church of God; two others, of the astonishing meeting on the road to Emmaus, because that manifestation was the most significant and the most affecting; three others, in fine, of his appearing to the eleven, because these were to be the foundations and the pillars of the church.

Moreover, you can perceive in their writings several traits which sufficiently indicate that, in giving an account of certain scenes, they knowingly abstain from mentioning others, the remembrance of which was no less dear to them, but which it was necessary to omit introducing, in order that their *Gospels* might be divinely short. Let us give some examples.

## GOD-BREATHED: THE DIVINE INSPIRATION OF THE BIBLE

You will hear Paul reminding the Corinthians (*1 Corinthians* 15:5) that Jesus "was seen first by Cephas, and then by the twelve;" yet, not one of the four evangelists has told us of this appearance of Jesus to Simon Peter. Certainly it is well that it so happens that we read afterward in *Luke* (24:34) these words, said in passing, "The Lord has appeared unto Simon." Without this expression (which occurs only casually in a conversation among the eleven and Cleopas), the adversaries of inspiration would not have failed to say that Paul was mistaken as to this fact, and that he had been a careless reader of his *Gospels*, seeing that not a word is said of this appearance in their fourfold account of the resurrection.

It is thus, too, that Luke, who (at the twelfth verse) speaks only of Peter, takes care, however, to make the disciples of Emmaus say afterward, "Certain of them that were with us went to the sepulchre."

It is thus, also, that Mark, who does not mention either the appearing of Jesus to the women or to Simon Peter, takes care, however, to insert in his account (16:9) a very few words which give us to understand that there were other manifestations, of which he was not to speak. "Jesus," says he, "appeared first [first!] to Mary of Magdala."

Finally, it is thus that John, whose sole purpose it was to complete the preceding *Gospels*, and who speaks only of Mary Magdalene, informs us, by a simple pronoun, that she, notwithstanding, was not alone: "They have taken away the Lord, and *we* know not where they have laid him."

Thus, then, in order to establish contradiction among the different parts of the quadruple statement, it were necessary that they should be proved irreconcilable with all the suppositions one must make on the unknown connecting links of the events of the day. But who can do this? On the contrary, it is easy to figure for ourselves the sequence of events in such a manner as that the separate details of the narrative should come to agree with each other. This is what several persons have attempted with success, and in different ways; so far is the problem from being incapable of being solved. All that was necessary for this was to make different but equally admissible suppositions on the number and the sequence of the visits made to the tomb by Mary, the disciples, and the women. Olshausen, Hess, and Griesbach reconcile the difficulties by assuming that at daybreak Mary of Magdala, while on the way to the sepulchre, parted from her companions, and arrived first. John LeClerc figured to himself rather that Mary, coming to the sepulchre a second time, with the two apostles, remained longer than them near the tomb, and that the other disciples went home. Hengstenberg has made other suppositions, more simple perhaps, and not less acceptable.

Such hypotheses, we shall be told, do not necessarily do away with the contradiction – they only show that *possibly* there may be none. What would we have more? The adversaries of inspiration only in their turn make contrary hypotheses.

Now, then, instead of replying separately to each of the eleven objections above adduced, we will content ourselves with exhibiting the course of events, such as we may conceive it to have been, according to the four accounts taken as a whole. What we give is very nearly the arrangement proposed by John LeClerc in his *Evangelical Harmony*.[38] Others will prefer, perhaps, that lately proposed by Olshausen, in his *Biblical Commentary*,[39] or that which Hengstenberg more recently still has exhibited in his *Evangelical Gazette*.[40] But it is of no consequence. Our account, it will be seen, dissipates, one after another, the eleven alleged contradictions. (The same letters that distinguish them in the objection will be reinserted here before the particulars that correspond with them and serve to solve them.)

A. Jesus had yielded up his spirit on the cross on Friday evening, at the ninth hour of the day. The Sabbath, which began three hours later, was doubly solemn (being both the weekly and the paschal Sabbath). As it grew late (*Matthew* 27:46, 57; *Mark* 15:34, 42), Joseph of Arimathea went to ask from Pilate the body of the crucified one. He obtained it, and, accompanied by Nicodemus, who saw to there being taken to the sepulchre about a hundred-weight of myrrh and aloes (*John* 19:39); he bought a pall, had the body of Jesus taken down, wound it in linen cloth with the spices (*John* 19:40), and wrapped it in a winding sheet (*Luke* 23:53; *Mark* 15:46; *Matthew* 27:59); then at last, for want of time, he hastened to deposit it in a sepulchre not far from Golgotha. One will see, therefore, that the godly women (who had beheld from a distance these funereal scenes down to the moment when a huge stone was placed on the entrance to the tomb), had very little time for going

---

38. Pages 224-231. Lugduni, 1620.
39. Volume 2, page 517, Kœnigsberg, 1834.
40. *Evangel. Kirchen-Zeitung*, August 1841, § 489-523.

home and preparing the perfumes which they had at their disposal. The Sabbath was about to commence; and whatever might be, in their eyes, the sacred nature of their occupations, they ceased from them; from the time of sunset nothing could withdraw them. From the repose and silence of that day (ἡσύχασαν, Luke 23:56). But as soon as it was over (that is to say, on Saturday at six o'clock at night), they ran to purchase aromatics to complete the pious preparations which they had been able only to commence. This funereal operation required a very considerable quantity of myrrh, aloes, and other substances; and, no doubt, in the evening, they could not have seen, from such a distance, that Nicodemus had already deposited in the sepulchre as much as a hundred-weight of perfumes.

Thus far, then, all is perfectly consistent — and it is by these touching details that Luke and Mark desired, each on his own side, to give prominence to the humble respect of these godly women for the law of the Sabbath; the one (Luke 23:56), by showing how submissively they at once intermitted the most sacred cares; and the other (Mark 16:1), with what scrupulous attention they resumed them only at the hour when they were again at liberty to work.

B. Meanwhile, they left their homes to go to the sepulchre. John names Magdalene only, because Jesus Christ had chosen her to be the first witness of the greatest of his miracles, and because she was the essential actor in his narrative. He takes care, however, to make her say, "We know not where they have laid him" (20:2)! In general, the evangelists show little anxiety about accumulating testimonies. And if the appearance with which the holy women were favored had not been the first, it is probable that the sacred historians would not even have mentioned it. This is what we might conclude by analogy from Paul's mode of procedure (1 Corinthians 15:5, 8), who speaks only of the apostles, and says not a word about the women. His complete silence sufficiently explains to us the partial silence of the evangelists.[41]

41. This is a remark of Hengstenberg's. We recommend his dissertation to readers desirous of a more ample explanation. In order to show, *a priori,* the improbability of the contradictions imputed to the Evangelists, he makes it certain that Mark had evidently Matthew's work before his eyes and John that of Luke. "An attentive comparison," says he, "of *Luke* 5:12 with *John* 3:6-10 does not permit us to doubt this. John in order to make his narrative, which is more complete, clearly harmonize with that of Luke, borrows from him almost all the terms he had employed."

## EXAMINATION OF OBJECTIONS

C. It was still almost night (*Mark* 16:1) when the women left their residence, carrying the spices, to go to the sepulchre (εἰς τὸ μνημεῖον, *Mark* 16:3); but the Sun had risen on their reaching it (ἐπὶ τὸ μνημεῖον, *Mark* 16:2). We know that in those southern latitudes the evening and morning twilights are of very short duration.

D. They asked themselves on the way how they should roll away the huge stone that covered the mouth of the sepulchral cave (*Mark* 16:3). During the repose and the silence of the Sabbath (*Luke* 23:56), how could they have known that guards had been appointed (*Matthew* 27:66)?

E. Meanwhile, there had been an earthquake (*Matthew* 28:2). An angel, whose countenance was like lightning, and his raiment white as snow, had come from Heaven and rolled away the stone. The guards were overcome with fear, and, after having become as dead men, fled. But what was not the astonishment of the women, when, on reaching the tomb, they found it open and empty! Only one young man, clothed in white, sat in the sepulchre, on the right side (*Mark* 16:5). Then two men presented themselves in shining raiment (*Luke* 24:4); these were angels (Mark and Matthew mentioning only the one that had rolled away the stone, and spoken to them).

F. Meanwhile, these holy women, hastening out of the sepulchre, fled, being overcome with feelings at once of terror and joy (*Matthew* 28:8; *Mark* 16:8). In returning to the city they were careful not to speak to anyone of what had happened. Did they dread the wrath of the Sanhedrin? At least, were they not unwilling to pour their emotions into the breasts of any but their brethren? Notwithstanding the early hour, they must have met a great many Israelites in the leading streets and squares of that immense city, where during festivals, there were reckoned to be no fewer than three million inhabitants. The governor Florus, in the year 65, reckoned two hundred fifty thousand paschal lambs, says Josephus; and this supposes at least two and a half million worshipers, without including the sick, unclean persons, and young children.[42]

---

42. *Jewish Wars*, 2:13.

G. On arriving among the eleven and the other disciples, the women told all that they had seen (*Matthew* 28:8; *Luke* 24:9), but this recital seemed to them nothing but an idle tale (*Luke* 24:10). Then Mary of Magdala, addressing herself more particularly to Peter and John, assured them that, at least, if their Master were not risen again, he must have been taken away (*John* 20:2).

H. According to the account itself of John, Mary must necessarily have said to those two disciples more than what that evangelist relates to us directly; for he adds that *they ran* to the sepulchre; and that no sooner had John seen the arrangement of the linen cloth than *he believed*. But, alas! this language of Mary: "They have taken away the Lord, and I know not where they have laid him!" was but too natural. The fleeting apparition of the angels had not produced so firm a conviction in her mind as not to have been violently shaken by the cold and incredulous reception her tale had met from the apostles. These men, according to whose directions she habitually conformed herself, had doubtless more than once repressed the warmth of her imagination. She saw them treat her heavenly vision as a mere revery. After that, she felt only enough of confidence in herself to attest the ordinary and material part of the fact. At least, says she, the tomb is open, and the body is no longer there.

I. Nevertheless, on hearing these words, and whilst Cleopas went away to Emmaus, Peter rose, Luke tells us (24:12), and ran to the sepulchre, but he did not run thither alone (24); and John tells us that he was accompanied by that "other disciple whom Jesus loved" (*John* 20:2-3). John, being the younger, arrived first; he did not go in; but stooping down he saw the linen cloths lying on the ground. Peter, stooping also, saw the linen cloths lying (*Luke* 24:12), and the napkin that was about his head not lying with the linen cloths, but wrapped together in a place by itself:. He had the courage to go in, and wondered at what had come to pass (*Luke* 24:12); but John did more; he entered in his turn and believed. They then departed unto their own home (*John* 20:10; *Luke* 24:12). Still there is nothing inconsistent in all this.

J. Meanwhile, Mary of Magdala, who had followed them, having returned to the sepulchre, remained alone at the spot, weeping and disconsolate at not even being able to find again her Master's remains. She stooped down to look into the interior of the sepulchre, and then it was that anew two angels clothed in white presented themselves to her sight. They were seated, the one at the head and the other at the foot of the place where the body of Jesus had lain (*John* 20:11,13). Soon after, Mary, having resumed her position, it was Jesus himself whom she saw behind her. "Go," said he to her, "to my brethren, and say unto them, I ascend unto my Father and your Father, and to my God and your God!" Mary hastened to go and tell the disciples that she had seen the Lord, and that he had spoken these things to her (*John* 20:18); but they believed not (*Mark* 16:10). Thus, then, was it, as Mark has said (16:9), that Jesus appeared *first* to Mary of Magdala.

The whole of this narrative is natural and harmonious; the historians here agree together in a manner which it is easy to comprehend. Only they relate each some one of the great facts of that incomparable day, without considering themselves called upon to relate the whole.

K. The two disciples on their departure from Jerusalem for Emmaus (*Luke* 24:21, 24), were as yet unaware of the events of the day beyond the first report of the women and of the two disciples, the opening of the sepulchre, the removal of the Lord, the appearing of the angels; but they had not yet learned the last news – the appearing of Jesus to Simon Peter and Mary's second report (*John* 20:18; *Mark* 16:10). Mark, however, what had afterward happened. Following the Magdalene's example, who had returned a second time to the sepulchre, after having informed the apostles of her first discoveries, the other women also had betaken themselves thither while Mary was returning to the disciples; they had found the tomb empty; and, as they were returning to give a farther attestation to their brethren that the body of Jesus could not be found there, Jesus himself had condescended to appear to them alive and full of sympathy. They had worshiped him, and he had said to them: "Be not afraid: Go tell my brethren, that they go into Galilee, and there shall they see me" (*Matthew* 28:9-10).

Such is the harmony of the sacred narratives. This concatenation seems to us satisfactory. One might, as we have said, propose some other; but this is enough. We must confess that we cannot understand the difficulties that have been found in it, or the noise that has been made about it.

## GOD-BREATHED: THE DIVINE INSPIRATION OF THE BIBLE

*Another Source of Precipitate Judgment.* Certain reigns, such as that of Nebuchadnezzar, that of Jehoiachim, and that of Tiberius, had two commencements; and the dates that relate to these are pronounced irreconcilable! The first, previous to mounting the throne, reigned three years with his father; the second reigned ten years with his; the third was assumed by Augustus as his associate in the Empire, from the twenty-eighth of August, of the second year of the Christian era, but succeeded him on the nineteenth of August, of the year 14 (Velleius Paterculus, 2. c. 121).

*Some examples:* See, for Jotham, *2 Kings* 15:33 (he reigned sixteen years alone; but four years also during the lifetime of his father, who was leprous). See for Joash, *2 Kings* 12:1 (he must have reigned two or three years with his father, as did Jehoshaphat and his son, *2 Kings* 8:16). See *2 Kings* 24:8; and *2 Chronicles* 36:9. See also *Daniel* 1:1; *Jeremiah* 25:1; *2 Chronicles* 36:5-7. See further, *Luke* 3:1.

*Another Source of Precipitate Judgment.* The design of the Holy Spirit in one of the *Gospels* is not often the same as his design in another *Gospel* while relating the same fact – yet some would have them all give the same turn to their narratives; nay, make bold, because of their differences, to declare them irreconcilable, and to assume that they are directly opposed to each other.

*Example:* "The Holy Spirit, in the genealogy of Jesus Christ, given in *Matthew* (1:16), would show the Jews that according to the strict rigor of their law, Jesus Christ is the son and the heir of all the kings of Judah, by a legal descent, while the same Holy Spirit, in the genealogy given by Luke (3:23-38), would show the Gentiles that Jesus Christ is the Son of David by a natural descent. And because, with this double object in view, they give us, the one his genealogy according to the law, by Solomon, the son of David, and by Jacob, the father of Joseph, the husband of Mary; and the other, his genealogy according to nature, by Nathan, another son of David, and by Heli, the father of Mary, people have thought, very absurdly, that they could make the one refute the other!"[43]

*Another Source of Precipitate Judgment.* A text mistranslated produces a meaning that is contrary to reason or to history; and forthwith the

---

43. This difficulty is hardly any longer insisted on. We can do no more here than point to the solution of it. Its exposition requires a development which would be inadmissible in these pages. It may easily be found elsewhere.

sacred writer is accused of committing the grossest blunder! People don't examine whether, in the simplicity of a literal translation, the same passage, better rendered, would not present itself free from every difficulty!

*First example* (again one of those adduced by M. Twesten): Luke, we are told (2:1), has no sooner spoken of the taxing ordained by a public decree issued by Augustus Caesar, at the time of the birth of Jesus Christ, than he adds these words at verse 2: "This taxing was first made when Cyrenius was governor of Syria."

Hence, it would follow that Luke is here caught in flagrant contradiction with contemporary history; for, at the birth of Jesus Christ, Judea was governed by Herod, and Syria either by Saturninus, or rather (from the seventh year of the Christian era) by Quintilius Varus, who replaced him, and during whose administration the death of Herod the Great took place. The Cyrenius (Publius Sulpicius Quirinius), under whom a second census took place, was not sent to the East until eleven or twelve years, at the least, after the birth of Jesus Christ. The historian Josephus[44] tells us in express terms that this census took place the thirty-seventh year after the defeat of Anthony; and Jesus Christ was born, at the latest, the twenty-sixth year after that great event. Luke, then, must have made a mistake of eleven years, and must have confounded these two epochs and these two censuses.

Before replying to this strange accusation, we would have the reader observe its extreme improbability, even taking Luke to have been a mere uninspired man. What! Luke, the only one of the evangelists that was a person of erudition – Luke, the physician – Luke, who subsequently resumes the mention of the census of Quirinius when he recalls that famous revolt of Judas the Galilean, which stirred up all Judea and caused the destruction of a great many people, who perished along with him[45] – Luke, writing for all nations, and in four and twenty pages, an historical work, which he knew would be immortal – Luke could make such a mistake as to place in the days of Herod the Great so very serious an event which had happened within the preceding thirty years! What should we say at the present day of a physician, who, even in a simple conversation, should put the battle of Austerlitz in the days of Catherine II and of the National Convention? And if this doctor were

---

44. *Ant. Jud.*, 17:15, 18:3.
45. *Acts* 5:37.

to publish a short narrative, in which such an absurdity should be found, what reception, think you, would he find even among his most unlettered contemporaries?

It is thus, then, that often, when people would make the sacred writers contradict themselves, they scruple not to impute to them such silliness as would be almost miraculous.

But let us return to the passage. There is nothing simpler than its translation: It is a parenthesis. According to the accent placed on the first word (αὐτη), it becomes either a demonstrative pronoun or a pronominal adjective; and, in this alternative, the phrase ought to be translated literally, in the former case, by "This first census" and, in the latter case, by "The first census itself." It is in this latter sense that the word has been rendered by the authors of the new version, published some months ago by a society of ministers in Switzerland,[46] and it is that also which we think ought to be adopted.

Thus, then, there is nought but what is quite natural and quite correct in Luke's narrative. After having spoken in the first verse of a decree from Augustus, which began to be executed under Herod's reign, he intimates (in the parenthesis of verse 2) that one must not confound what was done then with the too famous census of which all Judea still retained so tragical a recollection. *The first census itself,* says he, *was effected while Cyrenius was Governor of Syria.* Such is the plain literal translation of the Greek.[47]

Second example: Matthew (4:5), immediately after the first temptation, says, that "*then* the devil led Jesus into the holy city." And when this second temptation was over, he adds (verse 8) in beginning to relate the third, that "*again* the devil took him up into an exceeding high mountain," etc.

Luke, on the contrary (4:5), immediately after the first temptation, says, that "then took him up into an high mountain;" and when this second temptation was ended, he adds, in beginning to tell of the third, "He brought him also to Jerusalem."

Here, then, we find two of the evangelists manifestly at variance as to

---

46. Lausanne, 1839, page 105.

47. Others, taking πρώτη in the sense of προτέρα as in the πρῶτός μου ἦν of John the Baptist (*John* 1:15, 30), translate, "This census took place before Cyrenius was governor of Syria." This translation would still be legitimate, though perhaps less natural, because the Greek, with this meaning, would less resemble Luke's ordinary style.

the order in which the three temptations took place. One of the two must of necessity have been mistaken in putting the last before the second. Such is the objection.

You will see this difficulty equally vanish as soon as, instead of following Osterwald's version or Martin's, you seek only to give a more faithful rendering to the original text. We might here adduce a good many other passages (chiefly in the *Epistles*) which these two translators have darkened by not sufficiently marking the import of the conjunctions and adverbs καὶ, δὲ, γὰρ, οὖ, etc.

Everyone knows[48] that Luke, in writing his *Gospel,* did not restrain himself to the order of time, and that he had proposed to himself in his narratives to group together events and lessons rather according to the order of things (καθεξῆς). Both these methods of writing biography have their advantages. Among heathen writers, for example, Nepos has followed the first, and Suetonius the second. It was necessary, therefore, that the translators of Luke, marking well his language, should not make him appear to use adverbs of time, order, or events, which he had no thought of employing, and which come in much out of place to alter the meaning of what he has to say. Re-establish here the conjunctions of the Greek, and you will see forthwith the contradiction which the two French texts had presented to you disappear.

Matthew, who always follows the chronological order of the facts, takes care to employ very exact adverbs in proportion as he advances in his account of the temptation: τότε, τότε, πάλιν, τότε, τότε, *then, then, anew, then, then.* But Luke, on the contrary, who had not proposed to himself to follow the same course, and who confines his intention simply to letting us know the three attacks to which the Son of God found it proper and necessary to subject his holy humanity, studiously abstains from using any adverb of order or of time and contents himself with coupling, ten several times, the facts of his narrative by the copulative *and* (καὶ), which our translations have so improperly rendered by the adverb *alors,* or *ensuite* (English, *then,* or *afterward*).

The contradiction then does not belong to the sacred text.[49]

*Another Source of Precipitate Judgment.* It has not been sufficiently borne in mind that certain discourses and certain acts were repeated more

---

48. See Horne's *Introd.*, Volume 2, page 3, Book 2, § 4.
49. In the first edition of this work, we corrected here the faulty interpretation given of *Job* 37:8. We have suppressed it only to make room for other objections.

than once in the course of our Saviour's ministry. Hence the utmost rashness in concluding that certain detailed accounts given by two evangelists contradict each other, where there has been no more than an incomplete resemblance, and yet where people have imagined that the facts they read of were identically the same.

Examples: In the double miracle of the multiplication of the loaves we have a very striking instance of the ease with which one may in this way be led into error. On two occasions Jesus Christ, moved with compassion for the people, fed a famished multitude in the wilderness. Between these two miracles there are numerous and striking points of resemblance. Had it so happened that two of the evangelists had related only the first, and two others only the second, there would have been sure to be a cry that the two were but one, and that there was a contradiction in the statement of their details. What! in the one, five thousand men fed with five loaves; in the other, four thousand men fed with seven loaves! In the one twelve baskets (κοφίνους) taken away; in the other, seven hampers (σπυρίδας)! What a disagreement! Well it is that if Luke and John have mentioned the first only, Matthew and Mark, who relate the second, have also reported the first. But for this what a noise would not our adversaries have raised in the schools about such a passage!

This remark may be applied to several particulars of the New Testament; for example, to the Lord's Prayer, which was given twice, at least, to the disciples during our Lord's ministry (*Matthew* 6:9; *Luke* 11:2). (See also *Matthew* 12:39, and 16:1, 4; *Luke* 8:21, 11:27, and *Matthew* 12:49; *Luke* 9:1, 10:1, and *Matthew* 10:1.)

We shall adduce one further example.

It does not appear, on close examination, that the sermon called that *of the mount* (*Matthew* 5, 6, 7), and that given by Luke in the latter half of his sixth chapter, were delivered on the same occasion.[50] In fact, first, Luke omits many of the sentences reported by Matthew,[51] and he alone adds some others (6:24-26); second, Matthew lets us know that the sermon which he reports preceded the healing of the leprous person (8:3), and Luke that his followed it (*Luke* 5:12); third, Luke puts Matthew in the number of those whom Jesus called to the apostleship, and who came down with him from the mountain, before he addressed to

---

50. See Whitby on *Matthew* 5:5.
51. For example, *Matthew* 5:13, 39. The whole sixth and seventh chapter, 6-16.

them his discourse; whereas Matthew himself tells us that the sermon of which he speaks, long preceded his vocation; fourth, one of those discourses was delivered *on the mountain,* while Jesus, who had sat down, had his disciples ranged around him; the other, on the contrary, was delivered *on the plain,* and with other circumstances attending it. We pause at this remark in order to reassure such persons as may have heard adduced against the doctrine of inspiration the alleged contradiction of the sentence in which Matthew (5:40) makes Jesus say, "If any man will take away your coat ($\chi\iota\tau\hat{\omega}\nu\alpha$), let him have your cloak ($\iota\mu\acute{\alpha}\tau\iota o\nu$) also;" and of that in which, according to Luke, he had said, "Him that takes away your cloak, forbid not to take your coat also."[52] One can no more, then, we say, make an objection of this diversity, seeing these two sentences were pronounced on different days.

Nevertheless, we must not forget, at the same time, to observe, inasmuch as this remark applies to several other objections of the same nature. Even were it true that these two passages were cited as the same fragment of one and the same discourse, still their differing would not have anywise astonished us. We believe that the Holy Spirit, when he quotes the Holy Spirit, is not bound to use the same terms, provided the same meanings be retained. A man of an exact mind, in repeating what he has said before, or in quoting himself, by no means thinks himself bound to carry imitation thus far. And we think that here our Lord's whole idea is found equally in the sentences of Luke and Matthew.

*Another Source of Precipitate Judgment.* One may sometimes pay no attention to a various reading critically respectable, and which resolves a difficulty; and prefer imputing some contradiction to the sacred writer.

Example: According to the first three evangelists (*Mark* 15:25, 33, 34; *Matthew* 27:45-46; *Luke* 23:44-45), our Saviour was put upon the cross at the third hour of the day (that is to say, at nine o'clock in the morning); the Sun was darkened at the sixth hour, and Jesus gave up the ghost at the ninth hour; whereas, if we are to believe John (19:14), the execution did not begin until the *sixth hour of the day* (at noon). Palpable contradiction! say some objectors.

Before replying to this difficulty, we shall offer a remark, much like that already made on the census of Cyrenius. Was it likely that the

---

52. *Luke* 6:29.

Apostle John was ignorant of the length of time that his Master's execution lasted, and could he possibly have made a mistake of three hours out of six – he who had remained beside the cross!

But if we consult the Greek manuscripts of John, we shall find four in small letters, and three in uncial letters (among others, Beza's famous roll, preserved at Cambridge), which have here the *third* hour instead of the *sixth*. Numbers, in the Greek manuscripts, are often expressed in numerals; that is to say, in simple Greek letters; and 3 and 6 are expressed by two letters that are very easily confounded (the γάμμα and the ἐπίσημον): Several of the ancients thought that the variation might have arisen from this cause. Griesbach, who has marked this variation with a sign of preference, quotes Severus of Antioch and Ammonias in Theophylact; and he adds that the *Chronicle of Alexandria* appealed, in favor of this reading, to the best copies, and even to the original autograph (ἰδιοχείρῳ) of the *Gospel of John*.

*Another Source of Precipitate Judgment.* People fail to seize the meaning of certain particulars in a narrative and hasten to conclude that the author was mistaken!

First example: Jesus in *Matthew* 23:35-36 pronounced the most terrible judgments of God on the Jews, on account of the treatment they had given his saints, "in order," says he, "that upon this race (or this generation, γενεὰν) may come all the righteous blood shed upon the Earth, from the blood of righteous Abel unto the blood of Zacharias, son of Barachias, whom you slew between the temple and the altar!"

Here, certainly, we are told, there is an awkward inadvertence, not on the part of Jesus Christ, no doubt, but of the evangelist who reports these words, and whose memory must have failed him. We know, from the *Second Book of Chronicles* (24:21), that this Zacharias, who was stoned to death by the Jews in the holy place (ἱερῷ), was the son, not of Barachias, but of Jehoiada. Here, then, there is an evident error. It does not affect doctrine, and cannot in the slightest degree disquiet our faith; but it suffices to attest that the divine inspiration has not descended, as has been maintained, to the choice of expressions, or to matters of indifference, in the inspired narratives.

The answer is simple; would that we could make it as short as it is conclusive. We shall first briefly state what it is. The Zacharias here is not the Zacharias you speak of: The Evangelist, therefore, has made no mistake in not naming him, for he was not thinking of him. Is there not, in fact, a manifest incompatibility in such a supposition with the idea that occupied our Lord's mind? Was it not his purpose to recall the long succession of homicides for which the Jewish race will have to render an account? And when he takes his first instance of murder from times preceding the flood at the gate of paradise, to make them accountable for it, you would have him think it enough to adduce as the last a crime committed above eight centuries before! After commencing with a son of Adam, can you imagine that he could end with the son of Jehoiada; thus holding the Jews innocent of the blood shed during the 873 most scandalous years of their history? Would it not have been more rational to begin rather than to end with Jehoiada? Were not the Jews far more responsible for the murders they had committed during the last preceding nine centuries of their history than they could be for blood shed before the deluge? Had they not persecuted, for example, and slain with frightful atrocity the prophet Urijah, 240 years after Jehoiada? (*Jeremiah* 26:23). "Which of the prophets," said Stephen to them, "have not your fathers persecuted? They have even slain them which showed before of the coming of the Just One!" (*Acts* 7:52). In this passage of *Matthew*, then, it is not the son of Jehoiada that is spoken of.

Here our reply might close; but we shall no doubt be asked, Who then was the Zechariah spoken of by Jesus Christ? Even although we did not know, this could by no means be a difficulty, and we should content ourselves with replying: It was some just person whom the Jews slew, not only in the court of the temple (ἐν τῷ ἱερῷ) like the son of Jehoiada, but *between the temple* (τοῦ ναοῦ) *and the altar*; and this just person was *son of Barachias!* Nevertheless, one may go further still; for history speaks of two or three other Zachariahs, sons of Barachias (Βαραχίου or Βαρούχου), among whom the learned divide their suffrages.

The first was a man who had understanding in the visions of God (as he is called in the *Second Book of Chronicles*),[53] and who is believed to be the same as he that is spoken of by Isaiah, in his eighth chapter.[54] Be that as it may, he lived too short a time after the son of Jehoiada for our objections against the one not to be equally valid against the other.

53. 2 *Chronicles* 26:6.
54. Hieronymus, on *Isaiah* 8:2 (in the LXX, Ζαχαρίαν υἱὸν Βαραχίω).
55. *Prolegom.*, Walton, 12.

The second is the prophet "Zachariah, the son of Berechiah and the grandson of Iddo" (*Zechariah* 1:1), who returned from Babylon with Zorobabel, 325 years after the days of Jehoiada, and whose writings form the second last book of the Old Testament.

The Scripture, it is true, has not related his martyrdom to us, any more than that of the other prophets, who were almost all persecuted and put to death. But the temple and the altar were rebuilt by his care, as well that of Haggai (*Esdras* 4:14-15); and Zechariah, as it would appear, was slain "between that temple and that altar." We read in the *Targum,* or the Chaldee paraphrase of *Jonathan Ben-Uziel* (said to have been a contemporary of Jesus Christ),[55] the following passage, which attests to us what was even then, previous to the days of our Saviour, the tradition of the Jews with regard to this prophet, called indifferently the son of Hiddo and the son of Barachias (*Zechariah* 1:1; *Ezra* 5:1; 6:14): The paraphrast (*Lamentations* 2:20) introduces the "House of Judgment" replying to this complaint of Jeremiah: "Shall the priest and the prophet be slain in the sanctuary of the Lord?" "Was it well in you... to slay a prophet as you did Zechariah, the son of Hiddo in the home of the Lord's sanctuary, because he endeavored to withdraw you from your evil ways?"[56] Thus it will be seen that Jesus Christ might remind the Jews of the sacrilegious murder of that prophet, son of Barachias, and son of Hiddo, with whom the prophecy of the Old Testament was to close.

However, there is still a third Zacharias, son of Barachias, (or of Baruch, Βαρόυχου), to whom our Lord's saying might be applied with still more likelihood. Flavius Josephus has made him known to us in that inestimable *History of the Jewish Wars,* which confirms so many other prophecies of the New Testament. It was only three years before the final destruction of Jerusalem that people saw a Zacharias, son of Barach, slain by the Jewish zealots in the middle of the holy place (ἐν μέσῳ τῷ ἱερῷ)[57] and his body was thrown over the walls of the mount on which the temple stood. He was a just man, according to Josephus; he was hated for his virtues, for his influence, for his hatred of evil, and for his zeal for liberty.[58] At the close of that frightful night, which was, says Josephus, "the real commencement of the destruction of Jerusalem," (and in which the zealots butchered the chief of the nation, the

---

56. Whitby's Commentary on *Matthew* 23:35.
57. *Bell. Judaic.*, Book 4. chapter 19.
58. παρώξινα δ' αὐτοὺς τὸ λίαν τάνδρος μισοπονηρὸν καὶ φιλελεύθερον.

high priest Ananus, and, soon after, twelve thousand youths of the Israelitish nobility), these infuriated men, affecting the forms of justice, had him dragged before a court of seventy judges, all of whom, however, had the courage to declare him innocent. Then, maddened with rage at hearing his reproaches, and at the noble spirit in which he addressed them, they rushed upon him and massacred him "in the middle of the holy place." Here, as many commentators think, we behold the last of the just persons whose blood had to be required of that homicidal race. Abel is the first, Zacharias the last. Thus it is that Jesus Christ, assuming the style of the prophets in using the past for the future, speaks of this crime as already committed: "Whom you slew," he says to them, "between the temple and the altar!"

The historian Josephus, it is true, speaks of Zacharias only as a righteous man, and not as a Christian or as a prophet. But, being a Jew, he could not hold any other language. And we see at another place (*Antiquities,* Book 20, chapter 8), that as little does he speak of the Apostle James (who, nevertheless, was also a prophet) as more than a good man, whom the high priest Ananus caused to be stoned,[59] to the great regret of the more respectable classes, during the interregnum that followed the unexpected death of the governor Festus. No more does it appear to us that the difference in the terminations of the names *Barachias* and *Baruch* is enough to destroy the argument arising from their etymological and radical resemblance. We see, in fact, in the New Testament, how much people were accustomed, among the Jews, Hebrew or Hellenist, to change the termination of their proper names: Silas and Silvanus,[60] Prisca and Priscilla,[61] Rabba and Rabbath, Lucas and Lucius.[62]

Be this as it may, we conclude once more, that this passage could not refer to the son of Jehoiada; and we leave to the reader to decide which of the two personages whom we have pointed out was the one contemplated by Jesus Christ.

Second example: *Mark* 11:12-14: Jesus cursed a fig-tree which had only leaves; for the time for figs had not yet come.

Here, we are told, there is no doubt a mistake: Why look for fruit at a time when it could not reasonably be expected?

---

59. Ἐπιεικέστατων.
60. *2 Corinthians* 1:19; *Thessalonians* 1:1; *Acts* 15:22, 34; 16:25; 17:15.
61. *2 Timothy* 4:19; *Romans* 16:3; *Acts* 18:2, 26.
62. *Acts* 13:1; *Romans* 16:21; *Philemon* 24.

Yet there is nothing here but what is very simple. Had it been the season for gathering figs, the tree might have been stripped of all its fruit by the hand of man and, in that case, there was no evidence of its barrenness.

But is a tree (we mention the objection in passing) guilty because it bears no fruit? Why punish it? We reply that in this miracle, which is a type, the tree is as little a sufferer as it is a criminal, nor is its suffering more real than its morality. The one is symbolical, and so also is the other.

*Another Source of Precipitate Judgment.* In questions of chronology, regard has not been paid to the following rule (which we take pleasure in expressing here in the very words of the great reformer of Italy, the excellent Peter Martyr).[63]

(The great divisions of time in the history of the people of God are pointed out to us by numerical dates of great precision. From the passing of Abraham into Canaan to the entrance of his grandson into Egypt, 215 years; from that to the passage of the Red Sea 215 years more – hence in all 430 years (*Galatians* 3:17; *Exodus* 12:40); from that, further, to the foundation of the temple, 480 years (*1 Kings* 6:1); and from that, in fine, to the Babylonian captivity, 422 years more. But within these grand divisions of history the precise and co-ordinate arrangement of all the short intermediate dates, the reconciling of the numbers presented to us by books of an almost monumental conciseness, and of an age contemporary with the siege of Troy (that of *Judges, Kings,* and *Chronicles*), respecting the reigns and interregnums, first of the judges, then of the kings, especially after the subdivision of the twelve tribes into two distinct kingdoms; this arrangement, we say, presents numerous difficulties, for which we find the elements of an entire solution sometimes wanting.)

The following is the rule of Peter Martyr:

> Although obscure passages occur as to chronology, we must beware of pretending to reconcile them by imputing blunders to the inspired books. Therefore it is, that, should it sometimes happen that we know not how to account for the number of years, we ought simply to confess our ignorance, and consider that the Scriptures express themselves with so much conciseness that it is not always possible for us to discover at what

63. In his *Commentary* on *2 Kings* 8:17 and *1 Kings* 15:1.

epoch we ought to make such or such a computation commence. It often enough happens, that, in the history of the kings of Judah and of Israel, the respective numbers of their years are not easily reconciled; but these difficulties admit of explanation or adjustment in several ways. 1. The same year commenced by one of two, and finished by the other, is attributed to both. 2. Often the sons have reigned with their fathers during some years, which have been imputed sometimes to the fathers, sometimes to the sons. 3. There were often interregnums, which the Scripture attributes sometimes to the predecessor, sometimes to the successor. Finally, it sometimes happens that certain years, in which oppressive and profane princes have reigned, are not reckoned to them, being imputed to their immediate successor; thus, the last twenty years of Joram to his son Ahaziah (*2 Kings* 8:26; *2 Chronicles* 22:2)."

We think that the examples we have thus far adduced may suffice. We refrain from adducing more. What we have said may give one an idea of the weight to be attached to these difficulties,[64] for (we repeat) we have been careful to adduce those which have been held as the most serious. Warned by these examples, and by so many others, let us learn then, should any embarrassment of the same kind occur to us in the future, how to judge as did Origen's friend, Julius Africanus, sixteen hundred years ago, and as, before and after him, all the men of God have done. "Be that as it may (said he on the occasion of the two genealogies of Jesus Christ, which he had reconciled) be that as it may, the Gospel certainly everywhere speaks true!" – Τὸ μέντοι Εὐαγγέλιον πάντως ἀληθεύει.[65]

## Section VI
### Errors Contrary to Natural Philosophy

It will be admitted, we have been sometimes told, that the apparent or real contradictions in the dates, quotations, and narratives of the Holy Bible may possibly be removed by the resources of a more or less laborious exegesis; but there are others that you cannot reconcile: Such are all those expressions in which the sacred writers appear in manifest opposition to the now better known laws of nature. Nevertheless (these objectors desire to add), though this argument be irrefragable against

---

64. See for further details the authors whom we have quoted, and in particular the useful compilation of Horne, *Introduction to the Critical Study of the Bible.*

65. Eusebius, *Hist. Eccles.*, Book 1, chapter 7.

the verbal inspiration of the Scriptures, it compromises in nothing the divinity of their doctrines, any more than the great religious facts which they report to us. In inspiring his apostles and his prophets, God desired to make us, not scientific, but holy persons. Thus he could, without danger, allow the writers he employed to speak in ignorance of the phenomena of the material world; and their prejudices on such matters are innocent though incontestable. Do you not often find them expressing themselves as if the Earth were immovable and the Sun in motion? That star, according to them, rises and falls: "his going forth is from the end of the Heaven, and his circuit unto the ends of it" (*Psalm* 19); the Moon and the stars are equally in movement; the Sun, at the command of Joshua, became immovable in the midst of the heavens; it "stood still upon Gibeon, and the Moon in the valley of Ajalon" (*Joshua* 10:12); the earth is "founded on the seas (*Psalm* 24:2); "drawn from the water, it subsists amid the water" (*2 Peter* 3:5); "God has laid its foundations, it shall never be moved" (*Psalm* 104:5) – Can you admit that this is really the language of the Creator of the heavens and of the Earth, when addressing his creatures?

We proceed to reply to this objection, and we are delighted to meet it on our path, seeing that the examination of it can only redound to the glory of the Scriptures.

We most fully admit that were there some physical errors, duly ascertained, in the book of the Scriptures, it would not be entirely from God; but we proceed to put it beyond a doubt that there are no such errors; and we will venture to defy our adversaries to produce a single such error in the whole of the Bible. Indeed, we will even go much further; and will show how much latent science, on the contrary, betrays itself there, beneath the simplicity of its language.

We shall begin by saying a few words on Joshua's miracle, inasmuch as a disposition has often been shown to turn it to account in combating either the plenary inspiration or even the divine mission of the men of God. Several unbelieving writers have attacked it with that arrogance and irony which too often characterize them. But it is easy to reply to them. We have no thoughts of discussing here the methods by which the miracle might have been accomplished; we would only remark, from this example, how thoughtlessly people hasten to pronounce that because certain passages of Scripture are not understood, therefore they must be irrational.

## EXAMINATION OF OBJECTIONS

*The Sun,* on the day of the battle of Beth-horon, *stood still in the midst of Heaven,* we are told in the tenth chapter of Joshua; *and there was no day like that before it or after it.*

It has been said in Germany, "This phrase, taken in its natural sense, seems to us absurd; it is erroneous, therefore, and altogether human." Elsewhere it has been pronounced so absurd that another meaning must be given to it. But both opinions are drawn from false premises. The fact is far from being absurd; it is only miraculous.

We shall give the objection in the very words in which it has been stated: "The most fearless Methodist," it has been said, "will feel constrained to own that in the system of our globe, were the Sun to stop for an instant, or were the Earth's motion to be slackened, belligerent armies, and all that is on the Earth's surface, would be swept away like chaff before the wind!"

Nevertheless, it is this very objection that is an error. In point of fact, if the miracle, instead of stopping the rotation of the globe suddenly, in an indivisible instant, took only the short space of a few seconds to accomplish it, by a supple and continuous action, then you have enough in this feeble circumstance to be assured that such a phenomenon would have had no very sensible effect mechanically beyond that of raising the waters diffused over the surface of the Earth, and making them to flow from west to east. A child might tell you. Let a carriage in rapid motion meet a curb stone – it shatters itself upon it, because the stone is immovable; and all that are in the carriage are projected to a distance, and thrown with violence on the ground. But let it be stopped by a continuous resistance, operating in a successive manner, and consummating itself in three or four seconds: Then the smallest children seated in the carriage will remain in their seats; they will not even feel the impulsion which three seconds before was impressed on them by the impetuous movement of the horses, and which, without this precaution, would have sufficed to launch them to a distance.

The rotation of the Earth is, at the Equator, 1,426 feet per second; at Jerusalem, 1,212 feet. This is the initial speed of a cannon ball projected by a charge the fifth part of its own weight. It is capable (abstraction being made of the resistance of the air) of raising that projectile to the extreme height of 24,000 feet; and yet a child six years old would destroy, without danger, *in two-thirds of a minute,* the whole of this force by the continued action of his fingers. Put into his little hands a cannon ball of eight pounds' weight, and let him hold it against the action of its weight during two-thirds of a minute; during the same time, allow another bullet of quite the same weight to drop freely through the air, and from the height of the summit of the Himalaya range. When forty seconds only have expired, the force of gravitation, after having acted by the same impulsions upon both these projectiles, will not have done more with respect to the first than have fatigued the feeble hands that resist it, while it would have made the other acquire a speed equal to that which the rotation of the Earth impressed on the belligerent armies on the hill of Beth-horon. Since, then, a child might destroy, by the continuous effort of his little hands, a force capable (if concentrated on a single instant) of launching a cannon bullet to the height of Chimborazo, we can easily conceive that, if God, on the day of the battle of Beth-horon, had employed two-thirds of a minute to arrest, by short and successive resistances, the rotation of our globe, then the projectile impulsions which a mass of eight pounds of iron would have received continually during these forty seconds, would not even have been so strong as that a child might not have destroyed them by the sole effort of his fingers, and without expending more force than he would have to put forth in sustaining with his hands a weight of eight pounds during the same space of time. And if the mass, instead of having the form of a bullet, had had that of a quoit or a cube, it would not have had enough of that impulsion to make it overcome the resistance of friction, and to change its place on the surface of the ground.

It will be objected, perhaps, that the rotation of the Earth at Beth-horon was twenty-seven times more rapid than that of a steam-carriage on a railway. This is true; but since the retarding force necessary for exhausting a given impulsion is in the inverse ratio of the time employed in it, grant that the miracle took eighteen minutes for its consummation; take eighteen minutes (instead of forty seconds) for the entire stoppage of the movement of the terrestrial globe at the voice of Joshua; and then the belligerent armies, instead of being "swept away as if by a tempest," would not have felt more from what happened, than do the thousands of travellers that are stopped at each of the stations on a railway.

Other difficulties of a like kind have been started with regard to this miracle of Joshua. Had the Earth, it has been said, suspended its motion during ten hours, the attractive force of the Sun acting singly upon it, would in that time have made it fall 900 leagues in the direction of the Sun's blazing focus, and the annual conditions of our orbit would have been sensibly troubled.

This objection is no less futile than the preceding. The miracle, in fact, does not imply the slightest perturbation in the progressive movement of the Earth; it requires it only in its rotation. Now, according to the laws of the celestial mechanism, the rotation of a star upon its axis is entirely independent of the movement impressed on its center of gravity, and which makes it move onward in its elliptical course. Experience had attested this before it was demonstrated by calculation. It had long been observed that the speed of the Sun (or rather of the Earth) in its orbit, ceases not to vary from one end of the year to the other; and yet there does not exist in nature a more uniform movement than that which makes the whole celestial sphere daily revolve to our eyes. We are even assured, from the observations of the movement of the Moon, that for more than 2,000 years the sidereal day has not varied so much as the hundredth part of a second.

Let there be supposed, then, a double shock impressed upon the Earth above and below its center, and in two contrary and parallel directions, and we shall have explained how its rotation on its axis might have been suspended without any change in its onward movement. But here I check myself. It would be rash, do I say? it would be childish to pretend to enter into the details of the prodigy with the view of ascertaining its causes; and my only wish has been to show the futility of the objections. The true one, which people do not state, is that they find the miracle too great for its object. But, for men who believe in the great miracle of redemption by the Son of God, nothing is too great, and all things advance in due proportions in the divine revelations. Moreover, and I hasten to say it, it would not even be necessary, in order to account for this prodigy, to suppose so sovereign an act of Omnipotence as the suspension of the rotation of our globe. God might have employed for this purpose only one of those numerous means which divert the light from its paths, and produce the innumerable illusions of optics; some one of those refractions, for example, which daily displace to our eyes, in different measures, all the stars of the celestial sphere. Is it not matter of notoriety that in the polar regions the power of the horizontal refractions makes the Sun appear to the inhabitants of those cold countries ten days before he really rises above the horizon? Such might have been the cause of the miracle of Beth-horon. We decide nothing – we do not even venture on a hypothesis. We would only say, that the miracle was duly consummated (whatever the means by which it was produced), provided that the Sun to the eyes of the inhabitants of Palestine, *stood still upon Gibeon, and the Moon in the valley of Ajalon.*[66]

Meanwhile, the Scriptures are reproached with using a language on the daily phenomena of nature apparently betokening ignorance and incompatible with a plenary inspiration. According to the writers of the Bible, the Sun rises, the Sun sets, the Sun stands still, the Earth remains unmoved. People will have it that the Creator, in speaking to us in a book inspired by him, would have more clearly shown us that the Spirit that made the sacred historians speak knew before we did the rotation of our globe, its periodical revolution, and the respective immobility of the Sun.

Let us, then, examine this reproach.

We ask, first of all, of the persons who give utterance to it, if they would have had the Bible to speak like Sir Isaac Newton. Would they dismiss from their minds the consideration that if God, in speaking of the decrees of nature, were to express himself, I do not say only as he sees them, but as the scientific men of future ages will be able to see them, then even the great Newton could have understood nothing of what was said? Moreover, even the most advanced language of science is not yet, and never will be, after all, more than the language of appearances. The visible world, much more than you suppose, is a passing shadow, a scene of illusions and of phantoms. What you call reality is still in itself but a phenomenon considered in its relation to a more exalted reality, and to an ulterior analysis. In our mortal lips the word *reality* has nothing absolute; it is a term altogether relative, merely intimating that people think they have added one new step to the deep ladder of our ignorances. The human eye sees objects under only two dimensions, and projects them all as if on the same canvass, until touch and repeated experience have assured us of the reality of a depth, or of a third dimension. Colors are accidents, and it is only by reflection or illusion that they belong to the object which presents them to you. Even the impen-

---

66. One may read, besides, on this miracle, some striking historical and geological considerations in Chaubard's *Elements de Geologie*.

etrability of bodies, their solidity, their extension, are no more than an appearance, and present themselves as a reality only until the further progress of one science shall substitute another for it. Who would venture to say where this analysis ought to stop, and in what terms should we speak of creatures with which we are most familiar, were we but endowed with one more sense, with antennæ, for example, like ants and bees? The expression of appearances, accordingly, provided it be exact, is, among men, philosophically correct, and what was advantageous and proper for the Scriptures to employ. Would men have the Bible speak to us of the scenes of nature otherwise than we speak of them to one another, in our social or domestic intercourse, otherwise even than they are spoken of among the most enlightened persons? When Sir John Herschel tells his domestics to waken him precisely at midnight, to observe the passage of some star over his meridian telescope, does he feel himself called upon to speak to them about the rotation of the Earth, and of the moment when it will have brought their nadir into the plane of its orbit? I should think not; and were you even to hear him converse in Greenwich Observatory with the scientific Airey, you would find, that even in that sanctuary of science, the habitual language of these astronomers is still quite like that of the Scriptures. For them the stars rise, the equinoxes recede, the planets go forward and accelerate their speed, stop and go back. Would you, then, that Moses should speak to all the generations of men in a more scientific language than La Place or Arago?

But more than this. Here we would bid the reader notice two general facts that throw out a deal of light the moment we study them, and which soon betray in the Scriptures the pen of Almighty God. Here, as everywhere else, the objections, when narrowly examined, come back upon you, loudly retract themselves, and become arguments on the other side.

These two facts are analogous to what you might observe in the words of a scientific astronomer conversing with his sons in their boyhood, and pointing out the Earth and the heavens to them with his finger. If you follow him into these conversations, where his affection, stooping to their level, presents to their growing intelligence such images and words as it can comprehend, you will soon notice his respect for truth shown under a double character. First, he will never say anything to them that is not true; and, secondly, there will be many intimations in his words that he knows more on the subject than he wishes to tell them. He will make no pretension, it is true, to teach them science but, on the one hand, nothing in all he says will contradict its principles; and, on the other hand, several of his words will at once reveal that while he restrains himself from speaking about it, still he knows it. Afterward, when his children, grown up to manhood, come to recall his words, not only will they find them exempt from all error, but they will further recognize in them such a skilful choice of expression as to put them at once in a pre-established harmony with science, and to present it to them, while not aware of it, in its germ. In proportion to the gradual advance of their own knowledge, they will see with admiration, under the reserve and simplicity of his language, concealed marks of wisdom, instances of a scientific precision, a general phraseology and particular expressions harmonizing with events then unknown to them, but that had long been known to him.

Well, then, such also is the double observation which every attentive reader may make on the phraseology of the Scriptures. They speak poetically, but with precision, the true language of appearances. In them we hear a father condescending to address his youngest sons, yet in such a manner that the oldest can never find there a single sentence contrary to the true condition of the things he has created; and in such a manner also he suffers to escape from him, without affectation, enough to demonstrate to them that all that they have learned of his works during the last four thousand years, he knew before them and better than they. It is thus that, in the Bible, Eternal Wisdom addresses his children. In proportion as they advance in growth, they see that the Scripture is made for their age, is adapted to their development, appearing to grow with their growth, and always presenting the two facts which we have pointed out: on the one hand, the absence of all error; on the other, indirect yet incontestable indications of a science which preceded all that of man.

First fact: There is no physical error in the Word of God.

If there were any, we have admitted it, the book would not be from God. "God is not man that he should lie," nor the son of man that he should be mistaken. He finds it both advantageous and proper, no doubt, in order to his being understood, to stoop to our weakness, but without in the least partaking in it; and his language will always be found to witness to his condescension, never to his ignorance.

This remark is still more serious than one would suppose before having reflected on it. It becomes very striking on a close examination.

Examine all the false theologies of the ancients and moderns; read in Homer or in Hesiod, the religious codes of the Greeks; study those of the Buddhists, those of the Brahmins, those of the Mohammedans; you will not only find in these books repulsive systems on the subject of the Godhead, but will meet with the grossest errors on the material world. You will be revolted with their theology no doubt; but their natural philosophy and their astronomy also, ever allied to their religion, will be found to rest on the most absurd notions.

Read in the *Chou-king* and the *Y-king* of the Chinese their fantastic systems on the five elements (wood, fire, earth, metal, and water), and on their omnipotent influences on all divine and human affairs.[67] Read in the *Shaster* in the *Pouran,* in the four books of the *Vedham,* or law of the Hindus, their revolting cosmogony. The Moon is 50,000 leagues higher than the Sun; it shines with its own light; it animates our body. Night is caused by the Sun's setting behind the mountain Someyra, situated in the middle of the Earth, and several thousand miles high. Our Earth is flat and triangular, composed of seven stages, each with its own degree of beauty, its own inhabitants, and its own sea, the first of honey, another of sugar, another of butter, another of wine; in fine, the whole mass is borne on the heads of countless elephants which, in shaking themselves, cause earthquakes in this nether world![68] In one word, they have placed the whole history of their gods in relations at once the most fantastic and the most necessary with the physical world and all the phenomena of the universe. Thus, the missionaries to India have often repeated that a telescope, silently planted in the midst of the holy city of Benares, or in the ancient Ava, would prove a battery powerful as lightning for overturning the whole system of Brahma and the whole of that of Boudhou.

Read further the philosophers of Greek and Roman antiquity – Aristotle, Seneca, Pliny, Plutarch, Cicero. How many expressions of opinion will you not find there, any single one of which would be enough to compromise all our doctrines of inspiration if it could be met with in any book of Holy Scripture! Read Mohammed's Koran, making mountains to be created to prevent the Earth from moving, and

67. Panthier, *Les livres sacrés de l'Orient* (Paris, 1840), pages 15, 89, 94, 146, etc.
68. *Modern Universal History,* Volume 6, page 275.

to hold it fast as if with anchors and cables. What do I say? Read even the cosmogony of Buffon, or some of Voltaire's sneers on the doctrine of a deluge, or on the fossil animals of a primitive world. We will go much further. Read again, we do not say the absurd reasonings of the pagans, of Lucretius, of Pliny, or of Plutarch, against the theory of the antipodes, but even the fathers of the Christian church. Hear the theological indignation of the admirable Augustine, who says that it is opposed to the Scriptures; and the scientific eloquence of Lactantius, who considers it so opposed to common sense: "*Num aliquid loquuntur!*" he exclaims. "Is there any man so silly as to believe that men exist having their feet above their heads, trees with their fruit hanging downwards, rain, snow, and hail falling topsy turvy!" "They would answer you," he adds, "by maintaining that the Earth is a globe! *Quid dicam de iis nescio, qui cum semel aberraverint, constanter in stultitia perseverant, et vanis vana defendunt!*" One knows not what to say of such men, who, when they have once run into error, persist in their folly, and defend one absurdity by another![69]

Listen, further, to the legate Boniface, who brought Virgilius, for his opinion in this matter, as a heretic before the pope; listen to Pope Zachary treating that unhappy bishop as *homo malignus.* "If it be proved," says he, "that Virgilius maintains the existence of other men under this Earth, call a council, condemn him, put him out of the church, depose him from the priesthood!" Listen, at a later period, to the whole clergy of Spain, and especially to the imposing Council of Salamanca, indignant at the geographical system by which Christopher Columbus was led to look for a whole new continent. Listen, at the epoch of Newton's birth, to the great Galileo, who "ascended," says Kepler, "the highest ramparts of the universe," and who justified at once by his genius and by his telescope the disowned and condemned system of Copernicus; behold him groaning, at the age of eighty, in the prisons of Rome, for having discovered the movement of the Earth, after having had to pronounce these words, ten years before (June 28, 1633), before their Eminences, at the palace of the Holy Office: "I, Galileo, in the seventieth year of my age, on my knees before your Eminences, having before my eyes, and touching with my own hands, the Holy Scriptures, abjure, curse, and detest the error of the Earth's movement."

69. *On False Knowledge,* Book 3, chapter 24.

## EXAMINATION OF OBJECTIONS

What might we not have been entitled to say of the Scriptures had they expressed themselves on the phenomena of nature, as these have been spoken of by all the ancient sages? Had they referred all to four elements, as people did for so long a period? Had they said the stars were of crystal, as did Philoläus of Crotona; and had they, like Empedocles, lighted up the two hemispheres of our world with two Sun? Had they taught, like Leucippus, that the fixed stars, set ablaze by the swiftness of their diurnal movement round the Earth, feed the Sun with their fires? Had they, like Diodorus of Sicily, and all the Egyptian sages, formed the heavens and the Earth by the motion of the air and the natural ascent of fire? Or had they thought, like Philoläus, that the Sun has only a borrowed light, and is only a mirror, which receives and sends down to us the light of the celestial spheres? Had they, like Anaxagoras, conceived it to be a mass of iron larger than the Peloponnesus, and the Earth to be a mountain, whose roots stretched infinitely downward? Had they imagined the heaven to be a solid sphere, to which the fixed stars are attached, as was done by Aristotle, and almost all the ancients? Had they called the celestial vault a *firmamentum*, or a στερέωμα as their interpreters have done, both in Latin and in Greek? Had they spoken, as has been done so recently, and even among people professing Christianity, of the influence exerted by the movements of the heavens on the elements of this lower world, on the characters of men, and on the course of human affairs? Such is the natural proneness of all nations to this superstition that, notwithstanding their religion, the ancient Jews, and the Christians themselves, equally fell into it. "The modern Greeks," says D'Alembert,[70] "have carried it to excess; hardly do we find one of their authors who does not, on all occasions, speak of predictions by the stars, of horoscopes and talismans, so that there was hardly an edifice in Constantinople, and in all Greece, that had not been erected according to the rules of the *apotelesmatic astrology*." French historians observe that astrology was so much in fashion under Catherine de Médicis, that people dared not undertake anything of importance without having consulted the stars; and even under Henry III and Henry IV, the predictions of astrologers formed the engrossing subject of ordinary conversation at court. "We have seen, toward the close of the last century," says

---

70. *Encycl. ou Dict. rais. des Sciences*, etc., Volume 1, page 663 (Lucca, 1758).
71. *Encycl. ou Dict. rais. des Sciences*, etc., Volume 1, page 664.

Ph. Giulani,[71] "an Italian send Pope Innocent XI a prediction, in the manner of a horoscope, on Vienna, at that time besieged by the Turks, and which was very well received." And in our own days the Count de Boulainvilliers has written very seriously on the subject.

Open now the Bible; study its fifty sacred authors, from that wonderful Moses who held the pen in the wilderness, four hundred years before the war of Troy, down to the fisherman, son of Zebedee, who wrote fifteen hundred years afterwards, in Ephesus and in Patmos, under the reign of Domitian; open the Bible, and try if you can to find anything of this sort there. No. None of those blunders which the science of every successive age discovers in the books of those that preceded it; none of those absurdities, above all, which modern astronomy points out, in such numbers, in the writings of the ancients, in their sacred codes, in their systems of philosophy, and in the finest pages even of the fathers of the church; no such errors can be found in any of our sacred books; nothing there will ever contradict what, after so many ages, the investigations of the learned world have been able to reveal to us of what is certain in regard to the state of our globe or of that of the heavens. Carefully peruse our Scriptures from one end to the other in search of such blemishes there; and while engaged in this research, remember that it is a book which speaks of everything, which describes nature, which proclaims its grandeur, which tells the story of its creation, which informs us of the structure of the heavens, of the creation of light, of the waters, of the atmosphere, of the mountains, of animals, and of plants; it is a book that tells us of the first revolutions of the worlds and foretells to us also the last; a book that relates them in circumstantial narratives, exalts them in a sublime poesy, and chants them in strains of fervent psalmody; it is a book replete with the glow of oriental rapture, elevation, variety, and boldness; it is a book which speaks of the Earth and of things visible, at the same time that it speaks of the celestial world and of things invisible; it is a book to which nearly fifty writers of every degree of mental cultivation, of every rank, of every condition, and separated by fifteen hundred years from each other, have successively put their hand; it is a book composed first in the center of Asia, among the sands of Arabia, or in the deserts of Judea, or in the forecourt of the temple of the Jews, or in the rustic schools of the prophets of Bethel and of Jericho, or in the sumptuous palaces of Babylon, or on the idolatrous banks of Chebar; and afterwards, at the center of western civilization, amid the Jews with their manifold ignorance, amid polytheism and its ideas, as well as in the bosom of pantheism and its silly philosophy; it is a book the first writer of which had been for the space of forty years a pupil of the magicians of Egypt, who looked upon the Sun, and the stars, and the elements as endowed with intelligence, as re-acting upon the elements, and as governing the world by continual effluxes – it is a book the first chapters of which preceded by more than nine hundred years the most ancient philosophers of ancient Greece and of Asia, the Thaleses, the Pythagorases, the Zaleucuses, the Xenophaneses, the Confuciuses; it is a book which carries its narratives even into the field of the invisible world, even into the hierarchies of the angels, even into the remotest realms of futurity, and the glorious scenes of the last day; well then search through these 50 authors, search through these 66 books, search through these 1,189 chapters, and these 31,173 verses... search for one single error of those thousands with which ancient and modern books abound, when they speak either of the Heaven or of the Earth, or of their revolutions, or of their elements; search, but you will search in vain.

There is nothing constrained or reserved in its language; it speaks of all things and in all tones; it is the prototype, it is the unapproachable model; it has been the inspirer of all the most exalted productions of poetry. Ask this of Milton, of the two Racines, of Young, of Klopstock. They will tell you that this divine poesy is of all the most lyrical, the boldest in its flights, and the most sublime: It rises on a cherub and soars on the wings of the wind. And yet never does this book do violence to the facts or to the principles of a sound philosophy of nature. Never will you find it in opposition, in the case of a single sentence, with the correct notions which science has enabled us to reach with regard to the form of our globe, its size, or its geology; on the vacuum and on space; on the inert and obedient materiality of all the stars; on the planets, on their masses, on their courses, on their dimensions, or on their influences, on the suns that people the depths of space, on their number, on their nature, or their immensity. Just as in speaking of the invisible world, and of a subject so new, so unknown, and so delicate as that of the angels, this book has not one of its authors that, in the course of the 1,560 years which it took to write it, has varied in the character of charity, humility, fervor, and purity which belongs to those mysterious beings; just as in speaking of the relations of the celestial world with God, never has one of these fifty writers, either in the Old or in the New Testament, uttered a single word that favors that constant leaning to pantheism which characterizes the whole philosophy of the Gentiles; so likewise you will not find one of the authors of the Bible who, in speaking of the visible world, has suffered a single one of those expressions of opinion to escape him, which, in other books, contradict the reality of facts – not one which makes the Heaven to be a firmament, as has been done by the Septuagint, Jerome, and all the fathers of the church – not one that makes the world, as Plato did, an intelligent animal – not one that reduces all things here below to the four elements of the physical system of the ancients – not one that holds with the Jews, with the Latins, with the Greeks, with the finest minds of antiquity, with the great Tacitus among the ancients, with the great De Thou among the moderns, with the sceptic Michel Montaigne, that "the stars have domination and power, not only over our lives and the conditions of our fortune, but even over our inclinations, our discourses, our wills; that they govern, impel, and agitate them at the mercy of their influences; and that (according as our reason teaches us and finds it to be) the whole world feels the impulsion of the slightest celestial movements. *Facta etenim et vitas hominum suspendit ab astris;*"[72] – not one that peaks of the mountains as Mohammed has done, of the cosmogony like Buffon, of the antipodes like Lucretius, like Plutarch, like Pliny, like Lactantius, like Augustine, like Pope Zachary. Assuredly, were there to be found in the Bible a single one of those errors that abound among philosophers, as well ancient as modern, our faith in the plenary inspiration of the Scriptures would be more than compromised by it; we should have to acknowledge that there are errors in the Word of God, and that these delusive expressions are those of a fallible writer, not those of the Holy Spirit, for God is not man that he should lie; in him there is no variableness, neither shadow of falsity; and he to whom lying lips are an abomination, could not have been capable of contradicting himself and dictating that which is false.

There is no physical error, then, in the Scriptures; and this great fact, which becomes all the more striking the more narrowly we look into it, is the manifest proof of an inspiration carried into their choice of the smallest expressions they employ.

72. *Essays*, Book 2, chapter 12.

But we have more to say than this, and now come to the second fact.

Not only has the Bible not admitted any false statement of opinion or expression; but further, it has often allowed words to escape which enable us to see, beyond all possibility of our being mistaken, the science of the Almighty. His grand aim, no doubt, is to reveal to us the eternal glories of the invisible world, not the barren secrets of that which is doomed to perish. Meanwhile, however, it often happens that his language, when we listen to it with attention, allows a science to be seen which it is not his design to teach, but of which he cannot be ignorant, because *it is in him a great deep.* Not only will he never teach us anything false, even cursorily; but, further, you will often stumble on words which betray the voice of the Creator of all worlds. Often you will remark in these a wisdom, a forethought, an exactness, of which the ages of antiquity had no idea, and which nothing but the discoveries of the telescope, the calculating processes, and the science of the moderns have enabled us to appreciate; so that its language will be found to bear, by means of these traits, the evident character of the most entire inspiration. The discretion and departure from usual practice shown in its expressions, the nature of certain details, the perfect propriety and divine adaptation of which to the facts have remained unrevealed till three thousand years afterwards; the reserve of the language, sometimes its very hardihood, and its strangeness for the time in which it was written: All these signs will enable you to recognize the *savant par excellence,* the Ancient of days, who addresses himself to his children no doubt, but who speaks as the father of the family, and who knows the whole of his house.

When the Scripture speaks of the form of our Earth, it makes it a globe.[73] When it speaks of the position of this globe in the bosom of the universe, it hangs it upon nothing (על בלימה).[74] When it speaks of its age, not only does it place its creation, as well as that of the heavens, in the beginning that is, before ages which it cannot or will not number; but, further, it takes care to place before the disembroilment of chaos and the creation of man, that of angels and archangels, principalities and powers, their probation, the fall of some and their ruin,

---

73. *Isaiah* 40:22; *Job* 26:10; *Proverbs* 8:27.
74. *Job* 26:7 ($κρεμάζων\ γῆν\ ἐπὶ\ οὐδενός$).

the perseverance of others and their glory.[75] When it speaks, afterwards, of the origin of our continents, and of the last creation of plants, animals, and men, it then gives to our new world, and to this proud race of ours, so young an age, that men of all times, among all Earth's peoples, and even in our modern schools, have foolishly revolted at it; still it is an age to which they have been compelled to resign themselves since the labors of the De Lucs, the Cuviers, and the Bucklands, have so fully demonstrated that the state of the globe's surface, as well as the monuments of history and those of science, must compel alike the learned and the vulgar to submit to it.

When it speaks of the heavens, Scripture employs, in alluding to them and defining them, the most philosophic and the most beautiful expression; an expression that the Greeks in their Septuagint, the Latins in the Vulgate, and all the church fathers in their discourses, have made bold to correct, and which they have perverted from its proper meaning, because it seemed opposed to the science of their times. The heavens in the Bible are the expanse, *expansum,* רקיע;[76] that is to say, it is the void, or the ether, or the immensity, and not the *firmamentum* of Jerome; nor the στερέωμα of the Alexandrine interpreters; nor the *eighth heaven,* firm, solid, crystalline, and incorruptible of Aristotle and all the ancients. And although this, which is so remarkable a term of the Hebrew, recurs seventeen times in the Old Testament, and although seventeen times the seventy have rendered it by στερέωμα (*firmament*), never has the New Testament thought fit to make use, in this sense, of that expression of the Greek interpreters.[77] When Scripture speaks of light, it represents it to us as an element independent of the Sun, and as anterior by three epochs to that in which that great luminary was kindled;[78] thus anticipating the systems of the moderns, whom we have seen led, along with the great Newton, to suppose in the universe an ether, eminently subtle, powerfully elastic, and diffused everywhere, the contractions and dilatations of which would produce, not only the various phenomena of light, but those too of gravitation.[79]

75. *Nehemiah* 9:6; *Colossians* 1:16; *Daniel* 7:10; compare with *Jude* 6; *Genesis* 3:1, 13, 15; *Revelation* 20:2, 12:9, 12; *Genesis* 3:24; *John* 8:44; *2 Peter* 2:4, 9, 10; *John* 12:31.

76. *Genesis* 1:6; *Psalm* 19:6.

77. It has made use of it only once, and that in speaking of something quite different from the heavens, *Colossians* 1:5.

78. *Genesis* 1:4, 14.

79. This hypothesis of etherial pulsations and of a vibrating medium expanded

## EXAMINATION OF OBJECTIONS

When Scripture speaks of the creation of plants, it makes them vegetate, grow, and bear seed before the appearance of the Sun, and under conditions of light, heat, and humidity, which were not those under which our vegetables live at the present day;[80] and it is thus that it reveals to us, some thousands of years ago, an order of things which the fossil botany of these late times of ours has declared incontestable, and the necessary existence of which is attested by the gigantic forms of the vegetables lately discovered in Canada, and at Baffin's Bay; some, like M. Marcel de Serres,[81] having recourse, in order to explain it, to a terrestrial magnetism at that time more intense, or to more luminous *aurorae boreales*; others, like M. de Candolle,[82] to a great inclination of the ecliptic, although in reality (according to the famous theorem of La Grange) the mechanism of the heavens confines within very narrow limits this variation of the planetary orbs.[83] When it speaks of the air, the weight of which was unknown before the time of Galileo, it tells us that at the creation "God gave to the air its weight (משקל) and to the waters their just measure."[84]

When Scripture speaks of our atmosphere and of the upper waters,[85] it assigns to them an importance that the science of the moderns alone has been able to demonstrate;[86] seeing that, according to their calculations, the force annually employed by nature for the formation of clouds is equal to an amount of work which the whole human race could not do in less than 200,000 years.[87] And when it separates the

---

everywhere was the constant idea of this incomparable philosopher, in his most elevated views on the constitution of the universe. He even deduced from it the explanation of all the phenomena of combination, cohesion, elasticity, and of movement, which seem to be produced by intangible and imponderable principles. (See his *Letter to Dr. Boyle on the Cause of Weight;* his *Memoir* addressed to the Royal Society of London in December 1675; and two articles of Baron Meurice in the *Bibl. Uni. de Genève,* 1822, page 79).

80. *Genesis* 1:12.
81. *Memoires de Marcel de Serres.*
82. *Bibliotheque Universelle*, 58, 1835.
83. The oscillations of the ecliptic, including both sides of its mean position, cannot exceed 1 ⅓ degree.
84. *Job* 28:25.
85. *Genesis* 1:7.
86. See Leslie's *Calculations.*
87. *Annuaire du Bur. des Longitudes*, 1835, page 196. Arago, in this calculation, supposes that 800 million form the population of the globe, and that only half that number can work.

## GOD-BREATHED: THE DIVINE INSPIRATION OF THE BIBLE

higher waters from the lower, it is by *an expansion,* and not by a solid sphere, as its imprudent translators would do, both in Greek and in Latin.

When Scripture speaks of the mountains, it distinguishes them, in point of fact, into primitive and secondary; it speaks of them as generated, as raked, as notated like wax; it lowers the valleys; in a word, it speaks as a geological poet of our own days would do. "The mountains arose, O Lord, and the valleys went down unto the place which you had founded for them."[88]

When Scripture speaks of the human races of every tribe, of every color, and of every language, it gives one and the same origin, notwithstanding that the philosophy of all ages would so often have revolted against this truth; which we have seen that of the moderns forced at length to acknowledge.[89]

When Scripture speaks of the internal state of our globe, it declares to us two great facts, of which the learned were long ignorant, but now rendered incontestable by their last discoveries; the one relating to its solid crust, and the other to the great waters which it covers. When it speaks of its solid envelope, it informs us that if its surface gives us bread, underneath (תחתיה) the Earth is on fire;[90] that, besides, it is reserved unto fire, and that it will be burned in the last times, with all the works that are therein.[91] And when it speaks of the waters which our globe contains, it alone accounts, at least in this respect, for the immense cataclysms which (according to what we are told by men of science themselves) have completely, and for long periods, submerged it at different epochs. And while the latter tell us of the inconsiderable depth of the seas; while they assure us that a rise of two hundred meters only, or of one-and-a-half the height of the tower of Strasbourg, would suffice for the disappearance of the Baltic, the North Sea, the English and St. George's Channels; and that Mont Blanc, or at least Chimborazo, if thrown into the deepest part of the Pacific Ocean, would be found

---

88. *Psalm* 104:8, 6, 9; *Genesis* 2:14; 8:4; *Psalm* 90:2; *Proverbs* 8:25; *Psalm* 97:5; 144:6; *Zechariah* 14:4, 8; *Ezekiel* 47.

89. See Sumner, *The Records of the Creation,* Volume 1, page 286; and Professor Zimmerman, *Histoire Geographique de l'Homme;* Wiseman, *Third Discourse on the Natural History of the Human Race,* Volume 1, page 149.

90. *Job* 28:5; literally, "Underneath it is turned up, *and* as it were fire."

91. *2 Peter* 3:7, 10.

high enough to form an island; while La Place thought there was ground to conclude, from the size of the tides, that the mean depth of the ocean does not exceed a thousand meters (the height of the Saleve or of Hecla); while we have thus demonstrated to us the absolute insufficiency of the seas for these immense submersions which our globe has undergone;... the Scripture teaches us that the earth was taken out of the water, and subsists in the water,[92] "and that its solid crust covers a great deep (תהום), the waters of which were broken up (נבקעו), with surges and violence,[93] at the epoch of the deluge, as at that of chaos and of the countless ages that preceded it."

When Scripture speaks of the deluge, it supposes submersions and subversions, which all unbelievers of former times said were too great to be believed, and which at the present day geologists have found too insufficient rather to explain all the subversions which our Earth has disclosed to them. When it relates the preparative and the progressive steps of that immense cataclysm, it reveals facts that the science of the moderns may not yet have universally adopted, but neither has it been able to contradict them by other facts: It assumes the existence of an interior fire, which, by raising the temperature of the seas and of the deep waters, must have produced, on the one hand, an enormous evaporation and impetuous rains, as if the flood-gates of the heavens had been opened; and, on the other, a resistless dilatation, which not only raised the waters from their abysses, broke up the fountains of the great deep, and swelled them into mighty waves reaching to the top of the highest mountains,[94] but caused immense stratifications of carbonate

---

92. *2 Peter* 3:5.
93. *Genesis* 7:11.
94. Water dilates by $1/23$ in passing from the temperature of melting ice to that of boiling water: A rise of 16 or 17 degrees Réaumur will augment its Volume, then, by $1/111$. Now we find, by an easy calculation, that the quantity of water necessary to submerge the Earth to the height of $1/1000$ of the radius of our globe is equal to $1/333$ of its entire Volume, or to $1/111$ of its third. If, then, we suppose the third of the terrestrial globe to be metallic (at the specific mean weight of $12\frac{1}{2}$), that the second third is solid (at the weight of $2\frac{1}{2}$), and that the third third is water; then, first, the mean specific weight of the whole globe will be equal to $5\frac{1}{2}$ (according to the conclusions of Maskeline and of Cavendish); and, second, a rise of 16 degrees Réaumur in the mean temperature of the mass of the waters would suffice, in the days of the deluge, to submerge the Earth to the depth of 6,368 meters – that is to say, to 1,546 metres above Mont Blanc. This was very nearly the hypothesis previously suggested by Sir Henry Englefield. (René Antoine Ferchault de Réaumur was an eighteenth-century French

of lime, under the double action of an enormous heat and of a pressure equivalent to 80,000 atmospheres.

When Scripture describes the state of our globe in the days which preceded the bringing of order out of chaos, it assumes the existence in it of an internal heat, and of submarine fires, while covering the whole of it with water in a liquid stated.[95]

When Scripture speaks of the creation of birds and fishes, it assigns them a common origin; and we know that modern naturalists have ascertained that between those two classes of animals there are deep-seated points of resemblance, which there is nothing to indicate to our eyes, but which are revealed in their anatomy, and even in the microscopic form of the globules of their blood.[96]

When Scripture lays an arrest on the Sun – that is to say, on the Earth's rotation – in the days of Joshua the son of Nun, it takes care, too, to make the Moon to stop also, in the same proportion with the Sun, and from the same cause; a precaution, as Chaubard has shown,[97] which never would have been thought of by an astronomy that was a stranger to the knowledge of our daily movement; since, after all, nothing more was required for the purposes of this miracle than the prolongation of the day.[98] When it speaks of the Lord's coming as a flash of lightning, in the twinkling of an eye, at the last day, it once more bears witness to the rotation of the Earth, and to the existence of the antipodes; for, at that solemn moment, it says it will be day for one part of men, and it will be night at the same hour for another part.[99]

When Scripture describes the past and future riches of the land of Canaan, to which a marvelous force of vegetation is promised for the last times, it speaks of it as rich, not only in springs, but in subterranean

---

physicist who devised a thermometric scale in which the boiling point of water is 80° above the zero of the scale, and the freezing point is 0°. – *Editor.*)

95. *Genesis* 1:2.
96. *Memoires du Dr. J. L. Prevost*, à Genève.
97. *Elements de Geologie* par Chaubard; one octavo volume, Paris. The author establishes there, by numerous arguments, the chronological coincidence of Joshua's miracle with the deluges of Ogyges and Deucalion. He there remarks that these two cataclysms relate to the same epoch, lasted the same time, were accompanied with the same catastrophes, and produced currents in the same direction, flowing from west to east.
98. *Joshua* 10:12.
99. *Luke* 17:31, 34; *Matthew* 24:3, etc.

waters[100] and seems to anticipate the perforations by which the moderns have learned to fertilize an arid country, by boring the soil, so as to cause water to gush up.

When Scripture speaks of the language of men, it gives it a primitive unity, which a first study of our innumerable idioms seems to contradict, but which comes to be confirmed by a more profound examination.

When Scripture describes the deliverance of Noah, it gives to the ark dimensions which we at first sight pronounce to be too small, which we would have made a hundred times greater had we been charged with that narrative, but which a study of the fact has made appear sufficient.

When Scripture speaks to us of the number of the stars, instead of supposing them to be a thousand (1,022), as in the catalogue of Hipparchus, or as in that of Ptolemy; while, in both hemispheres taken together, the most practiced eyes are incapable of discovering more than five thousand; while, before the invention of the telescope, a man could not see, even in the finest night, more than a thousand, the Scripture calls them innumerable; it compares them, as Herschel would do, to sand on the seashore; it tells us that God has sown them with his hand in the immensity of space like dust, and that, nevertheless, "he calls them all by their name." When it speaks of that immensity, hark with what a learned and divine wisdom it portrays it to you! How guarded it remains in its noble poesy, and how wise in its sublimity! "The heavens declare the glory of God, and the expanse shows his handiwork. There is no speech nor language; nevertheless, we hear their voice."

When Scripture speaks of the relations borne by the stars to this sublunary world, instead of supposing them animated as the ancients did – instead of ever attributing to them some influence on human affairs, as was fondly imagined for so long a period even by the professedly Christian populations of Italy and France, down to the days of the Reformation – they are composed of inert matter, it tells you, shining no doubt, but passively acted upon. The heavens, even the Heaven of heavens, advance with the order, consistency, and unity of

---

100. *Deuteronomy* 8:7: "A land of brooks of water, of fountains, and depths that spring out of valleys and hills" (תהמה). See also *Isaiah* 35:6; *Ezekiel* 31:4; *Psalm* 78:15-16.

an army which advances to battle. "Lift up your eyes on high, and behold who has created these things, that brings out their host by number; he calls them all by names; not one fails. Why say you, O Jacob, My way is hid from the Lord, and my judgment is passed over from my God?"[101] When it describes the heavens, it takes care to distinguish three; first, the heaven of the birds, of tempests, of the powers of the air and spiritual wickednesses; next, the heaven of the stars; and, finally, the third Heaven, the Heaven of heavens. But when it speaks of the God of all this, mark how beautiful its language! The sound of his thunder is in the rotundity of the air, it tells us;[102] but the heavens, and even the Heaven of heavens, cannot contain him.[103] In what place would you enclose him? and what likeness will you compare unto him? He has set his glory above the heavens, and he even humbles himself when he beholds the heavens! Were you to take the wings of the morning, and fly with the speed of light, where should you go from his face, or where should you flee from his presence?[104] But after having deemed that it has said enough of all those visible grandeurs, it tells us that "these are but the skirts of his ways; and how small is the portion that we know of them!" And, finally, when holy Scripture thinks enough has been said of all the grandeurs even of the Creator of these immensities, listen to it further: "He tells the number of the stars," it says to you, "and he heals the broken in heart, and binds up their wounds."[105] "Wonderful in counsel, and magnificent in the means he employs, he puts your tears into his bottle, a sparrow falls not to the ground without his permission; the very hairs of your head are numbered."[106] "The eternal God is your refuge, and underneath are the everlasting arms."[107] "O, my God, how manifold are your works, and you have magnified your Word above all your name!"[108]

And now amid all these proofs of greatness…

> Where shall wisdom be found? And where is the place of understanding? The depth says, It is not in me; and the sea answers, It is not with me!

101. *Isaiah* 40:26-27.
102. *Psalm* 77:18.
103. *1 Kings* 8:27.
104. *Isaiah* 40:18; *Psalms* 8:1; 113:6; 139:7.
105. *Psalm* 147:3-4
106. *Psalm* 56:8; *Isaiah* 28:29; *Matthew* 10:29-30.
107. *Deuteronomy* 33:26-27.
108. *Psalm* 133:2.

God alone understands the way thereof, and he knows the place thereof.... He who looks unto the ends of the Earth, and sees under the whole Heaven; to make the weight for the winds; and he weighs the waters by measure. When he made a decree for the rain and a way for the lightning of the thunder; then did he see wisdom, and sound it to the bottom; and unto man he said, "Behold the fear of the Lord, that is wisdom; and to depart from evil, is understanding!"[109]

Such, then, is the inspiration of the holy Scriptures; and it is thus we may see there celestial reflections emanating from the very places where people had thought they might detect blemishes. If, with a calm and reverential hand, you uplift the veil of obscurity with which it required, on your account, to shroud its face, you will discover there a majestic brightness; for it comes down, as Moses did, from the holy mountain, and brings to you in its hands the tables of the testimony! At the very place where you had dreaded an obscurity, you find a splendor; at the place where people had noted an objection, God has turned it into a testimony; at the place where there was a doubt, you find an assurance.

We conclude, then, that with regard to this seventh objection, the difficulties become proofs; and that, on this head, as well as on so many others, we cannot fail at every page to recognize in the whole of the Bible a communication from God.

But let us listen further to a last objection.

## Section VII
### The Declarations of Paul Himself

It is idle to dream of disputing the fact of a partial and intermittent inspiration in the Scriptures (we are sometimes told) since the Apostle Paul himself has clearly decided the question. Has he not carefully, in point of fact, distinguished what he pronounced by inspiration from what he advanced in his own name only, as a simple believer? And do we not find him, in his *First Epistle to the Corinthians*, express this distinction in the clearest manner, and three several times, on the occasion of the several questions that had been addressed to him on the subject of marriage?

---

109. *Job* 28.

First of all, at the twenty-fifth verse of chapter seven, when he says in so many terms, "Now, concerning virgins, I have no commandment of the Lord; yet I give advice as one that has obtained mercy of the Lord to be faithful."

Next, at the tenth verse, when he writes, "And unto the married I command (not I, but the Lord), Let not the wife depart from her husband, and let not the husband put away his wife."

And finally, at the twelfth verse, where he adds, "But to the rest speak I, not the Lord (I, and not the Lord), If any brother has a wife that believes not,... let him not put her away," etc.

One sees clearly, then, say the objectors, from these three sentences, that there are in the apostle's epistles, passages that are Paul's, and other passages that are God's; that is to say, inspired passages and others that are not so.

The reply is easy.

No sooner do we examine more narrowly into the passages on which the objection is laid than we perceive that they cannot be legitimately employed against the doctrine of a plenary inspiration. Far from imposing limits on the divinity of the apostolic sayings, these verses, on the contrary, hold a language which the most entire and sovereign inspiration alone could authorize. Paul could not speak thus without putting his epistles, as Peter has done – I was about to say, "on a level with the other Holy Scriptures" – he must say above them (inasmuch as he gives utterance there to a more recent and more obligatory expression of the Lord's desires). We proceed to judge how far this is the case. What is it that, in this seventh chapter, the apostle of Jesus Christ does? He treats three cases of conscience. As to one of these cases, God, says he, has neither commanded nor interdicted anything. "He that marries his virgin sins not. I am not, therefore, charged with any order; but, in my character as an apostle, it is only an advice that I have to give you on the Lord's part," and he then takes care to add, at the fortieth verse, "And I think, also, that I have the Spirit of God." The Lord, therefore, here desires to leave you free, says the apostle; he would not lay a snare for you; and if you do not think yourselves bound to follow the general advice that is given you, you violate no commandment – you sin not. Only, he who marries does well; he who marries not, does better.

As for the other case, on the contrary, beware; for there is a commandment of the Lord. The Lord has already pronounced his will

(*Matthew* 5:31-32; *Malachi* 2:14-15); and I have nothing new to declare unto you: The Old Testament and Jesus Christ have spoken. It is not I, therefore, the apostle of Jesus Christ, it is the Lord who has already made known his will to you: "To such Christians as are married, I command (not I, but the Lord), that the wife depart not from her husband, and that the husband put not away his wife" (10-11).

But, as for the third case, that is to say, as respects the brethren who may find themselves united to unbelieving wives, you have a commandment of the Lord's under the Old Testament; "I have repealed it; and *I think that I have the Spirit of God!* I abolish, therefore, the old order of things, and am commissioned to put a contrary order in its place. It is not the Lord (verse 12) that tells you to keep with you an unbelieving wife; it is I, Paul, the apostle of Jesus Christ, not of men, neither by man, but by God the Father, and by Jesus Christ, whom he raised from the dead."[110]

Here, then, we see it as clear as noonday, that the apostle, instead of appealing to the Lord's utterance of old, repeals it, in order to substitute an opposite order in its place; so that this passage, far from invalidating inspiration, fully confirms it; seeing that it would amount to the most outrageous blasphemy if the apostle had not felt that in holding this language he was the mouth of God, and had he ventured to say of his own proper authority, "It is not the Lord, it is I! I, I say, and not the Lord – if any brother has an unbelieving wife, let him not send her away!" The Lord had said the very contrary.[111]

We must acknowledge, then, that these verses of Paul, far from giving their sanction to the supposition of any human mixture in the writings of the New Testament, stand there to attest to us that in their epistles, and in the most familiar details of their epistles, the apostles were the mouth of God, and placed themselves, not only in the same line with Moses and the ancient prophets, but, further, above them; inasmuch as a second expression of God's will ought to take precedence over that which went before it; and as the New Testament ought to surpass the Old, if not in excellence, at least in authority.

We have heard some persons still further oppose to us, as an admission of the intermittence and imperfection of his inspiration, those

---

110. *Galatians* 1:1.
111. *Deuteronomy* 7:3; *1 Kings* 11:2; *Ezra* 10:2-3, 11, 19.

words of Paul in which, after having told the Corinthians[112] of his having been caught up into the third Heaven, he adds, "Whether in the body or out of the body, I cannot tell: God knows." "Can it be supposed," it has been said, "that the Holy Spirit knew not how this miracle was performed? Necessarily, therefore, we must refer such a verse to Paul, not to God."

We reply, that though the Holy Spirit was not ignorant of it, Paul was; and that the Holy Spirit desired that Paul himself should tell us of his ignorance. Can it be forgotten that God has never ceased, in revealing himself to us in the Scriptures, to employ the personality of the sacred writers, and that it is under this form that he has desired almost constantly to instruct his church? When David, "speaking by the Spirit,"[113] exclaims in the *Psalms* "that he acknowledges his transgressions, and that his sin is ever before him, and that he was shapen in iniquity," it is not the Holy Spirit, doubtless, that acknowledges his own transgressions, and that has his own sin before his eyes; but it is the Holy Spirit that put, for our sakes, those expressions of repentance in the heart and on the lips of his humbled prophet. It was in an analogous sense, then, that he could make Paul say, "Whether in the body, I cannot tell: God knows."

We are not yet done, however, with these objections. There still remain three more, which we have called evasions; because, instead of resting, like the former, on some certain argument, or facts, they are rather systems by which people imagine they can withdraw a part of the Scriptures from the action of the divine inspiration. It remains for us, therefore, to examine these.

---

112. *2 Corinthians* 12:2-3.
113. *Mark* 12:36; *Acts* 4:25.

Chapter 5

# Examination of Evasions

SEVERAL systems of exceptions, we have said, have been proposed by some. There are persons who, while they fully admit that the thoughts found in Scripture have been given by God, would maintain, nevertheless, that its style and expressions are purely human; others have excluded the inspiration of the historical books; others, in fine, would make an exception of certain details at least, which to them have appeared too trite and too remote from edification to admit of our attributing them to the Spirit of God.

*Section I*
*Might Not Inspiration Pertain to the Thoughts Only,*
*Without Extending to the Words?*

"The prophets and the apostles," some say, "were, no doubt, inspired when they wrote their sacred books, in so far as respected their thoughts; but we must believe, that, beyond this, they were left to themselves as respects their language; so that in this written revelation the ideas are God's and the expressions those of a man. The task of the sacred writers resembles, in some sort, that of a man before whose eyes there have been successively passed some very highly colored pictures, while he has been charged to describe them merely in so far as they have passed before his eyes. It is thus that the Divine Spirit is considered to have presented the holy truths they announce to the view of the evangelists and the prophets, leaving them no more to do than simply to express them; and this mode of conceiving of what they did," it is added, "at once accounts for the striking differences of style which their writings exhibit."

We reply:

That this system is directly contrary to Scripture testimony. The Bible declares itself to be written "not with the words which man's

## GOD-BREATHED: THE DIVINE INSPIRATION OF THE BIBLE

wisdom teaches but which the Holy Spirit teaches."[1] It calls itself "the Word of God," "the words of God,"[2] "the voice of God," "the oracles of God,"[3] "the lively oracles of God,"[4] "the holy letters of God,"[5] "the scripture of God." A *scripture,* or writing, is made up of letters and words, and not of invisible thoughts only; but, we are told,[6] "all Scripture is given by inspiration of God." What is *written*, therefore, is inspired of God (θεόπνευστος); and that which is inspired of God is *all Scripture* – it is all that is written (πᾶσα γραφὴ).

While this system [merely of inspired ideas] is contradictory to the Bible, it is also most irrational. The ideas of our fellow-men embody themselves in words; and it is there only that you can seize them. Souls are revealed to us only in the flesh. You do not learn their character; you know nothing of their desires or their experiences; you do not even suspect their existence; and between you and them there are no ties until they have become clothed with bodies and have received organs, so that they can manifest themselves to you. My most intimate friend is known to me only by the language of his voice and his gestures. If he had no power of employing these, in vain might he remain for twenty years at my side: He would be to me as if he were not.

More than this. There exists, in so far as we are concerned, an inevitable dependence between souls and their organs, between their ideas and words. Not only do we come to know the existence of the former only by the language of the latter, but (even after they have spoken to us) we can but guess only at their true character, as long as we have not the assurance that the organ has been the faithful interpreter of the mind, that the word has truly reflected the idea, and the proposition the thought. And if we have some room to apprehend that language has not been the pliant and adequate servant of the will, we possess no certainty that we have not been mistaken. Though we might know that God himself had placed in the soul of a writer the purest thoughts of Heaven, still there would always be required, in order to our having through these words a certain revelation of them, that there should be given us

---

1. *1 Corinthians* 2:13.
2. Throughout.
3. *Romans* 3:2.
4. *Acts* 7:38.
5. *2 Timothy* 3:15.
6. *2 Timothy* 3:16.

the assurance that the language is exact, that the reflections are faithful, and that they reproduce to us without alteration the objects deposited in the secret chambers of that soul.

Language, then, is the wondrous mirror which reflects to us the depths of the soul.

Were you a son weeping for the loss of a mother, and were God, for your consolation, to desire that you should see again, for some moments, in a mirror, the ever-to-be-venerated features of that mother, would it be enough that she herself were made to come down behind you and occupy the place where the reflected light would come from the object to your eyes in most abundance? Doubtless not, it would further be necessary that the mirror should be without any twist, furrow, or blemish. Were it unequal and faithless, of what use would it be to you? You would have near you, it is true, the smiling features of your own mother; her inimitable look would bear toward you the ardent expression of her maternal good wishes and her august benediction; but all this would be in vain; you would have no better than a stranger before your eyes, one perhaps of a hideous expression – a deformed creature with features positively revolting! O, my good mother, it is, then, no longer you! you would exclaim. Thus would it also be for you with the thoughts of God, if left to receive them disfigured by the errors of the human language that reflected them to us. It is no longer you, O thought of my God! we should have to say to it. It is necessary then for our security that we should have the divine guarantee of the fidelity of the mirror as well as for the faithfulness of the objects.

These reflections will suffice, no doubt, to enable us to comprehend how irrational it is to think of receiving with exactness and certainty the thoughts of another through the medium of inexact and uncertain expressions. Can you lay hold of these thoughts otherwise than by words? And without God's words, how can you be sure of possessing his thoughts?

This theory of a divine revelation, in which you would have the inspiration of the thoughts without the inspiration of the language, is so inevitably irrational that it cannot be sincere, and proves false even to those who propose it; for, without their suspecting it, it makes them come much further down in their arguments than their first position seems at a first glance to indicate. Listen to them. Though the words are those of man, say they, the thoughts are those of God. And how will they prove this to you? Alas! once more, by attributing to this Scripture from God, contradictions, mistakes, proofs of ignorance! Is it then the words alone that they attack? Are not these alleged errors much more in the ideas than in the words? So true it is that we cannot separate the one from the other, and that a revelation of God's thoughts ever demands a revelation of God's words also.

This theory is not only anti-Biblical, irrational, and mischievous; further, it is taken up arbitrarily, and amounts at best to a gratuitous hypothesis. Besides, it is very useless; for it resolves no difficulty. You find it difficult, say you, to conceive how the Holy Spirit could have given the words in Holy Scripture; but can you tell us any better how he gave the thoughts? Will it be more easy for you, for example, to explain how God suggested to Moses the knowledge of the different acts of the creation, or to John that of all the scenes of the last day, than to conceive how he made them write the narrative of these things in the language of the Hebrews, or in that of the Greeks?

But we have much more to say than this. That which in this theory ought above all to strike every attentive mind, is its extreme inconsistency, seeing that those even who hold it most strenuously are forced withal to admit that, in its greatest part, the Scripture of necessity had to be inspired to the men of God even its words.

Suppose that the Holy Spirit were to call on you to go down this morning to the public street, there to proclaim, in Russian or in Tamil, "the wonderful works of God;" what would become of you, were he to be content with inspiring you with ideas, without giving you words? You might have the third Heaven before your eyes, and in your heart the transports of archangels; still you would have to remain as if dumb and stupid before the persons composing this multitude. In order to your inspiration being of any use to you, it would be necessary that the periods, the phrases, and even the smallest words of your discourse should be entirely given to you. What do I say? People might very well dispense with your own thoughts, provided you could make them hear, without even understanding them, the thoughts of God in the words of God. Well, then, let us carry this supposition into Jerusalem, and into the persons of the apostles. When the fishermen of Capernaum and Bethsaida met in their upper chamber on the day of Pentecost, received the command to come down and to go forth and publish before the people that had assembled from every region under Heaven the wonderful works of God in Latin, Parthian, Elamite, Chaldean, Coptic, and Arabic, would not the giving of the words be necessary? What could they have done on that occasion without the words? Why, nothing; while, with their words, they could convert the world!

When, afterward, in the church of Corinth, the faithful who had received miraculous powers spoke in the midst of the congregations in strange tongues, and found it necessary that some other, to whom the gift of interpretation had been given, should translate after them the unknown words which they had uttered in the ears of their brethren, was it not equally necessary that the words and all the phrases should be entirely dictated to them?[7] When all the prophets, after having written their sacred pages, set themselves to meditate upon them with so much respect and care as they would have done to the oracles of a strange prophet; when they meditated upon them night and day, searching what (as Peter tells us[8]) the Spirit of Christ which was in them did signify when it testified beforehand the sufferings of Christ, and the glory that should follow – was it not, then, also necessary that all the words should have been given them? When Moses gives an account of the creation of the world, and of the untangling of chaos; when Solomon describes the Eternal Wisdom; when David recites, a thousand years beforehand, the prayers of the Son of God on the cross; when Daniel relates in detail, and without very well understanding them himself, the remote destinies of the world and of the church; and when, in fine, John continues, in his own prophecies, the revelations of the prophet Daniel, was it not necessary that the smallest words should be given to them? And do not all interpreters, in reading them, acknowledge how far we might be led away from the true meaning by the smallest word being put in the place of some other word, by the tense of the verb being ill-chosen, by the imprudent placing of a particle?

From this, therefore, we must conclude, since so considerable a part of the Scriptures is necessarily inspired, even in its words, that the system of an inspiration of the thoughts without an inspiration of the language is inconsistent in the highest degree. There are not two kinds of the Word of God in the Holy Scriptures; there are not two sorts of God's oracles. If it was "as moved by the Holy Spirit that holy men

---

7. 1 *Corinthians* 14.
8. 1 *Peter* 1:10-11.

spoke," then all the sacred letters are divinely inspired; and that which is divinely inspired in the sacred letters is *all Scripture.*

But these last reflections are about to conduct us to something at once more simple and more important. Here let the utmost caution be observed, for the question has been misrepresented. It has been said that the sacred Scriptures were inspired by God; and people have asked themselves up to what point this was necessarily to be the case. The matter for inquiry, however, did not lie there.

We have said, that the question relates to the book, and not to the writers. You believe that God gave them the thoughts always, and not always the words; but the Scripture tells us, on the contrary, that God has given them always the words, and not always the thoughts. As for their thoughts, while they were in the act of writing, God might inspire them with ideas more or less lively, more or less pure, more or less elevated: That interests my charity alone, but has no bearing on my faith. The Scripture – the Scripture which they have transmitted to me, perhaps without themselves seizing its meaning, at least without ever entirely comprehending it – this is what concerns me.

Paul might have been mistaken in his thoughts, when, on appearing before the council of the priests, and not recognizing God's high-priest, he ventured to say to him, "God shall strike you, you whited wall!" This is of little consequence, however, provided I know that when he writes the Word of God, "it is Jesus Christ that speaks in him!"[9]

Peter might have been mistaken in his thoughts when, refusing to believe that God could send him among the heathen, he did not perceive and acknowledge that "in every nation, they who turn to God are accepted of him." He might have been still more grievously mistaken when, at Antioch, he compelled Paul to withstand him to the face, because he was to be blamed, and because he walked not uprightly according to the truth of the Gospel.[10] But how does this concern me, after all, I repeat, at least as respects my faith? For the question is not, How I can know at what moments, or in what measure, Paul, John, Mark, James, or Peter were inspired in their thoughts, or sanctified in their conduct; what, above all, interests me, is to know that all the sacred pages were divinely inspired; that their written words were the words of

---

9. *2 Corinthians* 13:3.
10. *Galatians* 2:11–14.

God, and that, in giving these to us, they spoke, not in the words which man's wisdom teaches, but which the Holy Spirit teaches,[11] (οὐκ ἐν διδακτοῖς ἀνθρωπίνης σοφίας λόγοις); that then it is not they that speak, but the Holy Spirit;[12] in a word, that "God has spoken by the mouth of his prophets since the world began"[13]

The sacred writers were sometimes inspired; but the Holy Scriptures were so always. Accordingly, the times, the measures, the degrees, the alternations of the inspiration of the men of God are not for us an object of faith; but that which is an object of faith is that the Scripture is divinely inspired, and that that which is divinely inspired is the whole Scripture. "Not one jot or tittle of it shall pass away."

There is doubtless an inspiration of thoughts, as there is an inspiration of words; but the first makes the Christian, while it is the second that makes the prophet.

A true Christian is inspired in his thoughts: The Spirit of God reveals to him the deep things of God;[14] it is not flesh and blood that have made him know the counsels of God and the glories of Jesus Christ, it is God the Father;[15] for the Holy Spirit leads him into all truth;[16] and he has been incapable of truly owning in his soul Jesus as Lord (the Lord of lords) but by the Holy Spirit.[17] Every true believer, then, is more or less inspired by God in his thoughts; but he is not so in his words. He is a Christian, but not a prophet. The holiest discourses of Cyprian, Augustine, Bernard, Luther, Calvin, Beza, and Leighton are only the words of men on the truths of God – venerable words, no doubt, precious and powerful words, and worthy of our utmost attention, because of the wisdom that has been given to them, and of the abundant expression which we find in them of the thought of God; still these, after all, are but the words of men – they form but a sermon. It is quite otherwise in the case of the prophet. The latter may have, and he may not have, the thought of God in his thought; but that which he will always have, as long as he shall speak as a prophet, is "the word of God in his mouth." The Spirit of God will speak by him, and the word of God will be on

11. *1 Corinthians* 2:13.
12. *Mark* 13:11.
13. *Acts* 3:21.
14. *1 Corinthians* 2:10.
15. *Matthew* 16:17.
16. *John* 16:13.
17. *1 Corinthians* 12:3.

his tongue.[18] He will be the mouth of God, a mouth intelligent or unintelligent, voluntary or involuntary – that is of little consequence, provided that God's oracles flow from him, and that I receive the thought of my God in the words of my God.

In a word, one may be a Christian without having on his lips the words of God, and one may be a prophet without having on his heart or in his understanding the thoughts of God; but one cannot be a Christian without having in his heart the thoughts of God, and one cannot be a prophet without having on his lips the words of God.

In the language of the Bible (this we shall before long establish), a prophet is a person in whose mouth God puts, for a time, the words that he wishes to have uttered upon Earth. Such a person prophesied only by intervals, "according as the Spirit gave him utterance."[19] One might not be a prophet, like King Saul, more than twice in his life; and, as his soldiers, more than once.[20] One might then pronounce the words of God while understanding them, or without understanding them, often even without having been previously apprised, and sometimes even without having wished it.

When Daniel had traced his last pages, he did not understand, he himself tells us, what the Spirit had made him write.[21] When Caiaphas uttered prophetic words, "he spoke not of himself," he had the will, but he had neither the consciousness nor the comprehension of what God caused him to pronounce.[22] When Balaam went up three times to the top of a hill to curse Israel, and when, three times, words of benediction proceeded from his lips, as it were in spite of himself, because "the Lord had met him and put a word into his mouth,"[23] he had the consciousness of what he did, but neither fully comprehended nor fully willed it. When Saul's armed followers went in search of David to Ramah, and when the Spirit of the Lord was upon them, so that they also prophesied; and when Saul, three successive times, sent others of them, who also three successive times prophesied; and when the profane Saul went himself likewise to the great well in Sechu, and when God (to illustrate

---

18. *2 Samuel* 23:2.
19. *Acts* 2:4.
20. *1 Samuel* 19:20-21.
21. *Daniel* 12:8-9.
22. *John* 11:51.
23. *Numbers* 23:16.

his power, and to manifest more clearly to us what it is to be a prophet and what his word is) had made his Spirit to come on that unbelieving man also; when he went on and prophesied; when the word of the Lord was in that ordinarily profane mouth, and he prophesied before Samuel all that day and all that night, "what was it that happened to the son of Kish? Was Saul also among the prophets?"[24] Yes, and Saul had the consciousness of his condition, and of the part he acted as a prophet; but of this he had neither the full will, nor the anticipation, nor probably the full comprehension. When the old prophet had seated himself amicably at table with the man of God, whom he had seduced from his road by an unbelieving and carnal kindness, and when, all of a sudden, under an impulse from on high, menacing words proceeded in a loud voice from his mouth against his imprudent and guilty guest, he prophesied with the consciousness of what he did, but he prophesied without having the wish to do so. What do I say? Did not God make his voice be heard in the empty air, in the presence of Moses and of all the people, on Mount Sinai? Did he not cause it to be heard by the couch of a child in the tabernacle at Shiloh? To the ears of the three apostles and of the two saints who had risen again from Hades on Mount Tabor? To John the Baptist, and to all the people, on the banks of the Jordan?

Be it well understood, then, it is the holy letters (τὰ ἱερὰ γράμματα, 2 Timothy 3:15); it is *all that is written,* that is to say, the *phrases* and the *words,* that are divinely inspired, that are θεόπνευστοι. The question, then, is about the words, and not about the men who have written. As to the latter, that concerns you little. The Spirit was able more or less to associate their individuality, their conscience, their recollections, their affections, with what he caused them to write, and you are nowise obliged to know how far this was the case; but that which it is necessary, proper, and advantageous for you to know is (as Peter has said), "that no written prophecy came by the will of man, but that it was as moved by the Holy Spirit, holy men of God spoke;" and just as at Belshazzar's feast people troubled themselves little about knowing what was passing in the fingers of that terrible hand which came forth from the wall over against the candlestick, while, on the contrary, all the thoughts of the guests were turned to the words that were traced on the plaster of the wall, *Mene, mene, tekel, upharsin,* because they knew well that these words were from

---

24. *1 Samuel* 19:23-24.

God; so likewise it concerns you little, in point of faith, to penetrate into what passed in the thoughts of Mark, the thoughts of John, the thoughts of Luke, the thoughts of Matthew, during the time that they were writing the roll of the *Gospels*. It is necessary and advantageous for you rather to direct your entire attention toward the words that they have written, because you know that these words are from God. Be the prophet holy like Moses, wise like Daniel, an enemy of God like Caiaphas, ignorant of the language in which he speaks like the prophets at Corinth, impure like Balaam – what do I say? – insensible, like the hand that wrote on the wall in the palace at Babylon; without form, without body, without soul like the empty air in which was heard the voice of God (on Sinai, on the banks of Jordan, on Mount Tabor…), it is of little consequence, once more (unless it be where their personality itself should be found so interested as to make an essential part of their revelation). Your thoughts, O my God, your thoughts and your words, these are what concern me!

## Section II
### Should We Except from Inspiration the Historical Books?

"One will admit," we are told, "that the inspiration of the Scriptures might have been extended to the choice of expressions, wherever this miraculous operation was necessary: in the laying down of doctrines, for example, in announcing the history of a past more ancient than the birth of the mountains, or in unveiling a future which God only can know. But would you proceed to maintain that men who lived at the time of the events they relate, had any need of the Holy Spirit in order to tell us facts of which they themselves were either agents or witnesses, or which they had heard related by others; the humble marriage of Ruth in the small town of Bethlehem, for example, or the emotions felt by Esther in the palace of Shusan, or the nomenclatures of the kings of Israel and Judah, their reigns, their lives, their deaths, their genealogies? Luke, who, from Troas, accompanied the apostle to Jerusalem, to Cesarea, to the isle of Malta, and as far as Rome, had he not enough of recollections of what had passed in order to tell us how Paul had been laid hold of under the porches of the temple; how his nephew revealed to him, in the castle, the conspiracy of the forty Jews; how the centurion took the young man to the chief captain, and how the chief captain took him by the hand, and went with him aside privately, and asked of him all that he knew? Did he then absolutely require for facts so simple and so well-known, a continual intervention of power from on high?" Some do not think so, and maintain, on the contrary, that it is neither necessary nor rational to believe that all the historical chapters of the two Testaments are divinely inspired.

To such objections our first answer will always be very simple. "All Scripture," we say, "is divinely inspired." "You have known the holy letters," O Timothy. Well then, "all the holy letters, all the Scriptures are given by the breath of God." We have not heard the Holy Spirit make an exception anywhere to these declarations; accordingly, neither in man, nor in angel, do we acknowledge any right to hazard any.

But we will say more. Were it allowable to place one book of God before another – if we must distinguish in the firmament of the Scriptures the more glorious constellations and stars of the first magnitude, we should certainly give the preference to the historical books. In fact:

It is to the historical books that the most striking and most respectful testimonies are rendered by the prophets in the Old Testament and by the apostles in the New. What is there more holy in the Old than the Pentateuch? What is there greater in the New than the four *Gospels*? Is it not solely of the historical books of the Bible that it is written: "The law of the Lord is perfect; his testimonies are wonderful; they are sure; they make wise the simple; they are pure; they are more to be desired than gold; the words of the Lord are pure words; they are like silver seven times refined. Blessed is the man who meditates on his law day and night."[25]

Besides, mark with what respect our Lord himself quotes them, and how in doing so he takes a pleasure in pointing to the smallest details in the divine decrees, and sometimes to the use of a single word.

The histories in the Bible have not been given us solely for the transmission to future ages of the memorials of past events: They are presented to the church of all ages for the purpose of making her know by facts the character of her God; they are there as a mirror of providence and grace; they are destined to reveal to us God's thoughts, God's designs, the invisible things of God, his Heaven, his glory, his angels, and

---

25. *Psalm* 19:7-10; 1:1-2.

those mysteries which the angels desire to look into.[26] For all this the most entire inspiration is requisite.

Remark further, that the historical Scriptures are given to us for the purpose of revealing to us the deep things of man. It has been said of the Word of God "that it pierces like a sword, to the division of the soul and spirit; that all is naked and open to it, and that it is a discerner of the thoughts and intents of the heart." This holds true of the written Word as well as of the personal Word of God, for the one is the language of the other; but it is especially true of the historical word. Do you not see that that word, in its narratives, is a two-edged sword, and that it tries men's consciences? And in like manner, as it describes to you what took place on our globe in the days of chaos, when the Spirit of God moved on the face of the abyss, it equally tells you of what takes place in the abyss of the human heart, the mysteries of the invisible world, the secret motives, the hidden faults, and many a thought which, but for it, would only have been known in the great day when the Lord will bring to light things hid in darkness, and will make manifest the purposes of men's hearts. Is it thus, then, that men write history?

The historical Scriptures were required on another account to have the most entire inspiration, namely, in order that they might relate to us without any error the mysterious interventions of the angels in this world's affairs, in those of the church, and in those of Heaven. Is there a subject more delicate, more novel, more difficult? Do not those ardent and pure, humble and sublime creatures, whose existence we know of only from the Bible, differ as much from man as the heavens differ from the Earth? Was anything similar to the angels ever conceived by the imaginations of the peoples, by their poets, or by their sages? No, they never even show the slightest approach to it. One will perceive, then, how impossible it was, without a constant operation on the part of God, that the Biblical narratives, in treating of such a subject, should not have constantly borne the all-too-human impression of our narrow conceptions; and that the sacred writers should not have often let slip from their pen imprudent touches, investing the angels by turns with attributes too divine, or affections too human. All nations have taken a fancy for figuring to themselves invisible beings, as the inhabitants of the celestial regions, whom they have tricked out with all those marks

---

26. *1 Peter* 1:12.

of superiority that charm the heart of man. But how have all their conceptions been creeping, childish, and vulgar, compared with what the angels are! How have all those creations of our fancy been comparatively earthly, passionate, selfish, impure, and often odious! See the gods, the demigods, and the whole Olympus of the ancients; see the fairies, the genii, and the sylphs of the moderns; see, even further, the angels of Scripture speedily disfigured in the books of man, in the *Apocrypha of Enoch,* for example, in several of the fathers, in the legends of Rome, and even in the more recent creations of several of the French poets. Winged passions, devout puerilities, sacrilegious idols, immortal egotisms, celestial wickednesses, deified impurities! But study the angels of Scripture; *there* not only is everything great, holy, and worthy of God; not only is that character at once ardent and sublime, compassionate and majestic, constantly recalled to us by their names, their attributes, their employments, their dwellings, their hymns, their contemplations of the depths of redemption, and the ineffable joys of their love; but that which above all ought to strike us is the perfect harmony of all this as a whole; it is that all these features accord together; it is that all these attributes correspond to each other, and maintain themselves in the justest proportions.

In a word, this whole doctrine, sustained from one end to the other of the Scriptures, throughout a course of fifteen hundred years, presents to us a unity which of itself alone will be found to attest the inimitable reality of its object, but which bears the most striking testimony to their entire inspiration.

While all the mythologies speak to us of the inhabitants of the Moon and of the planets, the Bible says not a word of them: It says nothing to us about the second heaven; but it pictures to us, with no less fulness than precision, the sublime inhabitants of the third Heaven, or of the Heaven of heavens. This subject recurs constantly there, and under the most varied forms. Descriptions of the angels are often found in the Bible, descriptions unembarrassed, full of details, independent of each other. They are exhibited to us in all situations in Heaven and on Earth, before God and with men, ministers employed in executing acts of mercy and sometimes also acts of vengeance, bathed in the radiance of the divine glory, standing before God and worshiping him night and day; but also engaged in ministering to the humblest believers, helping them in their distresses, in their travels, in their imprisonments, on their deathbeds; and finally coming, at the last day, on the clouds of Heaven with the Son of man, to remove all the wicked from his kingdom and to gather in his elect from the four winds.

And what were the historians of the angels? Let us not forget this: Some were shepherds; others were kings, or soldiers, or priests, or fishermen, or tax-gatherers; some writing in the days of Hercules, of Jason and the Argonauts, three hundred years before the war of Troy; others in the age of Seneca, of Tacitus, and of Juvenal. And yet we see that the relater has the same beings throughout before his eyes. Unlike men, they are always like themselves. We are defiled, they are perfect; we are selfish, they glow with love; we are haughty, they are gentle and meek. We are vain and proud in a body which will be gnawed by the worms, they are humble in their glory and immortality. We would sometimes desire to worship them; "See you do it not," they say to us, "I am but your fellow-servant!"[27] We are disquieted with lusts, they are fervent in spirit; they neither marry nor are given in marriage, for they cannot die.[28] We are hard-hearted, they are compassionate; we leave the poor Lazarus to groan as he lies famished at our gate and our dogs lick his sores, but they come to take him when he is dead, and convey him away to Abraham's bosom;[29] they utter shouts of joy at the conversion of a sinner; and yet, Jesus said, "the angel of one of these little ones continually beholds in the heavens the face of my Father."[30] Such is the angel of the whole of the Scriptures.

Now, let each ask himself: How, without a constant inspiration of all the historical books, it could have happened, that over a course of so many ages not one of the authors who had occasion to bring such beings before us has let slip, with regard to them, either words fraught with excessive respect, after the manner of the liturgies of Rome, or other words bearing too much of the impress of our humanity, after the manner of many of the fathers? And how not a single discordant trait falling from their pen spoils the perfect harmony of that inimitable character, or derogates from the ever amiable dignity of that sublime creation?

Once more, this unity, this purity, this perfection, comes not from

---

27. *Revelation* 22:9.
28. *Luke* 20:36.
29. *Luke* 16:22.
30. *Matthew* 18:10.

man: It is from God! And we ought to own that here, as well as elsewhere, it was necessary that the Holy Spirit should himself superintend all that is written by his historians, and make himself the guarantee of their slightest expressions.

But this is not all. See further how, even without the knowledge of the authors, the histories in the Bible are full of the future. Even in relating the events of the past, "they are types," says Paul, "for us upon whom the ends of the world are come."[31] They relate, it is true, national scenes or domestic scenes; but while they relate, Jesus Christ is incessantly and prophetically portrayed under all his aspects, and in all his characters. See the history of Adam, of Noah, of Abraham, of Isaac, of Joseph, of Moses, of the sacrificial lamb, of the deliverance from Egypt, of the pillar of fire, of the manna, of the rock which was Christ (1 *Corinthians* 10:4), of the goat Azazel, of all the sacrifices, of Joshua, of David, of Solomon, of Jonah, of Zorobabel. One would need to write a commentary on the whole history in order to do justice to this truth. Read over, in order that you may appreciate it, the pages of Paul on Agar, on Sarah, on Aaron, on Melchizedec.

If, then, one would reflect upon this, he would soon acknowledge with wonder the constant forth-putting of the power of inspiration in all parts of these Scriptures; and one would feel assured, that if there be pages in the Bible that have need to be inspired in every line and in every word, these are the historical books: They preach, they reveal, they set forth doctrine, they legislate, they prophesy. Compare them not, therefore, with other histories: They have quite another scope.

They necessarily possessed this full inspiration in order to recite without any error facts inaccessible to man's knowledge, the creation of the universe, the untangling of chaos, the birth of light, the rise of the mountains, the intervention of angels, God's secret counsels, the thoughts of man's heart and his secret faults; but they specially needed to have it in order that they might prefigure Christ by a thousand types unperceived by the writer himself, and thus exhibit even in their narratives of the past the character of the Messiah, his sufferings, his death, and the glories that were to follow. It was necessary for them, in order that they might speak in a suitable manner of those events even that were known to them, to pass some over in silence, to relate others, to characterize

---

31. *1 Corinthians* 10:6, 11.

them, to judge them, and thus to show in them the thought of God; but it was above all necessary for enabling them to describe in the just measure prescribed by that thought of God, and by the needs of the future church, the scenes, whether national or domestic, which were advantageous to carry along with them the types of the work of redemption, to prefigure the last times, and to take in a vast sweep of thousands of years posterior to them. They required it for the purpose of determining the measure of what they might confide to their readers, and what they should withhold, for the discreet use of their expressions, and for that admirable restraint upon themselves which they have uniformly preserved.

We could wish we had time to speak here of their dramatic power (if such an expression may be permitted), that divine and indefinable charm, that mysterious and ever-recurring attraction, which we find attached to all their narratives, which captivates man's soul under all climates, which makes us find in them, throughout all our lives, as in the scenes of nature, an ever fresh charm; and after being delighted and moved by these incomparable narratives in our early childhood, affects our tender feelings even in hoary age. Certainly, there must needs be something superhuman in the very humanity of these forms, so familiar and so simple. Men are incapable of telling a story thus. Who shall tell us the secret of this attractiveness? In what does it consist? We should find it not easy to say, perhaps: It seems to lie in an ineffable mixture of simplicity and depth, of the natural and the unlooked for, of local coloring and spirituality; it further lies in this, that the narratives are marked by rapidity and simplicity, that they are at once minute in detail and concise; it lies, finally, in the harmony and the truth of the sentiments; it presents man, it presents nature, in their inmost reality. In a word, you cannot fail to feel (even without being able to account for it) that he who speaks in this book has immediately before him all the most hidden strings of man's heart so as to be able to touch them at will, with a hand light or powerful, in the precise measure that his Spirit has proposed to itself. Read over the scenes in which Ruth and Boaz appear on the plains of Bethlehem, those where Abraham and Isaac meet on mount Moriah, those of David and Jonathan, those of Elijah and Elisha, those of Naaman the Syrian, of the widow of Zarephath, or of the Shunamite, and, above all, those of the life and death of the Son of man; and, after that, search everywhere else in the books of men, and see if

# EXAMINATION OF EVASIONS

you can find anything similar. Read, if you like, the four *Vedas*, and the voluminous collection of Pauthier, the sacred books of the East, Confucius, Manon, Mohammed;[32] and see if there are to be met with there eight lines that can be compared to these incomparable narratives of Scripture. But that we dreaded enlarging too far, we could have wished to make some comparisons here, and to take in turns the relations of the same facts in the Old Testament and in the Koran, in the New Testament and in the spurious Gospels, in the patriarchal scenes of *Genesis*, and in what has been made of them by men every time they have related them. Read over, for instance, in Moses, the life of Joseph, his infancy, his misfortunes, his temptations, and as far as that inimitable scene in which Jacob's eleven sons appear before their brother; as far as that "God be gracious unto you, my son!" (43:29), and as far as "I am Joseph (אֲנִי יוֹסֵף)!" which at no time of life can one peruse without fresh emotion; and, then, go and take up that history again in Mohammed; go read his twelfth chapter, titled *Joseph,* written at Mecca in one hundred eleven verses, and beginning with these words: "We have made this book come down from Heaven in the Arabic tongue, in order that people may understand it, and we proceed to relate the most beautiful story that we have revealed to you in this Koran."

"Let, then," says the celebrated Duplessis Mornay,[33]

> the hardest hearts, and the most squeamish palates in the world, come and read over these histories of our Bible;... they will feel their whole bodies thrill, their hearts move; and a tenderness of affection come over them in a moment, more than had all the orators of Greece and Rome preached to them the same matters for whole days. Let them go and read the same histories in Flavius Josephus, to whom the emperor Titus ordered a statue to be erected on account of the elegance of his history: He will leave them colder and less moved than he found them. What, then, if this Scripture has in its humility more elevation, in its simplicity more depth, in its absence of all effort more charms, in its grossness more vigor and point, than we know to find any where else of these qualities?

---

32. *Les Livres sacrés de L'Orient, comprenant le Chouking, ou Livre par excellence le Sse Chou, ou les Quatre livres moraux de Confucius et de ses disciples; les Lois de Manon, premier legislateur de l'Inde; le Koran de Mahomet,* par Pauthier, Paris, 1840.

33. *De la Vérité de la Religion Chrètienne,* pages 613-614.

Oh no! we must say of the historical Scriptures, even in this respect, that never have men related events as they have done, neither before nor after.

People have not perhaps sufficiently remarked, they have not sufficiently admired, their divine brevity. If you would, in this respect, appreciate the Scriptures, compare them with the biographies that men have written, or with the systems of doctrine which they have given, when left to do so. See, for example, the modern church of the Jews, and see that of the Latins. While the former has joined to the Scripture its two Talmuds, by attributing to them the same authority, one of which (that of Jerusalem) forms a large folio volume; and the other (that of Babylon), which is most followed, and which must be studied by all its doctors, is a work of twelve folio volumes;[34] and while the Roman Church in its Council of Trent declares "that it receives, with the same affection and reverence as the Holy Scripture, its traditions respecting faith and morals;" that is to say, the vast repertory of its synodal acts, of its decretals, of its bulls, of its canons, and of the writings of the holy fathers;[35] behold what the Spirit has done in the Bible, and there admire the celestial prudence of its inimitable brevity.

Who among us could have been, for three years and a half, the constant witness, the passionately attached friend, of a man like Jesus Christ, and could have been able to write in sixteen or seventeen short chapters, or in eight hundred lines, the history of the whole of that life – of his birth, of his ministry, of his miracles, of his preachings, of his sufferings, of his death, of his resurrection, and of his ascension into the heavens? Who among us would have found it possible to avoid saying a word of the first thirty years of such a life? Who among us could have related so many acts of kindness without an exclamation, so many miracles without reflections on them; so many sublime thoughts without any emphasis; so many sufferings without complaint; so many acts of injustice without bitterness; so many sinless infirmities in their Master, and so many sinful infirmities in his disciples, without any suppression; so much ingratitude in their cowardly abandonment of him; so

---

34. La dernière edition d'Amsterdam. Maimonides has made a learned extract from it in his *Yad Hachazakah*. See Prideau, *Histoire des Juifs,* Amsterdam, Volume 2, page 130.

35. Concile de Trent, session 4, first and second decrees, published April 28, 1546. Bellarmin, *De Verbo Dei,* Book 4, chapters 3, 5, 6. Coton, Book 2, chapters 24, 34, 35. Baile, *Traité,* 1, *du Perron contre Tilenus.*

many instances of resistance, so much ignorance, so much hardness of heart, without the slightest excuse or comment? Is it thus that man relates a history? Who among us, further, could have known how to distinguish what was necessary to be said cursorily from what required to be told in detail? Who among us, for example, could have thought that the whole creation of the world was properly related in a chapter of thirty-one verses; then the probation, the fall, and the condemnation of our race in another chapter of twenty-four verses; while he consecrated so very many chapters and pages to the construction of the tabernacle and of its utensils, because these presented to future ages a continual and typical view of Jesus Christ and of his redemption? Who among us, for the same reason, would have devoted the fifth part of the book of *Genesis* to relating the history of one alone of the twelve children of Jacob, while two chapters only had seemed to suffice for seventeen hundred years of the history of the human race, from Adam's fall to the deluge? Who among us would have thought, like Matthew, of mentioning only four women (and such women!) in the forty-two generations of the ancestors of Jesus Christ, and of their recording there the names of the incestuous Tamar, the impure Rahab, Ruth the Moabitess, and the adulterous spouse of Uriah, without tempering the scandal by a single reflection? Who among us would have consecrated but a single verse to the conversion of a Roman proconsul (*Acts* 13:12)? Who among us, after having shared, during ten years, in the labors of Paul, his perils, his imprisonments, his preachings, and his prophetical gifts, could have related twenty-two years of such a life without saying a word about himself, and without making known, except by the mere change of the personal pronoun (at chapter 16, verse 10) that from Troas to Jerusalem and Cesarea, and from Jerusalem and Cesarea to Malta and thence to Rome, he had been his suffering, faithful, indefatigable companion? It is necessary, in order to our being aware of this, that it should be Paul himself who, during his last imprisonment should write to Timothy: "At my first answer no man stood with me, but all men forsook me; Luke only is with me" (2 *Timothy* 4:16, 11; *Philemon* 24; *Colossians* 4:14). Holy and heavenly reserve, humble and noble silence, such as the Holy Spirit alone could have taught!

Where will you find, among all uninspired narrators, a man who could have written, like Luke, the *Acts of the Apostles*? Who could have contrived to relate within thirty pages the church history of the thirty noblest years of Christianity – from the ascension of the Son of man above the clouds of Heaven, to the imprisonment of Paul in the capital of the Roman world? Incomparable history! See, at once, how short it is and yet how full! What do we not find in it? Addresses delivered to the Jews, to the Greeks, before the tribunals, before the Areopagus, and before the Sanhedrin, in places of public resort and before a proconsul, in synagogues and before kings; admirable descriptions of the primitive church; miraculous and dramatic scenes witnessed in the midst of her; the interventions of angels, to deliver, to warn, or to punish; controversies and divisions in Christian congregations; new institutions in the church; the history of a first council and its synodic epistle; commentaries on the Scripture; accounts of heresy; judgments from God, solemn and terrible; appearances of the Lord in the highway, in the temple, and in prison; details of conversions, often miraculous and singularly varied – that of Eneas, that of the eunuch, that of Cornelius the centurion, that of the Roman jailer, that of the proconsul, that of Lydia, that of Apollos, that of a numerous body at Jerusalem; not to mention such as were only commenced, as in the emotion felt by King Agrippa, in the troubled state of Felix's mind, in the kind acts of the centurion Julius; missionary excursions; different solutions of sundry cases of conscience; permanent divisions with respect to external matters among different classes of Christians; mutual prejudices; disputes among the brethren and among the apostles; warm expressions, explanations, and yet triumphs of the spirit of charity over these obstacles, communications from one military officer to another, from one proconsul to another; resurrections from the dead; revelations made to the church in order to hasten the calling of the Gentiles; collections for the poor by one church for another; prophecies; national scenes; punishments consummated or prepared; appearances before Jewish tribunals or Roman municipalities, before governors and kings; meetings of Christians from house to house; their emotions, their prayers, their charity, their doubts; a persecuting king struck by an angel and eaten by worms, just as when, in order to gratify the populace, he had actually slain one apostle and was meditating the death of another – persecutions under every form – by synagogues, by princes, by municipalities, by the Jews, or by popular tumults; deliverances experienced by men of God through the instrumentality sometimes of a child, sometimes of an angel, sometimes of a Roman tribune or ship-captain! pagan magistrates or idolatrous soldiers, storms and shipwrecks described with a nautical exactness of detail which, as we ourselves have witnessed, continues to charm the sailors of our own day; and all this in thirty pages, or twenty-eight short chapters. Admirable brevity! Was God's Holy Spirit not necessary for this conciseness, for this choice of details, for this manner at once pious, varied, brief, richly significant, so sparing in the employment of words, and yet teaching so many things? Fullness, conciseness, clearness, unction, simplicity, elevation, practical richness; such is the book of church history needed for God's people. True; but once more, it is not thus that men compose histories.

Could you find upon the Earth a man capable of relating the murder of his mother with the calmness, the moderation, the sobriety, the apparent impassibility of that quadruple narrative of the evangelists, telling of the crucifixion of Jesus, of that Jesus whom they loved more than one loves his mother, more than one loves his life? Of that Jesus whom they had seen on his knees in Gethsemane; then betrayed, forsaken, dragged with his hands bound to Jerusalem, and finally nailed naked to a cross, while the Sun hid his light, and the Earth quaked and opened; and when he who had raised the dead to life again was himself reduced to the state of the dead! Was not God's Spirit then required at every line, at every word of such a narrative, in order to make a suitable choice of details, amid an age and a world of recollections?

There was a necessity, moreover, for an entire guidance by the Holy Spirit in order to maintain of that prophetical reserve which the sacred historians were enabled in so many respects to observe; and of that altogether divine prudence, which reveals itself not only in what they teach, but also in what they withhold; not only in the terms which they employ, but also in those they avoid.

And here, to enable one to form some estimate of this, observe them, for example, when they speak of the mother of Jesus. What divine foresight, and what prophetical wisdom, both in their narratives and in their expressions! How readily might they have been led, in their ardent adoration of the Son, to express themselves, when speaking of the mother, in terms of too much respect! Would not a single word, suffered to escape from the want of circumspection so natural to their first emotions, have forever sanctioned the idolatries of future ages toward Mary, and the crime of the worship that is paid to her? But they have never allowed themselves to drop any such word. Had they so much as merely called her the mother of God? No, not even that; although he was in their eyes Emmanuel, the God-Man, the Word which was in the beginning, which was with God, which was God, and which was made flesh. Listen to them. What do we find them say of her after the death and the resurrection of their Saviour? One single sentence, after which they say not a word more about her. "These all continued with one accord in prayer and supplication, with the women and Mary the mother of Jesus, and with his brethren" (*Acts* 1:14). (*Hi omnes erant perseverantes unanimiter in oratione cum mulieribus, et Mariâ et matre Jesu et fratribus eius.*) They name her neither first nor last; here she appears, as the mother of Jesus, among the brethren of Jesus, and the women of Galilee. And what do we find them say of her before the Lord's death? Note this carefully. Ah, it is not thus that men relate events! Of all that Jesus Christ may have said to his mother after the opening of his mission, they have selected but three sayings to be handed down to us. The first is as follows: "Woman [when she interfered with his commencing ministry, and asked of him a miracle], woman [woman!] what have I to do with you?"[36] Then, when a woman from among the people, in the warmth of her enthusiasm, cried out from amid the crowd: "Blessed is the womb that bore you, and the breasts which you have sucked!" "Yea, rather, blessed are they that hear the Word of God and keep it!"[37] Such is the second. Hear now the third: His mother and his brethren were shaken in their faith, and some of them had been heard to say, "He is beside himself [*dicebant enim, quoniam in furorem versus est*]; and one said unto him, 'Behold your mother and your brethren stand without desiring to speak with you.'" "Who is my mother?" was his reply; and stretching forth his hand toward his disciples he said: "Behold my mother...every woman that shall do the will of my Father which is in Heaven, the same is my mother." *Ecce mater mea.* And when, in his last agony, he beholds her from the cross, he no longer calls her by the name of mother; but he bequeaths her to the disciple whom he loved, saying, "Woman, behold your son; John, behold your mother;" and from that hour that disciple took her to his own home, not to worship her but to protect her as a weak and suffering creature whose soul had been pierced through with a sword.

36. *John* 2:4.
37. *Luke* 11:27-28.

## EXAMINATION OF EVASIONS

Is it thus, then, we again ask, that men relate events, and must not the prophetic Spirit alone have been the relater of these facts?

We could wish to give other examples: They at this moment crowd upon our mind, and it costs us a sacrifice to omit mentioning them, for the more narrowly we study these historical books, the more does the prophetical wisdom of God's Spirit who dictated them reveal itself there in details, at first sight far from obvious. We could wish to point out among others the altogether prophetic wisdom with which the Holy Spirit often, on coming to relate some one important fact more than once, is careful to vary his expressions, in order to prevent the false interpretations that might be put upon it, and to condemn beforehand the errors which were in a distant future to be attached to it. We would cite, for example, the manner so remarkable and so unexpected, in which the tenth law of the Decalogue is repeated in *Deuteronomy*,[38] with a remarkable transposition of its first terms; the Holy Spirit thus desiring to confound prophetically the artifice whereby the doctors of Rome were to endeavor, fifteen centuries afterward, to divide that commandment into two, in order to veil over the criminal omission they have dared to make of the second: "And you shall not make unto yourself any graven image, nor any likeness ...you shall not bow down to them, nor serve them." We could wish to point further to the variety of expression with which the Holy Spirit has related to us the divine institution of the holy Supper, and has paraphrased it several times for the purpose of enabling us better to comprehend what was the meaning of Jesus Christ, and to condemn beforehand the carnal sense which people were to give to these words: "This is my blood, this cup is the New Testament in my blood." He also said: "This cup is the communication of the blood of the New Testament." We would desire to call attention to the prophetic wisdom with which the Holy Spirit, in order to confound those who in the sequel were to allege that Judas Iscariot did not participate in the last Supper, and that he went out before, or did not come in till after it, has taken care to let us know, by Mark and Matthew,[39] that Jesus gave notice of the treachery of Judas before the communion, Judas being present; and by Luke, that he gave notice of it also afterward, Judas being present.[40] We could wish to show in the case

---

38. *Deuteronomy* 5:21; *Exodus* 20:17.
39. *Matthew* 26:21-25; *Mark* 14:18-20.
40. *Luke* 22:19-23.

of all the New Testament writers, the constant sobriety of their words when the subject in hand bears on the relations of pastors to the churches; and that admirable prudence with which they have always abstained from applying, even in a single instance, to the ministers of the Christian church the name *sacerdotes,* or sacrificers; reserving to them that title of elders or presbyters which was given to laymen in Israel, and distinguishing them always from the sacerdotal race (which represented Jesus Christ, and which necessarily ceased when the sole true priest had appeared). We could wish to point out, also, that prudence with which never do we find a soul conducted to any other pastor, any other director ($καθηγητής$)[41] than Jesus Christ, and with which, in recommending deference towards spiritual guides, the Scripture is careful to name them always in the plural, in order that none might ever have its authority to appeal to in support of that idea, so natural to pastors and to the members of the flock, that every soul ought to have its pastor among men. "Call no man on Earth your father; and do not make yourself be called director, for Christ alone is your director." What precaution, what reserve in the narratives, in order that too much might never be attributed to man, and to recount "the great things that God did by means of the apostles;"[42] in such a manner that self in all might be abased, that all glory might redound to God, and that all the Lord's servants may learn to say with the last prophet of the Old Testament and the first prophet of the New, "He must increase, and I must decrease."

We repeat it, one must do violence to his own feelings, with the volume of the Bible before him, not to cite more such examples from it.

From all these traits taken together, we are compelled to conclude, that, though the whole Scripture is divinely inspired, the historical books, more than all the rest, make this divine intervention most manifest; they show it to be most indispensable; they attest that for such pages it was necessary that the invisible and almighty hand of the Holy Spirit should be placed over that of the sacred writer, and guide it from the first line to the last. Here something more was necessary than learned men, than saints, than enlightened minds, than angels or archangels – here God was necessary.

41. *Matthew* 23:8-10.
42. *Acts* 14:27; 1 *Corinthians* 3:6.

## EXAMINATION OF EVASIONS

We will say, then, with Origen, that the sacred volumes breathe the plenitude of the Spirit, and that there is nothing either in *Prophets*, or in *Law*, or in *Gospels*, or in *Apostles*, which does not come down from the fullness of the majesty of God;[43] and with Ambrose,[44] "drink both the cup of the Old and that of the New Testament, for in both it is Christ that you drink. Drink Jesus Christ, that you may drink the blood by which you have been redeemed. Drink Jesus Christ, in order that you may drink in all his sayings. We drink holy Scripture, we devour holy Scripture, when the juice of the everlasting Word descends into the veins of our mind, and penetrates the energies of our soul." And with Augustine:[45] "Wonderful are the depths of your oracles! Behold how their surface charms little ones; but wonderful depth, O my God, what wonderful depth! One shudders at the contemplation of it – a thrill of reverence and trembling of love!"

But, how now (it has been sometimes said further), must we believe that the letter of the pagan Lysias,[46] or the harangue of the Jew Gamaliel,[47] or the discourses of Job's harsh friends were all inspired? No, without doubt. No more than those of Cain, or of Lamech, or of Rabshakeh, or of Satan. But the sacred writers were as really guided by God in order that they might transmit them to us as they were to tell us[48] the song of Mary in the hill country, or that of the seraphim in the year that king Uzziah died, or that of the celestial army at Bethlehem. The Holy Spirit is not always the author of the words which he reports, but he is always the historian.

Meanwhile another evasion is made in order to except a part of the Scriptures from the *Theopneustia*. If this is not the most serious objection, it is, at least, one of those that are most frequently advanced.

---

43. *Homilia 2, in Jeremiah,* cap.1.
44. "Utrumque poculum bibe Veteris et Novi Testamenti, quia ex utroque Christum bibis. Bibe Christum, ut bibas sanguinem quo redemptus es: bibe Christum, ut bibas sermones eius. Bibitur Scriptura sacra, et devoratur Scriptura divina, cum in venas mentis ac vires animi succus verbi descendit eterni" (*Ambrosius in Psalm 1 Enarratio*).
45. Mira profunditas eloquiorum tuorum, quorum ecce ante nos superficies blandiens parvulis; sed mira profunditas, Deus meus, mira profunditas! Horror est intendere in eam, horror honoris et tremor amoris! (*Confess.*, Book 12, chapter 14).
46. *Acts* 23:25.
47. *Acts* 5:34.
48. *Luke* 1:46.

## Section III
### Will the Apparent Insignificance of Certain Details in the Bible Authorize Their Being Excepted from Inspiration?

"Was it suited to the dignity of inspiration to accompany the thoughts of the Apostle Paul even into those vulgar details to which we see him descend in many of his letters? Could the Holy Spirit have gone so far as to dictate to him those ordinary salutations with which they close? Or those medicinal counsels which he gives to Timothy with respect to his stomach and his frequent infirmities? Or those commissions with which he charges him with respect to his parchments and a certain cloak which he had left with Carpus at Troas, when he quitted Asia?"

We beg the reader will allow us to beseech him to ponder well, when, on taking the Bible into his hands, he does not perceive, from his very first readings, the tokens of God in such or such a passage of the Word. Let not those reckless hands proceed to cast a single verse out of the temple of the Scriptures. They clasp an eternal book, all the authors of which have said, like Paul, "And I think that I also have the mind of the Lord." If then he does not as yet see anything divine in such or such a verse, the fault is in himself; not in the passage. Let him say rather, like Jacob, "Surely the Lord is in this place, and I knew it not."[49]

Let us examine more closely the passages alleged.

Paul, from the recess of his prison, asks for the return of his cloak; he had left it with Carpus at Troas; he begs Timothy to hasten before winter, and not to forget to bring it with him. This domestic detail, so many thousand times adduced as an objection to the inspiration of the Scriptures, from the days of the Anomeans spoken of by Jerome,[50] this detail seems to you too trivial for an apostolical book, or, at least, too insignificant, and too remote from edification, for the dignity of inspiration. Unhappy is the man, nevertheless, who does not perceive its grandeur!

Jesus Christ also, on the day of his death, spoke of his garment and his vesture. Would you have that passage dismissed from the number of inspired sayings? It was after a night of fatigue and anguish. He had

---

49. *Genesis* 28:16.
50. See *Proemium in epist. ad Philem.*

been led through the streets of Jerusalem for seven hours in succession, by torch-light, from street to street, from tribunal to tribunal, beaten and buffetted, blindfolded in mockery, and struck with sticks on the head. The morrow's Sun had not risen when they bound his hands to lead him further from the sacerdotal palace to Pilate's pretorium. There, his flesh torn with stripes, bathed with blood, then delivered over in order to his final execution into the hands of ferocious soldiers, he saw all his clothes taken from him that he might be arrayed in a purple robe, while people knelt before him, and put a reed in his hand, and spit in his face. Then, before placing the cross on his torn limbs, his garments were thrown over his wounds, in order to his being taken to Calvary, but, when they were about to proceed to his execution, they were taken from him for the third time; and it was then that, spoiled of everything, first of his upper garment, then of his very inner vesture, he was to die on the felon's gibbet, in view of an immense concourse of people. Was there ever found under Heaven a man who has not found these details deeply moving, sublime, inimitable? And was there ever found one who, from the recital of this death-scene, would think of retrenching, as useless or too commonplace, the account given of those garments which were parted, and of that vesture on which a lot was cast? Has not infidelity itself said, in speaking of it, that the majesty of the Scriptures astonished it, that their simplicity addressed itself to the heart, that the death of Socrates was that of a sage, but that the death of Jesus Christ was that of a God?[51] And if divine inspiration was reserved for a portion only of the holy books, would it not be for these very details? Would it not be for the history of that love which, after having lived upon the Earth more poor than the birds of the air and the foxes of the field, desired to die poorer still, despoiled of everything, of his upper and under garments, fixed to a felon's gibbet, with his arms extended and nailed to the tree? Ah! let your mind be at ease with respect to the Holy Spirit! He has not derogated from his dignity; and very far from having thought that he descended too far in reporting these facts to the Earth, he hastened to relate them; and it was a thousand years beforehand, it was in the age of the war of Troy, that he sang them to the harp of David: "They pierced my hands and my feet [he

---

51. Rousseau's *Emile*.

## GOD-BREATHED: THE DIVINE INSPIRATION OF THE BIBLE

said]; they look and stare upon me; they part my garments among them, and cast lots upon my vesture!"[52]

Well then, this is the same Spirit who has desired to show to us Paul writing to Timothy and asking for his cloak. Mark what he says. He, too, was spoiled of everything. Even while as yet but a youth, he was great among men, a favorite of princes, admired by all: He forsook all for Jesus Christ. For thirty years and more he has been poor; in labors more abundant than others, in stripes above measure, in prisons more frequent; of the Jews five times received he forty stripes save one; thrice was he beaten with rods; once was he stoned; thrice he suffered shipwreck; in journeyings often, in perils of waters, in perils in the city, in perils in the wilderness, in perils on the sea; in watchings often, in hunger and thirst, in cold and nakedness (we quote his own words).[53] Mark now what he says: Behold him advanced in years; he is in his last prison; he is in Rome; he is waiting for his sentence of death; he has fought the good fight, he has finished his course; he has kept the faith; but he is shivering with cold; ... winter has commenced; and he is in want of clothes! Buried in one of the dungeons of the Mamertine prisons, he lies under such a load of opprobrium that even all the Christians of Rome are ashamed of him, and when first called to appear before his judges, no man stood by him. The time was, ten years before, when already a prisoner in Rome, and loaded with chains, he had at least received some money from the Philippians, who, knowing his wretched state, had subscribed among themselves in their indigence something to be sent as alms to him there; but now behold him forsaken; nobody was with him but Luke; all had abandoned him; winter was at hand. He needed a cloak; he had left his two hundred leagues off, with Carpus at Troas; in the chilly dungeons of Rome there was nobody to lend him one: Had he not joyfully parted with all for Jesus?[54] Had he not counted all the world's glories as dung that he might win Christ? And does he not willingly endure all things for the elect's sake?[55] We were ourselves last year in Rome, in a hotel at the beginning of November, on a rainy day. With what a lively feeling, under the chill impressions of the evening, did we represent to ourselves the holy Apostle

---

52. *Psalm* 22:16-18; *John* 14:23-24.
53. *2 Corinthians* 11:23-27.
54. *Philippians* 3:8.
55. *2 Timothy* 2:10.

Paul in the subterranean prisons of the Capitol, dictating the last of his letters, expressing his regret at the want of his cloak, and begging Timothy to send it to him before winter!

Who is there now that would wish to retrench from the inspired epistles a trait so affecting and so pathetic? Does not the Holy Spirit take you as it were into Paul's prison, there to have instant ocular evidence of his affectionate self-renunciation and sublime poverty; so as to make us see also, as with our own eyes, what was the depth of his love, sometime before, when it made him write in his letter to the Philippians: "I tell you, even weeping, that there are many among you who mind only earthly things, and whose end is destruction!" Do you not seem to behold him in his prison, loaded with his chain, engaged in writing, and the tears dropping on his parchment? And do you not seem also to behold that poor body of his, one day ill-clothed, suffering, and benumbed; the next, beheaded and dragged into the Tiber, in expectation of "that day when the Earth will give up her dead, and the sea the dead that are in it, and when Christ shall change our vile body to be fashioned like unto his glorious body?" And if these details are beautiful, do you think they are not useful too? And if useful for the man who reads them as a simple historic truth, what do they not become for him who believes in their inspiration, and who says to himself: "O my soul, these words are written by Paul; but it is your God that addresses them to you!" Who could tell the strength and the comfort which, by their very familiarness and their actuality, they may have carried into prisons and cottages? Who could reckon up the poor men and the martyrs to whom such traits have imparted encouragement, example, and joy? We recollect, in Switzerland, in our day, the pastor Juvet, who was refused a coverlet, twenty years ago, in the prisons of the Canton de Vaud. One may call to mind in the universal church that Jerome of Prague, who was shut up for three hundred and forty days in the prisons of Constance, in the bottom of a dark, fetid tower, and never allowed to leave it except to appear before his murderers. No more has there been forgotten, among the English, holy Bishop Hooper, dragged from his damp, disgusting cellar, covered with wretchedly poor clothes and a borrowed cloak, as he proceeded to the stake, tottering on his staff, and bent double with rheumatism. Venerable fathers, blessed martyrs, you would no doubt call to mind your brother Paul, shut up in the prisons of Rome, suffering from cold and nakedness, and asking for his cloak! Ah!

unhappy he who feels not the sublime humanity, the tender grandeur, the provident and divine sympathy, the depth and the charm of such a mode of instruction! But more to be pitied still, perhaps, is he who declares it to be human, because he does not comprehend it! Here we would quote the noble words of the venerable Haldane[56] on this verse of Paul: "Here, in his solemn farewell address, of which the verse before us forms a part – the last of his writings, and which contains a passage of unrivaled grandeur – the apostle of the Gentiles is exhibited in a situation deeply calculated to affect us. We behold him standing upon the confines of the two worlds – in this world about to be beheaded, as guilty, by the Emperor of Rome – in the other world to be crowned, as righteous, by the King of kings – here deserted by men, there to be welcomed by angels – here in want of a cloak to cover him, there to be clothed upon with his house from Heaven."

Ah! rather than bring forward these passages in order to rob the Scriptures of their infallibility, one should have owned in them that wisdom of God, which so often, by a single stroke, has contrived to give us instructions for which, without that, long pages would have been necessary. One should have adored that tender condescension which, stooping to our feebleness, has been pleased not only to reveal to us the loftiest conceptions of Heaven in the simplest words of Earth, but also to present them to us in forms so lively, so dramatic, so penetrating, by often concentrating them, so as to enable us the better to seize them, in the narrow compass of a single verse.

It is thus, then, that Paul, by these words thrown out at random, among the very last commissions of a familiar letter, darts for us a sudden light on his ministry, and reveals to us with a word the whole of the apostle's life, as a single flash of lightning during the night illuminates in an instant all the summits of our Alps, and as some people reveal to you their whole soul by a look.

How many striking instances of this might we cite! They crowd upon us; but we are obliged to restrain ourselves; and it will be beneficial

---

56. *The Verbal Inspiration of the Old and New Testament Maintained and Established,* by Robert Haldane, Esq. Edinburgh, 1830. We warmly recommend to our readers the book of a man whose memory ought to be dear to our churches, and whose short residence at Geneva bore so much fruit. We would also refer, on the same subject, to a treatise by Mr. Alexander Carson: *The Theories of Inspiration, etc.* Dublin 1830. Both these works have been of much use to us.

to us rather to keep to the precise passages which have been adduced as objections.

Before proceeding further, we must, however, frankly show that we are almost ashamed to defend under this form the Word of the Lord; and for any such apology we experience, as it were, a disgust of conscience. Is it altogether becoming? And can we engage in it without some irreverence? We ought to look well at all times to the manner in which we defend the things of God, and see to it that we do not imitate the recklessness of Uzzah in putting forth his hand to the ark of God, and wishing to hold it, for the oxen stumbled. The anger of the Lord, we are told, was kindled against him for his error.[57]

If it be fully acknowledged, on both sides, that any word is contained in the oracles of God, then why defend it... as worthy of him, by man's reasonings? You may do so, no doubt, before unbelievers, but with men who own the divinity of the Scriptures, is it not to commit an insult on that Word – is it not to take up a false position, and to lay your hand on the ark, as Uzzah did? Did this Word present itself to your eyes as a root out of a dry ground; had it no form nor comeliness, and no beauty to make you desire it, still you ought to venerate it, and look for everything for it from him who has given it. Does it not imply, then, our being wanting in respect for him when he speaks, when we would prove the respect that is due to him? Should I not have been ashamed when shown my Saviour and my God rising from supper, taking a basin, laying aside his garments, girding himself with a towel, and proceeding to wash his disciples' feet – should I not have been ashamed to set myself to prove that, in spite of all this, still he was Christ! Ah, I should rather have wished to worship him more fervently than ever! Well, then, the majesty of the Scriptures desires to stoop to us! There do you not behold one who rises from the table, lays aside his garments, girds himself like a servant, and kneels before sinners, in order to wash their feet? "If I wash you not, you have no part with me!" Is there not in that very humiliation, which reveals itself to us with such a charm, as it were the voice of the Word in his humiliation?

As for us, it strikes us that there is no arrogance to be compared with that of a man who, owning the Bible to be a book from God, then makes bold to sift with his hand the pure in it from what is impure, the

---

57. *2 Samuel* 6:6-7.

inspired from what is uninspired, God from man. This is to overturn all the foundations of the faith; it amounts to placing it, no more in believing God, but in believing ourselves. It ought to be enough for us that a chapter or a word form part of the Scriptures, in order to our knowing it to be divinely good; for God has pronounced upon it as he has upon the creation, "I beheld all that I had made, and behold all was good." We will never say then, "I find this saying admirable, therefore it is from God"; and still less, "I see no use in it, therefore it is from man." God preserve us from so doing! But we say, it is in the Scriptures, therefore it is from God. It is from God, therefore it is useful, therefore it is wise, therefore it is admirable; and if I do not yet see it to be so, the fault lies only with myself. We hold there is an error in this protection which man's wisdom would accord to that of God; we hold there is an outrage involved in that clumsy stamp with which it sets itself to legalize the holy Scriptures, and in that absurd signature with which it dares to mark its pages.

If, then, we still go on here with the work of showing how the divine wisdom shines out in some passages that people dare to consider human, it is not for the purpose of establishing their divine origin on the judgments of our better informed wisdom, or to procure a tardy respect for them from the mere fact of the beauty they disclose. Our respect goes before; it was founded on the passage being written in the "Oracles of God." Henceforth, before having seen, we have believed. We have no thought, therefore, but that of refuting the objection by some examples of its temerity. Let us listen, further, to two or three passages to which people have made bold to refuse the honors of inspiration, because they have started with the idea that they are without any spiritual bearing. We will quote but a very small number here. It takes no time to pronounce of a sentence that it is useless or vulgar – to demonstrate that there is a mistake in the objection requires pages.

One of the passages which we have most frequently heard adduced, when people have wished to justify the distinction between what is inspired in the Word of God and what is not, is Paul's recommendation to Timothy with regard to the stomach complaints and ailings with which that young disciple was afflicted. "Drink no longer water, but use a little wine for your stomach's sake and frequent infirmities."[58]

---

58. *1 Timothy* 5:23.

## EXAMINATION OF EVASIONS

Nevertheless, examine this passage more closely; what an admirable and living revelation do we find in it of the grandeur of the apostolic calling, and of the amiability of the Christian character! Mark, first, that it was as it were in the temple of God that it was pronounced; for immediately before you hear those solemn words: "I charge you before God, and the Lord Jesus Christ, and the elect angels, that you observe these things, without preferring one before another, doing nothing by partiality. Lay hands suddenly on no man, keep yourself pure, drink no longer water." One sees that it is in the presence of their common Master and of his holy angels that Paul desired to speak to his disciple; let us enter then into the same temple, in order to comprehend him – let us place ourselves on the same heights "before the Lord and his holy angels," then shall we speedily perceive how many beauties are revealed by these words, both in the ministry of the apostles, and in the ways of the Lord. This the celebrated Chrysostom well understood, when, preaching on those very words, he observed how little the Lord's most useful servants should be surprised, should it so happen that their Lord should deem it fit to prove them, as he did Timothy, with complaints in their chest, or head, or stomach – should he put some thorn in their flesh and should he thus buffet them by some angel of Satan, in order to fashion them, on the one hand, for sympathy, for cordial affections, for tender compassions; and, on the other, for patience, self-denial, and, above all, for prayer. Read over seriously, and as if in the light of the last day, this beautiful passage of the apostle's; before long, within the small compass of this single verse, you will wonder how many precious lessons the Holy Spirit would give us, besides that pointed out by the pious bishop of Constantinople. How many words, and almost chapters, would have been required, in order that as much might be said to us under another form! Here you will learn, for example, Timothy's sobriety; he had wished, like Paul, to bring his body under – he abstained entirely from wine. You will see here, in the third place, with what a tender and fatherly delicacy the apostle reproved him, either for his imprudence, or for austerity carried too far. You will remark here with what wisdom the Lord authorizes, and even bids by these words, the men of God to pay the necessary attention to their health, at a time, nevertheless, in which he has thought fit to compromise it by sicknesses. In the fifth place, you will here admire the prophetic forecast with which these words, put in the mouth of an apostle, condemn beforehand those human traditions which were afterward to interdict the use of wine to believers as an impurity. Here you will see, in the sixth place, with what tender solicitude, and with what fatherly watchfulness, the apostle, in the midst of his high functions, and notwithstanding the cares with which all the churches overwhelmed him (from Jerusalem to Illyricum, and from Illyricum to Spain), directed his regards to the personal circumstances, to his health, to the weakness of his stomach, to his often infirmities, and to the imprudent habits of his daily regimen. You will further learn here an historical fact which will throw an useful light for you on the nature of the miraculous gifts. Notwithstanding all the interest felt by Paul in his disciple, he is incapable of re-establishing Timothy's health, even he who had so often healed the sick, and even raised the dead to life again; for the apostles (and we learn it again by this verse, as well as by the illness of Epaphroditus),[59] did not receive the gift of miracles for a continuance, any more than that of inspiration; it was a power that was renewed to them for every particular occasion.

But if these numerous lessons from the apostle are important, and if we thus receive them all in a single verse, and in a way the best fitted to affect us, oh how penetrating do they not become to the Christian soul from the moment he has the certain conviction that here we have not the words of a good man only; that they are not even those of an apostle only; but that it is the voice of his God who desires to teach him, under so affecting a form, sobriety, brotherly love, an affectionate interest for each other's health, the usefulness of infirmities and afflictions even for God's most zealous servants, and who, in order to convey so many precious lessons to him, condescends to address him by the mouth of a simple creature!

People, further, often object to those greetings that close the epistles of Paul, and which, after all, we are told, are of no more importance than those ordinary compliments with which we all usually conclude our letters. Here there is nothing unworthy of an apostle, no doubt; but no more is there anything inspired. Here the Holy Spirit has allowed Paul's pen to run on, as we ourselves would allow a clerk to conclude by himself, in the usual form, a letter, the first pages of which we had dictated to him. Look, for example, at the last chapter of the *Epistle to the Romans*. Is it not evident there that the apostle surrenders himself, in

---

59. *Philippians* 2:27.

the course of sixteen verses, to the purely personal reminiscences of his friendships? Was there any need of inspiration for the dry nomenclature of all those persons? The apostle mentions eighteen by their names, without reckoning all to whom he sent remembrances collectively in the house of Aquila, in that of Narcissus, or in that of Aristobulus. These verses require no inspiration; and, what would have sufficed at most, in order to their being written, would have been such a superintendence on the part of the Holy Spirit as that which he still exercised when he left them to their personality.

We are not afraid to avow that we delight to recall here these sixteen verses that have been so often objected to; for, far from furnishing any ground for objection, they belong to the number of passages in which the divine wisdom recommends itself by itself; and, if you will examine more closely, you will, before long, join us in admiring the fecundity, the condescension, and the elevation of this method of instruction; you will find in it, under the most practical and the most artless form, a living picture of a primitive church; and you will recognize in it to what an elevation, even the least known, and the most feeble among them, may rise in its bosom.

Listen first, with what an affectionate interest the apostle recommends to the kind regard of the church of Rome that humble woman, who, it would appear, undertook the voyage from Corinth to Rome for the sake of his temporal affairs. She was a sister well beloved, who had put herself at the service of the saints, and who had not been afraid to open her house to a great many of the believers, and to Paul himself, notwithstanding the perils of that hospitality. She was servant to the church of Cenchrea. It was proper that the brethren who were settled at Rome, therefore, receive her in the Lord, and to aid her in all her needs. Behold, then, what an example the apostle sets us, in some words, of that Christian urbanity which ought to characterize all the mutual relations of God's children. Admire, as he passes so rapidly under review the brethren and the sisters of the church of Rome, the manner in which he contrives to pour even over this list of names that is called dry, the sweet unction of his charity. He has some words of encouragement and affectionate esteem for each of them; he recalls in it the generous hospitality of Phebe, the risk of death which Aquila and his companion braved for him, the honor which Epenetus had of having been the first of the Achaians that were converted to Jesus Christ, the great labors of

Andronicus and of Junia, who were even in the faith before him; his Christian love for Amplias, the evangelical labors of Urbane, the proved fidelity of Apelles, the manifold labors of Tryphena and Tryphosa in the Lord, and those of the beloved Persis. What an appeal, too, to the conscience of every serious reader is there in this rapid catalogue! See, then, he ought to say to himself, who the faithful were to whom salutations were sent in the church of Rome! And were the same apostle to write a letter to the church in which I myself occupy a place for some days, what would he say of me? Would my name be found in it? Could he add that, like Phebe, I receive the saints into my house; that, like Aquila and Priscilla, I hold Christian meetings under my happy roof; that like Mary, I have bestowed much labor on the Lord's ministers; that, like Andronicus and Junia, I had suffered for Jesus Christ; that, like Rufus, I am chosen in the Lord; that, like Urbane, I am his helper; that, like Tryphena, and Tryphosa, I labor in the Lord; and that I even labor much, like the beloved Persis?

But behold, above all, what a lesson there is for Christian women in these admirable verses! In the unaffected familiarity that terminates this letter, what a lofty idea is given us of their vocation! What an important part, then, is assigned them in the church, and what a place in Heaven! Without having yet seen the city of Rome, Paul mentions there by their own names, no fewer than nine or ten women among his fellow-laborers. First we have, besides Phebe, that admirable Priscilla, who had even exposed herself to death for the apostle, and toward whom all the churches of the Gentiles felt so much gratitude. Then we have a lady called Mary, who had, he says, bestowed much labor on the apostles; there was Tryphena; there was Tryphosa, who labored also in the Lord; there was Persis, who was particularly dear to him, and who had labored much in the Lord; there was Julia; there was the sister of Nereus; there was Olympia, perhaps;[60] there was, in fine, the venerable mother of Rufus. And observe, in passing, with what respect he has named this lady, and with what delicacy he proceeds to salute her with the tender name of mother. Have we not here the very Christian politeness which he recommends to these same Romans in the twelfth chapter of this epistle: "Salute Rufus, chosen in the Lord," he writes, "and his

---

60. Or Olympias. This name might have been that of a woman; but it is probably that of a man.

mother, who also is mine!"⁶¹ What an affecting pattern do not these verses propose to husbands and wives in the persons of Aquila and of Priscilla! You see them here in Rome; you may have seen them, five years before, banished from Italy by the Emperor Claudius, arriving at Corinth, and receiving in their house the Apostle Paul; then, eighteen months afterward, setting off with him to Asia, and staying at Ephesus, where they already had a church in their house,⁶² and where they received with so much success the young and brilliant Apollos, who, notwithstanding his talents, thought himself fortunate in having it in his power to put himself in the school of their Christian conversation and their charity. Now that Claudius had died, so as to make way for Nero, you see them, when hardly returned to Rome, immediately consecrate their new residence to the church of God. It is in their house that it meets; and you learn here, further, as it were in passing, that these spouses had not hesitated to lay down their lives for the life of Paul.

But, besides all these lessons, which, in these sixteen short verses, are offered to our consciences, you may there learn further two facts of deep importance for the history of the church. And, first, you see there, with the most unsought and the fullest evidence, that at that time there was no question in Rome about Peter, or his episcopate, or about his popedom, or his primacy, or even his presence. Do you not perceive a prophetical foresight in the care taken by the Holy Spirit to do, for this *Epistle to the Romans*, what he has not done for any other of the fourteen of Paul's epistles, and to close it thus with a long catalogue of the women and of men that were the most esteemed at the time in the whole Roman church? Behold, then, the apostle of the Gentiles, who, twenty years after his conversion, writes to them with greetings addressed to as many as twenty-eight persons living in the midst of them, by their proper names, and many others besides by collective designations, and who has not a word to send them for the prince of the apostles, as he is called, for the vicar of Jesus Christ, for his superior, for the bishop of the universal church, for the founder of the Roman church! Peter was the apostle of the circumcision, and not of the Gentiles;⁶³ his place was at Jerusalem; there we have to look for him, and there Paul had always found him. In his first journey, three years after his

61. *Romans* 16:13.
62. *1 Corinthians* 16:19.
63. *Galatians* 2:7-9.

conversion, Paul visited him and abode fifteen days in his house.[64] In his second journey, to go to the first council, he again meets him there. In his third journey, in the year 44, at the time of the death of Herod Agrippa, again it is there that Peter has his residence.[65] In his fourth journey, seventeen years after his conversion,[66] Paul finds him still there, in the charge of an apostle, not of the Gentiles (mark this well) but of the circumcision. And when at last he was on the way accomplishing his fifth and last journey, he writes to the Romans and the Galatians; and then in order that the whole church might know well that Peter is not at Rome, and never was there, we find Paul taking care to salute by their names all the most eminent among the believers at Rome, even among the women. What bishop in our days, of the Latin sect, would dare to write a letter of sixteen chapters to the church of Rome, without saying to it a single word either about its pope, or about Peter, or about a vicar of Jesus Christ?[67]

But there is another historical fact, still more interesting, to the knowledge of which these very sixteen verses, said to be useless, conduct us by the most striking traits. See, in the very details of these short salutations, by what humble instruments, and yet how extensively, the Gospel had established itself in so short a time, in the mighty city of Rome. No apostle had set his foot there,[68] yet behold with wonder what progress had already been made by the Word of God, solely through the labors of artisans, merchants, women, slaves, and freedmen, who happened to be in Rome! Jesus Christ had his disciples there, even in the palaces of the Jewish princes who resided at the imperial court, and even among the pagans who served nearer the person of Nero. Paul asks that salutations should be sent from him, first (among other Christians) to those of Aristobulus' household; and, secondly, to those of the household of Narcissus "who are in the Lord." Now, the former of these two great personages was the brother of Agrippa the Great and of Herodias; the second was the all-powerful favorite of the Emperor Claudius. Agrippina caused him to be put to death only at the close of the year 54.

---

64. *Galatians* 1:18.
65. *Acts* 12:1, 3.
66. *Galatians* 2:7.
67. See on this subject the excellent dissertation of Pastor Bost: *Du pouvoir de St Pierre dans l'Eglise*. Geneva, 1833.
68. *Romans* 1:11, 13-15; 15:22.

Let all who call themselves Christians renounce, then, and forever, those rash systems in which people rise against the words of the Scriptures, to impugn their propriety; in which people take away from God's Bible such and such a passage, and such and such a word, in order to make (at least as respects that passage and that word) a Bible of man's; and in which people thus charge themselves with the responsibility of the temerities that shall be ventured upon besides, by doctors of greater hardihood, imitating upon a book what they shall have seen you do upon a verse! What idea can a man have of the sacred writers, when he would impute to them the mad audacity of mingling their own oracles with those of the Most High? We recollect the case of a man who had lost his reason, who was supported by our hospitals, whose handwriting, however, as a copyist, was so beautiful that one of the Geneva ministers engaged him to transcribe his sermons. Great was the confusion of the latter, when on looking at his papers again, he ascertained that the unhappy man had thought it his duty to enrich all the pages with his own thoughts. The distance is less, however, between a lunatic and a minister, even were he holy as Daniel and sublime as Isaiah, than between Daniel and Isaiah and the Eternal Wisdom!

Now, then, having advanced thus far, we would wish, before proceeding further, to recommend to our readers, in the practice of sacred criticism, three precautions, the importance and necessity of which ought to be impressed upon them by the theopneustic doctrine.

## Chapter 6
# Sacred Criticism, in the Relations It Bears to Divine Inspiration

Here we must not be misunderstood. Far from us be the idea of attaching the smallest disfavor to works of sacred criticism! These, on the contrary, we honor; we pronounce them necessary; we study them; we consider all ministers of the Gospel bound to know them, and that the Christian church is bound to be warmly grateful to them. That is indeed a noble science! It is so because of its object; to study the destinies of the divine text, its canon, its manuscripts, its versions, its witnesses, and the innumerable authors who have quoted it!... It is so because of the services it has rendered: how many triumphs achieved over infidelity, how many objections silenced, how many mischievous doubts forever dissipated!... It is so by its history: how many eminent men have consecrated to it either the devotedness of a pious life, or the might of the finest genius!... It is so, in fine, by its immense results, of which no one, perhaps, will ever know the measure if he has not studied it.

May God preserve us, then, from setting faith here against science; faith which lives on the truth, against science which studies it; faith which goes and lays hold of it in the hand of its God, against science which seeks it elsewhere more indirectly, and which often finds it! All that is true in one place is in pre-established harmony with all that is true in another more elevated place. Faith knows, then, from the first, and before having seen anything, that all truth will render testimony to it. All true science, be it what it may, is its friend; but sacred criticism is more than its friend – it is almost of its kindred. Nevertheless, it is all this only so long as it remains true, and as it keeps its own place. The moment it quits it, it must be kept down; it then ceases to be a science; it is but a silly piece of guesswork. Now, as there are three temptations to wander from it, we desire here to recommend three precautions to young men studying it.

## Section I
### Sacred Criticism Is a Scientific Inquirer, and Not a Judge

First of all, critical science does not keep its place when, instead of being a scientific inquirer, it would be a judge; when, not content with collecting together the oracles of God, it sets about composing them, decomposing them, canonizing them, decanonizing them, and when it gives forth oracles itself! Then it tends to nothing less than to subvert the faith from its foundation. This we proceed to demonstrate.

Employ your reason, your time, all the resources of your genius, to assure yourself whether the book which has been put into your hands, under the name of the Bible, contains, in fact, the same oracles, the first deposit of which was confided, under the divine Providence, to the Jewish people,[1] and of which the second deposit, under the same guarantee, was committed to the church universal of the apostolic times. Assure yourself, then, if this book be authentic, and if the copyists have not altered it. All this labor is legitimate, rational, honorable; it has been undertaken before you abundantly; and if the investigations of another have not satisfied you, resume them, follow them out, get all the information in your power; all the churches of God will thank you. But when this work is over, when you have ascertained that the Bible is an authentic book, and that the unexceptionable seals of God Almighty are attached to it, then listen to what science and reason alike call to you; then listen to God; then *sursùm oculi, flixi poplites, sursùm corda!* then down upon your knees! lift up your heart on high, in reverence, with profound humility! Then science and reason have no longer to judge, but to receive; no longer to pronounce, but to comprehend. There is still a task, and it is a science, if you will; but it is no longer the same; it is that of understanding and submission.

But if your wisdom, on the contrary, after having received the Bible as an authentic book, makes bold to constitute itself the judge of what is found contained there; if, from this Scripture, which calls itself inspired, and which declares that it is, at the last day, to judge you yourself,

---

1. Romans 3:2.

that wisdom of yours dares to take away anything; if, seating itself like the angels of the last judgment,[2] it drag the book of God to the seashore of science in order to collect in its vessels what it sees in it to be good, and to throw out what it finds in it to be bad, if it pretend to separate there the thought of God from the thought of man; if, for example (to adduce but one trait among a thousand) it venture to deny, like Michaëlis, that the first two chapters of *Matthew* are from God, because it does not approve the Scriptural quotations found in them; next, to deny the inspiration of *Mark* and that of *Luke*, because it has found them, it says, in contradiction with *Matthew*;[3] in a word, if it think it has the power of subjecting the book, acknowledged to be authentic, to the outrageous control of its ignorance and of its carnal sense; then, it is necessary that it should be reproved; it is guilty of revolt; it judges God. Here there is no longer science, there is fantasy; there is no longer progress, there is obscurantism.

One may judge of this, if he compare with this blundering of theologians on the Word of God the more rational procedure of physicians and naturalists in studying his works. Here, at least, people hold beforehand as an axiom that all objects in creation answer to ends that are full of wisdom and harmony. Here science sets itself, not to contest these ends, but to discover them. Here, what people call progress is not the daring rashness of controlling the works of their God; it is the good fortune to have sounded them, to have obtained a better recognition of their marvels, and to have been able to present them under some new aspects to the admiration of men.

Why, then, will Christians not do with the works of God in the works of redemption what naturalists do with the works of God in creation? Why, if, even among the pagans, a physician – the great Galen – could say "that in describing the different parts of the human body, he was composing a hymn in honor of him who has made us," will not the Christian comprehend that to describe with truth the various parts of the Word of God, would be always "composing a hymn in honor of him who has made it?" Thus thought the apostolic fathers; thus the pious Irenæus, the disciple of Polycarp, the pupil of John. "The Scriptures are perfect," said he. "In the Scriptures let God always teach, and

2. *Matthew* 13:48-49.
3. *Introduction to the New Testament*, by Michaëlis, Volume 2, page 17; Volume 1, pages 206, 214 (English translation).

let man always learn! Thus it is that from the confused polyphony of their instructions, one sole and admirable symphony will make itself heard in us, praising by its hymns the God who has made all things."[4]

Were we to be told there was a very studious nation in existence, among whom the science of Nature, taking a new direction, had begun immense works with the purpose of establishing that there are mistakes in creation; plants badly constructed, animals ill-conceived, organs ill-adapted – what would you think of such a people and their grand attempt? Would you say that they effected any advance in science? Would you not rather conceive that they darkened and degraded it, and that people there were putting themselves to a great deal of learned labor in finding out the art of being ignorant? While anatomists have been unable to explain the use of the liver in the human body, or of antennæ in that of insects, they have not on that account found nature in fault; they have put it all to the account of their own ignorance. Why, then, when you happen not yet to have discovered the use of something that is said in the Scriptures, do you lay the blame on any but yourselves, and why will you not wait?

This is no new idea. It is now sixteen hundred years since a godly man expressed it better than we have done, and preached it with unction to his contemporaries. "If ever, in reading Scriptures," says Origen, in the thirty-ninth of his homilies,[5]

> you happen to stumble on some thought which becomes for you a stone of stumbling and a rock of offense, blame none but yourself (αἰτιῶ σαυτόν) – doubt not that this stone of stumbling and rock of offense has some great meaning (ἔχειν νοήματα), and is to fulfil that promise, "He that believes shall not be confounded" (*Romans* 9:33). Begin, then, with believing; and soon you will find, under this imaginary stumbling block, a plentiful and holy utility?[6] If we have received the commandment not to speak idle words, for we shall give account thereof at the last judgment, how much more ought we to think, with regard to God's prophets, that every word proceeding from their mouth had its object to effect

---

4. "Sic, per dictionum multas voces, una consonans melodia in nobis sentietur, laudans hymnis Deum qui fecit omnia." According to the Greek, as preserved by John Damascenus: Διὰ τῆς τῶν λέξεων κολυφωνίας, ἓν σύμφωνον ἡμῖν αἰσθήσεται (*Adv. Hæreses*, Book 2, chapter 47).
5. *Origenes adamantius*, Hom. 39, in *Jeremiah* 44:22.
6. Παλλὴν ἀφέλειας ἁγίαν.

and its utility!⁷ I believe, then, that for those who know how to make use of the virtue of the Scriptures, each of the letters written in the oracles of God has its object and its use (ἐργάξεται) even to an iota and single jot.... And in like manner as among plants, there is not one which has not its virtue; and, nevertheless, it belongs only to those who have acquired a knowledge of botany to be able to tell us how each ought to be applied and prepared in order to its becoming useful; so likewise whoever is a holy and virtual botanist of the Word of God (τὶς Βοτανικὸς ἐστιν ὁ ἅγιος καὶ πνευματικός), he, collecting each iota and each element, will find the virtue of that Word, and will perceive that nothing in that which is written is superfluous (ὅτι οὐδὲν παρέλκει). Would you have another comparison? Every member of our body has its office for which it has been placed there by the great Architect. Nevertheless, it belongs not to all to be acquainted with its use and virtue, but only to those physicians who have occupied themselves with anatomy. Well,...then, I consider the Scriptures as the collection of the plants of the Word, or as the perfect body of the Word. But if you are neither botanist of the Scriptures nor anatomist of the prophetical words, do not imagine that there is anything superfluous there; and when you have been unable to find the reason for that which is written, blame not the holy letters; lay the blame on yourself alone.⁸

Thus spoke Origen; but we might have found thoughts quite to the same effect in other fathers, and particularly in Irenæus,⁹ who lived still nearer the apostolic times.

However, we must further bid the reader remark that this pretending to judge the Word of God overthrows all the foundations of the faith. It would even render it impossible in the hearts of all who are but a little consistent. This it is but too easy to demonstrate.

In order that a soul receive life, it must receive faith; in order that it may have faith, it must believe God; in order that it believe God, it must begin with renouncing the prejudices of its own wisdom on sin, on the future, on the judgment, on grace, on itself, on the world, on God, on all things.... Is it not written that the natural man receives not the things of the Spirit of God, that he even cannot receive them, and

---

7. Ἐργατικὸν ἦν.
8. And he adds, Τοῦτο μοι τὸ προοίμιον εἴρηται καθολικῶς χρήσιμον εἶναι δυναμένον εἰς ὅλην τὴν γραφὴν, ἵνα προτράπωσιν οἱ θέλοντις προσέχειν τῇ ἀνάγιωστι μηδὲν παραπέμπεσθαι ἀναξέταστον καὶ ἀνεξερεύνητον γραμμά.
9. Irenæus, *Adv. Hæ.*, Book 2, chapter 47.

that they are foolishness unto him?[10] The Gospel, accordingly, will shock his reason or his conscience, or both. And yet he must submit upon the sole testimony of God; and it is not until after having thus settled his relation to it that he will recognize it as being "the wisdom of God and the power of God unto salvation to everyone that believes." He must believe, then, without having seen; that is to say, the Gospel, before he has comprehended it, ought to confound his own wisdom, revolt his natural heart, buffet his pride, and condemn his own righteousness! How then would you ever get it to be accepted by men who would, like you, wait to have everything approved before receiving everything? Imbued with your principles, they will impute to man in the Scriptures everything that shocks their natural feelings. They will think that they ought to retrench from it the prejudices of the apostles on the consequences of Adam's sin, on the Trinity, on the expiation, on eternal punishments, on gehenna, on the resurrection of the body, on the doctrine of devils, on election, on the gratuitous justification of the sinner by faith, perhaps also on miracles. How shall a man, if he be unhappy enough to imitate you, ever find life, peace, and joy by means of faith? How shall he hope against hope? How shall he believe that he is ever saved, wretched man that he is? He will have to pass his days lost in vague, misty, uncertain doctrines! His life, his peace, his love, his obedience must remain, until death, such as his doctrines are! We conclude, then, with this first advice: Make critical science a learned inquirer; don't make it a judge.

## Section II
### Let Sacred Criticism Be an Historian, Not a Soothsayer

There is, in relation to the inspiration of the Scriptures, one other not less important precaution, which we must point out in the use that is made of science.

The task of sacred criticism is to collect facts on the Scriptures: Do not suffer her to engage you in vain hypotheses; there she will do you much mischief. She ought to be an historian; make her not a prophetess. When she divines, do not listen to her – turn your back upon her; for she will dissipate your time, and more than your time. Now,

---

10. *1 Corinthians* 2:14.

the believer's safeguard here is still the doctrine of inspiration such as we have exhibited it; I mean of the inspiration, not of the men, but of the book.

All Scripture is divinely inspired: Such is the declaration of the authentic book of the Scriptures. But as for what passed in the understanding and in the conscience of the sacred writers, that is hardly ever revealed to us, and it is what we are not required to know. Much time and many words have been lost owing to men having neglected this grand principle. Scripture is inspired, whether the author knew or did not know beforehand what God was making him write. In such researches, therefore, as studying in each book of the Bible the particularities of its style, of its language, of its reasoning, and all the circumstances of its sacred writer, we can see nothing but good; they are useful, legitimate, respectful; and it is in these, certainly, there is science. Should the student proceed to endeavor, by these same characters, to fix its date, and the occasion of its being written, still we can perceive nothing but what is instructive and becoming in such an investigation. It may be well, for example, to know that it was under Nero that Paul wrote to the Jews,[11] enjoining them "to be subject to the powers that be." It may be useful to know that Peter had been married more than twenty-three years when Paul reminded the Corinthians[12] that he (the first of the popes, as he is called) still continued, in all his apostolic journeyings, to lead his wife about with him, and that the other apostles, and James himself (who was reputed the first of the pillars of the church[13]), did the same thing. In this, too, there is science. We highly value, for the sake of the church of God, all labor which enables it to comprehend better a passage, aye, were it but a single word of holy Scripture. But to proceed from that to crude hypotheses on the sacred writers, to make what they say depend on the haphazard of their presumed circumstances, instead of considering their circumstances as prepared and willed by God for what they were to teach, to subordinate the nature, the abundance, or the conciseness of their teachings to the concurrence, more or less fortuitous, of their ignorances, or their recollections – this is to degrade inspiration; it is to lay the foundations of infidelity; it is to forget that

---

11. *Romans* 13:1.
12. *1 Corinthians* 9:5.
13. *Galatians* 2:9.

"the men of God spoke as they were moved by the Holy Spirit (φερό-μενοι), not with words which man's wisdom teaches, but with those which the Holy Spirit teaches."[14]

Did the evangelists, it has been asked, read each other? And of what consequence is this to me, provided they were "moved by the Spirit;" and if, after the example of the Thessalonians, I receive their book, not as the word of men, but as it is in truth, the Word of God?[15] The putting of this question, we may remark in passing, may be very innocent, but it is no longer so in the manner in which it is treated, and in the importance that is attached to it.

When people inquire whether John had read the *Gospels* of the other three; whether Mark and Luke had read the *Gospel of Matthew* before writing their own (as Dr. Mill[16] and Professor Hug[17] would have it, and as Dr. Lardner[18] and Professor Michaëlis[19] would not have it); when it is asked whether they only caused to be transcribed with discernment the most important portions of the oral tradition (as Dr. Gieseler[20] would have it); when on this huge volumes are written, in attack or defence of these systems, as if faith and even science were really interested in them, and as if great things were likely to result from them to the Christian church; when it is affirmed that the first three evangelists had consulted some original document now lost, Greek according to some, Hebrew according to others (an idea first conceived by LeClerc, and taken up sixty years after him by Messrs. Kopp, Michaëlis, Lessing, Niemeyer, Eichhorn, and others[21]); when people plunge still deeper into this romantic field; when they reach at last a drama so complicated as the Bishop of Landaff's,[22] with his first Hebrew historical document, his second Hebrew dogmatical document, his third document, his fourth document (a translation of the first), then his documents of the second class, formed by the translation of *Luke* and *Mark* and *Matthew*, which brings the sources at last to the number of seven,

---

14. *1 Corinthians* 2:13; *2 Peter* 1:21.
15. *1 Thessalonians* 2:13.
16. Millii, *Proleg.*, § 108.
17. *Einleitung in die Schriften des Neuen Testaments*. Stuttgart, 1821.
18. Volume 6, page 220-250.
19. *Introduction*, Volume 1, pages 112-129.
20. *Historisch-kritischer Versuch*. Minden, 1818.
21. Horne's *Introduction*, Volume 2, page 443, 1818 edition.
22. Bishop Marsh's *Michaëlis*, Volume 3, part 2, page 361.

without reckoning three more of them peculiar to *Luke* and *Mark*; or further still, with Mr. Veysie[23] in England, and Dr. Gieseler in Germany, we would trace up either the three first *Gospels*, or the four *Gospels*, to apocryphal narratives in previous circulation in the Christian churches; when, with the first of these doctors, people will have it that Mark copied them with a more literal exactness than Luke, on account, it is said, of his ignorance of Greek, while *Matthew*, first written in Hebrew, must, beyond doubt, have been afterwards translated into Greek by someone, who must have modified it out of *Mark* and *Luke*, and transmitted it to us at last in the state in which we possess it; when, not content with sketching these systems in a few phrases, as a task of passing curiosity, people have written thereon so many and such bulky volumes, as if the interests of the kingdom of God were involved in them! We cannot avoid saying that we experience, in the view of all this science, a profound sense of grief! But after all, is this science? No! these are no longer scientific inquirers – they have forsaken facts – they prophetize the history of the past; these are the astrologers of theology. It is thought, in astronomy, that a book of observations on the smallest satellite discovered near Uranus, or on the finding of a second of parallax in the case of some star, or on a single spot measured in the Moon is a precious acquisition for science, while all the writings of the Count de Boulainvilliers, and the three hundred volumes on the Barbaric sphere, on the influences, the aspects, or the horoscopes of the seven planetary bodies, can be for it no better than a piece of folly, or a useless encumbrance. Thus we should set a higher value on the pursuits of sacred criticism, on whatever might throw some surer light on the smallest passage of the Scriptures; but what end could all these crude hypotheses ever serve? In these, people desert the luminous paths of science, as well as those of faith; they weary themselves in the pursuit of empty nothings! Vain and noisy toil expended in misty conjectures formed upon the clouds! Nothing good can come down from them! Wretched pursuits, which teach men to doubt where God teaches them to believe! "Who is he;" says the Lord, "who darkens, by words without knowledge, the counsels of the Most High?"

In fact, would that we could say that there was nothing there beyond idle fancies, and an enormous loss of time! But in these, people do

---

23. Veysie's *Examination*, page 56.

much worse than waste their precious hours: They lose their faith. There they confuse their mind's eyes; they draw away young students from the great and first Author of the Scriptures. It is clear that these idle pursuits can proceed only from a lack of faith in the inspiration of the Scriptures. Believe, for one moment, that Jesus Christ had given to his apostles (the τῶς καὶ τί, *Matthew* 10:19-20) the *what* and the *how* that they were to speak; admit that the Holy Spirit made them relate the life of Jesus Christ, as he made them relate his sitting at the right hand of God, and you instantly perceive that all these hypotheses vanish into nothing. Not only *do* they teach you nothing, they *cannot* teach you anything; but they put your believing thoughts into a wrong track; they gradually undermine the doctrine of inspiration; they indirectly weaken God's testimony, its certainty, its perfection. They turn the thoughts of your piety from their true direction; they mislead those young persons who were looking for the living waters from the wells of the Scriptures, and who are drawn away to heal themselves amid the sands, far from the springs that gush up into eternal life. What, after all, will they find there? Broken cisterns, clouds without water, and at most, perhaps fantastic streams, gleaming to them for some days in the sun, like a deceitful mirage on the deserts of human thought.

What would you say of a learned divine who should endeavor to trace the discourses and the doctrines of Jesus Christ to the instructions of Joseph the carpenter, or to the lessons of the school at Nazareth? Idle and pernicious task, you would exclaim. Well, then, the same must be said of all those conjectural systems which would, on human principles, explain the composition of the Scriptures. Idle and pernicious, we say! Admit inspiration, and all this labor vanishes like an idle dream. The Scriptures are the Word of God; they are given by him, and we know that no prophecy ever came by the will of man; but holy men of God spoke as they were moved by the Holy Spirit.[24] The story of Paul's nephew giving warning to his uncle in the prison of Antonia is inspired by God, although Luke may have heard it twenty times from the mouth of the apostle before receiving it from the Holy Spirit. That story is inspired, equally with the account of the invisible angel who was commissioned by God to strike the king of the Jews upon his throne, in the city of Cesarea. The account given us of Jacob's ring-straked and speck-

---

24. *2 Peter* 1:21.

led sheep is from God, as well as that of the creation of the heavens and the Earth. The history of the fall of Ananias and Sapphira is as divinely inspired as is that of the fall of Satan and his angels.

No doubt the evangelists had one common document after which these holy men of God spoke; but as has been so well said by Bishop Gleig,[25] that document was neither more nor less than just the preaching and the life of our divine Saviour. That was their prototype.

Accordingly, when you hear it asked, from what documents Matthew could have taken his account of the birth of Jesus Christ? Luke, that of his early years? Paul, the Saviour's appearance to James, or the Saviour's words on the blessedness of giving? Whence Hosea took what he says of the tears of Jacob? And Jude, Enoch's prophecy? And Michael's contention about the body of Moses? – you may reply that they were derived from the same source from which Moses learned the creation of the Heaven and the Earth.

We have shown how sound views on the inspiration of the Scriptures, will preserve youthful students from being led into the two grand errors of modern criticism, and at the same time enable them to derive from that noble science the utmost possible amount of good. The former of these errors, we have said, consists in pretending to subject the Scriptures to our judgment, after having admitted their authenticity; the latter consists in indulging dangerous conjectures on the sacred books. But we have still to make an important reflection on the relations of learning to the great question which occupies us.

## Section III
### Sacred Criticism Is the Doorkeeper of the Temple, Not Its God

This reflection will present itself at once under the form of an advice and of an argument. But let not this alarm the reader. We venture on the advice only as a prelude to the argument; for we do not forget that our task in this book is to establish the fact of the divine inspiration, not to preach it. To begin with the advice, it is as follows:

Learning is a doorkeeper who conducts you to the temple of the Scriptures. Never forget, then, that she is not the God, and that her

---

25. Remarks on Michaëlis' *Introduction to the New Testament*, pages 32*ff.* Horne's *Introduction*, Volume 2, page 458. 1818 edition.

house is not the temple. In other terms, when you study sacred criticism, beware of keeping to that, even as regards learning. She leaves you in the street; you must enter. And now for the argument.

If you penetrate, in fact, into the sanctuary of the Scriptures, then not only will you find inscribed by the hand of God on all its walls that God fills it, and that he is everywhere there, but, further, you will receive the proof of it experimentally. There you will behold him everywhere; there you will feel him everywhere. In other terms, when one reads God's oracles with care, he not only meets with the frequent declaration of their entire inspiration, but, further, through unexpected strokes, and often through a single verse or the power of a single word, he receives a profound conviction of the divinity stamped upon it throughout.

As regards advice, it must not be imagined that we have given it with the view of discrediting learned investigations; we offer it, on the contrary, in their interest, and in order to their completion. In fact, it too often happens that a prolonged course of study, devoted to the extrinsic parts of the sacred book (its history, its manuscripts, its versions, its language), by entirely absorbing the attention of the men who give themselves to it, leaves them inattentive to its more intrinsic attributes, its meaning, its object, the moral power which displays itself there, the beauties that reveal themselves there, the life that diffuses itself there. And as there exist, nevertheless, necessary relations between these essential attributes and those exterior forms, two great evils result from this pre-occupation of the mind. By this absorption the student stifles his spiritual life as a man, and compromises final salvation. This, however, is not the evil we have to do with in these pages; as a learned inquirer, he compromises his science by it, and renders himself incapable of forming a sound estimate of the very objects of his studies. His learning is wanting in coherence and consistency, and from that very cause becomes contracted and creeping. How can a man become acquainted with the temple when he has seen but the stones and knows nothing of the Shekinah? Can the types be understood, when he has not even a suspicion of their antitype? He has seen but altars, sheep, knives, utensils, blood, fire, incense, costumes, and ceremonies; he has not beheld the world's redemption, futurity, Heaven, the glory of Jesus Christ! And, in this state, he has been unable so much as to comprehend the relations which these external objects have among themselves because he has not comprehended their harmony with the whole.

A learned man, without faith, living in the days of Noah, who had studied the structure of the ark, would have lost his soul, no doubt; but, further, he would have remained ignorant of a great part of the very objects which he pretended to appreciate.

Suppose that a Roman traveler, in the days of Pompey the Great, had wished to describe Jerusalem and its temple. Arriving in the city on a Sabbath day, he repairs to the holy place with his guide; he makes the tour of it; he admires its enormous stones; he measures its porticos; he inquires about its antiquity and the names of the architects; he passes through its gigantic gates, which two hundred men daily open at sunrise and shut again at noon; there he sees arriving by thousands, in regular order, the Levites and choristers in their linen habits; and while in the interior, the sons of Aaron perform their rites; while the *Psalms* of the prophet king resound under the sacred vaults, and thousands of choristers, accompanying them with their instruments, respond to each other in their sublime antiphonies; while the law is read, the word preached, and the souls that look for the consolation of Israel are lifted up with delight to the glories that are invisible, and filled with the deepest awe in contemplating that God "with whom there is plenteous redemption;" while aged Simeons are raising their thoughts to "that glorious salvation unceasingly waited for;" while sinners are turning to God; while more than one poor publican strikes upon his breast; while more than one poor widow, with joyous emotion, takes out her two mites for God's treasury; and while so many invisible but ardent prayers are rising toward Heaven; what may we suppose our traveler to be doing? Why, counting the pillars, admiring the pavements, measuring the courts, scrutinizing the congregation, taking drawings of the altar of incense, the candlestick, the table of shewbread, the golden censer; after which, he walks off, mounts to the battlements of the fortress, goes down to the Xystus and to the brook Kedron, makes the circuit of the walls, counting his steps as he goes, and then returns to his quarters, there to write out his observations and to prepare his book. No doubt, he might boast of his having seen the Hebrew nation, and their worship and temple; he might publish his journey, and find numerous readers; but, even with respect to the scientific knowledge which his book is meant to diffuse, how many errors of judgment will be found in it!

## ON SACRED CRITICISM

And how many errors would the worshipers in the temple have to refute in it!

Here, then, is the advice we proffer, in the sole interest of your theological learning. It necessarily follows, from the necessary relations that subsist between the eternal ends contemplated by God in his Word and its external forms, that, in order to judge correctly of the latter, you must first have made yourselves acquainted with the former.

If you would form a judgment of a physician, you would no doubt desire to know what country he is from, what has been his course of study, what universities he has attended, and what testimonials he can produce; but should he be the first to tell you what are your most latent disorders; should he reveal to you sensations in your system which you have hitherto vaguely felt, and the secret reality of which you recognize as soon as he has defined them to you; should he, above all, prescribe and supply the only remedy that could ever give you relief; would not such an experience tell you far more about him than his diplomas can do?

Well, then, the following is the counsel we venture to give to all such of our readers as have made any acquaintance with sacred criticism. Read the Bible, study the Bible by itself and for itself; ask it, if you like, where it has taken its degrees, and in what school its writers have studied; but come to its consultations as a sick person eager to be cured; be as careful to make the experience of its words as you can have been in studying its language and its history; and then, not only will you be healed (which is not the question at issue here), but you will be enlightened. "He that healed me said: Take up your bed and walk! Whether he be a sinner I know not: One thing I know, that whereas I was blind, now I see!"[26]

Here the author would take occasion to mention what a thirst he felt for apologetical books during his youthful studies; how Abbadie, Leslie, Huet, Turretin, Grotius, Littleton, Jennings, Ranhardt, and Chalmers formed his habitual reading; and how, while tormented with a thousand doubts, he came at last to be convinced and satisfied only by the word itself of the Scriptures. That Word gives testimony to itself, not only by its assertions, but by its effects, like light, like heat, like life, like health; for it carries in its beams health, life, heat, and light. A man might prove to me, by correct calculations, that at this moment the Sun ought

26. *John* 9:25.

## GOD-BREATHED: THE DIVINE INSPIRATION OF THE BIBLE

to be above the horizon; but can I have any need of these, if my eye behold him, if I am bathed in his beams and invigorated by them?

Read the Bible, then; do not be learned by halves; let everything have its proper place. It is the Bible that will convince you. It will tell you whether it came from God. And when you shall have heard a voice there, sometimes more powerful than the sound of mighty waters, sometimes soft and still as the sound that fell on the ear of Elijah: "The Lord, merciful and compassionate, the God who is pitiful, slow to wrath, abundant in mercy, the God of all consolation, the God who pardons so much, and more"... ah, then, we venture to tell you beforehand that the simple reading of a *Psalm*, of a story, of a precept, of a verse, of a word in a verse, will, before long, attest the divine inspiration of all the Scriptures to you more powerfully than could have been done by all the most solid reasonings of doctors or of books. Then you will see, you will know by experience, that God is everywhere in the Scriptures; then you will not ask of them if they are inspired; for you will know them to be quick and powerful searchers of the thoughts and desires of the heart, sharper than any two-edged sword, piercing to the dividing asunder of your soul and spirit, and of your joint and marrow, causing your tears to flow from a deep and unknown source, overthrowing you with resistless power, and raising you up again with such a tenderness, and such sympathies, as are found only in God.

All this is as yet mere advice; but we proceed to show in what respect, nevertheless, these considerations may be presented, if not as a proof, at least as a strong presumption, in favor of the inspiration of the very words of Scripture. In them, in fact, we indicate to our readers a threefold experience, which at all times has borne the fruit of profound convictions among other Christians, and the testimony rendered by which ought, at least, to strike them as demanding the most serious consideration.

One of the strongest proofs, no doubt, of the divine authority of the Scriptures, is that majesty of theirs which fills us with respect and awe; it is the imposing unity of that book, the composition of which extends over a period of fifteen hundred years, and which has had so many authors, some of whom wrote no less than two centuries before the fabulous times of Hercules, Jason, and the Argonauts; others in the heroic days of Priam, Achilles, and Agamemnon; others in the days of Thales and Pythagoras; others in the age of Seneca, Tacitus, Plutarch,

Tiberius, and Domitian; and who all, nevertheless, pursue one and the same plan, constantly advancing, as if they had all understood each other, toward one sole grand end, the history of the world's redemption by the Son of God, it is this vast harmony of all the Scriptures; this Old Testament filled with Jesus Christ, as well as the New; this universal history, which nothing stops, which tells of the revolutions of empires to the end of time, and which, when its scenes of the past have come to a close, continues them onward with those of the future, until the moment arrive when all the world's empires shall have become the possession of Jesus Christ and his saints: At the first page, the Earth created for the reception of sinless man; in the following pages, the Earth cursed for the reception of man ever sinning; at the last page, a new Earth for the reception of man who will never more sin! At the first page, the tree of life interdicted, paradise lost, sin entering into the world by the first Adam, and death by sin; at the last page, paradise found again, life again entering into the world by the second Adam, death vanquished, no more sorrow to be found, God's image restored in man, and the tree of life in the midst of the paradise of God. Assuredly there is in this majestic whole, commencing before there were men, and continued on to the end of time, a powerful and altogether heavenly unity; a convergence of long ages, universal, immense, whose grandeur captivates thought, transcends all our human conceptions, and proclaims its Author's divinity as irresistibly as, on a summer night, the view of a sky glittering with stars and the thought of all those shining worlds which resolve night and day in the immensity of space. "Myriads of things in perfect intimacy and symphony," says one of the earliest fathers of the church.[27] And yet over and above the beauties presented by the Scriptures, viewed thus as a whole, we have to contemplate something not less glorious, which reveals to us also the divine action in their smallest part, and attests to us their verbal inspiration.

Three orders of persons, or rather three orders of experiences, testify to this.

First, if you consult ministers who have spent their whole lives in meditating on the Scriptures, with the view of finding daily nourishment from them for the Lord's flocks, they will tell you that the more

---

27. "Μυρία φίλα καὶ σύμφωνκ." *Theophilus ad Autolyc.*, Book 1, chapter 36. See also Justin Martyr, *ad Græcos cohort.*, chapter 8.

they have given themselves to this blessed study, and have set themselves to look more narrowly into the oracles of God, the more also has their admiration of the letter of that Word increased. Surprised, as they proceed, by unexpected beauties, they have recognized in these, even in the most minute expressions, instances of divine foresight, profound mutual bearings, spiritual grandeurs which reveal themselves there by the sole fact of a more exact translation, or of the attention of the mind being longer directed to the detail of a single verse. They will tell you that the man of God who keeps for some time close to the eyes of his soul some text of that holy book soon feels himself called to adopt the language of the naturalist who, with the microscope, studies a leaf from the forest, with its integuments, its nerves, its thousand pores, and its thousand vessels. He that made the forest made the leaf! he exclaims; yes, says the Father, and he who made the Bible, made its verses also!

A second order of evidences, of which we would here cite the testimony, is that of the interpreters of the prophecies. All of them will tell you with what evidence, after one has bestowed some time on that study, it is perceived that in these miraculous pages every verse, every word without any exception, and even down to apparently the most indifferent particle, must have been guaranteed by God. The slightest alteration in a verb, in an adverb, or even in the simplest conjunction, might lead an interpreter into the most serious error. And it has often been remarked that if the prophecies that are now fulfilled were ill-understood before the events, this arose, in a great measure, from the circumstance that people had not examined, with sufficient attention, all the details of their text. Of this we might adduce many examples.

But there is yet another order of persons who attest to us more loudly, if possible, the divine inspiration of the Scriptures, even in their smallest parts; these are Christians who have experienced their power, first in their conversion, and afterward in the conflicts that followed. Go, and in the biographies of those who have been great in the kingdom of God, look for the moment at which they passed from death unto life; inquire around you about the same fact of the Christians who in their turn have experienced this virtue of the Word of God: They will all bear one unanimous testimony. When the holy Scripture, overmastering their conscience, made them lie low at the foot of the cross and there revealed to them the love of God, what seized hold of them was not the Bible as a whole, it was not a chapter, it was a verse; aye, a word, which was for them like the humble and powerful knob of the electric pile, the disks of which should mount to Heaven, or, as it were, the point of a sword wielded by the very hand of God. They found it quick and powerful. It was an influence from above which was concentrated in a single word, and which made it become for them, "as a fire, says the Lord, and as a hammer that breaks the stone."[28] They perused, in the moment of their need, a *Psalm*, or some words of the prophets, or some sentences from the epistles, or some narratives of sacred history – and as they were reading, behold, a word seized their conscience with an unknown, sweeping, irresistible force. It was no more than a single word, but that word remained upon their soul; there it spoke, there it preached, there it resounded, as if all the church bells of the City of God had been struck to call him to fasting, to the bending of the knee, to prayer, to meeting with Jesus Christ! It was but a word, but that word was from God. It was but one of apparently the meanest chords of the harp from Heaven, but that chord was so stretched as to be in unison with the heart of man; it gave forth unexpected sounds, all-powerful harmonies, which stirred their inmost souls, and then they felt that those tones are miraculous, that those harmonies proceed from Heaven. They knew it to be the call of Jesus Christ.

Such, then, is the voice of the church; such has been in every age the unanimous testimony of the saints. The inspiration which the Bible attributes to itself, they have said, we ourselves have experienced. We believe it, no doubt, because it attests it; but we believe it also because we have seen it, and because we ourselves can bear to it the testimony of a blessed experience, and of an irresistible impulse of feeling.

One might adduce such examples by thousands. Let us be content to name here two of the noblest minds that have ever served as guides to humanity. Let the reader call to his recollection how the two greatest lights of ancient and modern times were kindled. It was a word – a single word of the Scriptures – which, just at the moment that had been prepared by God, put into their souls the light of the Holy Spirit.

Luther, while as yet a monk, went off to Rome. He lay ill a-bed at Bologna in a foreign land, overwhelmed with the burden of his guilt, and believing himself to be at the gates of death. It was then that the seventeenth verse of the first chapter of the *Epistle to the Romans*, "*Justus*

---

28. Jeremiah 23:29.

## GOD-BREATHED: THE DIVINE INSPIRATION OF THE BIBLE

*ex fide vivet"* – "the just shall live by faith" – came like a beam from Heaven, and enlightened his whole being. These simple words seized him twice with a superhuman power; first at Bologna, there to fill him with inexpressible energy and peace; after that at Rome itself, there to check and elevate him, while with an idolatrous crowd he dragged himself on both knees up Pilate's fabulous staircase. It was with these words that the Reformation of the West commenced. "Words of creative power for the Reformer and the Reformation," exclaims on this subject my precious friend Merle D'Aubigné. It was by them that God then said, "Let there be light, and there was light."[29] "In truth," says the Reformer himself, "I felt as if entirely born again; and these words were for me the very gate of paradise." *"Hic me prorsus renatum esse sensi, et apertis portis in ipsum paradisum intrasse."*

Here, too, shall we not call to mind the greatest of the doctors of Christian antiquity (the admirable Augustine), when, in his garden near Milan, wretched, ill at ease, feeling, as Luther felt, a tempest in his soul, as he reclined under a fig-tree, *"jactans voces miserabiles et dimittens habenas lacrymis,"* groaning, and giving vent to a flood of tears, he heard from an adjoining house that youthful voice, which sang with a rapid repetition of the burden of the song: *"Tolle, lege! tolle, lege!"* "Take and read; take and read!" He went off to the neighborhood of Alypius for the roll of the epistles of Paul, which he had left there (*adripui, aperui et legi in silentio*) – he grasped it, opened it, and read in silence the first chapter that caught his eye. And when he came to the thirteenth verse of the thirteenth chapter of the *Epistle to the Romans*, then all was decided by a word. Jesus had overcome: The grand career of the holiest of the doctors began its course. A word, but a word from God, had lighted up that mighty beacon which was to illuminate ten centuries of the church's existence, and whose rays delight her still. After thirty-one years of revolt, of conflicts, of relapses, of wretchedness, faith, life, and peace had descended into that loving soul; a new light, but an everlasting light, had risen upon it. After these words, he wanted nothing more; he shut the book, he tells us; he no longer felt doubt. *"Nec ultra volui legere, nec opus erat;"* for with the close of that sentence, a stream of light and security was poured into his soul; and all the night of his doubts had vanished.

---

29. See Preface to the *History of the Reformation*.

*"Statim quippe cum fine hujus sententiœ quasi luce securitatis infusa cordi meo, omnes dubitationis tenebrae diffugerunt!"*

There is one experience more of the same kind with which we have been too deeply struck not to refer to it in these pages, although its testimony may probably be admitted by those only who are already pious men. The further a man advances in the Christian life – the more abundant the measure he receives of God's Spirit – the more, also, you must have observed what, in two contrary senses, on the one hand, our sacred books, and, on the other, the best writings of men, become for him. While you will see him ever more and more independent of the latter, because more fully aware that they have hardly anything more to teach him, or at least, because, after having read them once, he has received all that they have to give him, mark with admiration how very much otherwise it is for him with respect to the divine sayings, and with what a marvelous contrast he is seen to be ever more attached to the letter of the Scriptures, ever more convinced of the wisdom that is revealed there, and of the divine power put forth there, ever more eager to drink in their slightest expressions, ever more capable of deriving delicious nourishment, for whole days and nights, from a single passage, and from a single verse! Certainly, there is in this fact, to the person who has witnessed it, something peculiarly striking. We ourselves have seen it.

Such, then, is the triple testimony which we would invoke, and by which the church attests to us that an influence from God has been infused into the smallest parts of the sacred Word, in such wise, that "all Scripture is divinely inspired."

We must, however, be properly understood. We have made no pretension here to impose upon some the experience of others. Proofs from feeling are proof to those alone who have felt. They have, no doubt, an irresistible force for men who, having experienced them, have seen the testimonies of the Word confirmed in them with unquestionable evidence; but nothing would be less logical than to offer them as demonstrations to souls who are strangers to them. If you have had these experiences, you will be more than convinced, and we should have no more to say to you. Accordingly, we have presented them only as strong historical presumptions, to dispose you in this way to receive with readier submission the Scriptural proofs already put before you. A whole multitude of well-informed and pious persons, we say, attest to you for ages past, and by a threefold experience, that in the close study of the Word of God one is brought to recognize, on the clearest evidence, its inspiration, even in its words. Let this act, at least, as a powerful recommendation to listen with respect and candor to the testimonies in which the Bible itself has told you what it is. At least, let this voice of the church call to you, as it were from an adjoining house, *Take and read, take and read! Adripe, aperi, lege in silentio!* Read it in silence; and you yourself will feel how far its inspiration goes. No more doubt, you will say, like Augustine; for the morning star has risen in my heart; and you will not need to read more. *Nec ultra voles legere, nec opus erit; statim quippe cum fine unius sententiæ, quasi luce securitatis infusa cordi tuo, omnes dubitationis tenebræ diffugient!*

## Chapter 7
# Conclusion

THE QUESTION has been put, Is the Bible inspired, even in its language? We have affirmed that it is. In other words (for we have willingly consented to reduce our whole thesis to this second form, equivalent to the first), the question has been put, Have the men of God given us the Scriptures exempt from all error, great or small, positive or negative? We have affirmed that they have.

The Scriptures are composed of books, phrases, and words. Without stating any hypothesis as to the manner in which God has dictated them, we maintain, with the Scriptures, that this word is divine, without any exception. And were anyone to ask of us how God proceeded in order to guarantee all their words, we should wait, before replying to him, until he has let us know in what manner God proceeded in order to guarantee all their ideas; and we should be reminded of the child who said to his father, "Father, where does God get his colors when he dyes the cherries with such a beautiful red?" "My boy, I will tell you that when you have let me know how he paints all the leaves with so fine a green."

### Section I
### Retrospect

Divine inspiration, we have said, is not a system; it is a fact; and that fact, if attested by God, becomes to us a dogma. But it is the book that is inspired; it is with the book above all things, with which we have to do, and not with the writers. We might almost dispense with believing the inspiration of the thoughts, while we could not dispense with believing that of the language. If the words of the book are God's words, of what consequence to me, after all, are the thoughts of the writer? Whatever his mental qualifications, what proceeded from his hands would always be the Bible; whereas, let the thoughts be given him, and not the words, and it is not a Bible that he gives me; it is only something more than a sermon.

Nevertheless, we have been at great pains to make our reservations.

Scripture is entirely the word of man, and Scripture is entirely the word of God. O man, we have said, it is here especially that you are called to wonder and admire! It has spoken for you, and like you; it presents itself to you, wholly clothed in humanity; the Eternal Spirit (in this respect at least, and in a certain measure) has made himself man in order to speak to you, as the Eternal Son made himself man in order to redeem you. It was with this view that he chose, before all ages, men subject to the same affections with yourself.[1] He provided for this, and prepared their character, their circumstances, their style, their manner, their times, their way. And thus it is that the Gospel is the tenderness of God, and the sympathy of God; as it is, to speak with Paul, "the wisdom of God and the power of God."

Let it not be imagined, then, that the stamp of the individual character of the sacred writers in the several books of the Bible authorizes us to regard their inspiration as intermittent or incomplete. It matters little for the fact of their divine inspiration whether there be the absence or the concurrence of the sacred writer's emotions. God may either employ or dispense with them. If he uses second causes in all his other works, why should he abstain from doing so in divine inspiration? Besides, as we have remarked, this individuality, which is made the ground of objection, equally shows itself in those parts of Scripture which are most incontestibly dictated by God. This false system of a gradual and intermittent inspiration presents characters at once of complication, rashness, and childishness; but what, above all, condemns it, is its being directly contrary to the testimony which the Scripture has borne to its own nature. After all, think not that, in employing our personality, it has done so at random. No: All its several writers were chosen from before the foundation of the world for the work to which they were destined, and God prepared them for it, as he did Paul, "from their mother's womb." Oh, but the sacred books are admirable in this respect; how incomparable do they appear, and how soon do we abundantly recognize in them the divine power that caused them to be written!

1. *James* 5:17.

# CONCLUSION

Scripture is then from God; it is everywhere from God, and everywhere it is entirely from God. That is our thesis; and this is what we have done to establish it; this we could do only by Scripture.

If God reveals himself, it is for him to tell us, in that same revelation, in what measure he has been pleased to do so. Far from us be all idle hypotheses! In these we should meet only with our own fancies, and bewitch the eye of our faith. What then say the Scriptures? The whole question lies there.

First of all, we have said, they declare to us that all the words of the prophets are entirely given and warranted by God. In the second place, they attest to us that all the Scriptures of the Old Testament are the words of the prophets. Finally, they demonstrate to us that the New Testament Scriptures are no less so. All the words of the New Testament, then, are equally warranted by God.

This, too, was the conviction of the apostles of Jesus Christ. See what use they made of the Bible. What was it in their eyes? Did they not believe in its entire divine inspiration? Is it possible not to conclude from their whole conduct that for them the Scriptures were inspired of God, even to their most minute expressions?

But there is for us a proof still more decisive than all the rest. Let us consult the example of the Son of God himself. Let us attend to what he says of the Scriptures. Let us listen to him, especially when he quotes them. Assuredly (we must not be afraid to say it) among the most ardent defenders of their verbal inspiration, there is not one to be found who has ever expressed himself with more respect for the altogether divine authority, and the perpetuity of their most minute expressions, than has been done by the man Jesus. And when a modern writer happens to quote the Bible in the way that Jesus Christ quoted it, in order to deduce some doctrine from it, you will see him forthwith ranked among the most enthusiastic partisans of our doctrine of plenary inspiration.

Nevertheless, we have had objections to consider.

Some opposed to us the necessity for translations, and their unavoidable imperfection; others, the numerous various readings presented by the ancient manuscripts that had to be employed in printing our Scriptures. We replied that those two facts could nowise affect the question. It is the primitive text that we have to do with. Were the apostles and prophets commissioned to give us a Bible entirely inspired and without the admixture of any error? Such is the question. But, at the same time, we have been called to participate in the church's triumph at the state in which our sacred manuscripts are found and the astonishing insignificance of the various readings. The Lord's providence has watched over this inestimable deposit.

What was further adduced as an objection to the inspiration of the words was the use made by the apostles in the New Testament of the Septuagint; but we, on the contrary, pointed to the fact that in the independent and sovereign manner in which they have made use of it, you have a fresh proof (of the presence) of the Spirit who caused them to speak.

Finally, some have gone so far as to object to us, that, after all, there are errors in the Scriptures, and these errors they have specifically stated to us. This fact we denied. Because they have not at once understood some narrative, or some expression, some have rashly ventured to censure the Word of God! While willing to present some examples of the recklessness and erroneousness of such reproaches, we hastened at the same time to take note of this objection, for the purpose of showing its authors that they could not attack the inspiration of the language without imputing error to the thoughts of the Holy Spirit. Reckless indeed they are! At the very time that they say of the Bible, as Pilate said of Jesus Christ, "What evil has he done?" they put it on trial at the bar of their tribunal! To such objectors we would say, "What then would you do to those who smite him on the cheek, who spit upon him, and who say to him, 'Prophesy who it is that smote you?' Surely it is not for you to place yourselves on such a judgment-seat."

The language of Scripture has been blamed for erroneous expressions, betraying, on the part of the sacred authors, an ignorance (otherwise, it is said, pardonable enough) of the constitution of the heavens, and of the phenomena of nature. But here, as elsewhere, the objections, on being viewed more closely, pass into subjects of admiration. It is as if, in making us polish the diamonds of holy Scripture by a more diligent examination, they elicited unexpected splendors, and served only to dazzle us with more brilliant reflections of its divinity. At the same time that you cannot find in the Bible any of those errors which abound in the sacred books of all pagan nations, as well as in all the philosophical systems of antiquity, it in a thousand ways discloses in its language the knowledge of "the Ancient of Days;" and you will, before long, ascertain that – whether we look to the expressions which it employs,

## CONCLUSION

or to those which it avoids employing – that language maintained, throughout thirty centuries, a scientific and profound harmony with the eternal truth of facts. In that language it seems to say: What you learned only yesterday, I spoke not of to you, yet I knew it from eternity.

The words of Paul also were objected to us, in which that apostle distinguishes that which the Lord says from that which he himself says. We believe we have shown that, on the contrary, he could not have given a more convincing proof of his inspiration than is found in the boldness of such a distinction, seeing that, with an authority altogether divine, he repeals some of the laws of the Old Testament.

Still this was not all; we had to reply to other objections, presenting themselves rather under the form of systems, and which would make bold to exclude a part of God's book from being held to be inspired.

Some have been willing to admit the inspiration of the thoughts of the Bible, and to contest that of the language only; but we reminded such, first, that there exists so necessary a dependence between the thoughts and the words, that it is impossible to conceive a complete inspiration of the former without a full inspiration of the latter.

We charged this fatal system, besides, with being no better than a purely human hypothesis, fantastically assumed, without there being anything in Scripture to authorize it. Accordingly, we said that it led inevitably to suppositions that were most disparaging to the Word of God; while, at the same time, to our mind, it removed no difficulty, seeing that, after all, it but substitutes for one inexplicable operation of God another which is no less so.

But further, we added, what purpose does this system serve, since it is incomplete, and since, by the confession of even those who maintain it, it applies to only one portion of the Scriptures?

Others, again, have been ready sometimes to concede to us the plenary inspiration of certain books, but with the exclusion from these of the historical writings. Besides that every distinction of this kind is gratuitous, rash, and opposed to the terms of the Scriptures, we were compelled to show that these books are, perhaps, of the whole Bible, those whose inspiration is best attested, most necessary, most evident; those which Jesus Christ quoted with most respect; those that sound men's hearts and tell the secrets of their consciences. They foretell the most important events of the future in their most minute details; they constantly announce Jesus Christ; they describe the character of God;

they inculcate doctrines; they give forth laws; they make revelations. In a word, they exhibit the splendor of a divine wisdom, both in what they say, and in what they are silent about. In order to write them, more than men, more than angels, were called for.

We have been asked, finally, if we could discover anything divine in certain passages of the Scriptures, too vulgar, it has been said, to be inspired. We believe we have shown how much wisdom, on the contrary, shines out in these passages, as soon as, instead of passing a hasty judgment on them, we would look in them for the teaching of the Holy Spirit.

In fine, we besought the reader to go directly to the Scriptures for the purpose of devoting to the prayerful study of them that time which he might hitherto have given to judging them; and we assured him, on the testimony of the whole church, and after a threefold experience, that the divine inspiration of the minutest parts of the Holy Word will before long reveal itself to him, if he will but study it with reverence.

But we must draw to a close.

## Section II
## *The Bible Above Everything*

It follows from all we have said that there are in the Christian world but two schools, or two religions: that which puts the Bible above everything, and that which puts something above the Bible. The former was evidently that of Jesus Christ; the latter has been that of the rationalism of all denominations and of all times.

The motto of the former is this: The whole written Word is inspired by God, even to a single jot and tittle; the Scripture cannot be destroyed.

The motto of the second is this: There are human judges lawfully entitled to pass judgment on the Word of God.

Instead of putting the Bible above all, it is, on the contrary, either science, or reason, or human tradition, or some new inspiration, which it places above that book. Hence all rationalism; hence all false religions.

They profess to correct the Word of God, or to complete it; they contradict it, or they interdict it; they make it to be read without reverence by their pupils, or they prohibit the reading of it.

Those rationalists, for example, who, at the present day, profess *Judaism,* place above the Bible, if not their own reason, that at least of the

CONCLUSION

second, third, fourth, fifth, and sixth centuries; that is to say, the human traditions of their Targums, the Mishna, and the Gemara of their two enormous Talmuds. That is their Koran: Under its weight, they have smothered the *Law and the Prophets*.

Those rationalists who profess the *Roman religion*, will, in their turn, subject the Bible, not to their own reason, but, first, to the reason of the seventh, eighth, ninth, tenth, eleventh, twelfth, and thirteenth centuries, which they call tradition (that is to say, the reason of Dionysius the Little, Hincmar, Radbert, Lanfranc, Damascenus, Anastasius Bibliothecarius, Burkardt, Ives of Chartres, Gratian, Isidore Mercator); and next, to that of a priest, ordinarily an Italian, whom they call *Pope,* and whom they declare to be infallible in the definition of matters of faith.[2] Does the Bible require the adoration of the virgin, the service of angels, payment for pardons, the worshiping of images, auricular confession to a priest, forbidding to marry, forbidding the use of meats, praying in a foreign tongue, interdicting the Scriptures to the people[3] and that there should be a sovereign pontiff? And when it speaks of a future Rome,[4] is it otherwise (all the first fathers of the church are agreed about this[5]) than by pointing to it as the seat of the Man of Sin; as the center of a vast apostasy, as a Babylon drunk with the blood of the saints and the witnesses of Jesus Christ, which made all the nations to drink of the wine of the fury of her fornication; as the mother of fornications and abominations of the Earth?

2. This is the doctrine of the Ultramontanists, supported both by popes (Pascal, Pius, Leo, Pelagius, Boniface, Gregory) and by councils. Bellarmin, Duval, and Arsdekin assure us that it is the common sentiment of all theologians of any note. "Haec doctrina communis est inter omnes notæ theologos" (Arsdekin, *Theol.*, Volume 2, page 118. Antwerp, 1682).

3. Prohibemus etiam, ne libros Veteris Testamenti aut Novi laici permittantur habere, nisi forte psalterium, vel breviarium pro divinis officiis, aut horas beatæ Mariæ, aliquis ex devotione habere velit. Sed ne præmissos libros habeant in vulgari translatos, arctissime inhibemus. The fourteenth canon of the Council of Toulouse under Pope Gregory IX, 1229). *Concilia Labbæi*, Volume 2, paragraphs 1-8. Paris, 1771.

4. 2 Thessalonians 2:1-12; Revelation 13:1-8, 18:1-24. Jerome, *Exhortat. to Marcella* to induce her to emigrate from Rome to Bethlehem: "Lege Apocalypsim Johannis, et quid de muliere purpurata," etc.... "septem montibus, et Babylonis cantetur exitu, contuere,"etc.... "Tertullian: Sic et Babylon apud Johannen nostrum Romanæ urbis figura est,"etc. (*Adv. Judæos*, Parisiis, 1675).

5. Chrysostom (*Hom.* 4, in 2d epist. *ad Thessalonians*, c. 2). "What hindered," says he (of his own time), "the manifestation of the man of sin was the Roman Empire: ‘ωτέστιν ἡ ἀρχὴ Ῥωμαϊκή. Ὅται ὤρθη ἐκ μεσοῦ, ἐκεῖνος ἥξει.'"

## GOD-BREATHED: THE DIVINE INSPIRATION OF THE BIBLE

Those rationalists that profess an *impure Protestantism,* and who reject the doctrines of the Reformation, will put above the Bible, if not the reason of Socinus and Priestley, or of Eichhorn and Paulus, or of Strauss and Hegel, at least their own. There is a mixture, they will tell you, in the Word of God. They sift it, they "correct" it; and it is with the Bible in their hand that they come to tell you: There is no divinity in Christ, no resurrection of the body, no Holy Spirit, no devil, no demons, no Hell, no expiation in the death of Jesus Christ, no native corruption in man, no eternity in punishments, no miracles in facts (what do I say even?) no reality in Jesus Christ!

Those rationalists, in fine, who profess *Mysticism* (the Illuminati, the Shakers, the Paracelsists, the Bourignonists, the Labadists, the Bœhmists) will put above the text (of the Bible) their own hallucinations, their inward word, their revelations, and the Christ who (they say) is within them. They will speak with disdain of the letter, of the literal meaning, of the Gospel facts, of the man Jesus, or of the outward Christ (as they call him), of the cross of Golgotha, of preaching, of worship, of the sacraments. They are above all these carnal helps! Hence their dislike for the doctrine of God's judicial righteousness, of the reality of sin, of the divine wrath against evil, of grace, of election, of satisfaction, of Christ's imputed righteousness, of the punishments to come.

Disciples of the Saviour, hearken to what he says in his Word: There it is that he speaks to us; there is our reason, there our inspiration, there our tradition. It is the lamp for our feet. "Sanctify me by your truth, O Lord, your Word is truth!"

Let our reason, then, put forth all its energies, under the eye of God, first, in order to recognize the Scriptures as being from him, and then to study them. Let it every day turn more closely to these divine oracles in order to correct itself by them, not to correct them by it; there to seek for God's meaning, not to put our own in its place; to present itself before their holy utterances as a meek and teachable handmaiden, not as a noisy and conceited sybil. Let its daily prayer, amid the night that surrounds it, be that of the infant Samuel: "Speak, Lord, for your servant hears!" "The law of the Lord is perfect; the words of the Lord are pure words, as silver tried in a furnace of earth, purified seven times."[6]

---

6. *Psalm* 12:6.

## CONCLUSION

And, on the other hand, let us seek the Holy Spirit; "let us have the unction of the Holy One;" let us be baptized with him. It is the Spirit alone who will lead us into the whole truth of the Scriptures; which will by them shed the love of God abroad in our hearts, and will witness with our spirits that we are the children of God; by applying to us their promises, by giving us in these the earnest of our inheritance, and the pledges of his adoption. In vain should we bear in our hands, during eighteen hundred years, the holy Scriptures, as the Jews still do; without that Spirit we should never comprehend in them the things of the Spirit of God: "They would appear to us foolishness, because the natural man receives them not, and even cannot do so, seeing that they are spiritually discerned."[7] But at the same time, while we ever distinguish the Spirit from the letter, let us beware of ever separating them. Let it always be before the Word, in the Word, and by the Word, that we seek this divine Spirit. It is by it that he acts; by it that he enlightens and affects; by it that he casts down and raises up. His constant work is to make it understood by our souls, to apply it to them, and to make them love it.

The Bible, then, is in all its parts from God.

Still, no doubt, we shall have to meet with many passages of which we shall fail to perceive either the awe or the beauty; but the light of the last day will before long bring out their now hidden radiance. And as in the case of those deep crystalline caves into which torches have been brought after having been long consigned to darkness, the dawning of the day of Jesus Christ, bathing all things in a flood of light, will pierce into every part of the Scriptures, revealing everywhere gems unseen till then and causing them to dazzle us with innumerable splendors. Then will the beauty, the wisdom, the proportions, the harmony of all their revelations be manifested; and the prospect will fill the elect with ravishing admiration, with ever fresh raptures, with unutterable joy.

In this respect, the history of the past ought to lead us to anticipate that of the future; and we may judge, from what has already taken place, of the flood of light which we may look to see poured upon the Scriptures at the second coming of Jesus Christ.

Behold what beams of living light were at once diffused over all parts of the Old Testament at the first advent of the Son of God; and from this sole fact try to form an idea of what will be the splendor of both

---

7. *1 Corinthians* 2:14.

Testaments, at his second appearance. Then will God's plan be consummated, then will our Lord and our King, "fairer than any of the sons of men," be revealed from Heaven, upborne on the word of truth, meekness, and righteousness; then shall his brightness fill the hearts of the redeemed; and the awful grandeur of the work of redemption burst in all its glory on the contemplation of the children of God.

Mark how many chapters of Scripture, even as early as the age of Jeremiah, or later, during the long reign of the Maccabees, and during the whole time that the second temple lasted, from Malachi to John the Baptist; mark, we say, how many chapters of the Scripture, now radiant for us with the divinest luster, must have then appeared vapid and meaningless to rationalistic men in the ancient synagogue. How childish, commonplace, senseless, and useless must have seemed to them so many verses and so many chapters that now nourish our faith, that fill us with wonder at the majestic unity of the Scriptures, that compel us to weep, and that have before now led so many weary and heavy-laden souls to the feet of Jesus Christ! What would people say then of the fifty-third chapter of *Isaiah*? Doubtless, with the Ethiopian of Queen Candace: "How can I understand except some man should guide me? Of whom speaks the prophet this? Of himself, or some other man?" What purpose seems likely to be served by this mysterious history of Melchizedec? Why these long details about the tabernacle, Aaron's garments, things clean and unclean, worship, and sacrifices? What meaning could there be in the words – "Neither shall you break a bone thereof?" What meaning could be attached to the twenty-second, sixty ninth, and so many other *Psalms*: "My God, my God, why have you forsaken me"? "They have pierced my hands and my feet." Why (they must have thought) does David occupy himself at such length, in his *Psalms*, with the common incidents of his adventurous life? When was it, besides, that they parted his garments among them, and cast lots on his vesture? What mean those words, "All they that see me shake the head, saying, He trusted in the Lord that he would deliver him – let him deliver him, seeing he delighted in him"? What, then, is that vinegar, and what is the meaning of the gall, "They gave me also gall for my meat, and in my thirst they gave me vinegar to drink"? And those exaggerated and inexplicable words, "I hid not my face from shame and spitting; they smote me on the cheek, and the ploughers ploughed my back"? And what would the prophet mean, "Behold, a virgin shall be with child"? Who, again, is that king, lowly and mounted on an ass: "Rejoice greatly, O daughter of Zion; behold, your King comes unto you. He is just, and having salvation; lowly, and riding upon an ass, and upon a colt the foal of an ass"? What, then, is that sepulchre: "And he made his grave with the wicked, and with the rich in his death"?

How must all these expressions, and many others of a like kind, have appeared strange and little worthy of the Lord to the presumptuous scribes of those remote times! What humanity, would they have said, what individuality, what occasionality (to put into the mouths of those men of ancient times the language of the present day)! They were taught, no doubt, in their academies at that time, learned systems and long conjectural speculations on the conjunctures in which the prophets were placed when writing such details, and no more would be seen in their words than the ordinary impress of the entirely personal circumstances which had given rise to their emotions.

But what, then, was done by the true disciples of the Word of life? How did you act, Hezekiah, Daniel, Josiah, Nehemiah, Ezra – our brethren in the same hope and in the same faith? And you, too, holy women, who hoped in God and waited for the consolation of Israel? Ah! you bowed with respect over all those depths, as the angels of light still do; and desiring to see them to the bottom, you waited! Yes, they waited! They knew that in what was the most insignificant passage in their eyes, there might be, as was said by one of the church fathers, "mountains of doctrine." Thus it was that in "searching [as Peter has said] what the Spirit of Christ, which was in the prophets, did signify, when it testified beforehand of the sufferings of Christ and the glory that should follow," they never doubted that afterward, when time and events should have passed their hand over this sympathetic ink, there would come forth from it wondrous pages, and bearing the stamp of divinity, and all full of the Gospel. The day was to come, after the first appearance of the Messiah, when the least in the kingdom of God would be greater than the greatest of the prophets; and that day has arrived. But we ourselves know also, that the day is yet to come, after his second appearance, when the least among the redeemed shall be greater in knowledge than ever were the Augustines, the Calvins, the Jonathan Edwardses, the Pascals, and the Leightons; for then the ears of children will hear, and their eyes will see, "things which the apostles themselves desired to see and did not see, and to hear and did not hear."

Well, then, what doctors, prophets, and saints used to do with passages that were still obscure to them, and now luminous to us, we will do with passages that are still obscure to us, but which will before long be luminous to the heirs of life, when all the prophecies will be accomplished, and when Jesus Christ will appear in the clouds, in the last epiphany of his glorious advent.

What luster, as soon as it has been perceived, have we not seen shed on many a passage, many a *Psalm*, many a prophecy, many a type, many a description, the profound beauty of which had until then passed unobserved! What a wondrous Gospel has there not emanated from them! What appeals to the conscience! What a display of the love shown in redemption! Let us wait, then, for analogous revelations, but much more glorious still, on the day when our Master shall descend again from the heavens – "for in the Scriptures," says Irenæus, "there are some difficulties which even at present we can resolve by the grace of God; but there are others which we leave to him, not only for this age but for the age which is to come, in order that God may perpetually teach, and man also perpetually learn from God the things that are God's."[8]

If the lights of grace have eclipsed those of nature, how shall the lights of glory in their turn eclipse those of grace? How many stars of the first magnitude, as yet unseen by us, shall, at the approach of that great day, be kindled in the firmament of the Scriptures? And when, at last, it shall have arisen without a cloud over the ransomed world, what harmonies, what celestial tints, what new glories, what unlooked-for splendors, shall burst upon the heirs of eternal life!

Then will be seen the meaning of many a prophecy, many a fact, and many a lesson, the divinity of which, as yet, reveals itself only in detached traits; but the evangelical beauties of which will shine forth from every part of them. Then will be known the entire bearing of those parables, even now so solemnizing – of the fig tree, of the master returning from a far country, of the bridegroom and the bride, of the net drawn to the shore of eternity, of Lazarus, of the invited to the feast, of the talents, of the vine dressers, of the virgins, of the marriage feast. Then will there be known all the glory involved in such expressions as

---

8. Irenæus, *Adv. Hær.*, Book 2. chapter 47: "Ἵνα ὁ διδάσκῃ, ἄνθρωπος δὲ διὰ παντὸς μανθάνῃ παρὰ Θεοῦ.

the following: "The Lord said unto my Lord, Sit at my right hand, until I make your enemies your footstool." "Your people, O Lord, shall be willing in the day of your power, in the beauties of holiness from the womb of the morning: you have the dew of your youth." "He shall strike through kings in the day of his wrath." "He shall drink of the brook in the way; therefore shall he lift up the head."

Then, also, shall our eyes behold, in all his glory, Jesus Christ, the Saviour, the Comforter, and the Friend of the wretched, our Lord and our God! He that lives, and was dead, and is alive for evermore! Then all the knowledge of the heavens will be summed up in him. This was ever all the knowledge of the Holy Spirit, who comes down from Heaven; it was all the knowledge of the Scriptures, for the testimony of Jesus is the spirit of prophecy.[9] It is even now all the life of the saints; "their life eternal is to know him!"

The celebrated traveler who first brought to us from Constantinople the only horse-chestnut that the West had ever seen, and who planted it, they say, in the court of his mansion-house, could he have told all that he held in his hand, and all that was to come forth from it? The infinite in the finite! Forests innumerable in a humble nut, and within its insignificant shell trees in thousands, adorning with their majestic foliage and bunches of flowers our gardens and shrubberies, darkening with their shade our public squares, and the terraces and avenues of our cities; people celebrating their national festivals under their ample bowers; our children playing at their feet, and the house sparrow twittering to its mate in their branches; while each of those trees will itself produce, year after year, thousands of nuts similar to that from which it sprang, and all likewise bearing in them the imbedded germs of countless forests in countless generations!

Thus the Christian traveler, on passing from the church militant into his heavenly country, into the City of his God, to his Father's house, with one of the thousand passages of the Holy Bible in his mind, knows that in that he brings the infinite in the finite – a germ from God of the developments and the glory of which he may doubtless even now have a glimpse, but all the grandeurs of which he cannot yet tell. Possibly it may be the smallest of seeds; but he knows that there is to come forth from it a mighty tree, an eternal tree, under the branches

---

9. *Revelation* 19:10.

of which the inhabitants of Heaven will take shelter. As to many of these passages he can as yet, perhaps, see no more than their germ lying within a rough shell; but he knows, at the same time, that once admitted to the Jerusalem that is from above, under the bright effulgence of the Sun of Righteousness he will see beaming in those words of wisdom, on their being brought to the light of which the Lamb is the everlasting source, splendors now latent, and still enclosed in their first envelopment. Then it is that in an ineffable melting of the heart with gratitude and felicity he will discover agreements, harmonies, and glories which here below he but dimly saw or waited to see with lowly reverence. Prepared in God's eternal counsels before the foundation of the world, and enclosed as germs in his Word of life, they will burst forth under that new Heaven, and for that new Earth wherein will dwell righteousness.

The whole written Word, therefore, is inspired by God.

"Open my eyes, O Lord, that I may behold wondrous things out of your law!"

# Index

Aaron 68, 259, 296, 314
Abarbanel 137
Abbadie 297
Abbess of Port-Royal 42
Abel 214, 217
Aben-Ezras 137
Abraham 42, 99, 110, 189, 195, 218, 258-260
absolution(s) 121, 158
absurdities 230
Achaia 175
Achilles 298
*Ad Constant. Aug.* (Hilary) 144
*ad Græcos cohortatio* (Justin Martyr) 140, 299
Adam 60, 63–64, 97, 187, 215, 259, 263, 289, 299
adoration 27
adultery 114
*Advers. Hæreses* (Irenæus) 144, 288, 316
*Adv. Hæreses* (John of Damascus) 287
*Adv. Judæos* (Cyprian) 144
*Adv. Quirin.* (Cyprian) 144
*Advers. calumniantes S. Trinit.* (Basil the Great) 144
*Advers. Hermog.* (Tertullian) 144
*Advers. Marcion* (Tertullian) 141, 144
advice 242
Æsop's fables 131
Ætius 136

affections 50, 52–53, 62, 110, 126, 256
afflatu divino 57
Africa 155
Agabus 87
*Against Apion* (Josephus) 127, 129, 136
Agamemnon 298
Agar 189, 259
Agobard 135
Agrippa 264
Agrippa the Great 282
Ahaziah 219
Airey 225
Ajalon 224
Alcoran 131
Alexandria 144, 151
Alexandrine 164
allegory 138
Alps 274
Alypius 302
ambition 72
Ambrose 175
America 121
Ammon 116, 138
Ammonias 214
Amos 44, 50, 52
Amplias 280
Ananias 82, 294
Ananus 217
Anastasius Bibliothecarius 311
Anaxagoras 229
Andradius 131

Andronicus 280
angels 60, 62–65, 69, 97, 187, 200, 205-207, 231, 256, 258-259, 264, 268, 274, 277, 286, 293-294, 310, 315
*Annuaire du Bur. des Longitudes* 235
anointing 112
Anomeans 135-136, 270
Anthony 209
Antigone 117
Antioch 87-88, 114, 136, 182, 250
antipodes 31, 228, 232, 238
*Antiquities* (Josephus) 209, 217
antiquity 233
Antonia 293
Apelles 280
Apion 38, 90
*Apocrypha of Enoch* 257
apocryphal books 130
apocryphal writings 155
Apollo 68
Apollos 264, 281
apostasy 158, 311
apostles 32, 41, 45- 46, 69, 71, 74, 75, 77-79, 82–104, 107, 109, 113-115, 118-119, 125, 135-136, 140, 145, 150, 152-153, 183, 188, 195, 203-204, 206-207, 220, 243, 245, 248, 253, 255, 264, 268-269, 277-278, 289-290, 293, 307-308, 315
appearances 224–226
Appollinarius 136
Aquila 279–281
Arabia 230
Arabic 158
Arago 225, 235
archangel 104

*Archives du Christianisme* 182
Areopagus 264
Argonauts 258, 298
Arianism 178
Aristides 142
Aristobulus 279, 282
Aristotle 63, 70, 137, 227, 229, 234
arithmetic 150
Arius 136
ark 296
Armenian 158
Arminianism 129
Arminians 45
arrogance 220
Arsdekin 311
Artaxerxes 125
artisans 282
Asaph 103
ascension 262, 264
Asia 88, 131, 175, 230, 231, 281
Asia Minor 189
assurance 79, 180, 247
astrology 229, 292
astronomy 31, 225, 227, 230, 238, 292
Athalie 56
Athanasius 129, 144, 161
Athenagoras 140
Athenians 70
Athens 65
attractiveness 260
Augustine 46, 132, 143-144, 198, 228, 232, 251, 269, 304, 315
Augustus 208-210
auricular confession 121, 311
Austerlitz 209
authority 27, 79, 86, 89-90, 94-95, 102-104, 122, 131-132, 135, 138, 140, 144, 243, 262, 298, 307

INDEX

Ava  227
Averroës  137
Azazel  259

Babylon  54, 65, 122, 158, 216, 230, 254, 262, 311
Babylonian captivity  218
Baffin's Bay  235
Baile  262
Balaam  69, 108, 114, 115, 252, 254
Baltic  236
Barachias  214–216
Barberini Library  166
Barnabas  114
Barrett  192
Barrow  43
Bartimeus  195-196
Basil  141, 161, 175
Basil the Great  91, 144
Baumgarten  108
Bayli  131
beauty  47
begging the question  133
belief  31
Bellarmin  118-119, 131, 133, 262, 311
*Bellum Papale sive Concordia Discors Sexti V et Clementis VIII* (James)  119
Belshazzar  253
Benares  227
Bengel  156-157, 179, 181
Berechiah  216
Berlin  175, 193
Bernard  44, 46, 251
Bertrand  194, 195
Beth-horon  221–224
Bethel  35, 70, 230
Bethesda  99
Bethlehem  254, 260, 311

Bethsaida  248
Beza  181-182, 214, 251
*Bibl. Uni. de Genève*  235
Bible  256
Bible Societies  120-121, 162
*Bibliotheque Universelle*  235
biographies  262
blasphemy  103-104
Boaz  260
bodies  225
Bœhmists  312
Bologna  302
Bonaparte  58
Boniface  228, 311
Book of Life  94
books  39
Bost  282
botany  235, 288
Boudhou  227
Bourignonists  312
Brahma  227
brevity  262
British Museum  164
Buchanan, Claudius  159
Buckland  234
Buddhists  227
Buffon  228, 232
Burkardt  311

Caesar  65, 188
Caiaphas  53, 70, 252, 254
Caius  38
*Calculations* (Leslie)  235
Calcutta  193
Calvary  271
Calvin, John  46, 191, 193, 251, 315
Cambridge  159
Canaan  218, 238
Canada  235
Candace  314

*321*

canon 88-89, 132, 151, 284
Canton de Vaud 273
Capellus 116
Capernaum 248
Capitol 273
Carpus 270, 272
Carson, Alexander 274
Casca 188
Cassius 188
Castellio 137, 139, 191, 193
Cataphrygians 141
catechism 30
Catherine de Médicis 229
Catherine II 209
causation 142
Cavendish 237
celibacy 121, 158
Celsus 141, 191-192
Cenchrea 279
census 209-210, 213
Cerdo 135
certainty 32
Cesarea 87-88, 254, 263, 293
Chaldeans 54, 249
Chalmers 297
chaos 238, 259
charity 264
Charron 119
Chateaubriand 58
Chaubard 224, 238
Chebar 230
children 64, 121
Chimborazo 222, 236
China 31
Chinese 227
*Chou-king* 227
*Christian Observer* 160
Christianity 40
Christians 161, 229
*Christliche Glaube, Der* (Schleiermacher) 40

*Chronicle of Alexandria* 214
chronological order 211
chronology 218
Chrysostom 77, 131, 141, 144, 161, 277, 311
church 26, 32–33, 35, 38–39, 41, 46, 51, 62, 72, 76, 83, 85, 88, 90-92, 94, 102, 111, 120, 124-127, 129-132, 138-140, 142-143, 145, 151–152, 156, 174, 177, 181, 184, 201, 228, 230, 232, 249, 255-256, 260, 262, 264, 268, 279-282, 284-285, 290-291, 299, 301-304, 308, 310-311, 317
"church fathers" 25, 102, 111, 118-120, 130, 131, 139, 143-144, 156, 158, 161, 174, 178, 215, 228, 230, 232, 234, 257-258, 262, 268, 273, 286, 288, 299, 311, 315
church of Rome 280
Cicero 40, 227
circumstances 50
Claude 123
Claudius 281-282
Clement of Alexandria 175
Clement XI 120
Cleopas 62, 101-202, 206
clergy 173, 228
clouds 60
Cobbet, William 186
Coislin, Cardinal 164
colleges 173
Collins, Anthony 156, 163
colors 224
Columbus, Christopher 228
coming of the Lord 187
commandments 85
*Comment. on the Epistle to the Ephesians* (Jerome) 183

INDEX

*Comment. on the Epistle to the Galatians* (Jerome) 135, 183
*Comment. on the Epistle to Titus* (Jerome) 183
Commodus 91
common sense 228
condemnation 263
Confession of Faith (484) 178
Confession of Faith (French) 125
Confucius 231, 261
conscience 33, 53, 64
Constance 273
Constantinople 229, 277, 317
*Contra Apion* 124
*Contra Gentes* (Athanasius) 144
contradictions 138, 140, 142, 190-197, 202-204, 209, 211-213, 219, 248
controversies 264
conversions 264, 300
convictions 62
Copernicus 228
Coptic 249
copyists 155, 161, 285
Corinth 87, 108, 249, 254, 279, 281
Corinthians 202, 244, 290
Cornelius 87, 264
cosmogony 227-228, 232
Coton 118, 119
Council of Constantinople 134, 136
Council of Salamanca 228
Council of Toulouse 311
Council of Trent 118-119, 120, 130, 151, 262
councils 114, 118, 158
Count de Boulainvilliers 230, 292
creation 39, 64, 140, 230, 233-235, 238, 248, 249, 259, 263, 276, 286-287, 294

Creissenach 118
Cretans 70
Crete 70
*Critical Bible* 157
criticism 155, 162-164, 167, 181, 198, 283-304
critics 159
cross 32-33, 45, 80, 100-101, 203, 213, 265-266, 271, 300, 312
crucifixion 265
Cuvier 234
Cyprian 144, 251
Cyrenius 193, 209-210, 213

D'Alembert 229
Damascenus 311
Daniel 50, 52, 55, 75, 76, 191, 249, 252, 254, 283, 315
Darius 68
darkness 29
dates 192, 208, 219
David 58, 61, 71, 77, 86, 100, 101, 109-110, 114-115, 195, 208, 244, 249, 252, 259-260, 271, 314
*De Anima* (Tertullian) 144
*De Autor. Script.* 192
de Candolle 235
*De cognit. Dei* (Gregory of Nyssa) 144
*De consensu Evang.* (Augustine) 198
*De Discrimine Revelat. et Inspirationis* (Baumgarten) 108
*De Eccl.* (Bellarmin) 118
*De Incarnat. Christi.* (Athanasius) 144
*De la Verité de la Religion Chrètienne* (Mornay) 261
DeLuc 234

*De Opere et Eleemos* (Cyprian) 144
*DePerron contre Tilenus* (Coton) 119
*De Præscript. advers. hæret.* (Tertullian) 144
DeSacy 163
DeThou 232
*De Trinit.* (Hilary) 144
*De unitate Ecclesiæ* (Augustine) 144
*De Verbo Dei* (Bellarmin) 119, 262
DeWette 40, 116, 138, 147, 186
death 101, 266, 299
Decalogue 154, 267
decrees 255
decretals 158, 262
defend 275
*Defense of Dr. Haffner's Preface to the Bible* (Smith) 193
definitions 107–108
degrees 115
Deist 185
Delphos 67
demigods 122, 257
Demosthenes de Corona 90
denominations 310
Deucalion 238
Devil 97
devils 97-98, 151, 289, 312
*Dialog. De Anima et Resurrectione* (Gregory of Nyssa) 144
Dick, John 41, 51, 192
dictation 55–56, 58, 71, 73, 77, 83, 85, 103, 119, 122, 124- 125, 134, 140, 149, 150, 154, 156, 232, 249, 267, 270, 305, 306
different readings 162; *see also* various readings
Dinah 197

Diocletian 191
Diodorus of Sicily 229
Diogenes Laërtius 70
Dionysius 311
direction 41
disciples 69, 200
*Discourses on the Relations* (Wiseman) 157
dispersion 117, 128, 131
*Divarication of the New Testament* (Wirgmann) 186
diversity 142
divorce 99
doctors 88, 94-97, 104, 116, 118, 131, 134-139, 141-142, 144, 154, 188, 283, 292, 298, 316
doctrine 26, 30–32, 34, 38, 41, 46, 48, 50, 72, 76, 79, 92, 93, 103, 127, 133, 143, 145, 155, 174, 177, 262
*Doctrine of the Greek Article* (Middleton) 179
Domitian 230, 299
Douay 118
doubts 29, 264
dreams 107
Dresden 164
DuPin 135
*Du pouvoir de St Pierre dans l'Eglise* (Bost) 282
dullness 26
dungeons 272
Duval 311

Earth 34, 59, 62, 68, 74, 76, 79-80, 83, 95, 101-102, 118, 135, 149, 151, 178, 188, 220-224, 227-229, 231, 233–234, 236, 241, 252, 256-257, 265, 268, 271, 273-274, 294, 318

East Indies 150
*Ecclesiastical History* (Eusebius) 191
*Eccles. Writers* (Jerome) 191
Eckius 131
ecstasy 91, 141
Eden 64, 97
edification 49, 72
education 50
Edwards, Jonathan 45, 315
efficacious grace 44
Egypt 159, 218, 231, 259
Eichhorn, Joseph 116, 127, 138, 157, 181, 186, 291, 312
*Einleitung in das alte Testament* (Eichhorn) 138, 181
*Einleitung in die Schriften des Neuen Testaments* (Hug) 291
Elamite 249
elders 70, 268
Eleazar, Rabbi 117, 121
elect 28, 44, 76, 108, 258, 272, 313
election 289, 312
elements 229, 231-232
*Elements de Geologie* (Chaubard) 224, 238
elevation 41
Elijah 260, 298
Elisha 260
eloquence 58
Elzevir 162, 166, 181
*Emile* (Rousseau) 271
Emmaus 101, 201-202, 206-207
emotions 39, 43, 53, 62, 205, 261, 264, 306, 315
Empedocles 229
emperors 158, 189
Eneas 264
England 41, 193
Englefield, Henry 237

English Channel 236
Enoch 60, 60–61, 199, 294
enthusiasm 91
*Entwickelungs Geschichte des Mosaischen Ritual Besetzes* (Creissenach) 118
Epaphroditus 112, 278
Epenetus 279
Ephesians 83
Ephesus 87, 230, 281
Ephrem 164
Epicurus 62
Epimenides 70
Epiphanius 87, 91, 129, 136, 141, 144
*Epistle of Manichaeus* 132
epistles 41, 73, 78, 83, 157, 190
equinoxes 225
Er 197
Erasmus 90, 181, 182
errors 28, 30, 33, 41, 46-47, 51, 62, 139, 145, 147–148, 161, 186-188, 190-192, 219, 220, 230, 232, 247, 294, 296–297, 305, 308
erudition 209
Esau 189
*Esdras* 117, 124, 216
*Essay on the Inspiration of the Holy Scriptures, An* (Dick) 51
*Essays* (Montaigne) 232
Esther 254
eternal life 102
ether 234
*Ethicis regni* (Basil the Great) 144
Ethiopian 158
Europe 155
Eusebius 91, 129, 142, 191, 219
Eusebius of Cæsarea 143
Eutychus 112
*Evangel. Kirchen-Zeitung* 203

*Evangelical Gazette* 203
Evangelists 41
evasions 245–283
exaggeration 46, 51
*Examination* (Veysie) 292
excitation 91
exegesis 104
*Exhortat. to Marcella* (Jerome) 311
exhortation 72
experience(s) 40, 62, 224, 246
expiation 151, 289, 312
*Exposition of the Book of Job* (Gregory) 129
*Exsurge* (Leo X) 120
extension 225
Ezekiel 50, 53, 55, 58, 68, 75-76, 81
Ezra 315

facts 46, 145, 186, 190-191, 201, 211–212, 231
fairies 257
faith 27–29, 33, 38–39, 46–49, 51, 84, 96, 108, 111, 115-116, 119-121, 125, 127, 129, 132, 179, 184, 189, 201, 251, 254, 262, 266, 276, 284-285, 288-289, 292-293, 296, 302
fall 263
fallibility 145
false prophets 69
false religions 310
fanatics 138
feeling 303
Felix 264
Fénélon 58
Festus 82, 217
fishermen 258
flesh 36
flood 42, 60, 215
Florus 205

foresight 47
France 121
Fredigise 135
Free Thinkers 156
freedmen 282
freemasonry 32
Freiburg 60
French 162
frivolity 34
future 34

Gabler 116, 138
Galatians 33, 189, 282
Galen 286
Galilee 98, 207
Galileo 228, 235
Gamaliel 269
garments 271–273, 275, 314
Gauls 189
gehenna 289
*Gemara* 117, 311
genealogies 39, 142, 208, 219
Geneva 162, 196, 283
genii 257
Gentiles 87-88, 208, 232, 264, 274, 280-281
geologists 237
geometry 32, 58
*Georg.* 70
Gerard 192
Germain 164
Germany 25, 41, 121, 138, 181, 221
Gibeon 220, 224
Gieseler 291
gifts 71, 79, 85, 87, 108-114, 143, 263, 278
Giulani, Ph. 230
Gleig 294
glory 36, 316
Gnostics 134, 135, 140

# INDEX

God 44, 47, 49, 52, 55–57, 59, 62, 64–65, 151, 177, 182–183, 186, 188, 190, 220, 239, 241, 246, 249–251, 254, 259; the Father 30–32, 45, 62, 79, 94, 100–102, 104, 112, 136, 207, 243, 251, 258, 266, 300, 317; Holy Spirit 26, 29, 32–33, 38–41, 43–44, 46–47, 50, 53, 55, 58, 60, 65, 66–70, 72–74, 76–77, 79–83, 85–88, 91–92, 94, 97, 99, 100-101, 103, 106, 108, 110-114, 116, 118-119, 122-126, 132-135, 137, 140, 142, 146–148, 151, 153, 177-179, 188–189, 213, 232, 242, 244–246, 248-249, 251, 253-256, 259, 263, 265, 267-271, 273, 277-279, 281, 288, 291, 301, 303, 306, 308, 310, 312, 313, 315, 317; the Son 75-76, 78, 95, 306-307
gods 63, 68, 69, 104, 227, 257
Golgotha 203
Gomar 90
Gospel 33, 35–36, 41, 54, 58, 80, 82, 84, 89, 94, 97, 109, 114, 129, 132, 142, 183, 250, 282, 284, 289, 306, 315
*Gospels* 42, 73, 78, 83, 157, 164, 192, 194, 200–202, 208, 254-255, 269, 291–292
Gourgaud 194
grace 35, 61–62, 174, 255, 288, 312, 316
grammar 32
Gratian 311
gratitude 35
gravitation 222, 234
Greece 229, 231
Greek Church 182

Greeks 67–68, 70, 227, 264
Greenwich Observatory 225
Gregory 130, 311
Gregory Nazianzen 129
Gregory of Nazianzus 161
Gregory of Nyssa 144
Gregory the Great 144
Griesbach 157, 163-164, 167-168, 174-175, 176-180, 182, 202, 214
Grimaldi 186
Grotius 297
Guericke 48

Habakkuk 50
habits 50
Hades 253
Haggai 68, 216
*Hagiographa* 137
Haldane, Robert 274
Hales 192
Halley 43
hallucinations 312
Hamilton 152
harmony 299
healing(s) 71, 85
health 278
hearing 33
heart 55, 107, 256, 257, 259, 298
Heaven 34-35, 45, 59, 61, 64–65, 76, 80, 94, 96, 98, 101-102, 135, 140, 149, 151, 188, 205, 220, 240–241, 246, 248, 255-258, 261, 264, 266, 271, 274, 280, 295, 301, 314, 317-318
heavens 62, 74, 95, 104, 220, 225, 229-230, 233–235, 237, 239–240, 256, 294, 308
Hebrew 153, 160-161
Hecla 237
Hegel 312

Heli 208
Hell 151, 312
Hengstenberg 191-192, 203-204
Henry 90
Henry III 229
Henry IV 229
Hercules 258, 298
heresies 120, 134, 120, 136, 264
heretics 143, 178
hermeneutics 104
Herod 54, 209, 210
Herod Agrippa 282
Herod the Great 209
Herodias 282
Herschel, John 225, 239
Hesiod 227
Hess 202
Hezekiah 315
Hiddo 216
Hieronymus 141, 198, 215
Hilary 129, 144
Hillel 117
Hincmar 311
Hindus 227
Hipparchus 239
*Hist. Eccles.* (Eusebius) 142, 219
*Histoire des Juifs* (Prideau) 262
*Histoire Geographique de l'Homme* (Zimmerman) 236
historical books 42
historical writings 73
histories 255, 259, 261
*Historisch-kritischer Versuch* (Gieseler) 291
history 32, 41, 133, 139, 143, 155, 190, 215, 254–269, 281, 295, 301, 313
*History of the Council of Trent* (Paul) 119, 129–131
*History of the Jewish Wars* (Josephus) 216

*History of the Reformation* (Merle D'Aubigné) 302
holiness 32, 57, 64, 70, 110, 111
Holy Office 228
Holy Spirit 26, 29, 32–33, 38–41, 43–44, 46–47, 50, 53, 55, 58, 60, 65, 66–70, 72-74, 76-77, 79-83, 85-88, 91–92, 94, 97, 99, 100-101, 103, 106, 108, 110-114, 116, 118-119, 122-126, 132-135, 137, 140, 142, 146–148, 151, 153, 177-179, 188–189, 213, 232, 242, 244–246, 248-249, 251, 253-256, 259, 263, 265, 267-271, 273, 277-279, 281, 288, 291, 301, 303, 306, 308, 310, 312, 313, 315, 317
Homer 227
homicides 215
Hooper 273
Horeb 61, 65
Horne 153, 160, 192, 211, 219, 291, 294
horoscopes 229-230, 292
Hosea 50, 68, 75
hospitality 279
Houbigant 157
Huet 297
Hug 138, 157, 291
human eye 224
human races 236
human wisdom 180
hymns 64

idolatry 27, 127, 265
ignorance 25–26, 34, 40, 111, 116, 142, 183, 218, 220, 263, 286-287, 308
Illuminati 312
illumination 46, 57, 108-112, 114-116

illusions 224
Illyricum 88, 278
images 27, 121, 129, 158, 267, 311
imagination 50, 103, 256
Immanuel 30
immensity 239
immortality 258
imperfections 145
importance 52, 55, 139, 151, 177, 194
*In Dialogis.* 193
*In Reg.* 193
India 227
Indies 121
individuality 49–65, 72, 253, 306, 315
indulgences 122
infallibility 115, 117-118, 122, 145, 152, 274
infidels 185
infinity 150
innocence 29
Innocent XI 230
insignificance 270
inspiration 111; *afflatu divino* 57; degrees 48, 51, 57, 107, 112, 137, 139; direction 41, 107; elevation 41, 107; extraordinary excitation 57; infallibility 145; objections 145–244; plenary 49, 51, 55–56, 73, 77, 94, 104, 134, 139, 143-145, 182, 185, 187-188, 191-192, 220, 224, 232, 242, 307, 309; plenitude 42; suggestion 41, 107; superintendence 41, 50, 55, 107; universality 42; verbal 74, 94, 102, 104, 135, 141, 145, 151-152, 154, 220, 307
instruction 26, 64

*intellectus agens* 137
interpretation 71-72
*Introduction to the Critical Study of the Bible* (Horne) 153, 160, 211, 219, 291, 294
*Introduction to the New Testament* (Michaëlis) 41, 286, 291, 294
*Introduction to the New Testament Scriptures* (Hug) 138
*Introduction to the Reading of the Hebrew Scriptures* (Hamilton) 152
Irenæus 122, 140, 143, 144, 286, 288, 316
Isaac 259–260
Isaac, Rabbi 117
Isaiah 27, 50, 52, 55, 61, 74-75, 81, 86, 98, 186, 283
Isidore Clarius 119
Isidore Mercator 311
Israel 79, 80, 100, 138, 158, 198, 219, 252, 254, 296
Italy 121
Ives of Chartres 311

Jacob 35, 208, 261, 270, 293-294
Jacob, Rabbi 117, 121
James 90, 128, 187, 217, 290, 294
James, Thomas 119, 152
Jason 298
Jehoiachim 208
Jehoiada 214–215, 217
Jehovah 64, 68, 98, 113-114, 154; *see also* God
Jennings 297
Jeremiah 50, 55, 60–61, 61, 68, 75–76, 81, 86, 197–199, 216, 314
Jericho 193, 195, 196, 230
Jerome 91, 119, 130, 131, 135, 141, 142, 149, 151–152, 161,

175, 183, 191, 232, 234, 270, 311
Jerome of Prague 273
Jerusalem 65, 69, 79, 81, 87, 99, 118, 128, 196, 201, 207, 210, 216, 221, 248, 254, 262-265, 271, 278, 281, 296, 318
Jesuits 118
Jesus Christ 25-26, 29-31, 42, 45, 49, 53, 56-57, 60-61, 61, 63, 69-70, 72, 74-75, 76-80, 82, 84, 86-90, 94, 95- 98, 102-103, 108, 109-112, 114-115, 118-119, 122, 124, 126-127, 129-130, 132-136, 142, 150-151, 155, 158, 160-161, 177, 179-180, 186-188, 194, 195-196, 199-204, 207-209, 212-217, 219, 242, 250-251, 258-259, 262-263, 265-266, 268, 270-272, 277, 279-282, 293-295, 299, 301-302, 306-310, 312-314, 316-317; *see also* God
*Jewish Wars* (Josephus) 205
Jews 38, 48, 77, 79, 88, 95, 103, 117, 121, 124, 127-130, 136, 150, 153, 158-159, 161, 182, 189, 199-200, 215-217, 229-232, 254, 262, 264, 272, 281, 290, 293, 313
Joanna 199
Joash 208
Job 269
John 42, 44, 50, 52-53, 55, 58, 60, 84, 88-90, 94, 126, 155, 186, 200, 202, 204, 206, 212, 248-250, 254, 266, 286
John Damascenus 287
John the Baptist 35, 68, 84, 115, 210, 253, 314
Jonah 59, 259

Jonathan 260
Jonathan Ben-Uziel 216
Joram 219
Jordan River 59, 99, 253-254
Joseph 197, 208, 259, 293
Joseph Albo 137
Joseph of Arimathea 203
Josephus 38, 90, 124, 125, 127, 128-129, 136, 205, 209, 216, 217, 261
Joshua 75, 117, 220, 222, 238, 259
Josiah 315
Jotham 208
Juda 117
Judah 219, 254
Judaism 310
Judas 87, 196, 197
Judas Iscariot 267
Judas the Galilean 209
Jude 84, 186, 199, 294
Judea 79, 87, 99, 209-210, 230
judgment 60, 70, 287
Julius 264
Julius Africanus 142, 219
Junia 280
justification 29, 289
Justin Martyr 140, 144, 299
Juvenal 258
Juvet 273

Kennicott 157
Kepler 228
Keturah 189
keys 80
Kimchi, David 137
kingdom 94
kingdom of God 80, 110
kingdom of Heaven 82
kings 64, 219, 254, 258, 264
Klopstock 231

# INDEX

knowledge 31, 33, 46, 67, 71, 90, 94, 101, 110-112, 120, 122, 132, 140, 189, 315, 317
Kopp 291
Koran 131, 227, 261
Korholt 152

LaGrange 235
LaPlace 225, 237
Labadists 312
Lachman 174-176
Lactantius 228, 232
laity 120
Lamech 269
Lanfranc 311
language(s) 29, 31, 33, 46-47, 49-50, 63, 66, 70-71, 80-83, 91-92, 103, 106, 113, 116, 120, 122, 129, 135, 146-148, 155, 158, 185, 239, 245, 247, 254, 295
Lardner 152, 291
last judgment 287
Latin 32, 121, 158, 249
Latin Church 182
Law 41, 75, 137, 269, 311
law 29, 33, 102, 103-104
*Law and the Prophets* 311
Lawrence 157, 167
laws of nature 145, 219
Lazarus 56, 258, 316
LeClerc, John 116, 138, 202-203, 291
learning 30, 33, 35, 294-295
*Lectionaria* 157
*Lectures on the Evidences of Christianity* (Wilson) 51, 193
Lee 179
*Legatio pro Christianis* (Athenagoras) 140
legends 158

*Lehrbuch Anmerk* (De Wette) 40
Leibniz 133
Leighton 251, 315
Leo 311
Leo X 120
Leo XII 120
*Les Livres sacrés de L'Orient* (Panthier) 227, 261
Leslie 235, 297
Lessing 291
*Letter to Dr. Boyle on the Cause of Weight* (Newton) 235
Leucippus 229
Levites 296
liberty 216
libraries 181
life 65
light 230, 234, 259
Lightfoot 90
Littleton 297
liturgies 258
Livy 131
Locke 150
logic 155
longings 63
Lord's coming 238
Lord's Prayer 212
Lord's Supper 267
Louvain 118
Lucas 217
Lucius 217
Lucius of Cyrene 88
Lucretius 228, 232
Luke 42, 53, 55, 58, 86-88, 90, 195-196, 199, 202, 204, 209-213, 254, 263, 267, 272, 291-294
lusts 29
Luther, Martin 46, 120, 126, 147, 149, 251, 301, 302
Lydia 264

Maccabees 314
*Maccabees, Book of* 155
MacCaul 117
magicians 121, 231
magistrates 81
magnetism 235
Maimonides, Moses 137
majesty 36
Malachi 68, 75, 314
Malta 254, 263
Mamertine 272
man 256
Man of Sin 158, 311
Manaen 88
Manes 135, 136
Manichaeus 135
Manicheans 135
manna 259
manners 119
Manon 261
manuscripts 131, 145, 154-167, 173, 175-178, 180-181, 183, 198, 284, 295, 307–308
Marcel de Serres 235
Marcion 91, 135
Mark 42, 55, 57, 86-88, 90, 195-196, 202, 204-205, 212, 250, 254, 267, 291–292
marriage 99, 158, 241, 258
Marsh 291
Martha 56
Martin 149, 152, 162-164, 167, 211
martyrs 189, 273
Mary 207-208, 265–266, 269, 280
Mary Magdalene 199-202, 204, 206–207
Maskeline 237
mass 122
Massorethes 128, 160, 174
Matthæi 157, 164, 167

Matthew 42, 57, 61, 84, 89, 196, 198, 199-200, 204-205, 212-213, 254, 263, 267, 294
Maximin 178
meals 122
*Mécanique Céleste* 31
Mecca 261
Mede 199
Media 54
medicine 32
Medina 63
Mediterranean 194
Melchizedec 259, 314
*Memoir* (Newton) 235
*Memoires de Marcel de Serres* 235
*Memoires du Dr. J. L. Prevost* 238
memory 43, 116, 139
merchants 282
mercy 65, 257
merit 29
Merle D'Aubigné 302
Messiah 80, 100, 110, 118, 315
Meurice, Baron 235
Michael 294
Michaëlis, John Henry 41, 84, 89, 116, 133, 138, 181, 286, 291, 294
*Michaëlis* (Marsh) 291
Michaëlis, John Henry 157
Middle Ages 48, 137, 158
Middleton, Bishop Conyers 179
Milan 302
Mill 157, 167, 175-176, 179, 181, 182
Millii 291
Miltiades 91, 141
Milton 231
miracles 45–47, 54, 55, 71, 85, 112, 122, 138, 186, 204, 212, 218, 220–224, 238, 244, 262, 266, 278, 289, 312

*Mishna* 117, 311
mission 79
missionaries 227
*Modern Universal History* 227
Mohammed 63, 136, 227, 261
Mohammedans 135, 222
monasteries 159, 173
monks 154
Monod 196
monotheism 138
Mont Athos 159
Mont Blanc 236, 237
Montaigne, Michel 232
Montanists 141
Montanus 91
Montholon 194
Moon 220, 223-224, 227, 238, 257, 292
moral sense 34
*Moralia in Job* (Gregory) 144
morality 34, 121, 138, 262
*More Nebuchim* (Maimonides) 137
Moriah 260
Mornay, Duplessis 261
Moscow 182
Moses 41, 44, 52–54, 57–58, 61, 68–69, 75, 76, 78, 85, 95, 99, 101, 117, 128, 155, 186, 195, 225, 230, 241, 243, 248-249, 253-254, 259, 294
"mother of God" 266
Mount Athos 164
Mount Sinai 253
Mount Tabor 253, 254
mountains 236, 259
Munich 182
murder 63, 216, 265
Muses 68
myrrh 203, 204

mystery 80, 84, 94, 109, 112, 120, 123, 140, 177, 256
Mysticism 312
myths 186, 257

Naaman 260
Napoleon 149, 194, 195
Narcissus 279, 282
narratives 39, 41, 61, 64, 190-192, 194-196, 199, 201, 210-211, 219, 230, 260, 261, 265, 268, 292
Nathan 68, 208
National Convention 209
natural philosophy 219, 227
naturalists 286
nature 40, 308, 316
Nazareth 98
Nebuchadnezzar 159, 208
Nehemiah 52, 315
Nepos 211
Nero 82, 281-282, 290
Nestorianism 134
new birth 40, 112
New Testament 74, 78–91, 125, 127, 129-131, 135-136, 139, 151-153, 157, 161-162, 167, 173-176, 182, 186, 212, 216-217, 232, 234, 243, 255, 261, 267-269, 307-308
Newton, Isaac 43, 224, 228, 234
Nicias 70
Nicodemus 203-204
Niemeyer 291
Nineveh 59
Noah 239, 259, 296
Nolan 157, 167
North Sea 236
novelties 34
Nun 238

obscurity 26
*Œuvres Posthumes* (Claude) 123
Ogyges 238
Old Testament 74-75, 77-79, 83, 87, 89, 91, 94, 109, 118, 124, 127-129, 136-137, 139-140, 153, 157, 159-161, 186, 216, 232, 234, 243, 255, 261, 268, 299, 307, 309, 313
Olshausen 202–203
Olympus 257
omnipotence 223
*On False Knowledge* (Lactantius) 228
Onan 197
*Opera August.* 132
opinions 49, 58
oral tradition 291
ordinances 80
Origen 87, 129, 141, 144, 161, 191, 219, 269, 287–288
*Origenes adamantius* 287
orthodoxy 92
Osterwald 149, 152, 162-164, 166, 167, 211

pagans 141, 286
palaces 173
Palestine 224
pantheism 231-232
Panthier 227
parables 64, 316
Paracelsists 312
paradise 64, 215, 302
paradise lost 299
paralogisms 186
paraphrase 152-153
Paris 194
Parthian 249
Pascal 42, 129, 311, 315
Passionei, Cardinal 164

Patmos 60, 65, 230
patriarchs 197
patriotism 34
Paul 25–26, 28–29, 33, 38, 44-45, 50, 52, 55, 61, 66, 70, 72, 74, 77–78, 83–85, 87, 89, 91–93, 109, 111-115, 123-126, 142, 145, 151, 178, 183, 186, 187, 189-190, 202, 204, 241–244, 250, 254, 259, 263-264, 270, 272-273, 274, 276-277, 279, 280-281, 290, 293, 302, 306, 309
Paul, Father 119, 129–131
Paulus 116, 138, 192, 312
peace 65
Pelagianism 134
Pelagius 311
Peloponnesus 229
Pentateuch 135, 160, 191, 255
Pentecost 61, 78, 82, 87, 186, 248
persecutions 158, 264
Persia 54
Persis 280
Peter 50, 52, 55, 61, 67, 69-70, 73, 75, 77–78, 84, 87–89, 92, 94, 109, 113-114, 125, 186, 196, 200-202, 206-207, 242, 249, 250, 253, 281-282, 315
Peter Martyr 193, 218
phantoms 224
Pharaoh 65, 68
Pharisees 99-100
Phebe 279, 280
Philip 88
Philippians 45, 273
Philistines 158
Philo 38, 127, 136
Philoläus of Crotona 229
philosophers 65, 227, 231-232

## INDEX

philosophy 30, 63, 230
phraseology 54
Phrygia 91
physicians 286, 288
Pilate 54, 271, 302, 308
pillar of fire 259
Pius 311
planets 225, 231, 257
plants 54, 288
Plato 63, 67, 133, 136, 232
Pliny 227-228, 232
Plutarch 227-228, 232, 298
poem 136
poesy 231
poetry 61, 64, 103
poets 40, 68, 256, 257
Polycarp 286
polytheism 231
Pompey 188, 296
poor 35, 264
pope 27, 182, 228, 282
Pope Gregory IX 311
popes 118, 120, 138
popularity 34
Porphyry 48
Porphyry, Malchus 191
Pouran 227
poverty 98, 273
prayer 27, 33, 35, 42, 64, 121-122, 264, 277
pre-established harmony 226, 284
preaching 33, 83-84, 94, 98, 312
prediction 70, 229
*Preface on Job* (Jerome) 131
prejudices 46, 150, 183, 264
*Preliminary Manuals* (DeWette) 138
*Prepar. Evangel.* (Eusebius) 191
presbyters 268
preservation 156-157, 160-161, 173, 176

Priam 298
Prideau 262
priesthoods 122
Priestley 186, 312
priests 121-122, 129, 182, 258
*Principia* (Newton) 43
principles 34
Prisca 217
Priscilla 217, 280–281
prison 273
probation 263
Procopius 87
*Proemium in epist. ad Philem.* (Jerome) 270
progress 286
*Prolegom.* 215
promises 79, 80
prophecy 41-42, 54, 67, 71, 73, 84, 126, 137, 264, 293, 300, 316
prophesy 67
prophetesses 88
*Prophets* 75-76, 78, 85, 95, 101, 137, 269, 311
prophets 58–59, 62, 66–73, 75-77, 79, 81–91, 94, 107, 110-111, 113-115, 117-118, 121, 123-124, 127, 135, 140-141, 146, 149, 155, 183, 199, 216-217, 220, 230, 243, 245, 249, 251, 253, 255, 287, 307, 315-316
providence 54, 88, 95, 127-128, 130, 156, 158, 160-162, 185, 255, 308
*Provincial Letters* (Pascal) 42
psalmody 230
*Psalms* 72
Ptolemy 239
punctuation 166
pundit 194
punishment 151, 158, 312

purgatory 122
Pythagoras 231, 298
Python 69
Pythoness 57, 67

Quintilius Varus 209
Quirinius 209
quotations 35, 153, 156, 190, 219

Rabba 217
Rabbat 217
rabbins 48, 137
Rabshakeh 269
Racine 56, 231
Radbert 311
Rahab 263
Ramah 252
Ranhardt 297
rank 79
Rationalism 29, 310
Rationalists 62, 138, 164, 181, 311-312
reading 120, 158
readings 176
reality 224
reason 137, 310
reasoning 25, 29, 47-48, 50, 73, 77, 96, 135, 145, 155, 183, 185-186, 189-191, 228, 275, 290, 298
Réaumur, René Antoine Ferchault de 237
recollections 50–51, 53, 62
*Records of the Creation, The* (Sumner) 236
Red Sea 54, 218
redemption 38, 223, 257, 260, 263, 286, 296, 299, 314, 316
Reformation 129, 139, 144, 239, 302, 312

Reformers 26
regeneration 40
religion 30–34, 63
*Remarks* (Edwards) 45
repentance 244
reproof 26
Restig 116, 138
resurrection 49, 88, 94, 99, 151, 186, 199, 200-202, 262, 264, 266, 289, 312
Reus 181
revelation 28, 30, 72–73, 84, 108-109, 116, 133, 246, 307
righteousness 33, 65, 175, 312
righteousness of faith 190
rites 296
Roman Catholicism 257–258, 267, 311
Roman Catholic Church 117-118, 158, 162-163
Roman Empire 311
Romans 282
Rome 65, 87, 88, 254, 263, 272-274, 279-282, 301-302, 311
Rosenmuller 116
Rossi 157
rotation 221, 223, 225, 238
Rousseau 48, 63, 186, 271
Royal Society of London 235
Rudelbach 48, 135, 137, 139
Rufus 280
Russia 159, 164
Ruth 254, 260, 263

Sabbath 203–205
sacraments 312
sacrifices 259, 314
Sadducees 49, 99
Saint-Simon 63
saints 60, 115, 116-117, 129, 279, 299, 301, 316, 317

## INDEX

Saleve 237
Salome 199
salvation 32, 95, 114, 119, 139, 190, 289, 295, 315
Samaria 79, 87
Samuel 71, 253, 312
sanctification 40, 44
Sanhedrin 188, 205, 264
Sapphira 294
Sarah 259
Satan 29, 99, 187, 269, 277, 294
satisfaction 312
Saturninus 209
Saul 71, 88, 114, 252
Scaliger 116
scandal 34
scepticism 28
Schammai 117
Schleiermacher 40, 137
Scholz 157, 167, 174-175, 177, 179, 180, 182, 183
*Schultens' Compendium on the Proverbs* 138
Schuster 116, 138
science 31-33, 43, 46, 140, 164, 181, 220, 224-226, 230-231, 233-234, 236-237, 284-304, 310
scribes 117, 315
Sechu 252
second causes 54, 306
second coming 313
Second Council of Nicea 121
*Second Maccabees* 198
Seleucidæ 158
Semler 116, 127, 138
Seneca 63, 227, 258, 298
senses 60
sentiments 31
*Sentiments de quelques theologiens de Holland* 138

Septuagint 69, 145, 151-154, 160-161, 215, 232, 234, 308
Severus of Antioch 214
Shakers 312
Shaster 227
Shekinah 295
Shemaia 117
shepherds 64, 258
Shiloh 253
Shunamite 260
Shusan 254
sibyls 141
Silas 87, 217
Silvanus 217
Simeon 88
simplicity 61
sin 30, 62, 80, 100, 123, 128, 175, 244, 288-289, 299
Sinai 59, 98-99, 254
*Six Letters to Granville Sharpe* (Wordsworth) 178
Sixtus V 152
slaves 282
sloth 34
Smith, Pye 41, 193
Soccho 117
Socinians 136
Socinus 137, 139, 186, 192, 312
Socrates 133, 271
soldiers 258
Solomon 57, 61, 114, 136, 197, 208, 249, 259
Solomon Jarchi 137
Solomon's Porch 69, 102-103
Someyra 227
Sorbonne 135
sovereignty 142
Spain 121, 228, 278
speculations 31, 315
spirituality 28, 147, 260
spurious Gospels 261

*337*

St. George's Channel 236
St. Germain 166
St. Helena 194
Stapleton 131
stars 220, 223, 225, 229, 231-232, 239, 240
statistics 64
statues 129
Stephanus 178, 181
Stephen 74, 215
Strabo 70
Strauss 63, 150, 186-187, 191, 312
study 30, 33, 34, 120, 121, 144
style 49, 58, 62, 72, 135, 142, 245, 290
succession 119
Suetonius 211
sufferings 262
suggestion 41
suicide 197
Suidas 70
Sumner 236
Sun 220-224, 227, 231, 234-235, 238, 297
superintendence 41, 50, 55
superstitions 183, 185-187, 229
Switzerland 187, 210, 273
sybilline oracles 63
sylphs 257
sympathy 63
*Symposium* (Plato) 136
synagogues 81
Syria 209, 210
Syriac 158

tabernacle 263, 314
Tacitus 232, 258, 298
talismans 229
Talmud 117-118, 128, 137, 153, 262, 311

Tamar 263
Targum 216, 311
tax-gatherers 258
teachers 85
telescope 233, 239
temple 158, 215-217, 230, 254, 277, 295-297, 314
temptation 210
Ten Commandments 146
Terence 182
Tertullian 91, 141, 144
Thales 231, 298
Theodore of Mopsuestia 41, 134, 136
Theodoret 144, 161
*Theol.* (Arsdekin) 311
*Theologia Elenct.* (Turretin) 132, 138, 193
theologians 286
theology 30-34, 92, 143
*Theophilus ad Autolyc.* 299
Theophrastus 90
Theophylact 77, 214
*Theories of Inspiration, The* (Carson) 274
Thessalonians 291
thinking 62
*Third Discourse on the Natural History of the Human Race* (Wiseman) 236
thoughts 41, 73, 83, 91, 103, 105, 111, 122, 126, 146–148, 150-151, 245–254, 255, 256, 259, 270, 298, 305, 308-309
Tiber 189, 273
Tiberius 113, 208, 299
tides 237
Timæus 67
Timeus 195
Timothy 87, 112, 124, 255, 263, 270, 273, 276-277

# INDEX

Tittman 174-176
Titus 261
tongues 71, 85, 122, 158
touch 224
traditions 30, 34, 94, 117-120, 122, 129, 158, 160, 216, 262, 277, 310
*Traité* (Baile) 262
*Traité de la Religion* (La Chamb.) 138
translations 145–154, 166, 175, 209-210, 307
translators 145, 162
tree of life 64, 299
Trinity 289
Trinity College 43
Troas 254, 263, 270, 272
Trophimus 112
Troy 218, 230, 271
truth 30–33, 36, 41, 46, 50, 62, 64-65, 96, 108, 114, 123, 129, 251, 260, 284, 313-314
Tryphena 280
Tryphosa 280
Turkish Asia 159
Turks 230
Turretin, Francis 132, 138, 193, 297
Twesten 40–41, 52, 126, 193, 209
types 295, 316

*Über die Dogmatik* (Vories) 51
Ultra-Arians 136
Ultramontanists 311
unbelief 28–29
unbelievers 275
unction 27, 35, 108, 112, 313
understanding 40, 43, 55, 62, 108, 111
Unigenitus (Clement XI) 120

unity 64
universe 95
Urbane 280
Uriah 263
Urijah 215
Uzzah 275
Uzziah 269

Valentine 135
Van der Hooght 159
Vandals 178
various readings 145, 154–183, 307; *see also* different readings
Vatican 164
Vedas 261
Vedham 227
Velleius Paterculus 208
vengeance 257
*Verbal Inspiration of the Old and New Testament, The* (Haldane) 274
*Vérité* (Charron) 119
vernacular 120, 129
Veysie 292
Virgilius 228
virtue 63
visions 64, 107
*Vita Epimen.* 70
Volney 186
Voltaire 48, 163, 228
Vories 51
*Vorlesungen über die Dogmatik* (Twesten) 40, 193
Vossius 116
Vulgate 138, 161, 178, 234

water 237, 277
western civilization 231
Wetstein 157, 176, 179
Whitby 167, 175-176, 198, 212, 216

widow of Zarephath  260
will  40, 43
Wilson  41
wine  276, 278
Wirgmann  186
wisdom  28, 39, 46-47, 52, 54–55, 61, 78, 81-82, 97, 101, 106, 109, 127, 135, 137, 155, 189, 240–241, 246, 267, 276-277, 279, 289, 291, 303, 306, 310, 313, 318
Wiseman  157, 236; *Works: Discourses on the Relations of Science*  182
Wolfenbüttel  192
Wolff  133
women  106, 120, 200, 203-207, 282
words  39, 41–44, 46–47, 53, 57–59, 62, 67-73, 75-76, 79-80, 82-83, 85-86, 90-94, 97-98, 100-102, 104, 106-111, 114-117, 122, 126, 135, 141, 145-149, 151, 175, 179, 198, 225–226, 233, 244-255, 258, 268, 273-274, 277-279, 283, 287, 291-292, 298, 301, 304, 305, 308-309, 314, 318
Wordsworth  178
works  29, 33, 127, 174, 179

world  29
worship  121, 129, 182, 258, 265, 312, 314
wrath  128, 312, 317
writers  41, 306

Xenophanes  231
Ximenes  182

*Y-king*  227
*Yad Hachazakah* (Maimonides)  262
Yeates  159
Young  231

Zaccheus  196
Zachariah  77, 216
Zacharias  113, 214–215, 217
Zachary, Pope  228, 232
Zaleucus  231
zealots  216
Zebedee  230
Zechariah  215
*Zeitschrift für die gesammte Lutherische Theologie*  48
Zephaniah  50
Zimmerman  236
Zorobabel  216, 259
Zurich  187
*Zweite Verbesserte Auflage*  138

# Scripture Index

**Acts** 73, 88, 89, 199, 263
1:1 88
1:8 79
1:14 266
1:16 69, 77
1:18 196
1:20 75
2:4 70, 83, 113, 252
2:17 107
2:30 109-110, 77
3:12 111
3:18 69
3:21 69, 82, 251
3:21-22 75
4:25 44, 69, 77, 86, 244
4:27-28 54
4:31 83
5:34 269
5:37 209
7:14 197
7:35 75
7:37 75
7:38 74, 89, 246
7:52 215
8:15 87
8:17 87
8:28 75, 120
8:30-31 120
9:10-12 107
10:3 107
10:17 107
10:19 107
11:5 107
11:27 87
11:28 88
12:1 282
12:3 282
12:9 107
13:1 87, 217
13:1-2 88
13:2 92
13:6 69
13:12 263
13:33 86
14:27 268
15:18 59
15:21 128
15:22 217
15:28 91
15:29 120
15:32 87
15:34 217
15:39 114
16:7 179
16:9-10 107
16:10 87
16:25 217
17:15 217
18:2 217
18:26 217
19:1-6 72
19:6 112
19:6-7 87

19:11-12 112
20:28 177
20:35 199
21:9-10 88
23:25 269
24:14 124, 129
26:5 129
26:22 75
26:27 75
27:1 87
28:22 129
28:23 75
28:25 92

**Amos**
3:1 68

**Apocalypse** 55, 157

**1 Chronicles** 75, 124, 218
17:3 68
21:5 197

**2 Chronicles** 75, 124, 215, 218
8:18 197
22:2 219
24:21 214
26:6 215
27:1 197
36:5-7 208
36:9 208

*341*

**Colossians** *88*
1:5 *234*
1:16 *234*
1:17 *101*
2:3 *101*
4:14 *87, 88, 263*

**1 Corinthians** *85, 241*
1:1 *86*
1:23 *188*
2:10 *251*
2:13 *86, 107, 109, 246, 251, 291*
2:14 *189, 289, 313*
2:16 *86*
3:6 *268*
3:9-10 *126*
5:5 *187*
6:3 *187*
7:10 *242*
7:10-11 *243*
7:12 *242*
7:25 *242*
9:5 *290*
10:4 *259*
10:6 *259*
10:11 *259*
10:12 *243*
11:30 *187*
12 *71*
12:3 *251*
12:8-10 *71*
12:11 *72, 142*
12:19-20 *87*
12:28 *84, 85, 87*
14 *71, 87, 108, 249*
14:1 *72, 112*
14:1-3 *72*
14:4 *71*
14:9 *72*
14:26-31 *72*
14:31 *87*
14:32 *72, 91*
14:36-37 *85*
14:38 *87*
15:3 *124*
15:5 *202, 204*
15:8 *204*
15:22 *187*
16:5 *120*
16:19 *281*

**2 Corinthians**
1:1 *86*
1:19 *217*
2:17 *126*
3:15 *128*
5:20 *80*
8:3 *114*
8:18 *87*
11:23-27 *272*
11:28 *89*
12:1-2 *107*
12:2-3 *244*
13:3 *85, 111, 250*

**Daniel** *41*
1:1 *208*
1:17 *107*
2:6 *107*
5:5 *108*
5:25 *53*
7:1 *107*
7:10 *234*
12:4 *76*
12:8-9 *76, 252*

**Deuteronomy** *97, 159, 267*
4:12 *108*
5:21 *267*
6:13 *97*
7:3 *243*
8:3 *97*
8:7 *239*
10:20 *97*
10:22 *197*
18:21-22 *68*
33:26-27 *240*
34:10 *75*

**Ecclesiastes**
5:1-2 *188*

**Ephesians**
1:4 *60*
2:20 *84-85*
3:3 *109*
3:4-5 *83, 94, 113*
3:5 *84, 114*
3:10-11 *76*
4:7 *72*
4:8 *92*
4:11 *84-85, 113*
5:5 *178*
5:21 *179*

**Exodus**
3:6 *108*
4:10 *61*
4:11 *75*
4:12 *69*
4:13 *59*
4:15 *69*
4:16 *68*
4:30 *68*
7:1 *68*
12:40 *218*
19 *59*
19:3 *108*
20:4-5 *120-121*
20:17 *267*

## SCRIPTURE INDEX

**Ezekiel** 47, 236
1:3 68
3:4 68
3:10-11 68, 76
8:2-3 114
29:1 113
31:4 239

**Ezra**
5:1 216
6:14 216
10:2-3 243
10:11 243
10:19 243

**Galatians** 33, 175
1:1 86, 243
1:12 84, 109
1:15 60, 112
1:15-16 61
1:16 109
1:18 282
2:7 282
2:7-9 281
2:9 290
2:11-14 250
3:1 80
3:16 189
3:17 218

**Genesis** 93, 99, 261, 263
1:2 238
1:4 234
1:6 234
1:7 235
1:12 235
1:14 234
1:27 99
2:14 236
2:24 99

3:1 234
3:13 234
3:14 108
3:15 234
3:24 234
4:6 108
7:11 237
8:4 236
18:2 195
18:10 195
18:17 195
20:3 107
20:6 107
28:16 270
28:17 35
31:10 107
43:29 261
46:27 197

**Haggai** 93
1:1 68

**Hebrews** 50, 93
1:1 107, 111
1:5 86
1:8 92
2:8 93
2:11 93
3:2-6 93
3:7 86, 92
3:7-19 93
3:17 86
4:2 29
4:2-11 93
4:3 86
4:7 86
5-7 93
5:5 86
7 93
8:8-13 93
10 93

10:15 92
12:5-9 93
12:27 93

**Hosea** 124
1:1-2 68

**Isaiah** 41, 77
1:1 86
1:2 74
2:7 86
7:14 104
8 215
8:2 215
8:11 68
9:6 104
28:14 68
28:29 240
35:6 239
40:18 240
40:22 233
40:26-27 240
43:1 86
44:17 27
54:13 132
56:1 86
59:21 132

**James** 126
1:1 178
1:17 90
1:18 55
2:18 179
3:15 90
3:17 90
5:8 187
5:17 306

**Jeremiah** 124
1:1-2 68
1:2 86

1:5-7 *60*
1:9 *68, 76*
1:14 *68*
6:13 *69*
7:1 *68*
9:12 *68*
10:1 *68*
11:1 *68*
13:15 *68*
14:14 *114*
17:20 *68*
18:1 *68*
18:11 *199*
19:3 *68*
21:1 *68*
23:2 *199*
23:11 *114*
23:16 *114*
23:29 *301*
25:1 *208*
26:1 *68*
26:7-8 *69*
26:11 *69*
26:16 *69*
26:23 *215*
27:1 *68*
29:1 *69*
29:1-8 *69*
29:8 *69*
30:1 *68*
30:4 *68*
31:31 *93*
31:34 *110*
44:22 *287*
50:1 *68*
51:12 *68*

**Job** *119, 136*
7:14 *107*
26:7 *233*
26:10 *233*

28 *241*
28:5 *236*
28:25 *235*
33:15 *107*
37:8 *211*

**John** *42, 56, 214*
1 *266*
1:1 *178*
1:15 *210*
1:30 *210*
2:4 *266*
3:3 *90*
3:6-10 *204*
3:34 *112*
4:26 *120*
4:42 *132*
5:18 *103*
5:39 *99, 124*
6:27 *104*
6:45 *110*
7:15 *97*
7:38-39 *109*
8:44 *234*
8:56 *110*
9:25 *297*
10:23 *103*
10:34 *77, 102*
10:35 *101*
11:5 *56*
11:49-52 *53*
11:51 *70, 115, 252*
12:29 *59*
12:31 *234*
12:34 *102*
12:48 *96*
14:6 *126*
14:23-24 *272*
15:26 *108*
16:13 *251*
16:16-26 *109*

19:11 *90*
19:14 *213*
19:28-30 *101*
19:39-40 *203*
20:1 *199*
20:2 *200, 204, 206*
20:2-3 *206*
20:10 *206*
20:11 *207*
20:13 *207*
20:18 *207*
20:21 *79*

**I John**
2:20 *109-110, 112*
2:27 *109-110, 112*
4:2 *126*
5: 7-8 *178*

**Joshua**
10 *221*
10:12 *220, 238*
24:2 *68*

**Jude** *126*
4 *177-178*
6 *234*
14 *60*
14-15 *60, 199*

**Judges** *124, 218*

**I Kings** *73, 124, 218*
3:5 *107*
6:1 *218*
8:27 *240*
9:28 *197*
11:2 *243*
12:22 *68*
13:20 *70*
15:1 *218*

## SCRIPTURE INDEX

**2 Kings** *73, 124, 218*
  8:16 *208*
  8:17 *218*
  8:26 *219*
  12:1 *208*
  15:33 *208*
  18:19 *69*
  24:8 *208*

**Lamentations** *124*
  2:20 *216*

**Leviticus** *159*

**Luke** *42, 88, 89, 135, 196, 211, 286, 291–292*
  1:3 *91*
  1:41-42 *113*
  1:46 *269*
  1:59 *113*
  1:67 *113*
  1:70 *77*
  2:1-2 *209–210*
  3:1 *208*
  3:1-2 *113*
  3:2 *68*
  3:23-28 *208*
  4:5 *210*
  4:15-16 *98*
  4:21 *98*
  5:12 *204, 212*
  6:29 *213*
  7:22 *35*
  7:26 *87*
  7:27 *153*
  7:28 *84, 87*
  8:21 *212*
  9:1 *212*
  10:1 *212*
  10:16 *80*
  11:2 *212*
  11:27 *212*
  11:27-28 *266*
  11:33 *120*
  11:49 *84*
  12:11 *83*
  12:12 *81-82*
  16:16 *75, 124*
  16:17 *102*
  16:22 *258*
  16:29, 31 *75, 124*
  17:31, 34 *238*
  18:35 *195*
  19:48 *63*
  20:36 *258*
  20:42 *75*
  21:14 *81*
  21:15 *81, 109*
  21:33 *102*
  22:19-23 *267*
  23:44-45 *213*
  23:53 *203*
  23:56 *199, 204-205*
  24:4 *195, 200, 205*
  24:9 *206*
  24:9-10 *200*
  24:10 *199, 206*
  24:12 *200, 202, 206*
  24:21 *207*
  24:23-24 *200*
  24:24 *206-207*
  24:25 *75*
  24:27 *75, 101*
  24:29 *201*
  24:32 *101*
  24:33 *201*
  24:34 *202*
  24:36 *201*
  24:44 *74-75, 85, 101*

**Malachi**
  1:1 *68*
  2:14-15 *243*
  3:1 *153*

**Mark** *42, 89, 286, 291–292*
  1:2 *153*
  7:9 *118, 122*
  7:13 *118*
  10:46 *195*
  11:12-14 *217*
  12:24 *49*
  12:27 *49*
  12:36 *77, 244*
  13:11 *81, 251*
  14:18-20 *267*
  15:25 *213*
  15:33-34 *213*
  15:34 *203*
  15:42 *203*
  15:46 *203*
  16:1 *199, 204-205*
  16:2 *199, 205*
  16:3 *205*
  16:5 *194, 200, 205*
  16:8 *200, 205*
  16:9 *202, 207*
  16:10 *207*
  16:5 *200*

**Matthew** *42, 286, 291–292*
  1:16 *208*
  1:20 *107*
  1:22 *69, 77*
  2:5 *69*
  2:6 *153*
  2:12 *107*
  2:15 *69*
  2:22 *107*

2:23  *69*
3:17  *108*
4:1-11  *97*
4:5, 8  *210*
4:14  *69*
5-7  *212*
5:5, 13  *212*
5:17  *75*
5:18  *101-102*
5:31-32  *243*
5:39  *212*
5:40  *213*
6  *212*
6:9  *212*
6:24-26  *212*
7:6-16  *212*
7:12  *75*
8:3  *212*
8:17  *69*
10:1  *212*
10:10  *153*
10:19  *83*
10:19-20  *80-81, 293*
10:29-30  *240*
11:5  *35*
11:9  *84*
11:11  *84, 110*
11:13  *75*
12:6  *99*
12:17  *69*
12:39  *212*
12:49  *212*
13:35  *69, 76*
13:48-49  *286*
15:3-9  *118*
16:1  *212*
16:4  *212*
16:17  *112, 251*
16:19  *80*
17:5  *108*
17:9  *107*
18:10  *258*
18:18  *80*
19:4-6  *99*
19:17  *180*
19:28  *80*
20:30  *195*
21:4  *69*
21:42  *124*
22:31-32  *99*
22:40  *75*
22:43  *77*
23:8-10  *268*
23:35  *216*
23:35-36  *214*
25:31  *96*
26:21-25  *267*
26:54  *124*
27:5  *196*
27:9  *69, 197*
27:10  *197*
27:45-46  *213*
27:46  *203*
27:59  *203*
27:66  *205*
28:5  *200*
28:8  *200, 205-206*
28:9  *200*
28:9-10  *207*
28:19-20  *79*
28:2  *205*

**Micah**
4:4  *68*
5:2  *153*

**Nehemiah**  *124*
9:6  *234*

**Numbers**  *93*
11:23-29  *70*
12:6  *107*

20:6  *107*
23:5  *69*
23:16  *252*
24:4  *107*

**1 Peter**
1:1  *86*
1:10-11  *249*
1:10-12  *76*
1:11  *110*
1:12  *60, 84, 256*
1:24-25  *36, 97*
5:13  *87*

**2 Peter**
1:1  *86, 178*
1:20  *67, 124*
1:21  *70, 77, 94, 107, 113, 291, 293*
2:4  *234*
2:9-10  *234*
2:16  *108*
3:5  *220, 237*
3:7, 10  *236*
3:15-16  *79, 109*

**Philemon**
24  *87, 217, 263*

**Philippians**  *272*
2:13  *45, 55*
2:27  *112, 278*
3:8  *272*
4:13  *180*

**Proverbs**  *73, 77*
3  *93*
4:18  *112*
8:22  *98*
8:25  *98, 236*
8:27  *233*

## SCRIPTURE INDEX

**Psalms** *42, 75, 76, 77, 85, 95, 100, 101, 102, 103, 109, 110, 119, 244, 296, 301, 316*
1 *269*
1:1-2 *255*
8:1 *240*
12:6 *75, 312*
19 *220*
19:6 *234*
19:7 *63, 75*
19:7-10 *255*
22 *100*
22:11 *93*
22:16-18 *272*
24:2 *220*
40 *93*
45 *26*
56:8 *240*
69 *101*
77:18 *240*
78 *76*
78:15-16 *239*
89:19 *107*
90:2 *236*
95 *93*
97:5 *236*
104:5 *220*
104:6, 8-9 *236*
110 *100*
113:6 *240*
133:2 *240*
139:7 *240*
144:6 *236*
147:3-4 *240*

**Revelation** *55, 83, 157*
1:8 *180*
1:11 *180*
1:17 *60*

8:13 *179*
12:9 *234*
12:12 *234*
13:1-8 *311*
18:1-24 *311*
19:10 *126, 317*
20:2 *234*
22:9 *258*
22:13 *180*
22:18-19 *94*
22:20 *60*

**Romans** *42, 50, 84, 88, 163–164, 165, 167, 168, 175–177, 278, 281*
1:1 *86*
1:2 *75, 124*
1:11 *87, 282*
1:13-15 *282*
1:17 *301*
2:16 *96*
3:1-2 *161*
3:2 *74, 89, 127, 246, 285*
3:19 *77, 102*
3:21 *75*
4:17 *175*
4:21 *89*
4:26 *175*
5:6 *174*
5:19 *176*
6:16 *175*
9:1-4 *53*
9:25 *92*
9:33 *287*
10:5 *75*
10:17 *46*
11:6 *174*
12:11 *174*
13:1 *290*

14:15 *89*
15:4 *124*
15:19 *87-88*
15:22 *282*
15:29 *87*
16:3 *217*
16:5 *175*
16:13 *281*
16:21 *87-88, 217*
16:25-27 *84*

**Ruth** *124*

**1 Samuel** *124*
10:6 *72*
10:11 *71*
18:10 *72*
19:20-21 *252*
19:23-24 *253*

**2 Samuel** *124*
6:6-7 *275*
23:1-2 *44, 68, 77, 114*
23:2 *86, 252, 71*
28:8 *197*
29:9 *197*

**Song of Solomon**
*26, 42, 136*

**1 Thessalonians**
2:13 *29, 85, 86, 89, 291*
2:15 *84*
2:16 *128*
4:8 *86*
4:15 *187*
5:2 *120*

**2 Thessalonians**
1:12 *178*

|   |   |   |
|---|---|---|
| 2  *187* | 3  *255* | **Titus** |
| 2:1-12  *311* | 3:1  *38* | 2:3  *178* |
|  | 3:15  *124, 246, 253* | 2:13  *178* |
| **1 Timothy** | 3:16  *56, 57, 66,* |  |
| 1:1  *178* | *76, 246* | **Zechariah** |
| 3:16  *177* | 3:16-17  *26* | 1:1  *216* |
| 4:14  *87* | 4:1  *178* | 1:4  *199* |
| 5:23  *112, 276* | 4:5  *89* | 3:8  *199* |
| 6:20  *140* | 4:11  *87, 263* | 11:13  *198* |
|  | 4:16  *263* | 13:2  *69* |
| **2 Timothy**  *124* | 4:17  *89* | 14:4  *236* |
| 1:6  *87* | 4:19  *217* | 14:8  *236* |
| 2:10  *272* | 4:20  *112* |  |

# The Crisis of Our Time

HISTORIANS have christened the thirteenth century the Age of Faith and termed the eighteenth century the Age of Reason. The twentieth century has been called many things: the Atomic Age, the Age of Inflation, the Age of the Tyrant, the Age of Aquarius; but it deserves one name more than the others: the Age of Irrationalism. Contemporary secular intellectuals are anti-intellectual. Contemporary philosophers are anti-philosophy. Contemporary theologians are anti-theology.

In past centuries, secular philosophers have generally believed that knowledge is possible to man. Consequently they expended a great deal of thought and effort trying to justify knowledge. In the twentieth century, however, the optimism of the secular philosophers all but disappeared. They despaired of knowledge.

Like their secular counterparts, the great theologians and doctors of the church taught that knowledge is possible to man. Yet the theologians of the twentieth century also repudiated that belief. They too despaired of knowledge. This radical skepticism has penetrated our entire culture, from television to music to literature. *The Christian at the beginning of the twenty-first century is confronted with an overwhelming cultural consensus – sometimes stated explicitly but most often implicitly: Man does not and cannot know anything truly.*

What does this have to do with Christianity? Simply this: If man can know nothing truly, man can truly know nothing. We cannot know that the Bible is the Word of God, that Christ died for his people, or that Christ is alive today at the right hand of the Father. Unless knowledge is possible, Christianity is nonsensical, for it claims to be knowledge. What is at stake at the beginning of the twenty-first century is not simply a single doctrine, such as the virgin birth, or the existence of Hell, as important as those doctrines may be, but the whole of Christianity itself. If knowledge is not possible to man, it is worse than silly to argue points of doctrine – it is insane.

The irrationalism of the present age is so thoroughgoing and pervasive that even the Remnant – the segment of the professing church that remains faithful – has accepted much of it, frequently without even being aware of what it is accepting. In some circles this irrationalism has become synonymous with piety and humility, and those who oppose it are denounced as rationalists, as though to be logical were a sin. Our contemporary anti-theologians make a contradiction and call it a Mystery. The faithful ask for truth and are given Paradox. If any balk at swallowing the absurdities of the anti-theologians, they are frequently marked as heretics or schismatics who seek to act independently of God.

There is no greater threat facing the true church of Christ at this moment than the irrationalism that now controls our entire culture. Totalitarianism, guilty of tens of millions of murders – including those of millions of Christians – is to be feared, but not nearly so much as the idea that we do not and cannot know the truth. Hedonism, the popular philosophy of America, is not to be feared so much as the belief that logic – that "mere human logic," to use the religious irrationalists' own phrase – is futile. The attacks on truth, on revelation, on the intellect, on words, and on logic are renewed daily. But note well: The misologists – the haters of logic – use logic to demonstrate the futility of using logic. The anti-intellectuals construct intricate intellectual arguments to prove the insufficiency of the intellect. Those who deny the competence of words to express thought use words in their denials. The proponents of poetry, myth, metaphor, and analogy argue for their theories by using literal prose, whose competence they deny. The anti-theologians use the revealed Word of God to show that there can be no revealed Word of God – or that if there could, it would remain impenetrable darkness and Mystery to our finite minds.

## *Nonsense Has Come*

Is it any wonder that the world is grasping at straws – the straws of experientialism, mysticism, and drugs? After all, if people are told that the Bible contains insoluble mysteries, then is not a flight into mysticism to be expected? On what grounds can it be condemned? Certainly not on logical grounds or Biblical grounds, if logic is futile and the Bible unintelligible. Moreover, if it cannot be condemned on logical or Biblical grounds, it cannot be condemned at all. If people are going to have a religion of the mysterious, they will not adopt Christianity: They will have a genuine mystery religion. The popularity of Eastern mysticism, of drugs, and of religious experience is the logical consequence of the irrationalism of the twentieth century. There can and will be no Christian reformation – and no reconstruction of society – unless and until the irrationalism of the age is totally repudiated by Christians.

## *The Church Defenseless*

Yet how shall they do it? The spokesmen for Christianity have been fatally infected with irrationalism. The seminaries, which annually train thousands of men to teach millions of Christians, are the finishing schools of irrationalism, completing the job begun by the government schools and colleges. Some of the pulpits of the most conservative churches (we are not speaking of the apostate churches) are occupied by graduates of the anti-theological schools. These products of modern anti-theological education, when asked to give a reason for the hope that is in them, can generally respond with only the intellectual analogue of a shrug – a mumble about Mystery. They have not grasped – and therefore cannot teach those for whom they are responsible – the first truth: "And you shall know the truth." Many, in fact, explicitly deny it, saying that, at best, we possess only "pointers" to the truth, or something "similar" to the truth, a mere analogy. Is the impotence of the Christian church a puzzle? Is the fascination with pentecostalism, faith healing, Eastern Orthodoxy, and Roman Catholicism – all sensate and anti-intellectual religions – among members of Christian churches an enigma? Not when one understands the studied nonsense that is purveyed in the name of God in the colleges and seminaries.

## *The Trinity Foundation*

The creators of The Trinity Foundation firmly believe that theology is too important to be left to the licensed theologians – the graduates of the schools of theology. They have created The Trinity Foundation for the express purpose of teaching the faithful all that the Scriptures contain – not warmed over, baptized, secular philosophies. Each member of the board of directors of The Trinity Foundation has signed this oath: "I believe that the Bible alone and the Bible in its entirety is the Word of God and, therefore, inerrant in the autographs. I believe that the system of truth presented in the Bible is best summarized in the *Westminster Confession of Faith*. So help me God."

The ministry of The Trinity Foundation is the presentation of the system of truth taught in Scripture as clearly and as completely as possible. We do not regard obscurity as a virtue, nor confusion as a sign of spirituality. Confusion, like all error, is sin, and teaching that confusion is all that Christians can hope for is doubly sin.

The presentation of the truth of Scripture necessarily involves the rejection of error. The Foundation has exposed and will continue to expose the irrationalism of the twentieth century, whether its current spokesman be an existentialist philosopher or a professed Reformed theologian. We oppose anti-intellectualism, whether it be espoused by a Neo-orthodox theologian or a fundamentalist evangelist. We reject misology, whether it be on the lips of a Neo-evangelical or those of a Roman Catholic charismatic. To each error we bring the brilliant light of Scripture, proving all things, and holding fast to that which is true.

## The Primacy of Theory

The ministry of The Trinity Foundation is not a "practical" ministry. If you are a pastor, we will not enlighten you on how to organize an ecumenical prayer meeting in your community or how to double church attendance in a year. If you are a homemaker, you will have to read elsewhere to find out how to become a total woman. If you are a businessman, we will not tell you how to develop a social conscience. The professing church is drowning in such "practical" advice.

The Trinity Foundation is unapologetically theoretical in its outlook, believing that theory without practice is dead, and that practice without theory is blind. The trouble with the professing church is not primarily in its practice, but in its theory. Churchgoers do not know, and many do not even care to know, the doctrines of Scripture. Doctrine is intellectual, and churchgoers are generally anti-intellectual. Doctrine is ivory tower philosophy, and they scorn ivory towers. The ivory tower, however, is the control tower of a civilization. It is a fundamental, theoretical mistake of the practical men to think that they can be merely practical, for practice is always the practice of some theory. The relationship between theory and practice is the relationship between cause and effect. If a person believes correct theory, his practice will tend to be correct. The practice of contemporary Christians is immoral because it is the practice of false theories. It is a major theoretical mistake of the practical men to think that they can ignore the ivory towers of the philosophers and theologians as irrelevant to their lives. Every action that "practical" men take is governed by the thinking that has occurred in some ivory tower – whether that tower be the British Museum; the Academy; a home in Basel, Switzerland; or a tent in Israel.

## *In Understanding Be Men*

It is the first duty of the Christian to understand correct theory – correct doctrine – and thereby implement correct practice. This order – first theory, then practice – is both logical and Biblical. It is, for example, exhibited in Paul's *Epistle to the Romans,* in which he spends the first eleven chapters expounding theory and the last five discussing practice. The contemporary teachers of Christians have not only reversed the order, they have inverted the Pauline emphasis on theory and practice. The virtually complete failure of the teachers of the professing church to instruct the faithful in correct doctrine is the cause of the misconduct and spiritual and cultural impotence of Christians. The church's lack of power is the result of its lack of truth. The *Gospel* is the power of God, not religious experience or personal relationship. The church has no power because it has abandoned the Gospel, the good news, for a religion of experientialism. Twentieth-first-century American Christians are children carried about by every wind of doctrine, not knowing what they believe, or even if they believe anything for certain.

The chief purpose of The Trinity Foundation is to counteract the irrationalism of the age and to expose the errors of the teachers of the church. Our emphasis – on the Bible as the sole source of knowledge, on the primacy of truth, on the supreme importance of correct doctrine, and on the necessity for systematic and logical thinking – is almost unique in Christendom. To the extent that the church survives – and she will survive and flourish – it will be because of her increasing acceptance of these basic ideas and their logical implications.

We believe that The Trinity Foundation is filling a vacuum in Christendom. We are saying that Christianity is intellectually defensible – that, in fact, it is the only intellectually defensible system of thought. We are saying that God has made the wisdom of this world — whether that wisdom be called science, religion, philosophy, or common sense — foolishness. We are appealing to all Christians who have not conceded defeat in the intellectual battle with the world to join us in our efforts to raise a standard to which all men of sound mind can repair.

The love of truth, of God's Word, has all but disappeared in our time. We are committed to and pray for a great instauration. But though we may not see this reformation in our lifetimes, we believe it is our duty to present the whole counsel of God because Christ has commanded it. The results of our teaching are in God's hands, not ours. Whatever those results, his Word is never taught in vain, but always accomplishes the result that he intended it to accomplish. Professor Gordon H. Clark has stated our view well:

> There have been times in the history of God's people, for example, in the days of Jeremiah, when refreshing grace and widespread revival were not to be expected: The time was one of chastisement. If this twentieth century is of a similar nature, individual Christians here and there can find comfort and strength in a study of God's Word. But if God has decreed happier days for us, and if we may expect a world-shaking and genuine spiritual awakening, then it is the author's belief that a zeal for souls, however necessary, is not the sufficient condition. Have there not been devout saints in every age, numerous enough to carry on a revival? Twelve such persons are plenty. What distinguishes the arid ages from the period of the Reformation, when nations were moved as they had not been since Paul preached in Ephesus, Corinth, and Rome, is the latter's fullness of knowledge of God's Word. To echo an early Reformation thought, when the ploughman and the garage attendant know the Bible as well as the theologian does, and know it better than some contemporary theologians, then the desired awakening shall have already occurred.

In addition to publishing books, the Foundation publishes a monthly newsletter, *The Trinity Review.* Subscriptions to *The Review* are free to U.S. addresses; please write to the address on the order form to become a subscriber. If you would like further information or would like to join us in our work, please let us know.

The Trinity Foundation is a non-profit foundation, tax exempt under section 501 (c)(3) of the Internal Revenue Code of 1954. You can help us disseminate the Word of God through your tax-deductible contributions to the Foundation.

JOHN W. ROBBINS

# Intellectual Ammunition

THE Trinity Foundation is committed to the reformation of philosophy and theology along Biblical lines. We regard God's command to bring all our thoughts into conformity with Christ very seriously, and the books listed below are designed to accomplish that goal. They are written with two subordinate purposes: (1) to demolish all non-Christian claims to knowledge; and (2) to build a system of truth based upon the Bible alone.

### PHILOSOPHY

*Ancient Philosophy*
Gordon H. Clark                               Trade paperback $24.95
    This book covers the thousand years from the Pre-Socratics to Plotinus. It represents some of the early work of Dr. Clark – the work that made his academic reputation. It is an excellent college text.

*Behaviorism and Christianity*
Gordon H. Clark                                Trade paperback $5.95
    *Behaviorism* is a critique of both secular and religious behaviorists. It includes chapters on John Watson, Edgar S. Singer, Jr., Gilbert Ryle, B. F. Skinner, and Donald MacKay. Clark's refutation of behaviorism and his argument for a Christian doctrine of man are unanswerable.

*A Christian Philosophy of Education*                       Hardback $18.95
Gordon H. Clark                               Trade paperback $12.95
    The first edition of this book was published in 1946. It sparked the contemporary interest in Christian schools. In the 1970s, Dr. Clark thoroughly revised and updated it, and it is needed now more than ever. Its chapters include: The Need for a World-View; The

Christian World-View; The Alternative to Christian Theism; Neutrality; Ethics; The Christian Philosophy of Education; Academic Matters; and Kindergarten to University. Three appendices are included: The Relationship of Public Education to Christianity; A Protestant World-View; and Art and the Gospel.

*A Christian View of Men and Things*              Hardback $29.95
Gordon H. Clark                       Trade paperback $14.95

No other book achieves what *A Christian View* does: the presentation of Christianity as it applies to history, politics, ethics, science, religion, and epistemology. Dr. Clark's command of both worldly philosophy and Scripture is evident on every page, and the result is a breathtaking and invigorating challenge to the wisdom of this world.

*Clark Speaks from the Grave*
Gordon H. Clark                        Trade paperback $3.95

Dr. Clark chides some of his critics for their failure to defend Christianity competently. *Clark Speaks* is a stimulating and illuminating discussion of the errors of contemporary apologists.

*Ecclesiastical Megalomania: The Economic and Political*
*Thought of the Roman Catholic Church*          Hardback $29.95
John W. Robbins                     Trade paperback $19.95

This detailed and thorough analysis and critique of the social teaching of the Roman Church-State is the only such book available by a Christian economist and political philosopher. The book's conclusions reveal the Roman Church-State to be an advocate of its own brand of global religious Fascism. *Ecclesiastical Megalomania* includes the complete text of the *Donation of Constantine* and Lorenzo Valla's exposé of the hoax.

*Education, Christianity, and the State*
J. Gresham Machen                  Trade paperback $9.95

Machen was one of the foremost educators, theologians, and defenders of Christianity in the twentieth century. The author of several scholarly books, Machen saw clearly that if Christianity is to survive and flourish, a system of Christian schools must be established. This collection of essays and speeches captures his thoughts on education over nearly three decades.

*Essays on Ethics and Politics*
Gordon H. Clark                              Trade paperback $10.95
Dr. Clark's essays, written over the course of five decades, are a major statement of Christian ethics.

*Gordon H. Clark: Personal Recollections*
John W. Robbins, editor                      Trade paperback $6.95
Friends of Dr. Clark have written their recollections of the man. Contributors include family members, colleagues, students, and friends such as Harold Lindsell, Carl Henry, Ronald Nash, and Anna Marie Hager.

*Historiography: Secular and Religious*
Gordon H. Clark                              Trade paperback $13.95
In this masterful work, Dr. Clark applies his philosophy to the writing of history, examining all the major schools of historiography.

*An Introduction to Christian Philosophy*
Gordon H. Clark                              Trade paperback $8.95
In 1966 Dr. Clark delivered three lectures on philosophy at Wheaton College. In these lectures he criticizes secular philosophy and launches a philosophical revolution in the name of Christ.

*Language and Theology*
Gordon H. Clark                              Trade paperback $9.95
There are two main currents in twentieth-century philosophy – language philosophy and existentialism. Both are hostile to Christianity. Dr. Clark disposes of language philosophy in this brilliant critique of Bertrand Russell, Ludwig Wittgenstein, Rudolf Carnap, A. J. Ayer, Langdon Gilkey, and many others.

*Logic*  Hardback $16.95
Gordon H. Clark  Trade paperback $10.95
 Written as a textbook for Christian schools, *Logic* is another unique book from Dr. Clark's pen. His presentation of the laws of thought, which must be followed if Scripture is to be understood correctly, and which are found in Scripture itself, is both clear and thorough. *Logic* is an indispensable book for the thinking Christian.

*Logic Workbook*
Elihu Carranza  Oversize paperback $11.95
 Designed to be used in conjunction with Dr. Clark's textbook *Logic*, this *Workbook* contains hundreds of exercises and test questions on perforated pages for ease of use by students.

*Lord God of Truth, Concerning the Teacher*
Gordon H. Clark
and Aurelius Augustine  Trade paperback $7.95
 This essay by Dr. Clark summarizes many of the most telling arguments against empiricism and defends the Biblical teaching that we know God and truth immediately. The dialogue by Augustine is a refutation of empirical language philosophy.

*The Philosophy of Science and Belief in God*
Gordon H. Clark  Trade paperback $8.95
 In opposing the contemporary idolatry of science, Dr. Clark analyzes three major aspects of science: the problem of motion, Newtonian science, and modern theories of physics. His conclusion is that science, while it may be useful, is always false; and he demonstrates its falsity in numerous ways. Since science is always false, it can offer no alternative to the Bible and Christianity.

*Religion, Reason and Revelation*
Gordon H. Clark  Trade paperback $10.95
 One of Dr. Clark's apologetical masterpieces, *Religion, Reason and Revelation* has been praised for the clarity of its thought and language. It includes these chapters: Is Christianity a Religion? Faith

and Reason; Inspiration and Language; Revelation and Morality; and God and Evil. It is must reading for all serious Christians.

*The Scripturalism of Gordon H. Clark*
W. Gary Crampton                    Trade paperback $9.95
Dr. Crampton has written an introduction to the philosophy of Gordon H. Clark that is helpful to both beginners and advanced students of theology. This book includes a bibliography of Dr. Clark's works.

*Thales to Dewey: A History of Philosophy*          Hardback $29.95
Gordon H. Clark                    Trade paperback $21.95
This is the best one-volume history of philosophy in print.

*Three Types of Religious Philosophy*
Gordon H. Clark                    Trade paperback $6.95
In this book on apologetics, Dr. Clark examines empiricism, rationalism, dogmatism, and contemporary irrationalism, which does not rise to the level of philosophy. He offers an answer to the question, "How can Christianity be defended before the world?"

*William James and John Dewey*
Gordon H. Clark                    Trade paperback $8.95
William James and John Dewey are two of the most influential philosophers America has produced. Their philosophies of instrumentalism and pragmatism are hostile to Christianity, and Dr. Clark demolishes their arguments.

*Without a Prayer: Ayn Rand and the Close of Her System*
John W. Robbins                    Hardback $27.95
Ayn Rand has been a best-selling author since 1957. *Without a Prayer* discusses Objectivism's epistemology, theology, ethics, and politics in detail. Appendices include analyses of books by Leonard Peikoff and David Kelley, as well as several essays on Christianity and philosophy.

## THEOLOGY

*Against the World: The Trinity Review 1978-1988*
John W. Robbins, editor                Oversize hardback $34.95
This is a clothbound collection of the essays published in *The Trinity Review* from 1978 to 1988, 70 in all. It is a valuable source of information and arguments explaining and defending Christianity.

*The Atonement*
Gordon H. Clark                Trade paperback $8.95
In *The Atonement*, Dr. Clark discusses the covenants, the virgin birth and incarnation, federal headship and representation, the relationship between God's sovereignty and justice, and much more. He analyzes traditional views of the atonement and criticizes them in the light of Scripture alone.

*The Biblical Doctrine of Man*
Gordon H. Clark                Trade paperback $6.95
Is man soul and body or soul, spirit, and body? What is the image of God? Is Adam's sin imputed to his children? Is evolution true? Are men totally depraved? What is the heart? These are some of the questions discussed and answered from Scripture in this book.

*The Changing of the Guard*
Mark W. Karlberg                Trade paperback $3.95
This essay is a critical discussion of Westminster Seminary's anti-Reformational and un-Biblical teaching on the doctrine of justification. Dr. Karlberg exposes the doctrine of justification by faith and works – not *sola fide* – taught at Westminster Seminary for the past 25 years, by Professor Norman Shepherd and others.

*The Church Effeminate*
John W. Robbins, editor                Hardback $29.95
This is a collection of 39 essays by the best theologians of the church on the doctrine of the church: Martin Luther, John Calvin, Benjamin Warfield, Gordon Clark, J. C. Ryle, and many more. The essays cover the structure, function, and purpose of the church.

*The Clark-Van Til Controversy*
Herman Hoeksema                              Trade paperback $7.95
　　This collection of essays by the founder of the Protestant Reformed Church – essays written at the time of the Clark-Van Til controversy – is one of the best commentaries on those events in print.

*Cornelius Van Til: The Man and The Myth*
John W. Robbins                              Trade paperback $2.45
　　The actual teachings of this eminent Philadelphia theologian have been obscured by the myths that surround him. This book penetrates those myths and criticizes Van Til's surprisingly unorthodox views of God and the Bible.

*The Everlasting Righteousness*
Horatius Bonar                               Trade paperback $8.95
　　Originally published in 1874, the language of Bonar's masterpiece on justification by faith alone has been updated and Americanized for easy reading and clear understanding. This is one of the best books ever written on justification.

*Faith and Saving Faith*
Gordon H. Clark                              Trade paperback $6.95
　　The views of the Roman Catholic Church, John Calvin, Thomas Manton, John Owen, Charles Hodge, and B. B. Warfield are discussed in this book. Is the object of faith a person or a proposition? Is faith more than belief? Is belief thinking with assent, as Augustine said? In a world chaotic with differing views of faith, Dr. Clark clearly explains the Biblical view of faith and saving faith.

*God and Evil: The Problem Solved*
Gordon H. Clark                              Trade paperback $4.95
　　This volume is Chapter 5 of *Religion, Reason and Revelation,* in which Dr. Clark presents his solution to the problem of evil.

## INTELLECTUAL AMMUNITION

*God-Breathed: The Divine Inspiration of the Bible*
Louis Gaussen                                   Trade paperback $16.95
   Gaussen, a nineteenth-century Swiss Reformed pastor, collected
   the hundreds of passages in which the Bible claims to be the Word
   of God. This is a massive defense of the doctrine of the plenary and
   verbal inspiration of Scripture.

*God's Hammer: The Bible and Its Critics*
Gordon H. Clark                                 Trade paperback $10.95
   The starting point of Christianity, the doctrine on which all other
   doctrines depend, is "The Bible alone, and the Bible in its entirety,
   is the Word of God written, and, therefore, inerrant in the autographs." Over the centuries the opponents of Christianity, with
   Satanic shrewdness, have concentrated their attacks on the truthfulness and completeness of the Bible. In the twentieth century
   the attack was not so much in the fields of history and archaeology
   as in philosophy. Dr. Clark's brilliant defense of the complete
   truthfulness of the Bible is captured in this collection of eleven
   major essays.

*The Holy Spirit*
Gordon H. Clark                                  Trade paperback $8.95
   This discussion of the third person of the Trinity is both concise
   and exact. Dr. Clark includes chapters on the work of the Spirit,
   sanctification, and Pentecostalism. This book is part of his multi-
   volume systematic theology that began appearing in print in 1985.

*The Incarnation*
Gordon H. Clark                                  Trade paperback $8.95
   Who is Christ? The attack on the doctrine of the incarnation
   in the nineteenth and twentieth centuries has been vigorous,
   but the orthodox response has been lame. Dr. Clark recon-
   structs the doctrine of the incarnation, building and improving
   upon the Chalcedonian definition.

*The Johannine Logos*
Gordon H. Clark                                   Trade paperback $5.95
   Dr. Clark analyzes the relationship between Christ, who is the
   truth, and the Bible. He explains why John used the same word to
   refer to both Christ and his teaching. Chapters deal with the
   Prologue to John's Gospel; *Logos* and *Rheemata;* Truth; and Saving
   Faith.

*Justification by Faith Alone*
Charles Hodge                                    Trade paperback $10.95
   Charles Hodge of Princeton Seminary was the best American
   theologian of the nineteenth century. Here, for the first time, are
   his two major essays on justification in one volume. This book is
   essential in defending the faith.

*Karl Barth's Theological Method*
Gordon H. Clark                                  Trade paperback $18.95
   *Karl Barth's Theological Method* is perhaps the best critique of the
   Neo-orthodox theologian Karl Barth ever written. Dr. Clark discusses Barth's view of revelation, language, and Scripture, focusing
   on his method of writing theology, rather than presenting a com-
   prehensive analysis of the details of Barth's theology.

*Logical Criticisms of Textual Criticism*
Gordon H. Clark                                   Trade paperback $3.25
   Dr. Clark's acute logic enables him to demonstrate the inconsis-
   tencies, assumptions, and flights of fancy that characterize the
   science of New Testament criticism.

*New Testament Greek for Beginners*                  Hardback $16.95
J. Gresham Machen                                Trade paperback $10.95
   Long a standard text, *New Testament Greek for Beginners* is extremely
   helpful in the study of the New Testament in the original Greek.
   It may profitably be used by high school, college, and seminary
   students, either in a classroom setting or in self-study. Machen was
   Professor of New Testament Literature and Exegesis at Princeton
   Theological Seminary and the founder of Westminster Theologi-
   cal Seminary and the Orthodox Presbyterian Church.

*Predestination*
Gordon H. Clark                           Trade paperback $10.95
> Dr. Clark thoroughly discusses one of the most controversial and pervasive doctrines of the Bible: that God is, quite literally, Almighty. Free will, the origin of evil, God's omniscience, creation, and the new birth are all presented within a Scriptural framework. The objections of those who do not believe in Almighty God are considered and refuted. This edition also contains the text of the booklet, *Predestination in the Old Testament*.

*Sanctification*
Gordon H. Clark                            Trade paperback $8.95
> In this book, which is part of Dr. Clark's multi-volume systematic theology, he discusses historical theories of sanctification, the sacraments, and the Biblical doctrine of sanctification.

*Study Guide to the Westminster Confession*
W. Gary Crampton                         Oversize paperback $10.95
> This *Study Guide* may be used by individuals or classes. It contains a paragraph-by-paragraph summary of the *Westminster Confession*, and questions for the student to answer. Space for answers is provided. The *Guide* will be most beneficial when used in conjunction with Dr. Clark's *What Do Presbyterians Believe?*

*A Theology of the Holy Spirit*
Frederick Dale Bruner                    Trade paperback, $16.95
> First published in 1970, this book has been hailed by reviewers as "thorough," "fair," "comprehensive," "devastating," "the most significant book on the Holy Spirit," and "scholarly." Gordon Clark described this book in his own book *The Holy Spirit* as "a masterly and exceedingly well researched exposition of Pentecostalism. The documentation is superb, as is also his penetrating analysis of their non-scriptural and sometimes contradictory conclusions."

## GOD-BREATHED: THE DIVINE INSPIRATION OF THE BIBLE

*The Trinity*
Gordon H. Clark                                     Trade paperback $8.95
   Apart from the doctrine of Scripture, no teaching of the Bible is more fundamental than the doctrine of God. Dr. Clark's defense of the orthodox doctrine of the Trinity is a principal portion of his systematic theology. There are chapters on the Deity of Christ; Augustine; the Incomprehensibility of God; Bavinck and Van Til; and the Holy Spirit; among others.

*What Calvin Says*
W. Gary Crampton                                    Trade paperback $7.95
   This is a clear, readable, and thorough introduction to the theology of John Calvin.

*What Do Presbyterians Believe?*
Gordon H. Clark                                    Trade paperback $10.95
   This classic is the best commentary on the *Westminster Confession of Faith* that has ever been written.

### CLARK'S COMMENTARIES
### ON THE NEW TESTAMENT

| | | |
|---|---|---|
| *Colossians* | Trade paperback | $6.95 |
| *Ephesians* | Trade paperback | $8.95 |
| *First Corinthians* | Trade paperback | $10.95 |
| *First John* | Trade paperback | $10.95 |
| *First and Second Thessalonians* | Trade paperback | $5.95 |
| *New Heavens, New Earth* (*First* and *Second Peter*) | Trade paperback | $10.95 |
| *The Pastoral Epistles* | Hardback | $29.95 |
| (*1* and *2 Timothy* and *Titus*) | Trade paperback | $14.95 |
| *Philippians* | Trade paperback | $9.95 |

All of Clark's commentaries are expository, not technical, and are written for the Christian layman. His purpose is to explain the text clearly and accurately so that the Word of God will be thoroughly known by every Christian.

INTELLECTUAL AMMUNITION

## *The Trinity Library*

We will send you one copy of each of the 56 books listed above for $450 (retail value over $600), postpaid to any address in the U.S. You may also order the books you want individually on the order form on the next page. Because some of the books are in short supply, we must reserve the right to substitute others of equal or greater value in The Trinity Library. This special offer expires October 31, 2004.

# Order Form

NAME _____

ADDRESS _____

_____

TELEPHONE AND E-MAIL _____

Please:

- ❏ add my name to the mailing list for *The Trinity Review*. I understand that there is no charge for *The Review* sent to a U.S. address.

- ❏ accept my tax deductible contribution of $ _____ .

- ❏ send me ____ copies of *God-Breathed: The Divine Inspiration of the Bible*. I enclose as payment $ _____ .

- ❏ send me the Trinity Library of 56 books. I enclose US $450 as full payment.

- ❏ send me the following books. I enclose full payment in the amount of $ _____ for them.

_____

_____

_____

_____

The Trinity Foundation
Post Office Box 68, Unicoi, Tennessee 37692
Website: www.trinityfoundation.org
United States of America

Please add $5.00 for postage. For foreign orders, please enclose 20 percent of the total value of the books ordered for shipping and handling.